Making Minds

Benjamins Current Topics

Special issues of established journals tend to circulate within the orbit of the subscribers of those journals. For the Benjamins Current Topics series a number of special issues have been selected containing salient topics of research with the aim to widen the readership and to give this interesting material an additional lease of life in book format.

Volume 4

Making Minds
Edited by Petra Hauf and Friedrich Försterling

These materials were previously published in *Interaction Studies* (6:1 and 6:3, 2005), under the guidance of Editor-in-Chief Kerstin Dautenhahn

Making Minds

The shaping of human minds
through social context

Edited by

Petra Hauf

St. Francis Xavier University, Antigonish, Canada

Friedrich Försterling

Ludwig-Maximilians-Universität, München, Germany

John Benjamins Publishing Company

Amsterdam / Philadelphia

^{TM} The paper used in this publication meets the minimum requirements of
American National Standard for Information Sciences – Permanence of
Paper for Printed Library Materials, ANSI z39.48-1984.

Library of Congress Cataloging-in-Publication Data

Making minds : the shaping of human minds through social context/ edited by Petra
        Hauf and Friedrich Försterling.
     p.   cm. (Benjamins Current Topics, ISSN 1874-0081 ; v. 4)
     Previously published in Interaction studies (6:1 and 6:3, 2005)
     Includes bibliographical references.
        1. Social interaction--Congresses. 2. Social psychology--Congresses.
     HM1111 .M35   2007
302--dc22   2007060744
ISBN 978 90 272 2234 3 (Hb; alk. paper)

John Benjamins Publishing Co. · P.O. Box 36224 · 1020 ME Amsterdam · The Netherlands
John Benjamins North America · P.O. Box 27519 · Philadelphia PA 19118-0519 · USA

Table of contents

Foreword

Making Minds: The shaping of human minds through social context

The contributions to this volume are based on an interdisciplinary conference held at the Monastery at Irsee, Germany in January, 2004. While planning this interdisciplinary meeting about the social making of minds we tried to address a question of crucial significance for any theory that somehow believes in the shaping of human minds through social context: how the shaping of individuals' mental structures and dispositions is determined by the way they perceive themselves understood and/or treated by other individuals. Further we were interested in the psychological mechanisms underlying the social construction of individual minds. Though many large-scale theories emphasize that the human mind is shaped through social context, it is fair to say that small-scale theories about the mechanisms, through which such shaping is actually done, are still largely lacking. To this end, we brought together researchers from various fields of empirical study, e.g. social psychology, personality theory, clinical psychology, ethology, developmental psychology, as well as scholars who address the conceptual issues cross-sectioning the empirical fields.

Accordingly, this volume about the "Making of Minds through Social Context" examines the notion that social communication and interaction may perhaps play a stronger and more deep-rooted role than the standard model provides – a role not only for the build-up of mental contents such as beliefs, motives, and attitudes, but of mental form and structure as well. In fact there are two claims here. One is that people may be able to perceive and understand, through communication and interaction, how they are perceived and understood by others. The second is that their perception of being perceived in a particular way may be constitutive for their becoming that way – thereby adopting, or appropriating the mental organization others impute to them. In this sense the volume starts with an introduction by *Wolfgang Prinz*, *Friedrich Försterling*, and *Petra Hauf* providing a detailed outline of the underlying theoretical ideas about the more local mechanisms involved in the social making of minds. The contributions of this volume are taken from a broad variety of empirical domains and related research traditions. For that reason the overarching conceptual coincidence is discussed from a philosophical perspective by *Martin Kusch* and from a perspective on social coordination in relationships by *Robin Vallacher, Andrzej Nowak,* and *Michal Zochowski.*

The next contributions focus on the impact of expectancy confirmation on the social making of minds. *Mark Snyder* and *Olivier Klein* consider the role that the behavioural confirmation phenomenon can play in shaping the social perception of perceivers, targets, and outside observers. Identity negotiation is one additional process through which perceivers and targets come to agreements regarding the identities that targets are to assume in the interaction which is emphasized by *William Swann.* Furthermore, *Lee Jussim* and colleagues critically challenge empirical evidence apparently which has been interpreted as support for the assumption that social reality makes the social mind.

After that the contributions concentrate on the communication of emotions, evaluations, and attributions. *Denis Hilton, Gaëlle Villejoubert* and *Jean-François Bonnefon* draw our attention on the performative functions of logical expressions. *Sandra Graham* shows impressively the role of attributions for peer harassment and *Kurt Hahlweg* demonstrates with research on Expressed Emotions in schizophrenic patients that the shaping of individuals' mental structures and dispositions by others is in some cases not only dramatic, but even more a struggle for existence.

The issue of the self in groups and social exchange is highly related to the question of how the shaping of individuals' mental structures and dispositions is determined by the way they perceive themselves understood and/or treated by other individuals. In this framework *Kipling Williams* and *Jonathan Gerber* explore the powerful consequences of ostracism – being ignored and excluded – at the neurophysiological, emotional, cognitive and behavioural levels. *Caryl Rusbult* and colleagues present one more example for self processes in interdependent relationships – the Michelangelo phenomenon – which describes the manner in which close partners shape one another's dispositions, values, and behavioural tendencies.

The remaining contributions of this volume focus on ethological perspectives and on the development of emotions and self-understanding. On this note, *Jeremy Carpendale, Charlie Lewis, Ulrich Müller,* and *Timothy Racine* start with a more general account on the constructing perspectives in the social making of minds thereby focusing on the development of joint attention in infants.

On the face of ethological perspectives the processes involved in the social making of minds are not restricted to human beings. *Lucie Salwiczek* and *Wolfgang Wickler* demonstrate that even animals' minds are shaped throughout several social processes. They present examples illustrating basically different mind-shaping processes as well as common mind-shaping phenomena with implications for the understanding of human minds. In line with this *Josep Call* suggests that chimpanzees are even sensitive to some of the psychological states of others. They can gauge the motives of a human experimenter and distinguish his intentional from accidental actions indicating that they interpret the perceptions and actions of others from a psychological perspective.

Whereas the former contributions addressed the question of how far and how deep mental structures are shaped through the social context, the last contributions raise the question how the underlying processes start. *Petra Hauf* and *Wolfgang Prinz* consider the bidirectional exchange between self-performed actions and perceived actions of others during infancy. *Jaqueline Nadel, Ken Prepin,* and *Mako Okanda* argue that precursors of inferential capacities concerning self and others' understanding are found in the early experience of social contingency and emotion sharing. *György Gergely* and *Gergely Csibra* critically re-examine the dominant role attributed to imitative learning in the intergenerational transmission of human cultural knowledge. *Josef Perner* and *Johannes Brandl* introduce a new theory of cognitive changes around 4 years of age by trying to explain why the understanding of false belief and the understanding of alternative naming emerge at this age. All these contributions highlight that cognitive development is more than just an increase in processing capacity but involves profound changes in how we understand the external world and that of our minds.

The aim of the interdisciplinary conference on "Making Minds" was to come a step closer on the way to a broad and coherent theoretical framework for better understanding the input of social context in the formation of the self. Even though we did not fully succeed in this we explored synergies. We considered these synergies being worthwhile leaving the Conference and distributing among other interdisciplinary interested colleagues. Accordingly, we published the contributions firstly as two separated special issues in *Interaction Studies: Social Behaviour and Communication in Biological and Artificial Systems*; an international journal speaking especially to an interdisciplinary interested audience. Now, the book highlights the significance of the contributions to the interdisciplinary discussion about the social making of minds by bringing together both special issues into one volume. The contributions show converging evidence for the important impact of social exchange. No doubt, our mental structures and/or dispositions are shaped through social interaction. But, social interaction is by definition bi-directional. Therefore, we still have to keep in mind, that not only is our self shaped by others, but also that we are the others who shape social minds…

Enjoy being put into others' shoes…

Petra Hauf and Friedrich Försterling

Of minds and mirrors

An introduction to the social making of minds

Wolfgang Prinz, Friedrich Försterling and Petra Hauf
Max Planck Institute for Human Cognitive and Brain Sciences, Leipzig /
University of Munich / University of Antigonish, Canada

Minds

Psychology is about people. Psychological explanations seek to explain how individuals think, feel, and act. For both folk psychology and scientific psychology, individual minds are the natural units of analysis and investigation. For example, we explain an individual's actions by resorting to mental operations preceding those actions. These operations, in turn, may be drawn from the various representational resources that pertain to permanent motives, transient needs, stored knowledge about the world, or perceptually mediated knowledge about the current environment. All of these operations and resources are thought to work in individual minds, bringing forth thoughts, feelings, and actions.

As has occasionally been pointed out, psychology's preoccupation with isolated, individual minds may be traced back to the roots of this discipline in social and political individualism that started dominating European thought in the 18th century — and continues to do so now. Since the study of individual minds is fairly constitutive of psychology, this discipline may even be considered the scientific counterpart of individualism in ethics, law, and politics (Barnes, 2000; Danziger, 1990; Kusch, 1999; Markus, Kitayama, & Heiman, 1996).

One of the obvious observations about individual minds is that they are different from each other. People may deeply differ in their beliefs and attitudes, in their needs and desires, in their talents and skills. Still, no less obvious is the observation that, despite deep-going differences, all these minds have something in common as well — that which makes them human minds, that which gives them the power to bring forth thoughts, feelings, and actions. We are thus faced with the issue of how psychological explanations can accommodate the dialectics of unity and diversity entailed in these seemingly conflicting observations.

To answer this question, psychology has come up with a simple standard model for the making of minds, which is largely based on intuitions borrowed from folk psychology. Central to that model is a distinction between two basic aspects of mental life: *universal form* and *specific content*. According to the model, universal mental form, or structure, emerges from internal sources, whereas specific mental content is acquired through interaction with external sources.

As concerns the build-up of *universal form*, or structure, the long history of psychology has seen a rich variety of classifications, models, and metaphors. For instance, medieval Christian philosophy believed in three faculties of the mind — reason, desire, and volition. 19th century phrenological systems believed in more than 30 such faculties. Others, like Wilhelm Wundt, replaced mental faculties by mental elements like sensations and feelings. In recent textbooks we no longer encounter such coherent systems of the mind's basic make-up. Still, we do encounter various building blocks for such systems. They either come as neutral devices for storage (like episodic and semantic memory) and processing (like working memory, attention, and executive control), or as dedicated devices for particular representational purposes (e.g., for faces, actions, self and other). Even if there is no consensus across textbooks about how universal functions and devices should be individuated and classified, there is consensus that such universals do exist and that they make up the basic structure of the human mind as it unfolds in each and every individual. Universal structure is typically thought to arise from our biological nature, rooted in our genes and expressed in the functional architecture of our brains.

As concerns the build-up of *specific contents*, psychological theories resort less to genes, but rather focus on the individual's learning history. Since the early days of psychological research, learning mechanisms have attracted a vast amount of attention. This is not surprising, since it is through these mechanisms that individual minds become shaped; not only by their physical environments but also by the social and cultural environments they live in. It is through social communication and interaction that universal form gets filled with specific socio-cultural content, be it culture-specific, group-specific, family-specific, etc. Individual minds become social minds by learning to share their mental contents with others — their beliefs, attitudes, norms, and behaviors.

In sum, the standard model for the making of individual minds holds that whereas specific content is acquired from external environmental sources, universal form emerges from internal sources in the individual herself. Therefore, it is widely believed that the universals of mental structure can be studied in isolated minds whereas the specifics of mental contents need to be explored in minds interacting with their environments.

Mirrors

In this volume about the *"Social Making of Minds"* we wish to examine the notion that social communication and interaction may perhaps play a stronger and more deep-rooted role than the standard model provides– a role not only for the build-up of mental contents such as beliefs, motives, and attitudes, but of mental form and structure as well.

How could this happen? How could it be at all that the make-up of a thing depends on the way we talk about or interact with it? Of such things like, for instance, tigers, trees, or tulips, we would certainly not believe that the way we deal with them, or talk about them — or even talk to them (!) — makes any contribution to their make-up. To such *natural kinds* the constructivist credo that reality is created by social practice cannot be applied — at least not in an obvious and straightforward way. However, it can be applied, at least in principle, to *social kinds* like human minds; that is, to kinds that are themselves sensitive to communication and interaction directed at them. Human minds are special in that respect, because they can take two roles at the same time: the active role of talking about, talking to, or interacting with somebody else, and the passive role of perceiving communications and interactions directed at themselves. Active minds and passive minds are both of the same kind. Not only do they communicate and interact with others in a particular way — they also perceive others of the same kind communicating and interacting with themselves in a particular way.

In fact there are two claims here. One is that people may be able to perceive and understand, through communication and interaction, how they are perceived and understood by others. The second is that their perception of being perceived in a particular way may be constitutive of their becoming that way — thereby adopting, or appropriating the mental organization others impute to them.

These two claims have been used to explain both the diversity and the unity of human minds. *First*, as regards diversity, sociologists, ethnologists, and cultural psychologists have long been claiming that the cultural diversity of the human mind does not only pertain to beliefs, attitudes, and motives. It touches upon more fundamental features of its structural make-up as well, such as the notion of self, boundaries between self and others, personal uniqueness, and identity (see Barnes, 2000; Bruner 1986, 1990; Geertz, 1973, 1975; Markus & Kitayama, 1998; Markus et al., 1996; Mauss, 1950; Shweder & Bourne, 1984; Shweder & Miller, 1991). For instance, one of the programmatic statements by *Clifford Geertz*, cited over and over in that literature, reads as follows:

> "... the Western conception of the person as a bounded, unique, more or less integrated motivational and cognitive universe, a dynamic center of awareness,

emotion, judgment, and action organized into a distinctive whole and set contrastively both against other such wholes and against a social and natural background is, however incorrigible it may seem to us, a rather peculiar idea within the context of the world's cultures..." (Geertz, 1975, p. 48).

In a similar vein, *Jerome Bruner* claimed that:

"Culture is not a set of responses to be mastered, but a way of knowing, of construing the world and others. To enter culture is not to *add* some element to one's 'natural' repertory but to be transformed." (Bruner, 1993, p. 516).

Second, some philosophers have even advocated the more radical claim that the social making of human minds may not only touch upon cultural specifics but on human universals as well. In defending that idea, they come up with some fundamental principles and mechanisms of human communication and interaction — fundamental in the sense that they should apply to all human beings. Let me just quote from three of such philosophical voices — A. Smith, G. W. F Hegel, and R. A. Sharpe.

In his "Theory of Moral Sentiments" (1759/1976) *Adam Smith* was concerned with two major issues. One was how we come to "approve or disapprove of the conduct of another man." Smith suggested that we do it by simulating that conduct, that is, by putting ourselves in the other man's shoes and viewing the case from his perspective. The second issue, which is more relevant for our present context, was how we come to approve or disapprove of our own conduct. At first glance, this appears to be a much simpler task than approving or disapproving of the conduct of others — just because we are already in our own shoes. However, Smith suggested that we do it in an even more complex way, which is actually based on simulating other simulators:

"We can never survey our own sentiments and motives [...], unless we remove ourselves [...] from our own natural station, and endeavor to view them as at a certain distance from us. But we can do this in no other way than by endeavoring to view them with the eyes of other people ..." (Smith, 1759/1976, p. 110).

This is in fact a remarkable claim, invoking that people can perceive their own sentiments and motives only through the eyes of others. Even more remarkable is that Smith, in a further step, extended that principle beyond the domain of moral conduct proper and applied it to the way in which we perceive and shape our own minds:

"Were it possible that a human creature could grow up to manhood in some solitary place, without any communication with his own species, he could no more think of his own character, of the propriety or demerit of his own sentiments and conduct, of the beauty or deformity of his own mind, than of the beauty or deformity of his own face. All these are objects which he cannot easily see, which naturally he does not look at, and with regard to which he is not provided with [a] mirror. [That mirror] is placed in the countenance and behavior of those he lives with [....]; and it is here that he first views the propriety and impropriety of his own passions, the beauty and deformity of his own mind." (p.110).

This is where the mirror comes in that helps us to perceive and portray ourselves (Figure 1). For Adam Smith that mirror is provided by the others we live with. It is their looking at us that helps us to look at ourselves in the same way as others do. And it is only through that looking at ourselves through that mirror that we come to build up our own minds.

Figure 1. Mirrors help individuals to perceive and portray themselves. Taken from Giovanni Boccaccio, Des clères et nobles femmes (c. 1402). *The paintress Marcia portraying herself.* Cliché Bibliothèque Nationale de France, Paris, MS. Fr. 598, fol. 100v. — The picture is particularly remarkable because it depicts not only one of the earliest self-portraits in European art but also the process of portraying oneself with the aid of a mirror.

A similar notion is entailed in *Hegel's* discussion on the constitution of self-consciousness. Hegel's pertinent ideas are laid down in the *"Enzyklopädie der Philosophischen Wissenschaften"* (1817 /1830) and in *"Die Phänomenologie des Geistes"* (1807/1980). We will be brief on Hegel, since we find that it is not easy to understand his user-unfriendly style and terminology (even in German, let alone to translate it correctly). For Hegel, human self-consciousness does not emerge as a brute fact of nature. Rather, it develops in social context. The mechanism, which in Hegel's system takes the role of Adam Smith's mirror, is the mechanism of "Anerkennung" (usually translated with *recognition*, sometimes perhaps better with *acknowledgement*). According to Hegel, self-consciousness can only develop under conditions in which individuals recognize, or acknowledge, each other — and do so in a way that they recognize others as those who recognize themselves and others as well. Here is a short quotation from Hegel and a provisional translation that hopefully captures the gist of what is being said.

> "Das Selbstbewußtseyn ist *an* und *für sich*, indem, und dadurch, daß es für ein anderes an und für sich ist; d.h. es ist nur als ein Anerkanntes." (Hegel, 1807/1980, p. 109).

> "Self-consciousness exists in and for itself, by virtue of the fact that it exists in and for itself for some other (self-consciousness), that is, it only exists as being recognized."

Accordingly, the mechanism of recognition is based on strict mutuality and reciprocity. Humans become intentional subjects only through their mutual attributions of intentionality. Intentionality arises in reciprocal recognition and attribution, and it cannot exist outside our social embeddedness (Pinkard, 2004). Communication and social interaction are prerequisites for the build-up of such key features of the human mind, like conscious awareness and intentionality.

A similar view has recently been advocated by R. A. Sharpe (1990), who provides a blueprint for an evolutionary scenario for the making of the human mind. Like Smith and Hegel, Sharpe contends that conscious beliefs about one's own mind are derived from beliefs about the minds of others. His blueprint language takes the pivotal role of the mirror which links others to self:

> "Once I have language what I can recognize in others I can describe in them and what I can describe in them I will soon describe of myself. I can recognize my intentions in my behavior just as others can. [...] Our conscious beliefs are prompted first by our seeing them in others' actions and then by our describing them first in others, then in ourselves." (Sharpe, 1990, p. 1).

Accordingly, access to our own mental life is much more indirect than is commonly believed:

"What I can recognize in others I can describe in myself, and it is from this point that a mental life can develop. For I can recognize my intentions in the behavior from which others identify my intentions. And from this point on my intentions become available to me by direct inspection, so to speak." (Sharpe, 1990, p. 119).

Accordingly, there can be others without self, but no self without others. The self is parasitic on others: First we understand and describe others, and only then can we describe and understand ourselves.

Making Minds

The claims raised by Smith, Hegel, and Sharpe are certainly well compatible with the constructivist *Zeitgeist*, which hallmarks major present-day theories in the social sciences. Still, *Zeitgeist* notwithstanding, it is fair to say that these global claims have so far not been matched by more local mechanisms explaining how the shaping of individual minds through social context actually works.

To be sure, we certainly do dispose of a rich body of evidence supporting strong correlations between the make-up of individual minds in different cultures and social beliefs, and the practices these cultures share about those individuals (cf., e.g., Markus et al., 1996; Shweder & LeVine, 1984). Though this evidence is certainly suggestive of strong links between minds and their social context, it faces one serious limitation. Since it is correlational by nature, it cannot unequivocally solve the hen-and-egg problem: Is it really the case that the structure of an individual mind is formed through perceiving beliefs and practices directed at it — or is it just the case that those beliefs and practices mirror a mental structure that has formed independently of them?

In this volume we will not focus on global claims and principles. Rather, we would like to step back from global ideas and study more local mechanisms in greater detail — mechanisms that are believed to actually realize the shaping of mental structures through social context. Those local examples are taken from a broad variety of empirical domains and related research traditions. Each of them may come with its own style of method and theory, and they may even not know each other very well. This is the risky part of the enterprise. Still, we believe that those research programs have more in common than they know so far, and we hope that this common ground will become apparent in the volume. This we consider the promising part of the enterprise.

Common ground is provided, we believe, by a three-fold focus that many contributions share: on structures and dispositions, on perceivers' perspectives, and on knowledge about self.

Mental Structures and Dispositions: As stated before, social shaping and modulation of the mind may apply to both transient mental contents and behaviors. These apply to concrete situations on small time-scales, as well as more permanent mental structures and dispositions that generalize over a range of situations over larger time-scales. Contributions to this volume are meant to focus on the social construction of more permanent mental structures and dispositions. *How can social context contribute to the shaping of individuals' mental structures and dispositions?*

Perceiver's Perspective: Research questions pertaining to the social shaping of minds can be phrased from two perspectives: that of the target individual whose dispositions are being shaped, and that of the individuals forming the social context involved in that shaping. This volume is meant to focus on the first of these two perspectives: *How can individuals' mental structures and dispositions be shaped by their perception of other individuals' actions, cognitions, and communications?*

Focus on Self-Related Knowledge: From perceiving other individuals' communications and actions, individuals may derive knowledge about (i) the physical world, (ii) the social world, and — eventually — (iii) about themselves. This volume is meant to focus on that latter domain; that is, on contributions of social context to the build-up of mental structures pertaining to self-related knowledge. *How can individuals' mental structures and dispositions be shaped by the way they perceive themselves treated and/or understood by others?*

So much about common ground. The study of local mechanisms on that ground should help us to delineate the scope of our global claims and answer the question about how far the impact of social context reaches and how deep it goes. Again it was Adam Smith who made particularly strong claims regarding the depth of the impact of social mirroring on the formation of human minds:

> "To a man who from his birth was a stranger to society, the objects of his passions, the external bodies which either pleased or hurt him, would occupy his whole attention. The passions themselves, the desires or aversions, the joys or sorrows, which those objects excited, though of all things the most immediately present to him, could scarce ever be the objects of his thoughts. [...] Bring him into society, and all his own passions will immediately become the causes of new passions. [...]; his desires and aversions, his joys and sorrows [...] will now [...] interest him deeply, and often call upon his most attentive consideration." (p. 110 f).

This claim was advocated 250 years ago. We thought it may be time to go ahead and fill in some details. Naturally, we cannot expect that the empirical investigations will be able to provide direct answers to the abstract conceptual questions asked in the passage above. In order to conduct empirical research, far-reaching conceptual issues need to be broken down into "smaller" manageable empirical research questions. Some of the research we present in the contributions to this volume was not explicitly designed to answer the "big issues" of the making mind question. However, the empirical findings and conceptual analyses originating from more "small grained" theoretical approaches shed light on the more global questions that underlie our topic. Accordingly, this volume about the "*Social Making of Minds*" consist of intra- and interdisciplinary contributions addressing the making mind question from empirical (often experimental) and conceptual perspectives. The areas to be represented are clinical, social and developmental psychology, as well as ethology and philosophy.

Most of the presented empirical contributions use paradigms in which an aspect of the social situation (e.g., behaviors, expectations, or effects of a perceiver), are experimentally or quasi-experimentally varied as independent variables. As dependent variables, changes in the targets' behaviors, states and/or traits are assessed. This orientation is informatively illustrated in the classical experimental paradigm for demonstrating behavioral confirmation (see Snyder & Klein, 2004). Participants ("perceivers") receive information about a stimulus person ("target"), e.g., one group is led to believe that the target is extraverted whereas the other group is informed that the target is introverted. Subsequently, target and perceiver engage in a taped conversation. On the basis of the taped interaction, independent judges rate the behavior of the target. Behavioral confirmation has occurred when the targets' behavior reflects the expectations induced in the perceiver.

The "*Social Making of Minds*": Which phenomena might be susceptible to social fabrication and modulation?

Despite the considerable range of phenomena addressed in the various research programs reported in this volume, most contributions share a focus on self-perceptions or self-schemata, and the psychological processes guided by these concepts. Taking a philosophical perspective, *Kusch* suggests that the fundamental, honorific status of the responsible and free agent needs continuous creation in and through social interaction. He maintains that socialisation, classification of self and others, and the deference emotion system take on major roles in the formation of this mental structure. When the self is built in a social construction, then self (-esteem-related) emotions (such as pride) should be inconceivable outside of a social context.

Even though Kusch's theoretical analysis is not substantiated with empirical evidence, other empirical research programs reported here have — consistent with Kusch's conceptual analysis — demonstrated that the way one perceives oneself perceived by others influences a wide range of self-perceptions as well as self-related thoughts, behaviors and emotions. For instance, the above-mentioned behavioral confirmation studies showed that perceivers' expectations shape targets' behaviors (e.g., extraverted or introverted, respectively). In addition, *Snyder and Klein* reported that such findings are not limited to the laboratory but also occur in more naturalistic settings, especially in the context of stereotype maintenance and inter group-relations. They conclude that perceivers' beliefs with respect to a target are powerful determinants of the psychological reality of that person.

Other research has directly assessed resulting self-perceptions or behavioral reactions of targets exposed to social influence. *Graham*, for instance, studied reactions to peer harassment. Victims of peer harassment blame themselves (their character) more for episodes in which they are attacked by their peers than non-victims. These attributions, in turn, reduce the victim's self-esteem and lead to depression, social anxiety, and loneliness. Hence, the experience of victimization in connection with certain attributions can have detrimental effects for the self.

Hahlweg summarizes research about the impact of schizophrenics' relatives' emotions on relapse, indicating that the probability of relapse drastically increases when family members express strong emotions, especially anger, toward the patient. These findings indicate that — under certain conditions — the social context can create severe disturbances of the mind.

Hence, we can summarize that the way one perceives oneself perceived by others influences a wide range of psychological variables: Trait relevant behavior (Snyder & Klein), self-relevant thoughts such as characterological versus behavioral self blame, as well as affective states such as depression and social anxiety (Graham), and even debilitating psychological disorders such as schizophrenic relapse (Hahlweg).

The "*Making Minds Effects*": How far and how deep do they go? How strong and how long lasting are they?

The susceptibility to social influence of psychological phenomena ranging from trait-relevant behaviors to deep psychological disturbances such as schizophrenia might, at first glance, be interpreted as strong support for the notion of the social construction of the mind. However, a word of caution might be in order: *Jussim et al.* (this volume) argue that social psychology tends to portray social perceivers as inaccurately informed individuals who are guided by stereotypes imputing unrealistic expectations on targets and thus creating a deformed social reality. In this context, the mind is often conceived of as a product of shortcomings and distortions. This picture has been implemented by classical studies such as Rosenthal und

Jacobson's (1968) "pygmalion in the classroom" or Rosenhahn's findings on the labelling of psychiatric (pseudo-) patients (1973). These studies apparently showed that students' intelligence and individuals' mental health are strongly determined by (teachers' or psychiatrists', respectively) unrealistic expectations, or more generally, that inaccurate perceivers arbitrarily create minds. Jussim et al., however, argue that the mind typically reflects rather than produces social reality and that self-fulfilling prophecies and expectancy confirmation, when they occur, are rather small and unstable, whereas social reality creates strong and stable effects. They base their arguments on evidence gathered by reviewing the literatures on self-fulfilling prophecies, expectancy confirmation and on accuracy in social perception, and they introduce the "goodness of judgment index" to assess the degree of imperfection of social judgments.

The *"Social Making of Minds"*: Is it confined to specific content or does it also affect universal form?

These contributions provide clear evidence for the making of mind with regard to specific content (e.g., high vs. low self-esteem, depression, introversion). Possibly the influence of expressed emotions on schizophrenic relapse might be taken as an example for social influence on psychological structure, as this disturbance involves changes in very basic cognitive processes. However, researchers on Expressed Emotions do not assume that family members' emotions influence the "universal structure" of the schizophrenic patient. By contrast, Hahlweg suggests — in his diathesis-stress model — that Expressed Emotions (external input; "stress") only has such a profound influence on psychological functioning (schizophrenic relapse) for individuals with specific internal predispositions (internal processes; diatheses).

However, one could argue that the social making of universal structure might specifically occur in the early stages of human development. Naturally, Kusch's analysis of the status of the self as responsible and free agent refers to processes that have occurred long before the age of the typical experimental participant (college age). Therefore, the search for the fabrication of structures might be especially promising in the domain of developmental psychology. In addition, ethologists have investigated different species throughout the animal kingdom to especially address the question about specific contents, as well as about the universal forms of self-development through social interaction.

The *"Social Making of Minds"*: What processes are involved?

Kusch differentiates the classification of natural objects from the classification of individuals, and points out that individuals are both classifiers as well as objects of classification. Humans do both, they respond to and participate in their own social classification. Self-classifications (e.g., as a responsible and free agent) depend on how others classify the self.

In line with these general ideas, *Swann's* research program focuses on the reciprocal nature between mind makers and minds in the making. He asks whether behavioral confirmation is a ubiquitous phenomenon. Obviously, individuals do not change — like chameleons — their psychological structures as soon as they are exposed to different views about themselves. Rather, they maintain a certain degree of stability in their self-assessments. Without such stable self-schemas it would be difficult to predict the future. Swann points out that exposure to others' false conceptions or expectations about us lead to active attempts to disconfirm these expectations. This phenomenon is labelled "self-verification". Shifting the focus of attention from the perceiver to the target, Swann analyses causes and consequences of self-verification. Self-verification is documented in various ways. For instance, there is a desire to interact with individuals who view the person the same way as one sees oneself. In addition, individuals actively strive to get their partners to see them as they view themselves, and failure to have one's self-views verified results in distress, and might lead to withdrawal from the ("self-falsifying") relationship. Notably, the desire for self-verification is not only present for positively valued traits (i.e., persons with high self-perceived ability preferring to interact with individuals who consider them smart) but also applies to negative self-views (individuals low in self-perceived ability prefer individuals estimating their ability to below).

In a similar vein, Hahlweg points out that the analysis of communication sequences between discharged schizophrenics and their family revealed that the "making of the schizophrenic mind" might not be a unidirectional process. High "expressed emotions" (EE-) family members showed critical behavior to which the (former) patient responded to, in turn, in a critical manner. Hence, bi-directional escalation, which resulted in an increase of the patients' autonomous arousal, took place. Such escalation was not observed in low EE patients.

Similarly, studies on victimization have documented the interplay between victimization and targets' attributions for victimization (Graham); her studies showed that personal factors (i.e., characterological attributions) together with situational social stimuli (i.e., rejection) give rise to a change of mind.

From the contributions of Snyder and Klein, Swann, Graham, as well as Hahl-weg, one may draw the conclusion that the "making of minds" is possibly most properly understood as an interactive affair in which both perceivers and targets shape the minds of one another through a process of identity negotiation. More-over, behavioral confirmation and self-verification mark two opposite poles of the making mind process: susceptibility and resistance to social influence, respec-tively. Therefore, the question is raised about under which conditions self-views adapt to others' perceptions and when they are defended against the views of the social environment? Snyder and Swann suggest that when certainty (and possibly importance) about the attribute in question is high, self-verification wins over be-havioral confirmation.

In the same vein, *Vallacher et al.* maintain that coordination between individ-uals in close relationships has not yet received sufficient attention. They present a dynamical systems model to capture the emergence, maintenance and disruption of coordination in such relationships.

To summarize: The making of minds is not a one-way route but should be con-ceived of as an interactive process involving the perceiver and the target. Kusch points out that individuals are not only classified, they are classifiers as well. The idea of such an interactive process was echoed in the research programmes on victimiza-tion, expressed emotions, and, most explicitly, in research on self-verification.

The *"Social Making of Minds"*: What local mechanisms are involved?

As has already been indicated, we expected implicit or explicit attribution, indirect communication of such attributional assumptions and unintentional processes (e.g., social situations providing particular behavioral roles for the individual) to be operative in this context.

Snyder and Klein alluded to the possible role of targets' attributions in the mind making process. For instance, in the behavioral confirmation paradigm, a target might realistically make a situational attribution of his (e.g., extraverted) be-havior, which occurred in response to communication with a perceiver in whom a false expectancy about his extraversion was induced. In this case, he might dis-count his own dispositions as a cause for his behavior and leave the situation with an unchanged mind. However, if such an external explanation is not made (for in-stance, when the situational determinant of behavior is not salient), the expectancy confirming behavior might be attributed to internal dispositions (and disconfirm-ing behavior attributed to the situation). As a consequence, the person's self con-cept may be changed (an idea already referred to in Bem's (1967) self perception theory). Similarly, Graham explicitly addresses the role of attributions in the making of minds. Her findings suggest that perceivers' beliefs about targets can shape the targets' mind if these beliefs create target behaviors that are internally attributed. Moreover, Graham shows that social situations, which provide particular behavioral roles for the individual, shape such (target-) attributions. She found that the psychological consequences of being victimized (i.e., characterological self-blame, and the subsequent social anxiety and loneliness) were stronger for victims belonging to the ethnic majority (!) group than for those who are minorities.

Kusch focuses on the importance of perceivers' assignment of responsibility to the target. He suspects that self-perception as a responsible agent is a social creation which could not exist without such attributions being made by others. Moreover, Hahlweg has alluded to the possibility that the anger of schizophrenic family members might convey to patients that they are held responsible for their behavior, and that this information might play an important role in the process leading from high Expressed Emotions to schizophrenic relapse. More specifically, he points out that nonverbal communication, i.e., emotional expressions (such as anger or pity) can inform a target how a perceiver explains the target's behavior through factors controllable or uncontrollable by the target. Hence, perceivers' emotions can be used by targets to infer whether one is being perceived as responsible for one's actions.

Can the attributions which might be responsible for the making of minds be communicated in regular verbal communication? *Hilton et al.* (this volume) address such verbal communication mechanisms, i.e., specific aspects of language use. They present research indicating that quantifiers (e.g., few, many) or probability expressions are primarily communicated because of their pragmatic function, rather than in order to describe an objective state of affairs. For instance, a travel agent might tell a customer "there are <u>few</u> seats left on the plane" or, alternatively, "there are <u>a few</u> seats left". Although both statements do not communicate different information about the exact number of seats available on the plane, they communicate advice about the course of action to take ("buy immediately" or "you can wait"). Hence, in everyday communication, probability statements and quantifiers often convey causal arguments for or against a course of action.

In summary, the contributions show that the way we perceive ourselves understood can have, under certain circumstances, severe impact on our mind; ranging from the cross-situationally stable changes of extraverted behaviors, which targets showed in behavioral confirmation experiments (Snyder), self-esteem, depression (Graham), to schizophrenia (Hahlweg). Whether these effects reflect entirely inaccurate processes might be doubted. The spectacular findings reported by Rosenthal or Rosenhahn indicating that inaccurate perceivers' attitudes strongly influence human minds must be viewed with caution (Jussim et. al). In addition, the making of mind is probably not to be conceived of as a one-way route but rather as a process of identity negotiation involving both the perceiver as well as the target. Attributional processes might be good candidates for important mechanisms to be involved in the making of mind: Attributions targets make for external events and their own, perceiver-induced, behavioral changes might determine whether or not stable changes in the self occur. In addition, perceivers' attributions might be transmitted quite indirectly via emotions and they are communicated implicitly and explicitly in our language.

Psychology is about people, and these people act in or interact with their social environment. Accordingly, it is of special importance to understand other individuals, their actions, thoughts, desires, and feelings. Understanding the way other people's minds work — and knowing that those minds are linked to our own — is crucial to our interaction with these people. In view of that, the volume about the "Social Making of Minds" focuses on the processes involved in the shaping of mental structures through social context. The volume brings together researchers from various fields, like clinical, social, and developmental psychology, as well as ethology and philosophy, which are addressing the challenging topic of *Making Minds*.

Wolfgang Prinz, Friedrich Försterling, and Petra Hauf

References

Barnes, B. (2000). *Understanding agency. Social theory and responsible action.* London: Sage Publications.

Bem, D. J. (1967). Self-perception: An alternative explanation of cognitive dissonance phenomena. *Psychological Review, 74,* 183–200.

Bruner, J. (1986). *Actual minds, possible worlds.* Cambridge, MA: Harvard University Press.

Bruner, J. (1990). *Acts of meaning.* Cambridge, MA: Harvard University Press.

Bruner, J. (1993). Do we "acquire" culture or vice versa? A reply to M. Tomasello, A. Cole Kruger, & H. Horn Ratner ("Cultural learning"). *Behavioral and Brain Sciences, 16*(3), 515–516.

Danziger, K. (1990). *Constructing the subject. Historical origins of psychological research.* Cambridge: Cambridge University Press.

Geertz, C. (1973). *Interpretation of cultures.* New York: Basic Books.

Geertz, C. (1975). On the nature of anthropological understanding. *American Scientist, 63,* 47–53. [Also in: Basso, K., & Selby, H. (Eds.) (1976). *Approaches to symbolic anthropology* (pp. 221–237). Albuquerque, NM: University of New Mexico Press.]

Graham, S. (this volume). Attributions and peer harassment.

Hahlweg, K. (this volume). The shaping of individuals' mental structures and dispositions by others: Findings from research on expressed emotion.

Hegel, G. W. F. (1830). *Encyclopädie der philosophischen Wissenschaften im Grundrisse. Zum Gebrauch seiner Vorlesungen* (3rd edition/3. Ausgabe). Heidelberg: Verwaltung des Oßbald'schen Verlags, C. F. Winter. (Original ed. 1817)

Hegel, G. W. F. (1980/1807). *Phänomenologie des Geistes* [Band 9 der historisch-kritischen Ausgabe G. W. F. Hegel: Gesammelte Werke]. Hamburg: Felix Meiner. (First ed., 1807, titled *System der Wissenschaft. Erster Theil, die Phänomenologie des Geistes*. Bamberg, Würzburg: Joseph Anton Goebhardt.)

Hilton, D., Villejoubert, G., Bonnefon, J. F. (this volume). How to do things with logical expressions: Creating collective value through co-ordinated reasoning.

Jussim, L., Harber, K. D., Crawford, J. T., Cain, T. R., & Cohen, F. (this volume). Social reality makes the social mind: Self-fulfilling prophecy, bias, and accuracy.

Kusch, M. (this volume). How minds and selves are made. Some conceptual preliminaries.

Kusch, M. (1999). *Psychological knowledge: A social history and philosophy.* London: Routledge.

Markus, H. R. & Kitayama, S. (1998). The cultural psychology of personality. *Journal of Crosscultural Psychology, 29,* 63–87.

Markus, H. R., Kitayama, S., & Heiman, R. J. (1996). Culture and "basic" psychological principles. In E. T. Higgins & A. W. Kruglanski (Eds.), *Social psychology: Handbook of basic principles* (pp. 857–913). New York, London: Guilford Press.

Mauss, M. (1950). *Sociologie et anthropologie.* Paris: Presses Universitaires de France. [English transl. publ. 1979 in London: Routledge & Kegan Paul]

Pinkard, T. (2004). Reason, recognition, and historicity. In B. Merker, G. Mohr, & M. Quante (Eds.), *Subjektivität und Anerkennung* (pp. 45–66). Paderborn: Mentis.

Rosenhahn, D. L. (1975). On being sane in insane places. *Science, 179,* 250–258.

Rosenthal, R. & Jacobson, L. F. (1968). *Pygmalion in the classroom: Teacher expectations and intellectual development.* New York: Holt.

Sharpe, R. A. (1990). *Making the human mind.* London: Routledge.

Shweder, R. A., & Bourne, L. (1984). Does the concept of the person vary cross-culturally? In R. A. Shweder & R. A. LeVine (Eds.), *Culture theory: Essays on mind, self and emotion* (pp. 158–199). Cambridge, New York: Cambridge University Press.

Shweder, R. A., & Miller, J. G. (1991). The social construction of the person: How is it possible? In R. A. Shweder (Ed.), *Thinking through cultures: Expeditions in cultural psychology* (pp. 156–185). Cambridge, MA: Harvard University Press.

Shweder, R. A., & LeVine, R. A. (1984). (Eds.), *Culture theory: Essays on mind, self and emotion* (pp. 158–199). New York: Cambridge University Press.

Smith, A. (1976/1759). *The theory of moral sentiments.* Reprinted: The Glasgow edition of the works and correspondences of Adam Smith, Vol. 1, Eds.: D. D. Raphael & A. L. Macfie. Oxford: Clarendon Press.

Snyder, M., & Klein, O. (this volume). Construing and constructing others. On the reality and the generality of the behavioral confirmation scenario.

Swann, W. B. (this volume). The self and identity negotiation.

Vallacher, V. R., Nowak, A., & Zochowski, M. (this volume). Dynamics of social coordination: The synchronization of internal states in close relationships.

How minds and selves are made

Some conceptual preliminaries

Martin Kusch
University of Cambridge

This paper aims at a conceptual clarification of some of the mechanisms that are involved when human selves are made in interactions with each other. Four such broad mechanisms are distinguished: socialisation, classification of self and others, the deference-emotion system, and the attribution and manipulation of the status of the responsible agent. The first two mechanisms are modelled with simple mechanical machines like clocks and signalling devices. Regarding the status of the responsible agent, the paper offers a proposal as to why we have conflicting intuitions about freedom of the will.

1. Social interaction

It is a truism that human selves are, to a considerable degree, formed by social interactions. No-one doubts that a substantial part of our mental structures and dispositions, and the ways in which we understand ourselves, are shaped by our perceptions of how we are understood and treated by others. That the social making of minds is widely accepted does not of course mean that it is well understood in its details. Undoubtedly, there is scope for progress regarding the identification and study of many of the psychological and social mechanisms involved.

Naturally, much of this progress must come from empirical work in cognitive and social psychology, sociology and anthropology.[1] As a philosopher I have no new empirical observations to report, at least none that are systematic or based on experimental investigations. Fortunately, the possible contribution of philosophy lies in any case elsewhere: at its best it can offer abstract concepts and models that may be of some use in identifying and conceptualising some of the desiderata and results of empirical investigations. In an attempt to make such kind of contribution here, I shall, in what follows, sketch some models and ideas for understanding four areas that must loom large in any research on the social shaping of minds and selves: socialisation, classification, sanctioning, and the status of the free and responsible agent. Not all of the models and concepts I shall be discussing are altogether new: I hope, however, to have developed them in some new ways. I am also mindful of the fact that numerous social psychologists have preceded me in arguing for the social construction of personal reality. This paper merely redevelops the philosophical foundations of an issue that has been, and continues to be, of critical importance to psychology in general, and social psychologists in particular.

2.   Socialisation

I begin with *socialisation*. Socialisation is the process in and through which individuals become competent members of a social group. By speaking of 'modes of socialisation' I want to draw attention to the fact that this process can take different forms. One useful dichotomy is 'deistic' versus 'continuous' socialisation. The underlying metaphor comes from the medieval and early-modern distinction between two conceptions of creation: the 'deistic' and the 'continued-creation' views. According to the first, God is like a clockmaker: after the world has been created, it runs its predetermined course without any further divine intervention. After the initial creation the creator is a *Deus otiosus* (an idle God). According to the continued-creation view, however, creation and preservation of the created order are one and the same process; creation is moment-by-moment creation. God is never idle. In analogous fashion we can distinguish between deistic and continued-creation views and phenomena of socialisation. Some social theorists (e.g. Parsons, 1937) take socialisation to be a deistic process, with the community taking the place of God; other social theorists conceive of socialisation as a continuous process (e.g. Garfinkel, 1967). As ever, the truth lies somewhere between the extremes: some aspects of our socialisation are once and for all, many others are continuous.

The conception of socialisation as a continuous process can be analysed further. I shall do so by using a mechanical metaphor already alluded to above: clocks.[2] I shall simplify matters by assuming that socialisation can be thought of as a practice in which communities create uniformity or consensus amongst their members. Consider then a population of clocks. Assume that each clock has a certain degree of mechanical individuality; that is, each clock runs a little faster or slower than the others. Imagine that we are trying to set up a form of interaction between the clocks that would make their behaviour more uniform, that is, that would reduce the differences in their respective times. Let us stipulate that we want a solution that does not involve repeated human intervention. Many different such uniformity-creating systems of interaction are of course possible. But the following three are particularly salient.

The 'way of the single authority' is to designate one clock as the standard for all. At regular intervals, this master clock sends a signal to all other clocks, thereby setting them all to its time. In between such interventions each clock displays again its individuality of running faster or slower than the other clocks.

The 'way of the single consensus' is to have all clocks linked up to one consensus-forming mechanism. At regular intervals, this mechanism simultaneously receives information about the times of all clocks. The mechanism calculates the average of all of the readings it receives and resets the clocks to this time. So, for example, if four clocks show 5 to, 10 to, 5 past, and 10 past twelve, the average time will be twelve.

Finally, according to the 'way of the multiple, local, consensus' we allow our clocks to move about freely, and without being linked up to any kind of master device. The space in which they move about is limited, however, and thus they randomly bump into each other. Whenever two (or more) of them collide, they perform the following operation. They observe each others' and their own times, calculate the average of these two (or more) readings, and set themselves to this value. They then continue their journey until they collide with another clock.

It is of course this third scenario that best approximates ordinary continuous socialisation. The 'third way' models the scenario of social institutions in which no member has access to the actions of all, and where some degree of conformity co-exists with divergence. Indeed, only under special circumstances will all clocks ever show the same time. But their mechanical individuality will not be able to express itself without limitation. Given a sufficient frequency of encounters between the clocks, they all will end up within a limited *bandwidth* of times.

Each of the three 'ways' models one way of organising socialisation and social consensus. And in order for each way to work, we need to presuppose specific abilities and dispositions in each of the participating clocks. In the first case, the way of the single consensus, the demands on the construction of each subordinate clock are minimal. It is enough that we have one mechanism that links each clock to the master device. Through this mechanism the master clock's time is transferred to the subordinate clock. There is little in this case that even begins to approximate — even by way of a mechanical analogy — the ways in which my mental structures and dispositions, and the ways in which I understand myself, are shaped by my perceptions of how I am understood and treated by others.

Things get more interesting, however, as we turn from the first to the third scenario, leaving the second as an intermediate case to one side. In the third case, each clock needs the following devices:

1. a *system of mobility*, that is, a means of moving about within the confined space;

2. a *system for the perception of others*, that is, a mechanism that detects the position of the hands on the dial of the other clocks;
3. a *system of self-monitoring*, that is, a mechanism that detects the position of the hands of its own dial;
4. a *system of comparison and mediation*, that is, a mechanism that calculates the averages; and
5. a *system of self-adjustment*, a mechanism that brings it about that the clock resets the hands of its dial to the calculated average time.

It is obvious that these five abstract systems — appropriately refined and developed — do not just characterise clocks in the way of the local consensus: they can be found in most social animals. Possessing instances of these systems is a precondition for a social life in and through which individuals' mental structures and dispositions are shaped and modified.

3. Classification

I now turn to my second topic: *classification*. There are two distinctions I want to develop: natural versus social classification on the one hand, and other-regarding versus self-regarding classification on the other hand. The game I am after is a better understanding of the constitution of social statuses and institutions.

Again it seems useful to work with a simple mechanical model. Since it is hard to think of clocks as classifiers, let us replace them with a different sort of machine.[3] I call these machines 'classifiers' and distinguish between 'natural' and 'social classifiers'. Natural classifiers first. Natural classifiers move around in their environment until they encounter physical objects other then themselves. Call these objects '*X*s'. A natural classifier consists of two subsystems, a *pattern recognition system* and a *signal emission system*. The pattern recognition system contains a stored pattern ($= P$); the system matches incoming Xs against this P. Think of the stored patterns as patterns for physical properties like 'square' or 'round'. Natural classifiers check all Xs they encounter. Those that do not fit P do not lead to further action. But if the pattern recognition system detects an X that fits P then this causes the second system, the signal emission system to produce a beep. The machines I am describing obviously model one stereotype of concept application: the case where we apply natural kind terms. In other words, this is the case where the classifier is attentive and responsive only to physical, non-social properties of the things classified. Hence the name 'natural classifiers'.

Contrast natural classifiers with *proto-social classifiers*. Proto-social classifiers lack a pattern recognition system. Instead, they have an *signal-detection system*, a *memory*, and a *tracking device* that follows and records the movements of the Xs. Assume that all proto-social classifiers as well as the Xs, move in close proximity of one another: this not only enables each proto-social classifier to detect signals emitted by all the other proto-social classifiers, it also makes it possible that each proto-social classifier can keep track of all Xs. The Xs move about at random, but they regularly bump into one or another of the proto-social classifiers (they then move on, before colliding with another social classifier). When such a collision with a particular X occurs, proto-social classifiers either emit, or do not emit, a signal on the basis of the following rule: they emit a signal if and only if their memory tells them that all (or most) other proto-social classifiers have previously emitted a signal when colliding with the same particular X. They do not emit a signal when their memory tells them that not all (or not most) proto-social classifiers emitted a signal under this circumstance. Obviously, proto-social classifiers attend to what we might call proto-social properties. Put differently, the acts of signalling have a clear self-referential character: each signalling with respect to a given X signals the existence of all of the prior signallings with respect to the same X by the same and all other social classifiers. This self-referential character of signalling models the self-referential character of our own, human referential activities when we constitute social statuses and institutions. I call a given (type or token) metal disc a coin (say a one-pound coin) because everyone else in my community does so. In referring to the disc as a coin I am ultimately referring to all other community members' acts of referring to the disc as a coin. And because of our collective referential practices the disc has the social status of a coin.

The way I have described the scenario up to this point models only the constitution of social statuses of objects encountered by the classifiers, it does not model the constitution of social statuses for the classifiers themselves. Let us modify the scenario so as to include this further possibility. First, every social classifier $(= SC_i)$ is able to detect and remember the signals that other social classifiers have emitted with respect to SC_i in the past. And second, every social classifier has to decide at regular intervals whether to emit a signal with reference to itself. A social classifier SC_i will be able to do so only if all other social classifiers have emitted such a signal when classifying SC_i in the past.

We have here a new phenomenon: one social classifier responds to other social classifiers' responses to it. Some acts of signalling are now acts in which a social classifier responds to, and participates in, the constitution of its own status. This models the process in and through which our self-understanding is dependent upon how we are understood and treated by others. My self-classification as a member of a club is in good part dependent upon how other club members classify me.

4.   Social emotions

Of course, one of the many features not captured by my mechanical models is the emotional effect of being classified in certain ways by others and oneself. Social life is about more than the collective constitution of statuses, it is also about social emotions like pride and shame, and about sanctions and pain. None of these phenomena are easily captured with mechanical models. One clock can determine the position of hands on the dial of another clock, but no clock can literally be said to sanction another clock. The concept of sanction becomes applicable only once we have reached the level of biological systems that can suffer losses and enjoy gains.

Sanctions come in many different forms. My main distinction amongst *modes of sanctioning* parallels my main distinction in the realm of socialisation: deistic versus continuous. Some types of sanctioning are deistic in character: they are severe, fundamental, and their effects stay with us for a long time. Think of a prison sentence or acts of physical torture. Such sanctions do have a substantial and dramatic effect on those that encounter them. But they are also costly and risky for the one who is doing the sanctioning. Keeping people in prison is expensive and potentially dangerous to the judges and the guards. Continuous sanctioning usually works differently: it reaches its goals not because of its severity but because of its very continuity. It is obvious that most systems of sanctions involved in the making of selves are of the continuous kind.

The most important case of such a system of continuous sanctioning is the 'deference-emotion system'.[4] The precondition of this system is our emotional need to continuously monitor how others treat us and think of us. We respond to our assessments of this treatment by changing our position on an internal scale that ranges from pride to shame. When we believe that others treat us with deference, we feel pride (and related feelings) and move ourselves up on the pride-shame scale. When we suspect that such deference is missing, we tend to feel bad about ourselves and slide downwards towards the shame end of the scale.

This emotional dependence on others is exploited by the deference-emotion system. The granting or withholding of deference constitutes a subtle system of social sanctions, a system that we barely notice. The deference-emotion system is easy to overlook because it is all-pervasive and routine. Almost without knowing it we signal each other our degree of deference; we get others to fulfil our wishes by manipulating their perception of where they stand on the scale between pride and shame; and we endlessly seek to improve our standing in our own eyes. Moreover, producing the sanctions of the deference-emotion system is not costly and carries little risk. Precisely because the sanctions are informal, routine and minute, they can be generated at little cost and risk to their producer. Finally, the deference-emotion system is crucial for understanding how our mental structures and dispositions, and the ways in which we understand ourselves, are often, if not always, shaped by our perceptions of how others understand and treat us. Since others' deference matters to us, we are usually only too willing to change our mental structures and dispositions in ways that increase our chances of moving up on the pride-shame scale.

5. The status of the free and responsible agent

Up to this point I have treated modes of socialisation, modes of classification, and modes of sanctioning as if they were isolated or isolatable issues. Of course they are not. The deference-emotion system as a continuous mode of sanctioning is inseparable from continuous socialisation. And neither continuous socialisation nor the deference-emotion system can be understood without considering social classification and social statuses.

This brings me to my fourth and final topic, the *status of the free and responsible agent*. 'Free and responsible agent' is a social status that plays a key role in our continuous socialisation and in the deference-emotion system. Commenting on this social status thus constitutes a case study in the interdependence of socialisation, sanctioning and social classification.

Recall the standard distinction between the main positions regarding free will and determinism (Figure 1). Compatibilism allows an action to be free even when it is causally determined. Only certain kinds of causes, coercion for example, remove an action from the realm of freedom. Incompatibilism insists that freedom and determinism do not mix. An action cannot be both causally determined and free. Incompatibilism comes in two forms. 'Libertarianism' holds that freedom of the will is possible since certain phenomena are exempt from causal determinism. Such phenomena are, first and foremost, acts of choosing and freely chosen actions. 'Hard determinism' responds to the incompatibility of freedom and determinism in a less compromising fashion. According to hard determinism there is no freedom of the will at all; there is only causal determination. The attribute 'hard' is used in order to distinguish this form of determinism from compatibilism. Compatibilism is a 'soft' form of determinism since it allows causal determination to go (at least sometimes) hand-in-hand with freedom of the will. Hard determinism leaves no space for this possibility. Hard determinists do of course recognise that we often speak as if libertarianism or compatibilism were true. Some hard determinists therefore call for a reform of language. More typically, hard determinists advocate 'illusionism': they regard our libertarian or compatibilist ways of speaking and thinking as useful illusions. They believe that people will be more likely to act co-operatively if they believe themselves to possess internal states of choice and rationality.

Here is a second way to put the differences between the three positions. Compatibilism, hard determinism and libertarianism are different responses to the 'Paradox of Free Will' (Schiffer, 2002):

(1) We have free will; at least some of the things we do we do freely, of our own free will;
(2) Everything we do is such that we were caused to do it by factors over which we have no control, perhaps factors that obtained even before we were born;
(3) If (1) is false, (2) is true.

Different philosophical positions regarding the freedom of the will resolve the paradox by denying different premises: compatibilism rejects (3), libertarianism (2), and hard determinism (1).

Let us say that a paradox has a 'happy-face solution' if and only if we can escape it by rejecting one of its premises (Schiffer, 2002). Compatibilism, libertarianism and hard determinism all believe that the Paradox of Free Will has a happy-face solution. The philosopher Stephen Schiffer disagrees. As he sees it, none of the three options has a satisfactory account of the initial plausibility of its chosen 'odd-guy-out'. On Schiffer's analysis, there is a fundamental tension in our concept of free will, a tension that expresses itself in our acceptance of the incompatible propositions [1] to [3].

I find this analysis persuasive: there is no happy-face solution to the paradox of free will. But I do not think that we should stop here. We need to go further and explain why there is this tension in our concept of free will. I submit that this explanation must focus on the ways in which my self-understanding is shaped by my perceptions of how I am understood and treated by others.

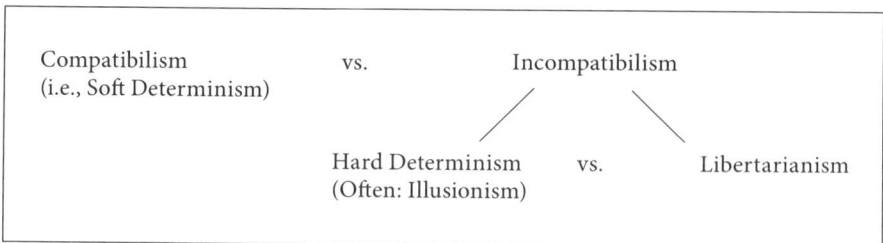

Figure 1. The main positions regarding free will and determinism.

6. Voluntary actions

Much of this explanation is contained in the work of the sociologist Barry Barnes (2000) — even though he fails to do full justice to his own insight.[5] Consider the distinction between actions that are done voluntarily and actions that are done involuntarily. Dictionary definitions suggest that we see a close connection between voluntary actions, freedom from external or internal coercion, rationality and responsibility. Voluntary actions are actions performed by rational agents who have made their own independent and free decisions. Sometimes we are willing to go so far as to say that voluntary agents are the uncaused causes of their actions. They are starting points of causal chains, but their decisions are not themselves caused. To explain a voluntary action is to appeal to reasons rather than causes. Involuntary actions are actions that the agent cannot help doing, actions that the agent was forced to do. Involuntary actions are caused and coerced actions. And to explain an involuntary action is to marshal causes rather than reasons.

Although we sometimes put great emphasis on the distinction between caused and uncaused actions, in other contexts we happily ignore it. We have no difficulties, for instance, holding people responsible for actions that are not voluntary in the strong sense of being uncaused. We punish criminals even though we recognise that the deprivations of their childhood were partial causes of their decisions to commit crimes, and we continue to speak of voluntary actions despite the fact that we learn more and more about the myriad ways in which nature and nurture shape our thinking and behaving.

There must then be two kinds of criteria at work in our thinking about voluntary actions. On the one hand, we have strict criteria for voluntary actions, criteria that demand that voluntary actions are the product of an uncaused causer, of a metaphysically free will. On the other hand, we also seem to admit more diffuse and pragmatic criteria, criteria that allow that voluntary actions and free decisions are the products of all sorts of causal intervention. This duality of criteria raises two questions: What, if anything, underlies the pragmatic set of criteria? And why do we have these two different ways of thinking about free actions?

To answer the first question (concerning the unity underlying the pragmatic criteria), it helps to consider the issue of what kinds of action and decision classifications must be important to beings whose relationships with each others are marked by continuous socialisation of the third way; who relate to one another through the deference-emotion system and who are relentless in their classification of one another and themselves. A little reflection shows that such creatures must find it important to distinguish between two kinds of decisions by others: decisions by others they can influence by means of symbolic interventions and decisions by others that they cannot so influence. I can bring about your decision to bring me a glass of water by asking for it or by explaining how important the water is to me. 'Bringing a glass of water' is a type of action that typically can be brought about by symbolic intervention. However, if you are pathologically obsessive about washing your hands, then typically I cannot stop you from doing so by asking you to stop. Your decision to wash your hand thus falls on the other side of the divide.

The suggestion is that we see our distinctions between voluntary and involuntary actions, and between free and coerced decisions, in light of the distinction between decisions susceptible to change via communication, and decisions not so susceptible. What unifies our set of pragmatic criteria for attributing free decisions and voluntary actions is the idea of being susceptible to verbal intervention. A careful look at the decisions that we end up classifying as either free or coerced suggests that susceptibility to change on the basis of symbolic intervention is central. Put differently, it seems that for us a decision is free if it 'could have been otherwise if symbolic intervention had occurred'. If this is correct, then as 'folk metaphysicians' we are compatibilists concerning causality and freedom: what makes a decision free is not that it is uncaused but that it is not causally insulated from one specific kind of cause: verbal intervention.

If all this is true, why is it that we do not spontaneously produce 'susceptibility to change through communication' as the decisive criterion for free actions? And why do we have such strong intuitions concerning the importance, for voluntary decisions, of rationality, responsibility and uncaused causes?

To find the answers to these questions, we have to remain firmly focused on the fact that we constantly seek to influence each other through interaction in general and communication in particular. Let us call 'causal discourse' the modes of speech in which we centrally rely on the language of 'causes' and 'coercion'; and let us reserve 'voluntaristic discourse' for modes of speech in which we employ the categories of 'responsibility', 'rationality', 'free action' or 'free decision'. Now, which of these discourses is central when we seek to influence others to co-operate with us and to act in ways we would like them to act? Obviously, the answer must be 'voluntaristic discourse'. The best way for you to convince me to change my ways is for you to appeal to my sense of honour and freedom. In so doing you both invoke and manipulate the most important social status of all: the social status of being a responsible and free agent. We constantly hint and imply that we take each other to be the rational and responsible uncaused causes of our actions, and we do so while suggesting that the best way to retain this status is to yield to our demands. We get each other to change our mental structures and dispositions by continuously hinting and implying that such change is precisely the sort of change that a free and responsible agent would aim for.[6]

Here then lies the key to understanding why we do not openly abide by our pragmatic criteria: the strict criteria are an important tool — a tool that is absolutely central to the ways in which we go about influencing one another. Operating the strict criteria for freedom is central to the discourse by which we seek to influence others. In so doing we try to increase the domain of decisions that are free in the pragmatic sense. And at the heart of the operation of strict criteria lies the central honorific status that we constitute collectively but manipulate individually: the social status of the responsible and free agent. This status exists only in and through a myriad of references to it — it is the product of social classification. But it is also the status that we cannot but identify with, and that we need in order to maintain a tolerable position on the pride–shame scale.

We can now see why Schiffer's 'Paradox of Free Will' cannot have a 'happy-face solution': our intuitions regarding freedom have to be contradictory. By calling each other free we both grant each other the most basic honorific status, and seek to bend each other's will to our own.[7]

7. Conclusions

Let me try to sum up. We are trying to understand the psychological and social mechanisms that are involved when human selves are made in their interactions with other human selves; that is, we are trying to understand the ways in which our mental structures and dispositions, and the ways in which we understand ourselves, are, to a considerable degree, shaped by our perceptions of how we are understood and treated by others.

I have made an effort to add to our understanding of some of these mechanisms and ways by first isolating them analytically, and then putting them back together again in order to understand their interdependence. Human selves are made and remade primarily in continuous socialisation and interaction. This continuous socialisation and interaction is local, does not have one single overriding standard, and results in a bandwidth, rather than a unique set, of calibrated behaviours. Continuous and local socialisation invariably involves the deference-emotion system, and it is circularly related to the constitution of social statuses, and the social classification of others and oneself. We are continuously being socialised into classifying ourselves and others in ways that fit with how others continuously classify others and themselves — and to act upon such classifications. We are socialised so as to fit with various statuses, and socialised to monitor both ourselves and others for adherence to these statuses.

The responsible and free agent is our most fundamental honorific social status. This status needs continuous creation in and through interaction. And it is the status that emotionally we cannot do without. That is why we maintain the status even when the action in question is clearly causally determined. However, precisely because the status is so important to us, we can be moved — by promises and threats regarding it — to change ourselves, our mental structures and dispositions.

Needless to say there are many other ways in which minds and selves are made in and through interaction. But the way that involves the interrelation of continuous interaction, the deference-emotion system, and the status of the free agent is both intriguing and important.

Notes

1. See the other papers in this volume.

2. I am not the first to use this reification of social life; Pierre Bourdieu (1990, p. 59) used the same metaphor some years back. But my way of developing this idea owes little to his work (cf. Kusch, 1999, pp. 270–272).

3. My original inspiration here was Barnes (1983), cf. Kusch (1999, pp. 255–275).

4. This was first described in detail by Scheff (1988, 1990).

5. As I have tried to show elsewhere; cf. Kusch (2004).

6. Barnes is here indebted to the seminal work on 'face' and 'face-maintenance' by Goffman (1967). See also Brown and Levinson (1987).

7. My discussion of Schiffer's Paradox will not satisfy the philosopher who insists on a *philosophical* answer to the question 'are we — metaphysically speaking — free or not?' I have attempted a *genealogy* of our intuitions regarding freedom in an attempt to explain why philosophers have been unable to agree on a solution to the Paradox of Free Will. But of course a philosopher might insist that he or she has found such a solution.

References

Barnes, B. (1983). Social life as bootstrapped induction. *Sociology, 17*, 524–545.
Barnes, B. (2000). *Understanding agency: Social theory and responsible action*. London: Sage.
Bourdieu, P. (1990). *In other words: Essays towards a reflexive sociology*. Cambridge: Polity Press.
Brown, P. and S. C. Levinson (1987). *Politeness: Some universals in language usage*. Cambridge: Cambridge University Press.
Garfinkel, H. (1967). *Studies in ethnomethodology*. Englewood Cliffs, NJ.: Prentice-Hall.
Goffman, E. (1967). *Interaction ritual: Essays on face-to-face behavior*. New York: Doubleday.

Kane, R. (Ed.). (2002). *Oxford handbook of free will*. Oxford: Oxford University Press.

Kusch, M. (1999). *Psychological knowledge: A social history and philosophy*. London: Routledge.

Kusch, M. (2002). *Knowledge by agreement: The programme of communitarian epistemology*. Oxford: Oxford University Press.

Kusch, M. (2004). Barnes on the freedom of the will. Forthcoming in M. Mazzotti (Ed.), *Festschrift for Barry Barnes*.

Parsons, T. (1937). *The structure of social action*. New York: Free Press.

Scheff, T. J. (1988). Shame and conformity: The deference-emotion system. *American Sociological Review, 53*, 395–406.

Scheff, T. J. (1990). *Microsociology: Discourse, emotion, and social structure*. Chicago and London: University of Chicago Press.

Schiffer, S. (2002). Skepticism and the vagaries of justified belief. Paper available at: http://www.umass.edu/philosophy/events/contextualism_conference_files/SchifferPaper.pdf

Dynamics of social coordination

The synchronization of internal states in close relationships

Robin R. Vallacher, Andrzej Nowak and Michal Zochowski
Florida Atlantic University / Warsaw University / University of Michigan

Close relationships are described in terms of the temporal coordination of behavior based on the similarity of partners' internal states (e.g., moods, personality traits). Coupled nonlinear dynamical systems (logistic equations) were used to model the emergence, maintenance, and disruption of coordination in such relationships. For each system (partner), there was a control parameter corresponding to an internal state and a dynamical variable corresponding to behavior. Computer simulations investigated how the temporal coordination of behavior in a relationship reflects the similarity of partners' control parameters and the strength of coupling (mutual influence between partners). Several types of coordination were observed, with in-phase synchronization occurring for strong coupling and similarity in internal states. In a variation of the model, each system could adjust its own control parameter to synchronize its dynamics with that of the other system. Simulation results provide insight into several topics in the study of close relations and group dynamics.

Interpersonal relations are established through the coordination of people's thoughts, moods, and actions. Coordination is necessary for any type of sustained relationship, from those defined in purely instrumental terms to those defined in terms of romance and commitment. Lay people clearly recognize the importance of coordination to their relations with one another. Two individuals with a positive relationship are commonly described as "being on the same wavelength" or "resonating with one another," whereas individuals in problematic relationships are said to "be out of synch with each other." Yet despite the centrality of coordination in people's implicit psychology of relationships, this construct has received surprisingly little attention in scientific psychology. Our aim in this article is to document the role of coordination in close relationships and to present a dynamical model, implemented in computer simulations, that illustrates how this dynamic component develops in interpersonal contexts.

The importance of coordination to social relations has not been entirely lost on social scientists. The prevalent approach, however, has been to conceptualize interactions and relationships with respect to global variables that characterize the interaction or relationship as a whole. The interactions of dyads and groups, for example, are often investigated in terms of dimensions such as cooperation versus competition, compatibility of motives and goals, and the structure of norms and roles (e.g., Biddle & Thomas, 1966; Dawes, 1980; Levine & Moreland, 1998; Berkowitz & Walster, 1976; Wish, Deutsch, & Kaplan, 1976). Some approaches emphasize the temporal aspects of social interaction, but the focus is typically restricted to the development of strategies for achieving personal or shared goals (e.g., Axelrod, 1984; Messick & Liebrand, 1995; Thibaut & Kelley, 1959).

Social coordination takes on a different meaning when viewed from the perspective of dynamical systems. In this account, two (or more) people are coordinated to the extent that the actions, thoughts, and feelings of one person are related over time to the actions, thoughts, and feelings of the other person or persons (cf. Nowak & Vallacher, 1998; Vallacher, Read, & Nowak, 2002). With this in mind, we suggest that the concepts and methods used to characterize temporal coordination in physical systems may be relevant to coordination in interpersonal systems. In particular, we argue that coupled non-linear dynamical systems capture the essence of the temporal coordination of individual dynamics in relationships. We employ coupled logistic equations — the simplest dynamical systems capable of chaotic behavior — to study the temporal aspects of coordination. Our focus is how coordination changes as a function of the strength of influence between individuals, and of the degree of similarity of their respective internal states.

The coordination of behavior and internal states

The most basic form of social coordination is the synchronization of motor behavior. This phenomenon has been examined in the context of movement coordination (e.g., Beek & Hopkins, 1992; Schmidt, Beek, Treffner, & Turvey, 1991; Turvey, 1990), with most research focusing on the synchronization of the leg movements of two people. In this approach, one person is asked to swing his or her legs in time to a metronome and the other person tries to match those movements. Two forms of coordination are typically observed: in-phase synchronization (people swinging their legs in unison) and anti-phase synchronization (people swinging their legs with the same frequency but in the opposite direction). Sometimes the individuals are instructed to synchronize out-of-phase and up to a certain frequency they are able to do so. Beyond a critical tempo, however, the individuals can no longer synchronize in this manner and switch to in-phase synchronization. Hysteresis, which is a sign of non-linear dynamical systems, is also commonly observed in this line of research (cf. Kelso, 1995). Thus, when the tempo decreases, at some value the individuals are able to reestablish anti-phase coordination, but this tempo is significantly lower than the point at which they originally started to coordinate in-phase.

In-phase coordination is the easiest form to achieve and maintain. Indeed, this may become the only form that can be sustained as coordination becomes more difficult (e.g., as the tempo of behavior is increased). This restriction on coordination possibilities may generalize to social situations. Under high stress (e.g., a panic situation), for example, it may prove impossible for people to coordinate their behavior in any form other than in-phase. In a crowded theater that suddenly bursts into flames, the occupants are unable to take turns in exiting through the doors, even though this is the only form of coordination that would make evacuation possible. Similarly, two people engaged in conversation may find it impossible to take turns speaking if the level of emotionality reaches a critical point.

Coordination of overt behavior is certainly important in interpersonal relations, but of greater interest from a psychological perspective is the coordination of people's internal states (cf. Nowak, Vallacher, & Zochowski, 2002; Tickle-Degnen & Rosenthal, 1987). Internal states cover a wide ground, from those that are highly variable, such as mood or arousal, to those that reflect fairly enduring properties of a person, such as personality traits, values, goals, and temperament. Achieving coordination with respect to such psychological features as opposed to physical movements is especially important in close relationships. Empathy, perspective taking, and emotional compatibility capture necessary components of a relationship in which the partners are on the same wavelength. Indeed, people are often motivated to adjust their own internal state to match that of their interaction partners, presumably in service of facilitating smooth interaction. Research has shown that people sometimes prepare for social interaction by changing their internal state to match the anticipated state of the interaction partner, even if this means toning down a positive mood in favor of a more subdued mood (e.g., Erber, Wegner, & Thierrault, 1996). Accordingly, we propose a formal model that depicts the emergence of synchronization of both overt behavior and internal states in social relationships. We present the results of computer simulations that test key assumptions in the model regarding the development of synchronization between two people as they develop a progressively closer relationship.

Humans as nonlinear dynamical systems

A dynamical system is a set of interconnected elements that undergo change by virtue of their mutual influences. This means that even in the absence of external influences, a dynamical system may display a pattern of change in some system-level property that reflects the mutual adjustment of elements at each moment in time. Recent research in several areas of science has shown that very simple rules of interaction among system elements can produce highly complex dynamics on the system level if the interactions are nonlinear in nature. Nonlinearity means that the effects of changes in one element — represented as a variable — are not reflected in a proportional manner in other elements (variables). Non-linearity also means that the relations among variables usually depend on the values of other variables in the system, and thus are interactive rather than additive in nature (cf. Nowak & Lewenstein, 1994). In more formal terms, a dynamical system is composed of a set of *dynamical variables* (x) that change in time, and one or more *control parameters* (r) that play a critical role in influencing the dynamical variables.

Humans can be viewed as dynamical systems in the sense that they display change over time in the absence of external influence. There clearly is no shortage of variables capable of promoting constant change in people's thoughts, emotions, and actions. Any element of human experience, after all, can be analyzed with respect to myriad potential genetic, hormonal, familial, dispositional, and cultural factors. The abundance of potential interactions among these variables, meanwhile, suggests that humans can be profitably viewed as nonlinear systems. In recognition of the dynamic, complex, and non-linear nature of human experience, recent years have witnessed the ascendance of the dynamical perspective in personality and social psychology (e.g., Nowak & Vallacher, 1998; Vallacher & Nowak, 1994, 1997; Vallacher, Read, & Nowak, 2002).[1]

The simplest dynamical system capable of complex behavior is the logistic equation or map (Feigenbaum, 1978). The logistic map involves repeated iteration, which means that the output value of the dynamical variable (x) at one step (n) is used as the input value at the next step ($n + 1$). The current value of the dynamical variable (which varies between 0 and 1), in other words, depends on the variable's previous value — that is, $x_{n+1} = f(x_n)$. This dependency is represented in two opposing ways. First, the higher the previous value, the higher the current value; specifically, x_{n+1} equals x_n multiplied by the value of r. Second, the higher the previous value, the lower the current value; specifically, x_{n+1} equals $(1 - x_n)$ multiplied by the value of r. The combined effect of these competing tendencies is expressed as $x_{n+1} = rx_n(1 - x_n)$. Depending on the value of r, the logistic equation may display qualitatively different patterns of behavior (pattern of changes in x), including the convergence on a single value, oscillatory (periodic) changes between two or more values, and very complex patterns of behavior resembling randomness (i.e., deterministic chaos).

The logistic equation provides a useful way of conceptualizing human dynamics (cf. Nowak & Vallacher, 1998; Nowak, Vallacher, & Zochowski, 2002). In this approach, the dynamical variable (x) represents a person's behavior, and changes in x represent variations in the intensity of the behavior. The control parameter, r, corresponds to internal states (e.g., moods, values, traits) that shape the person's pattern of behavior (changes in x over time). The notion of opposing forces represented in the logistic equation captures the idea of conflict, which has proven to be a key concept in many psychological theories. In the approach-avoid situation (Miller, 1944), for example, movement toward a goal increases both approach and avoid tendencies. The work on achievement motivation (e.g., Atkinson, 1964), in turn, has identified two concerns, the desire for success and the fear of failure, that combine in different ways to produce resultant motivation. Research on the dynamics of suppression, meanwhile, suggests that attempts at action or thought suppression activate an ironic process that works at cross-purposes with the attempted suppression (cf. Wegner, 1994). The assumption that conflicting forces or tendencies are central to human dynamics, in fact, represents a common theme in most issues of psychological interest (e.g., impulse vs. self-control, autonomy vs. social identity, short-term vs. long-term self-interest, egoism vs. altruism).

Social interaction as the coupling of nonlinear dynamical systems

If an individual is conceptualized as a dynamical system, then social interaction can be investigated as the coupling or synchronization of two (or more) dynamical systems. Accordingly, we employed coupled logistic equations, an approach which has successfully modeled the synchronization of physical systems (e.g., Shinbrot, 1994), to model the synchronization of people in social interaction. The basic idea is that when the value of the dynamical variable (x) for one equation depends not only on its previous value but also to some degree on the value of x for the other equation, the two equations tend to synchronize in their behavior over time. This idea has straightforward application to human interaction. Quite simply, the behavior of each partner depends not only on his or her preceding behavior but also on the preceding behavior of the other person. Formally, such influence is introduced by the assumption that the behavior of each partner in the next moment in time depends to a certain degree on the behavior of the other partner at the preceding moment in time. The coupling is done in a simple way, according to the following equations:

$$x_1(t+1) = \frac{r_1 x_1(t)(1 - x_1(t)) + \alpha\, r_2 x_2(t)(1 - x_2(t))}{1+\alpha} \qquad [1]$$

$$x_2(t+1) = \frac{r_2 x_2(t)(1 - x_2(t)) + \alpha\, r_1 x_1(t)(1 - x_1(t))}{1+\alpha} \qquad [2]$$

To the value of the dynamical variable representing one's own behavior (x_1), one adds a fraction, denoted by α *(alpha)*, of the value of the dynamical variable representing the behavior of the partner (x_2). The size of this fraction *(alpha)* corresponds to the strength of coupling and reflects the mutual influence or interdependency of the partners. When the fraction is 0, there is no coupling on the behavior level, whereas a value of 1.0 corresponds to the situation where one's own behavior is determined equally by one's preceding behavior and the preceding behavior of the partner. Intermediate values of *alpha* correspond to intermediate values of coupling.

Modeling the synchronization of behavior

When the control parameters of each system have the same value, the dependence between their respective dynamical variables causes the systems to synchronize completely, so that the temporal changes in x_1 and x_2 become identical (e.g., Kaneko, 1984). Of course, the respective control parameters of two individuals are rarely (if ever) identical, nor do all relationships display the same degree of mutual influence or interdependence. Our first set of simulations, then, investigated how the coordination of dynamical variables (corresponding to individuals' behavior) depends on the similarity of control parameters (corresponding to individuals' internal states) and the strength of coupling (corresponding to the strength of influence between individuals).

For each simulation, we started from a random value of the dynamical variables for each person, drawn from a uniform distribution that varied from 0 to 1. The control parameter for one system (corresponding to one partner) was held constant at a value of 3.67, which corresponds to low levels of chaotic behavior. We systematically varied the value of the control parameter for the other partner between values of 3.6 and 4.0, which corresponds to the highest value of the chaotic regime. We let the two systems run for 300 steps, so that each system had a chance to come close to its pattern of intrinsic dynamics (i.e., pattern of changes in x) and both systems had a chance to synchronize. For the next 500 simulation steps, we recorded the values of the dynamical variables for each system and measured the degree of synchronization (i.e., the difference between the dynamical variables).

The primary results were straightforward and in line with the intuitions expressed earlier. The degree of synchronization tended to increase both with increases in *alpha* and with increasing similarity in *r*. This suggests that interdependence and similarity in internal states can compensate for one another in achieving or maintaining a particular level of synchronization in people's behavior. Thus, two people can achieve a high degree of synchronization despite relatively weak mutual influence if their respective internal states are similar. By the same token, if the partners have different internal states, high mutual influence (e.g., constant monitoring, communication, mutual reinforcement) is necessary to maintain the same level of synchronization.

The simulation results also revealed less straightforward, but quite interesting effects for coordination as a result of variation in *alpha*. For very high values of *alpha*, the predominant mode of coordination was in-phase synchronization and what varied was the strength of the behavior matching. For low values of *alpha*, however, different modes of coordination were observed. In addition to in-phase synchronization, the coupled systems displayed anti-phase synchronization (analogous to complementarity or turn-taking in behavior), independence in behavior, and other complex forms of coordination. This suggests that a richer repertoire of modes of coordination is available when mutual influence is relatively weak. There was also a tendency under relatively weak coupling for the systems to stabilize each other, so that each system behaved in a more regular (e.g., less chaotic) manner than it would have without the weak influence (cf. Ott, Grebogi, & York, 1990). With respect to close relationships, these results suggest that for strong mutual influence and control (e.g., constant monitoring and control), the behavior of one partner largely tends to mirror the behavior of the other partner. For relatively weak mutual influence and control, in contrast, interpersonal coordination can take more complex and less obvious forms. Because coordination in this case may reflect a complex, non-linear pattern, observers may find it difficult to note or understand the ways in which the behaviors of the partners are synchronized.

Taken together, these results suggest that the mutual influence commonly associated with close relationships (cf. Thibaut & Kelley, 1959) may be a mixed blessing. To be sure, if two people are highly dissimilar in their internal states, they may nonetheless achieve a fair degree of coordination by directly influencing one another's behavior. This scenario, though, creates the potential for instability in the relationship. As soon as the influence is curtailed, the dynamics of the two people will immediately diverge. On the other hand, a high degree of similarity in the setting of control parameters preserves synchronization for a considerable period of time when mutual influence is broken. Even if the partners' behaviors do not synchronize in time, the overall form of their respective dynamics will remain similar, so that reestablishing coordination at a later time will be relatively easy. In couples characterized by similarity of internal states, then, relatively little influence or communication is needed to maintain coordination and thus preserve the relationship. Couples characterized by weak similarity of internal parameters, on the other hand, may be able to maintain their behavioral coordination, but only through strong and sustained attempts at mutual influence. Such couples thus have a heightened risk for a breakdown in coordination. To prevent this from occurring, they may engage in events together that induce a common mood and also bring about coordination on a behavioral level. Events that are affectively positive (e.g., dancing, sexual relations) can clearly have this effect, but in principle so can negatively toned events, such as a heated argument or witnessing a tragic event.

Modeling the synchronization of internal states

In principle, modeling the direct coordination of control parameters is fairly straightforward. All one needs to assume is that on each simulation step, the values of each person's control parameter drifts somewhat in the direction of the value of the partner's control parameter. The rate of this drift and the size of the initial discrepancy between the values of the respective control parameters determine how quickly the control parameters begin to converge. This mechanism assumes, however, that both partners can directly observe or estimate the settings of one another's control parameters. Direct observation of the internal states of an interaction partner may be difficult, or even impossible in some cases. Indeed, considerable effort is typically devoted to communicating or inferring one another's dispositional qualities and other internal states (cf. Jones & Davis, 1965; Kunda, 1999; Nisbett & Ross, 1980; Wegner & Vallacher, 1977). Even with the multiplicity of cognitive means available to people, the precise nature of a person's momentary state or relevant chronic disposition may be impossible to determine.

Lacking insight or clear inferences into one another's internal states, interaction partners may nonetheless achieve similarity in these states by means of behavioral coordination. Various lines of social psychological research are relevant to this idea. Research on the facial feedback hypothesis, for example, has shown that when people are induced to mechanically adopt a specific facial configuration linked to a particular affective state (e.g., disgust), they tend also to adopt the corresponding state (e.g., Strack, Martin, & Stepper, 1988). The matching of internal states to overt behavior is enhanced for behavior that is interpersonal in nature. Research has shown that even role-playing, in which a person follows a scripted set of actions *vis a vis* another person, commonly produces noteworthy changes in attitudes and values on the part of the role player to match his or her overt actions (cf. Zimbardo, 1970).

We implemented this mechanism in our model by allowing each system to modify the value of its own control parameter in order to match the other system's pattern of behavior. The exact value of the partner's control parameter is invisible to the person. Each person, however, remembers the partner's most recent set of behaviors (i.e., the most recent values of x), as well as his or her own most recent behaviors. The person compares the partner's pattern with his or her own, and adjusts his or her own control parameter until the respective behavior patterns match (cf. Zochowski &Liebovitch, 1997). If the partner's observed behavior pattern is more complex (e.g., more chaotic) than the person's own behavior pattern, he or she adjusts (increases) the value of his or her own control parameter until similarity in their respective behavior patterns is achieved. On the other hand, if the partner's behavior is less complex than the person's own behavior, the person decreases slightly the value of his or her own control parameter. Each person, in effect, can discover the internal state of the other person by monitoring and matching the dynamics of the other person's behavior.

In Figure 1, we show how the internal states of two systems become progressively similar in accordance with this scenario. This simulation was run for relatively weak coupling ($alpha = .25$). The x-axis corresponds to time in simulation steps, and the y-axis portrays the value of the difference between the two systems in their respective control parameters (thick gray line) and in their dynamical variables (thin black line). The figure shows that over time, the two systems become similar in the values of their control parameters and perfectly synchronized in their behavior. This suggests that attempting behavioral synchronization under weak levels of mutual control over one another's behavior facilitates the matching of one another's internal state.

Different results were obtained when the simulations were performed with a relatively high value of coupling ($alpha = 0.7$). Figure 2 displays the results of this simulation. Although virtually perfect coordination in behavior develops almost immediately, the control parameters of the two systems fail to converge, even after 1,000 simulation steps. This disparity occurs because strong coupling causes full synchronization of behavior, even for systems with very different values of their respective control parameters. Once their behavior is fully synchronized, the two systems do not have a clue that their control parameters are different. Hence, if the coupling were suddenly removed, the dynamics of the two systems would immediately diverge. This suggests that using very strong influence to obtain behavioral coordination is likely to hinder synchronization at a deeper level.

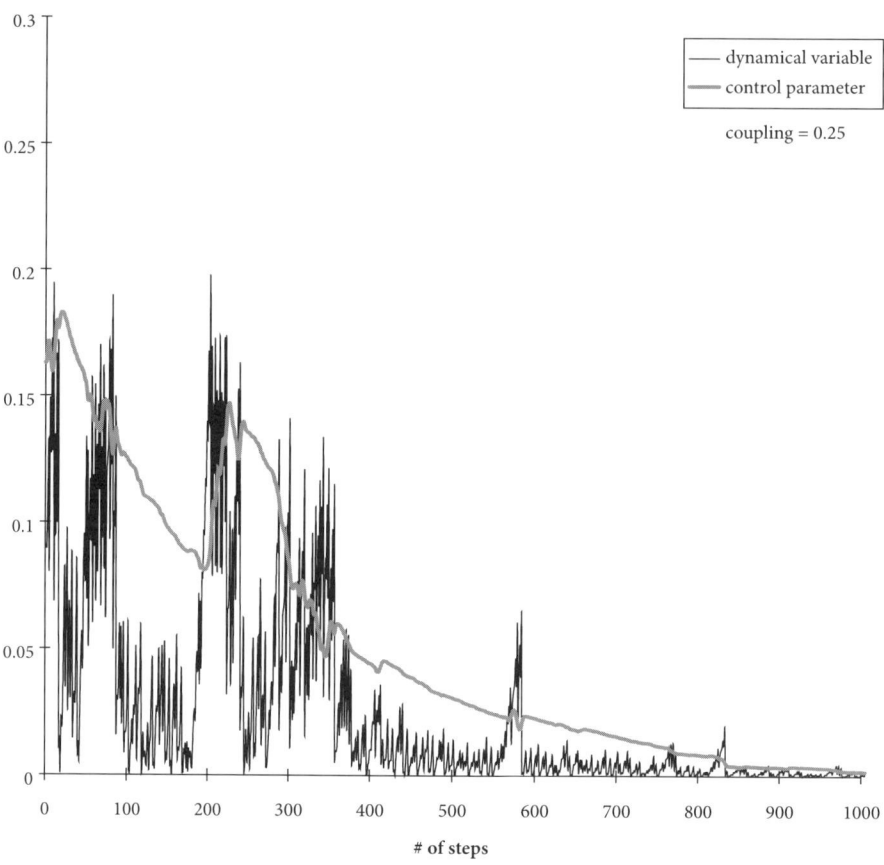

Figure 1. Development of synchronization under relatively weak coupling (mutual influence)

The results of these simulations have interesting implications for interpersonal dynamics. First of all, they suggest that there is an optimal level of influence and control over behavior in social relationships. If influence is too weak, synchronization may fail to develop at all. Very strong influence, on the other hand, is likely to prevent the development of a relationship based on mutual understanding and empathy. Highly monitored and controlled partners may fully synchronize their behavior, but they are unlikely to adopt the internal states necessary to maintain such behavior in the absence of social influence. As noted earlier, moreover, high values of coupling restrict the range of possible modes of coordination in a relationship. Too strong a coupling may therefore result in a relationship that is experienced as highly predictable and therefore boring. On balance, the most desirable degree of coupling is one that allows for effective coordination, but keeps direct

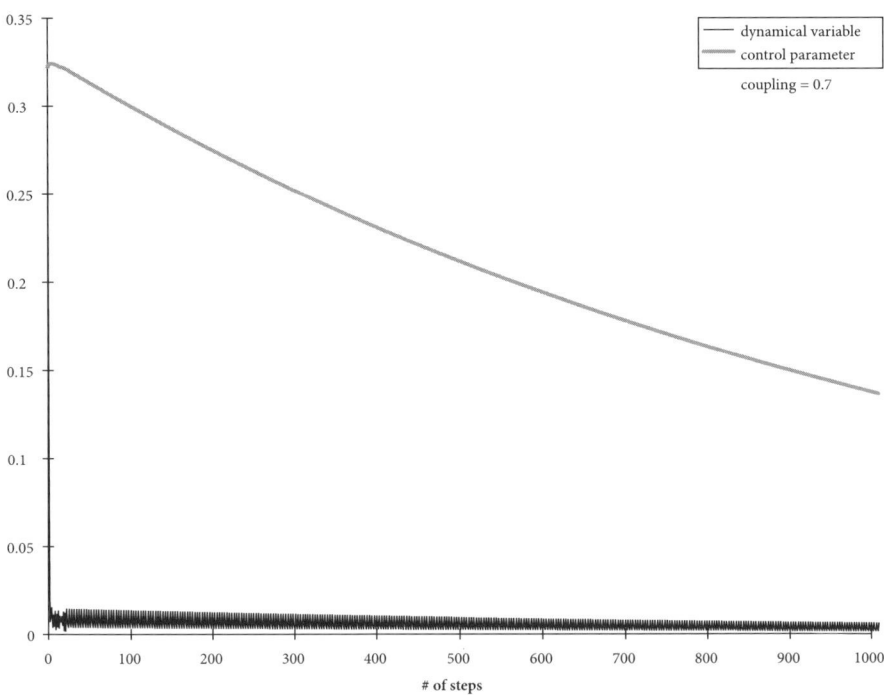

Figure 2. Development of synchronization under relatively strong coupling (mutual influence)

influence at a relatively low level. This moderate degree of coupling allows for the internalization of common internal states in a relationship. Under such conditions, relationships may develop rich dynamics and switch between different modes of coordination. The most advantageous degree of coupling, in sum, is the minimal amount necessary to achieve synchronization.

The simulation results also shed light on a controversial and somewhat puzzling conclusion regarding the relative impact of parents and peers on personality development in children (e.g., Harris, 1995; Scarr, 1992). Although children spend far more time with their parents than with any single peer when they are very young and thus highly impressionable, considerable research suggests that children develop personality traits that are more similar to those of their peers than to those of their parents. This conclusion, though certainly controversial, is not particularly surprising in light of our model. The parent-child relationship, after all, is characterized by strong coupling, so that children have little need to internalize the settings of their parents' control parameters in order to achieve and maintain behavioral coordination with them. When parents monitor a child's behavior, praising it when it is considered appropriate and providing discipline when it is less so, they are exerting fairly constant and strong influence over what the child does. To the extent that the parents' behavior control is apparent to the child, he or she learns to act in accordance with the relevant reinforcement contingencies, expectations, rules, and so forth.

Children obviously internalize certain lessons from these experiences and thus may develop control parameters that resemble their parents'. But the need to adopt parents' internal states pales in comparison to the strategic value of matching the internal states of their peers. Unlike parents, peers are not in a position to monitor a child's behavior, let alone control it on a daily basis. Peers make for considerably less faithful interaction partners too, and the surface structure of their behavior tends to be more erratic as well. These characteristics of peer relations — relatively weak coupling, relationship instability, and potential for unpredictable behavior — all point to the practical value of learning the internal bases for peers' behavior. Beyond that, it is simply easier to resonate with the interests, moods, and thoughts of someone who is similar to oneself in age, life experiences, competencies, and power. Children certainly love and admire (and may even appreciate) their parents, but they are less likely to empathize and identify with them than they are with their peers. Synchronization with peers, in short, has all the ingredients for convergence on common control parameters, and thus may be more influential in establishing children's characteristic ways of thinking and acting.

Caveats and conclusions

In dynamical terms, a close relationship represents the achievement and maintenance of coordination between two people. Models of coupled non-linear dynamical systems, originally developed in mathematics and the physical sciences, provide important insight into the dynamics of close relationships. We employed coupled logistic equations to model such dynamics. Coordination occurs both with respect to dynamical variables, representing overt behavior, and control parameters, representing internal states (e.g., moods, values, personality traits, attitudes). The strength of coupling (*alpha*) corresponds to mutual influence, which can represent direct communication, promises of reward or threats of punishment, or other forms of control. To simulate the coordination of internal states, we adopted a model of synchronization dynamics (Zochowski & Liebovitch, 1997; see also Nowak et al., 2002), in which a feedback loop exists such that each system changes its own control parameter to match the level of complexity in the dynamical variable of the other system.

The computer simulations revealed that coordination of internal states in a relationship facilitates the coordination of behavior. Results also revealed that difficulty in achieving behavioral coordination may be used as a guide for achieving coordination with respect to internal states. Ironically, very strong behavioral coordination resulting from strong mutual control (i.e., very high values of *alpha*) was found to hinder rather than facilitate the development of similarity in partner's internal states. A close relationship is most likely to develop and endure, in other words, if there is similarity of internal states and partners' mutual control is not too strong.

This approach is new to psychology, so caution should be exercised when generalizing the results to human relationships. At this preliminary stage, it is not clear which coordination phenomena we observed are reflective of coupled nonlinear systems generally, and which are specific to the coupling of logistic equations. Although we believe the logistic equation captures important features of human systems (e.g., conflicting forces), the robustness of the results we obtained will ultimately depend on their generality across different instantiations of dynamical systems.

It is also the case that our model greatly simplifies the complexity of human behavior and people's internal (psychological) states. Overt behavior can be reduced to a single dimension (e.g., intensity) by a variety of means, but the multidimensionality of emotions, values, plans, and other internal states raises questions concerning the appropriateness of reducing these states to a single control parameter. Finally, certain coordination phenomena in social relations may be unique to humans, reflecting the influence of social and cultural norms, social motives and orientations, or perhaps expressing the unique biological properties of humans. Some coordination phenomena, on the other hand, may be generic to different types of coordinating systems. Although computer simulations may prove useful in discovering and illuminating the nature of the generic phenomena, empirical research with humans is critical to decide which findings may be extended to human interpersonal experience.

These caveats notwithstanding, the results of our simulations point to striking parallels between the dynamics of coupled logistic equations and the dynamics of close relationships. The finding that strong influence can compensate for differences in people's internal states, for example, corresponds with intuitions regarding control in close relationships. The computer simulations also produced results that are consistent with research demonstrating that psychological changes obtained under relatively weak influence and subtle means tends to be more enduring than are the more rapid changes obtained through excessive (rewarding and aversive) control (cf. Vallacher, Nowak, & Miller, 2003). Empirical research nonetheless is necessary before one can accept the results of the computer simulations as applicable to intimate human relationships. Computer simulations can prove useful in generating the hypotheses to be tested in such endeavors, and they can highlight those phenomena (e.g., modes of coordination and transitions between them) that are worthy of special attention. In sum, framing human interpersonal dynamics in terms of coordination phenomena prevalent in the natural world provides a bridge between psychological intuitions and the precision afforded by physical science.

Acknowledgement

The research presented in this article was presented in *Making minds: An interdisciplinary conference*, in Kloster-Irsee, Germany, January, 2004. We thank Petra Hauf, Wolfgang Prinz, and an anonymous reviewer for their insightful and constructive comments on an earlier draft of this article.

Note

1. Psychological systems clearly differ from physical systems in important respects, and it is an open question whether certain unique features of human thought and action (e.g., consciousness, intentionality) can be meaningfully reframed in terms of formal properties that are common to dynamical systems in other areas of science. Because the dynamical approach has spawned a set of rigorous methods and tools, however, this question is also an empirical one. We refer the interested reader to Nowak and Vallacher (1998) for a more thorough consideration of this issue.

References

Atkinson, J. W. (1964). *An introduction to motivation*. Princeton, NJ: Van Nostrand.
Axelrod, R. (1984). *The evolution of cooperation*. New York: Basic Books.
Beek, P. J., & Hopkins, B. (1992). Four requirements for a dynamical systems approach to the development of social coordination. *Human Movement Science, 11*, 425–442.
Berkowitz, L., & Walster, E. (Eds.) (1976). *Advances in experimental social psychology* (Vol. 9). New York: Academic Press
Berscheid, E. (1983). Emotion. In H. H. Kelley et al. (Eds.), *Close relationships* (pp. 110–168). New York: W. H. Freeman.
Biddle, B. S., & Thomas, E. J. (Eds.) (1966). *Role theory: Concepts and research*. New York: Wiley.
Dawes, R. M. (1980). Social dilemmas. *Annual Review of Psychology, 31*, 169–193.
Erber, R., Wegner, D. M., & Thierrault, N. (1996). On being cool and collected: Mood regulation in anticipation of social interaction. *Journal of Personality and Social Psychology, 70*, 757–766.

Feigenbaum, M. J. (1978). Quantitative universality for a class of nonlinear transformations. *Journal of Statistical Physics, 19*, 25–52.

Harris, J. R. (1995). Where is the child's environment? A group socialization theory of development. *Psychological Review, 102*, 458–589.

Jones, E. E., & Davis, K. E. (1965). From acts to dispositions: The attribution process in person perception. In L. Berkowitz (Ed.), *Advances in experimental social psychology* (Vol. 2, pp. 220–266). New York: Academic Press.

Kaneko, K. (1984). Like structures and spatiotemporal intermittency of coupled logistic lattice: Toward a field theory of chaos. *Progress in Theoretical Physics, 72*, 480.

Kelso, J. A. S. (1995). *Dynamic patterns: The self-organization of brain and behavior.* Cambridge, MA: The MIT Press.

Kunda, Z. (1999). *Social cognition: Making sense of people.* Cambridge, MA: MIT Press.

Levine, J. M., & Moreland, R. L. (1998). Small groups. In D. T. Gilbert, S. T. Fiske, & G. Lindzey (Eds.), *The handbook of social psychology* (4th ed., Vol. 2, pp. 415–469). New York: McGraw-Hill.

Messick, D. M., & Liebrand, V. B. G. (1995). Individual heuristics and the dynamics of cooperation in large groups. *Psychological Review, 102*, 131–145.

Miller, N. E. (1944). Experimental studies of conflict. In J. M. Hunt (Ed.), *Personality and the behavior disorders* (pp. 431–465). New York: Ronald.

Nisbett, R., & Ross, L. (1980). *Human inference: Strategies and shortcomings of social judgment.* Englewood Cliffs, NJ: Prentice-Hall.

Nowak A., & Vallacher, R. R. (1998). *Dynamical Social Psychology.* New York: Guilford Press.

Nowak, A., Vallacher, R. R., & Zochowski, M. (2002). The emergence of personality: Personal stability through interpersonal synchronization. In D. Cervone & W. Mischel (Eds.), *Advances in personality science* (pp. 292–331). New York: Guilford Press.

Ott, E., Grebogi, C., & York, J. A. (1990). Controlling chaos. *Physics Review Letters, 64*, 1196–1199.

Scarr, S. (1992). Developmental theories for the 1990s: Development and individual differences. *Child Development, 63*, 1–19.

Schmidt, R. C., Beek, P. J., Treffner, P. J., & Turvey, M. T. (1991). Dynamical substructure of coordinated rhythmic movements. *Journal of Experimental Psychology: Human Perception and Performance, 17*, 635–651.

Schuster, H. G. (1984). *Deterministic chaos.* Vienna: Physik Verlag.

Shinbrot, T. (1994). Synchronization of coupled maps and stable windows. *Physics Review E, 50*, 3230–3233.

Strack, F., Martin, L. L., & Stepper, S. (1988). Inhibiting and facilitating conditions of the human smile: A nonobtrusive test of the facial feedback hypothesis. *Journal of Personality and Social Psychology, 54*, 768–777.

Thibaut, J. W., & Kelley, H. H. (1959). *The social psychology of groups.* New York: Wiley.

Tickle-Degnen, L., & Rosenthal, R. (1987). Group rapport and nonverbal behavior. *Review of Personality and Social Psychology, 9*, 113–136.

Turvey, M. T. (1990). Coordination. *American Psychologist, 4*, 938–953.

Vallacher, R. R., & Nowak, A. (Eds.) (1994). *Dynamical systems in social psychology.* San Diego: Academic Press.

Vallacher, R. R., & Nowak, A. (1997). The emergence of dynamical social psychology. *Psychological Inquiry, 8*, 73–79.

Vallacher, R. R., Nowak, A., & Miller, M. E. (2003). Social influence and group dynamics. In I. Weiner (Series Ed.) & T. Millon & M. J. Lerner (Vol. Eds.), *Handbook of psychology: Vol. 5. Personality and social psychology* (pp. 383–417). New York: Wiley.

Vallacher, R. R., Read, S. J., & Nowak, A. (2002). The dynamical perspective in personality and social psychology. *Personality and Social Psychology Review, 6,* 264–273.

Vallacher, R. R., & Wegner, D. M. (1987). What do people think they're doing? Action identification and human behavior. *Psychological Review, 94,* 1–15.

Wegner, D. M. (1994). Ironic processes of mental control. *Psychological Review, 101,* 34–52.

Wegner, D. M., & Vallacher, R. R. (1977). *Implicit psychology.* New York: Oxford University Press.

Wish, M., Deutsch, M., & Kaplan, S. J. (1976). Perceived dimensions of interpersonal relations. *Journal of Personality and Social Psychology, 33,* 409–420.

Zimbardo, P. G. (1970). The human choice: Individuation, reason, and order versus deindividuation. In W. J. Arnold & D. Levine (Eds.), *Nebraska Symposium on Motivation* (Vol. 17, pp. 237–307). Lincoln: University of Nebraska Press.

Zochowski, M., & Liebovitch, L. (1997). Synchronization of trajectory as a way to control the dynamics of the coupled system. *Physics Review E, 56,* 3701.

Construing and constructing others

On the reality and the generality of the behavioral confirmation scenario

Mark Snyder and Olivier Klein
University of Minnesota / Université Libre de Bruxelles

When individuals (as perceivers) hold expectations about other people (as targets), they can elicit from these targets behaviors that are consistent with their expectations, even if these expectations are independent of the target's real characteristics. In this paper, we consider the role that this phenomenon, known as behavioral confirmation, plays in shaping the social perceptions of perceivers, targets, and outside observers. As well, we address the value of laboratory research on behavioral confirmation for understanding the dynamics and outcomes of social interactions in naturally occurring settings. Building on these considerations, we then examine the role of behavioral confirmation phenomena in shaping intergroup relations, with particular reference to delineating conditions in which such phenomena serve to preserve these relations. Based on this analysis, we suggest that dyadic confirmation phenomena are likely to occur in naturally occurring settings and may contribute to the maintenance and perpetuation of social stereotypes and societal structures.

At the time of this writing, in mid-2004, it is not difficult to imagine an American soldier serving in Iraq holding negative expectations about the Iraqi people. This soldier might believe that the people of Iraq are extremely aggressive and do not adhere to the same moral standards as Americans. In dealing with individual Iraqis, this soldier may act in offensive ways, perhaps by threatening them physically, or by placing them in degrading postures. As a result of being treated in such a fashion, these Iraqis may in turn experience heightened hostility towards this soldier. As a consequence, given the opportunity, these Iraqis may actually act in aggressive ways towards this soldier and other Americans. If so, the American soldier's expectations may be confirmed as a result of interactions with Iraqis.

In this example, a belief that was "subjectively" real (from the American soldier's perspective) instigated a series of behaviors on the part of the perceiver (the soldier) and these behaviors induced the targets of these expectations (individual Iraqis) to enact the perceiver's initial beliefs, thereby making them "objectively" real. This sequence of events illustrates a reality-constructing process by which an individual's beliefs about another person may, in the course of social interaction, come to be confirmed by the behavior of that other person. This process is referred to as behavioral confirmation (Snyder & Stukas, 1999).

Behavioral confirmation processes have been studied using a laboratory paradigm designed to capture a scenario in which beliefs create reality. It involves an individual (the perceiver) whose expectations about another person (the target) are manipulated (e.g., through a picture or a personality profile purportedly of the target), after which perceiver and target engage in a getting acquainted conversation. After the interaction, the perceiver is asked to rate the target's personality on the dimensions that defined the expectation; in some studies, the target also provides self-ratings on these dimensions. Recordings of the target's contribution to the exchange are later played to independent judges (unaware of the perceiver's expectation), who rate the target's behavior on these same dimensions. *Behavioral confirmation* is said to occur when the target's behavior reflects the expectations induced in the perceiver. *Perceptual confirmation* occurs if the perceiver's evaluation of the target is similarly affected, such that the perceiver regards the events of the interaction as confirmation of the initial expectations. *Behavioral disconfirmation* and *perceptual disconfirmation* are evidenced when the judges' and the perceiver's ratings are influenced in a direction *opposite* to the perceiver's expectations.

Several decades of research using this paradigm (for reviews, see: Jussim, 1986; Miller & Turnbull, 1986; Snyder & Stukas, 1999) have revealed that behavioral confirmation is a phenomenon that reliably occurs in a variety of contexts. In this paper, we have two sets of inter-related goals. *First*, we consider the ways in which confirmation (and disconfirmation) phenomena can be said to shape both the perceiver's and the target's "minds", as well as the minds of outside observers to interactions between perceivers and targets. *Second*, we consider the relevance of behavioral confirmation as it has been observed in laboratory contexts for understanding such "making minds" phenomena as they occur in naturalistic settings. In so doing, we hope to "calibrate" the extent to which findings can be translated beyond the laboratory, and the ways in which procedural paradigms for investigating behavioral confirmation can be enriched to maximize this translation from the possibly "artificial" laboratory to the "real" world and the social interactions and intergroup relations that occur in it.

The behavioral confirmation scenario as a setting for making minds

Let us first consider the ways in which behavioral confirmation phenomena contribute to "making minds" and the construction of social and objective realities. There are several ways in which such processes can occur, depending on which actor's mind and whose representations of "reality" are involved — those of the perceiver, the target, and outside observers.

Starting with the perspective of the perceiver, behavioral and perceptual confirmation clearly shape the mind of the perceiver. These phenomena, singly and together, serve to bolster the perceivers' prior expectations and to increase their certainty. Thus, not only do the perceiver's beliefs instigate the events that culminate in their confirmation, but these beliefs are consolidated and strengthened as a result of the process, thus shaping the perceiver's mind. Moreover, as a result of these mind-making consequences, the likelihood that perceivers will act on these beliefs in the future should be increased. Indeed, there is evidence that, when certain of their expectations, perceivers are more likely to generate behavioral confirmation in targets (Swann & Ely, 1984).

What about the mind of the target? When behavioral confirmation occurs, it is clear that the behaviors of the target have come to match the beliefs of the perceiver. But, do the target's own beliefs come to match the perceiver's expectations? Here, the evidence suggests that the target may be affected by even brief encounters. For example, Smith, Neuberg, Judice, and Biesanz (1997) have observed that targets who confirmed a perceiver's expectation maintain their expectation-confirming behavior in a second interaction with another perceiver, even if this second perceiver does not share the first perceiver's expectations (see also: Snyder & Swann, 1978; Stukas & Snyder, 2002). This perpetuation of the target's confirmatory behaviors is especially evident in circumstances that promote the "internalization" of these behaviors into corresponding self-conceptions (Fazio, Effrein, & Falender, 1981; Smith et al., 1997). Such internalization might be a consequence of behavioral confirmation through "self-perception" processes. According to self-perception theory (Bem, 1972), individuals use their behavior to infer self-views if their behavior cannot be situationally explained. It is therefore conceivable that targets' perceptions of their confirmatory behaviors may lead them to internalize the expectations of perceivers.

It is an open question whether these mind-making outcomes are translated into long-lasting changes in the target's underlying personality. However, the behavioral confirmation scenario can produce stability across time and contexts in the target's behavior. For example, Snyder and Swann (1978) observed that behavioral confirmation persisted from the initial interaction to a new interaction in a new setting with a new perceiver, with the correlations of the target's behavior across interactions being as high as .90 when targets attributed their confirmatory behaviors to their own dispositions. Such findings suggest that the consequences of behavioral confirmation may extend to the level of the traits and dispositions of the target; stability over time and across situations are often considered to be indicators of traits and dispositions of personality (Snyder & Ickes, 1985).

Let us turn now to the perspective of outside observers of interactions between perceivers and targets. The independent judges who code the behavior of the target for evidence of behavioral confirmation can be considered as functionally comparable to bystanders who observe interactions between perceivers and targets in natural settings. Thus, the occurrence of behavioral confirmation is testimony to the fact that outside observers' minds may be shaped by perceivers' expectations (see Claire & Fiske, 1998 for a related point).

We should note that, as well documented as behavioral confirmation is in the psychological literature, instances of behavioral "disconfirmation" (in which perceivers' expectations are actively disconfirmed by targets' behavior) have also been noted (Miller & Turnbull, 1986). However, the "making minds" effects of behavioral disconfirmation may not be contrary to those of behavioral confirmation. First, behavioral disconfirmation may occur without perceptual disconfirmation, or even with perceptual confirmation, because of perceivers' tendency to preferentially attend to expectation confirming behavior (Olson, Roese, & Zanna, 1996). Second, behavioral disconfirmation, even if accompanied by perceptual disconfirmation, may fail to modify the perceiver's general stereotypes: indeed, the target's stereotype-inconsistent behavior may be attributed to membership in a "subtype" of his or her social category, thereby reducing the relevance of the target's behavior to the stereotype (Kunda & Oleson, 1995). The target's disconfirming behavior may also be seen as attempts to be perceived as different from the typical group member (especially if the group is stigmatized); ironically, this voluntary distancing from the stereotype may lead the perceiver to endorse it even more (Kunda & Oleson, 1995, 1997).

Thus, beliefs and expectations can lead to the emergence, and bolstering, of a variety of representations in the minds of perceivers who hold those expectations, in the minds of targets of those expectations, and in the minds of observers of interactions between perceivers and targets. The ways that individuals construe other people and themselves, as well as their generalization to stereotypes, are some of the most crucial cognitive tools that people use in their social lives. By affecting these construals, behavioral confirmation processes are involved in making the minds of perceivers, targets, and observers of their interactions.

Making minds: In the laboratory and in naturalistic settings

As much as behavioral and perceptual confirmation may be involved in the making of minds, there are limitations to be acknowledged, especially when extrapolating from observations in the laboratory to events that occur in naturalistic settings. Accordingly, we now consider the translation from studies in the laboratory to the realities of social interaction and inter-group relations as they naturally occur. We shall address three features of laboratory studies that may constrain their generalization.

Much research on behavioral confirmation has been conducted in experimental analogs of first encounters between strangers. Typically, pairs of previously unacquainted individuals are brought together to engage in brief conversations. In these interactions, one person is assigned to receive an expectation, thus making that person the perceiver and the other person, by default, the target. Moreover, the target typically does not know about the expectation (e.g., the target doesn't receive a personality profile or a picture, and hence has no reason to infer that the perceiver has one), and (since expectations are randomly assigned) may not actually belong to the group signified by the expectation. Typically, the parties expect no further interaction; thus, the interactions being studied have neither a past nor a future. In these respects, the behavioral confirmation scenario as it is played out in the laboratory may be atypical of interactions as they naturally occur. Accordingly, these features may limit the generalizability of such studies. Or do they? Let us examine the evidence.

That laboratory studies have focused on first encounters between strangers raises the possibility that behavioral confirmation may be a phenomenon limited to such encounters. If so, laboratory studies would be providing an over-estimate of the importance of behavioral confirmation in ongoing interactions and relationships. However, if anything, the relevant evidence suggests that laboratory studies, as they are typically conducted, may be an *under*-estimate of the impact of behavioral confirmation. For, when initial encounters include the prospect of future interaction, the likelihood of confirmation may be enhanced. Thus, when Haugen and Snyder (1995) told participants that their getting acquainted conversations were the prelude to further interactions, behavioral confirmation effects were greater than when it was made absolutely clear that there would be no further interactions. Moreover, Stukas and Snyder (2003) have found that, when perceivers interact with the targets of positive expectations, even the possibility of future interaction increases their sociability, which in turn elicits increased sociability from their interaction partners; however, in interactions with the targets of negative expectations, the possibility of future interaction has no comparable effect on perceivers and targets. Finally, studies that move beyond first encounters have identified circumstances in which targets demonstrate "carry over" effects such that they continue to confirm the expectations of perceivers in subsequent interactions (Smith et al., 1997; Snyder & Swann, 1978; Stukas & Snyder, 2002). Conversely, over the course of multiple encounters, perceivers become more confident in the validity of their beliefs, even if these beliefs are initially inaccurate (Gil, Swann, & Silvera, 1998). Thus, in their interaction with targets, they are likely to keep engaging in the behaviors that facilitate the persistence of behavioral confirmation.

What are we to make of the fact that, in laboratory experiments, the target is typically unaware of the perceiver's expectation? To be sure, there is evidence that, at times, targets will actively disconfirm negative expectations when they are made aware of them (e.g., Hilton & Darley, 1985). However, the "typical" case may be one in which targets are not aware of negative expectations; for a variety of reasons relating to social etiquette and politeness, perceivers may be less likely to reveal negative expectations than positive ones; and, if they do reveal their negative appraisals, they are likely to do so in their non-verbal behaviors only (Swann, Stein-Seroussi, & McNulty, 1992), which makes them hard to detect by targets. Accordingly, to the extent that they are unaware of negative expectations, targets may have little opportunity to actively disconfirm them, both inside and outside the laboratory.

Moreover, even targets who are aware of negative expectations may nonetheless behave in ways that confirm these expectations, or at least not actively disconfirm them, particularly when these expectations are held by powerful perceivers who might retaliate against those who challenge their views (Copeland, 1994). Even when interacting with perceivers of equal power, and even when made aware of their expectations, targets may still confirm these expectations (Stukas & Snyder, 2002). Such outcomes may reflect motivations to have smoothly flowing interactions; challenging the expectations of perceivers exposes targets to the risk of disrupting (or terminating) the interaction. Finally, targets may be motivated to confirm negative expectations that happen to be consistent with their self-concepts, as work on self-verification suggests (Swann, this volume).

Much of the intrigue of the behavioral confirmation scenario comes from the self-fulfilling impact of *erroneous* beliefs, such as those stemming from stereotypes whose endorsement exceeds their validity. Indeed, in laboratory experiments, perceivers receive their expectations as a result of their random assignment to experimental conditions, effectively de-coupling expectations about targets from the actual attributes of targets, and effectively setting the stage for documenting the causal impact of perceivers' beliefs on targets' behaviors. As a result, laboratory investigations may be particularly well suited to studying the effects of initially erroneous expectations.

However, not all beliefs are inaccurate, and accurate beliefs may be powerful predictors of future behavior, not necessarily because of behavioral confirmation, but because the perceiver's beliefs and the target's behaviors may both be reflections of the target's prior behaviors. Indeed, in studies of teachers and students, Jussim (1993) has documented that expectation effects (defined as associations between teachers' expectations and students' performance) are smaller than "accuracy" effects (defined as associations between students' prior performance and current performance).

Although it may be tempting to infer that accuracy effects are the way of the real world and that expectation effects are limited to the laboratory (a state of affairs that would limit the applicability of laboratory studies of behavioral confirmation to the outside world), it is important to note that the predictors of the size of expectation effects in naturalistic settings are quite consistent with known moderators of expectation effects in the laboratory. Thus, the search for a "powerful self-fulfilling prophecy" (Madon, Jussim, & Eccles, 1997) in dealings between teachers and students has revealed that the effects of teachers' expectations are larger for students who are low in status, power, and advantage relative to their teachers. Such findings are clearly convergent with those of laboratory experiments in which behavioral confirmation is particularly evident when targets have less power and status than perceivers (Copeland, 1994; Virdin & Neuberg, 1990).

Thus, as much as laboratory experiments have focused on the consequences of false expectations and as conducive as naturalistic settings may be to accuracy effects, the two investigative strategies offer converging messages about conditions that promote the confirmation of expectations. That these messages concern status, power, and advantage take on particular meaning when behavioral confirmation processes are considered in the larger context of inter-group relations.

Behavioral confirmation, stereotype maintenance, and intergroup relations

Much of the interest in the reality-constructing aspects of behavioral confirmation stems from their possible role in the maintenance of shared social stereotypes and, more generally, the relations between groups in society. When these stereotypes are repeatedly confirmed by targets' behavior, they become "legitimized"; but also, they can legitimize the actions of advantaged groups and the actual balance of power and prestige between advantaged and disadvantaged groups in society (Jost & Banaji, 1994). Consider again our opening example: if the stereotype about Iraqis held by our American soldier is shared by many other soldiers, and if Iraqis react in a uniformly hostile way to soldiers' actions guided by these stereotypes, the stereotype of Iraqis as "dangerous" will be bolstered. Moreover, the behavior of Iraqi targets could be taken as evidence that the "war on terror" was a legitimate enterprise and that a foreign presence in Iraq is necessary for protecting the people of Iraq.

But, is it appropriate to perform such a translation from the behavioral confirmation scenario (in which expectations about individual targets are directly manipulated in individual perceivers) to encounters between members of different groups as they occur in naturalistic settings (in which expectations often stem from widely shared social stereotypes)? To answer this question, we shall consider several factors that address this translation from the interpersonal to the intergroup level of analysis.

Targets who belong to stigmatized groups are typically aware of the stereotypes that perceivers use to form expectations: They are, so to speak, "stigma conscious" (Pinel, 1999). As we have seen, an awareness of the perceiver's expectation does not necessarily preclude behavioral confirmation. Nevertheless, it may influence the strategies that the target will employ to deal with the perceiver. Consider three such strategies (see Klein & Snyder, 2003, for a more detailed account). A target may engage in *stereotype compensation* by putting forward an *individual* image of self that is radically different from the stereotype of the group. For example, an obese person, who (because of the stereotype attached to the obese in the US) may be viewed as having few social skills, might try to project a very cheerful image. Alternately, a target may attempt *stereotype change* by putting forward a different image of the target's *group* than the one held by the perceiver. For example, at the end of a dinner with a man, a woman may refuse to have her meal paid for in an effort to show that women as a group are not financially dependent on men. Or, a target may engage in *stereotype enactment* by overtly accepting the stereotype and displaying behaviors that are consistent with it. For example, as happened in a study by Zanna and Pack (1975), a woman may behave in a gender-stereotypical way when anticipating interaction with an attractive man who holds "traditional" views of women.

However, the target's choice of strategy may be constrained by situational factors, the foremost of which may be the perceiver's power. Consider stereotype compensation and stereotype change, both of which involve openly challenging the perceiver's views, which may disrupt the flow of interaction and even jeopardize the relationship with the perceiver. In an effort to maintain a smooth flow of interaction, and the relationship itself, the target may abide by and play out the conversational scenario laid down by the perceiver, a scenario likely to be geared toward confirming the perceiver's views (e.g., Copeland, 1994; Smith et al., 1997).

In addition, the relevance of a stereotype to an interaction may be a function of the situation in which perceiver and target interact. For example, if this situation calls for skill in a particular domain, stereotypes relevant to the relative competence of groups are likely to be activated. In turn, the activation of such stereotypes may prompt the perceiver to adopt a behavioral style that may facilitate the confirmation of these stereotypes. Thus, knowing that the target belongs to an out-group perceived as "incompetent" may lead perceivers to rely on a dominant style (Berger, Cohen, & Zelditch, 1972). In doing so, they may self-define in terms of the relatively positive, "competent" social identity attached to their in-group. Relevant to these considerations, Vescio, Snyder, and Butz (2003) have examined interactions between powerful holders of stereotypes and powerless targets of their expectations, and found that stereotypes of groups to which the powerless belong influence powerful people *only* when those stereotypes are both contextually relevant *and* provide information of relevance to powerful peoples' beliefs about the relation between subordinates' personal attributes and their goal attainment.

Of course, the fact that the confirmation of stereotype-based expectations is possible in natural settings does not guarantee that behavioral confirmation actually plays a role in maintaining stereotypes. Given that stereotypes are, by definition, shared within a particular social group or even across an entire society, it is essential to determine when behavioral confirmation effects are likely to influence members of a target group in a uniform way, that is when members of a target group will be *collectively* exposed to conditions that facilitate behavioral confirmation of these stereotypes. For such collective processes to occur, perceivers must categorize targets as belonging to an out-group and view them in terms of a shared stereotype. Moreover, targets belonging to a common in-group must repeatedly abide by the expectation-confirming interactional scenario instigated by the perceiver (Snyder & Haugen, 1994).

These conditions seem particularly likely to be met when targets belong to a stigmatized group. For, in their dealings with each other, members of stigmatized groups are likely to have less power than members of nonstigmatized majority groups (Klein & Snyder, 2003; Ramirez & Soriano, 1993; Smith-Lovin & Mc Pherson, 1991). Hence, they may have limited opportunities to challenge the perceiver's views, even if they are aware of being stigmatized. Members of disadvantaged groups are also likely to be categorized and viewed in an undifferentiated way (Lorenzi-Cioldi, 1993; Sedikides, 1997). Moreover, individuals belonging to low power, stigmatized groups objectively display less behavioral flexibility than those who belong to high power, advantaged groups (Guinote et al., 2002). For these reasons, behavioral confirmation effects may be particularly likely to be uniform when they concern interactions between nonstigmatized perceivers and targets belonging to stigmatized groups.

Another way to address the question of stereotype maintenance is to assume that it is most likely to occur when targets do *not* engage in the strategy of stereotype change. The success of this strategy is itself dependent on the existence of common self-views of the target group that could be held by many targets in their interactions with members of a nonstigmatized group. According to social identity theory (Tajfel & Turner, 1986), such a strategy will be adopted when members of the stigmatized group perceive the boundaries between the in-group and the out-group to be impermeable (i.e., it is not possible to move from the disadvantaged to the advantaged group) and when they collectively perceive that the status system that disadvantages them is either unstable or illegitimate. Although these conditions are sometimes present, they may be limited by beliefs such as the "Protestant work ethic" (Weber, 1904–5) or the ideology of individual achievement through individual effort. They may therefore be quite scarce in societies in which such beliefs are widespread.

On the other hand, when they perceive that boundaries are permeable, members of disadvantaged groups may be motivated to seek individual mobility. This is likely to result in the adoption of a stereotype compensation strategy in their interactions with members of nonstigmatized groups. Such a strategy serves to dissociate the individual from the group, and may therefore inadvertently bolster group stereotypes through a contrast effect (Kunda & Oleson, 1997). However, when boundaries are perceived as permeable, but the position of the target group is still perceived as legitimate and unlikely to change (e.g., because the advantaged group is very powerful), targets are likely to accept negative views of their group and to enact the stereotypes espoused by the perceiver's group (Tajfel & Turner, 1986). In such a situation, behavioral confirmation may contribute to stereotype maintenance.

Although dyadic behavioral confirmation processes may contribute to stereotype maintenance, their role should not be over-estimated. Jussim and Fleming (1996) have argued that stereotype maintenance often occurs as a result of "institutional" rather than "dyadic" self-fulfilling prophecies. That is, individuals may take on specific roles and positions by virtue of their group memberships. These roles may be associated with specific traits (Eagly & Steffen, 1984) and form the basis of stereotypes by being attributed to dispositions shared by all members of the target group. Such a distribution of social roles may limit opportunities for engaging in stereotype-inconsistent behavior. For example, if members of a group are systematically refused access to intellectually rewarding occupations, it may be difficult for them to demonstrate their intellectual skills. As a result, they may come to confirm the expectations that led to the distribution of roles. However, such "institutional" forces may also work their way through individual and dyadic processes. In this regard, dyadic behavioral confirmation processes may take on particular importance in the maintenance of social systems when they occur in settings (such as job interviews or schools) that offer opportunities for social mobility to members of stigmatized groups. In these contexts, behavioral confirmation may contribute to institutional self-fulfilling prophecies; for example, if members of minority groups tend to confirm interviewers' stereotypes (e.g., Word, Zanna, & Cooper, 1974), they may be denied more prestigious jobs and be "trapped" in occupations that do not match their qualifications.

Conclusion

The behavioral confirmation scenario represents, we believe, a compelling instance of the influential role that people play in constructing their social worlds. By acting on their beliefs and expectations, individuals can and do elicit the evidence that confirms those beliefs and expectations. As such, the behavioral confirmation scenario serves as a potent reminder that the reality of how people behave is not only a reflection of who they are, but also of who others believe them to be. For these reasons, we believe that studies of behavioral confirmation in social interaction teach powerful lessons about why it is so important to understand what people believe about others, for such beliefs have powerful consequences, including creating their own reality.

Studies of behavioral confirmation, we have argued, provide one laboratory for understanding the making of minds — the minds of perceivers, targets, and observers of their interactions. Moreover, the research procedures employed in this laboratory, we suggest, are appealing for their use of methodologies that capture the unfolding drama of belief creating reality in social interactions and interpersonal relationships. And, as we also have argued, it is possible to build bridges between the reality constructing features of the behavioral confirmation scenario as it is examined in the laboratory and as it occurs in naturalistic settings. In so doing, it becomes possible to understand the processes by which beliefs are confirmed at the level of dyadic interactions and by which stereotypes are confirmed at the level of intergroup relations.

Acknowledgement

Research on behavioral confirmation in social interaction has been supported by grants from the National Science Foundation to Mark Snyder.

References

Bem, D. J. (1972). Self-perception theory. In L. Berkowitz (Ed.), *Advances in experimental social psychology* (Vol. 6, pp. 1–62). New York: Academic Press.

Berger, J., Cohen, B. P., & Zelditch, M. (1972). Status characteristics and social interaction. *American Sociological Review, 37,* 241–255.

Claire, T., & Fiske, S. T. (1998). A systemic view of behavioral confirmation: Counterpoint to the individualist view. In J. Schopler (Ed.), *Intergroup cognition and intergroup behavior.* (pp. 205–231). Mahwah, NJ: Lawrence Erlbaum Associates.

Copeland, J. T. (1994). Prophecies of power: Motivational implications of social power for behavioral confirmation. *Journal of Personality and Social Psychology, 67,* 264–277.

Eagly, A. H., & Steffen, V. J. (1984). Gender stereotypes stem from the distribution of women and men into social roles. *Journal of Personality and Social Psychology, 46,* 735–754.

Fazio, R. H., Effrein, E. A., & Falender, V. J. (1981). Self-perceptions following social interaction. *Journal of Personality & Social Psychology, 41,* 232–242.

Gill, M. J., Swann, W. B., & Silvera, D. H. (1998). On the genesis of confidence. *Journal of Personality and Social Psychology, 75,* 1101–114.

Guinote, A., Judd, C. M., & Brauer, M. (2002). Effects of power on perceived and objective group variability: Evidence that more powerful groups are more variable. *Journal of Personality and Social Psychology, 82,* 708–721.

Haugen, J. A., & Snyder, M. (1995). *Effects of perceiver's beliefs about future interactions on the behavioral confirmation process.* Paper presented at the annual meeting of the American Psychological Society.

Hilton, J. L., & Darley, J. M. (1985). Constructing other persons: A limit on the effect. *Journal of Experimental Social Psychology, 21,* 1–18.

Jost, J. T., & Banaji, M. R. (1994). The role of stereotyping in system-justification and the production of false consciousness. *British Journal of Social Psychology, 33,* 1–27.

Jussim, L. (1986). Self-fulfilling prophecies: A theoretical and integrative review. *Psychological Review, 93,* 429–445.

Jussim, L. (1993). Accuracy in interpersonal expectations: A reflection-construction analysis of current and classic research. *Journal of Personality, 61,* 637–668.

Jussim, L., & Fleming, C. (1996). Self-fulfilling prophecies and the maintenance of social stereotypes: The role of dyadic interactions and social forces. In C. N. Macrae; M. Hewstone, M., & C. Stangor (Eds.), *Stereotypes* (Vol. 161–192). New York: Guilford.

Klein, O., & Snyder, M. (2003). Stereotypes and behavioral confirmation: From interpersonal to intergroup perspectives. In M. P. Zanna (Ed.), *Advances in experimental social psychology* (Vol. 35). San Diego, CA: Academic Press.

Kunda, Z., & Oleson, K. C. (1995). Maintaining stereotypes in the face of disconfirmation: Constructing grounds for subtyping deviants. *Journal of Personality and Social Psychology, 68,* 565–579.

Kunda, Z., & Oleson, K. C. (1997). When exceptions prove the rule: How extremity of deviance determines the impact of deviant examples on stereotypes. *Journal of Personality and Social Psychology, 72,* 965–979.

Lorenzi Cioldi, F. (1993). They all look alike, but so do we …sometimes: Perceptions of in-group and out-group homogeneity as a function of sex and context. *British Journal of Social Psychology, 32,* 111–124.

Madon, S., Jussim, L., & Eccles, J. (1997). In search of the powerful self-fulfilling prophecy. *Journal of Personality and Social Psychology, 72*, 791–809.

Miller, D. T., & Turnbull, W. (1986). Expectancies and interpersonal processes. *Annual Review of Psychology, 37*, 233–256.

Olson, J. M., Roese, N. J., & Zanna, M. P. (1996). Expectancies. In E. T. Higgins & A. W. Kruglanski (Eds.), *Social psychology: Handbook of basic principles* (pp. 211–238). New York, NY.: Guilford Press.

Pinel, E. (1999). Stigma consciousness: The psychological legacy of social stereotypes. *Journal of Personality and Social Psychology, 76*, 114–129.

Ramirez, A., & Soriano, F. I. (1993). Differential patterns of intra- and interethnic interaction in social power systems. *Journal of Social Psychology, 133*, 307–316.

Sedikides, C. (1997). Differential processing of ingroup and outgroup information: The role of relative group status in permeable boundary groups. *European Journal of Social Psychology, 27*, 121–144.

Smith, D. M., Neuberg, S. L., Judice, T. N., & Biesanz, J. C. (1997). Target complicity in the confirmation and disconfirmation of erroneous perceiver expectations: Immediate and longer term implications. *Journal of Personality & Social Psychology, 73*, 974–991.

Smith-Lovin, L., & Mc Pherson, J. M. (1991). You are who you know: A network perspective on gender. In P. England (Ed.), *Theory on gender/feminism on theory* (pp. 223–251). New York: Aldine.

Snyder, M., & Haugen, J. A. (1994). Why does behavioral confirmation occur? A functional perspective on the role of the perceiver. *Journal of Experimental Social Psychology, 30*, 218–246.

Snyder, M., & Ickes, W. (1985). Personality and social behavior. In G. Lindzey & E. Aronson (Ed.), *Handbook of Social Psychology* (Vol. II, pp. 883–943). New York: Random House.

Snyder, M., & Stukas, A. A., Jr. (1999). Interpersonal processes: The interplay of cognitive, motivational, and behavioral activities in social interaction. *Annual Review of Psychology, 50*, 273–303.

Snyder, M., & Swann, W. B. (1978). Behavioral confirmation in social interaction: From social perception to social reality. *Journal of Experimental Social Psychology, 14*, 148–162.

Stukas, A. A., Jr., & Snyder, M. (2002). Targets' awareness of expectations and behavioral confirmation in ongoing interactions. *Journal of Experimental Social Psychology, 38*, 31–40.

Stukas, A. A., Jr., & Snyder, M. (2003). *The influence of possible future interactions on first encounters.* Unpublished manuscript: La Trobe University.

Swann, W. B., & Ely, R. J. (1984). A battle of wills: Self-verification versus behavioral confirmation. *Journal of Personality and Social Psychology, 46*, 1287–1302.

Swann, W. B., Stein-Seroussi, A., & McNulty, S. (1992). Outcasts in a white lie society: The enigmatic words of people with negative self-conceptions. *Journal of Personality and Social Psychology, 62*, 618–624.

Tajfel, H., & Turner, J. C. (1986). The social identity theory of intergroup behavior. In W. G. Austin (Ed.), *The psychology of intergroup relations* (pp. 7–24). Chicago: Nelson-Hall.

Vescio, T. K., Snyder, M., & Butz, D. A. (2003). Power in stereotypically masculine domains: A social influence strategy X stereotype match model. *Journal of Personality and Social Psychology, 85*, 1062–1078.

Virdin, L. M., & Neuberg, S. L. (1990). *Perceived status: a moderator of expectancy confirmation.* Manuscript presented at the annual meeting of the American Psychological Association.

Weber, M. (1904–1905). *The protestant ethic and the spirit of capitalism* (T. Parsons, Trans.). New York: Scribner.

Word, C. O., Zanna, M. P., & Cooper, J. (1974). The nonverbal mediation of self-fulfilling prophecies in interracial interaction. *Journal of Experimental Social Psychology, 10,* 109–120.

Zanna, M. P., & Pack, S. J. (1975). On the self-fulfilling nature of apparent sex differences in behavior. *Journal of Experimental Social Psychology, 11,* 583–591.

The self and identity negotiation

William B. Swann, Jr.
University of Texas at Austin

Identity negotiation refers to the processes through which perceivers and targets come to agreements regarding the identities that targets are to assume in the interaction. Whereas past work has focused on the contribution of perceivers to the identity negotiation process, I emphasize the contribution of targets to this process. Specifically, I examine the tendency for targets to work to bring perceivers to verify their self-views. For example, people prefer and seek self-verifying evaluations from others, including their spouses and employers — even when this means attaining evaluations that validate negative self-views. Moreover, receiving self-verification has adaptive consequences, even improving the performance of workers in diverse groups. Some boundary conditions of self-verification strivings as well as implications for making of minds are discussed.

As a graduate student I became interested in the self-fulfilling effects of people's expectations about one another. With Mark Snyder, I studied a phenomenon we referred to as "behavioral confirmation." In a series of studies, we showed that perceivers' expectations about targets channeled their interactions so as to make those expectations come true (for reviews, see Snyder, 1984; Snyder & Klein, this volume). We concluded that perceivers might systematically shape the minds of targets.

Yet as robust as these findings seemed to be, I noticed that sometimes targets actively resisted the label with which they had been tagged and attempted to alter the impressions of perceivers. This suggested that the process of "making minds" was not a one-way street; not only did perceivers shape the minds of targets, but targets shaped the minds of perceivers. Apparently, the "making of minds" was an interactive and dynamic process in which both perceivers and targets actively influenced one another. Through this process of *identity negotiation* perceivers and targets interactively forge agreements regarding the identities of targets.

In this essay I focus on the target's contribution to the identity negotiation process. In the tradition of the early symbolic interactionists (e.g., Cooley, 1902;

Mead, 1934), I assume that people form self-views as a means of making sense of the world, predicting the responses of others, and guiding behavior. From this vantage point, self-views represent the "lens" through which people perceive their worlds and organize their behavior. As such, it is critical that these "lenses" remain stable. This explains why people are motivated to stabilize their self-views (e.g., Secord & Backman, 1965; Lecky, 1945) through a series of active behavioral and cognitive activities I dubbed *self-verification processes.*[1]

In what follows, I first identify several distinct forms of self-verification processes. I then examine the consequences of these processes. Finally, I conclude with some remarks about the implications of these processes for the making of minds.

Forms of self-verification

All living organisms inhabit "niches" that routinely satisfy their basic needs (e.g., Clark, 1954). Human beings satisfy their need for self-verification by attempting (consciously or not) to construct self-confirmatory social environments (McCall & Simmons, 1966). To this end, they engage in several distinct activities. First, people seek self-verifying interaction partners. Even if they fail to find such partners, people may elicit self-verifying reactions by enacting behaviors that tend to bring others to see them as they see themselves. And what if the first two strategies fail and people find themselves with partners or in contexts in which they fail to receive verification? Under such circumstances, they may withdraw either psychologically or in actuality. I consider each of these strategies of self-verification in turn.

Seeking self-verifying partners

An especially important form of self-verification occurs when people choose partners who see them as they see themselves, thereby creating social environments that are likely to support their self-views. In one study, for example, we asked people with positive and negative self-views whether they would prefer to interact with evaluators who had favorable or unfavorable impressions of them. As can be seen in Figure 1, participants with positive self-views preferred favorable partners and people with negative self-views preferred unfavorable partners (e.g., Swann, Stein-Seroussi, & Giesler, 1992).

Over a dozen replications in different laboratories using diverse methodologies have left little doubt that people with negative self-views seek negative feedback as well as negative interaction partners (e.g., Hixon & Swann, 1993; Robinson & Smith-Lovin, 1992; Swann, Hixon, Stein-Seroussi, & Gilbert, 1990; Swann, Pelham, & Krull, 1989; Swann, Wenzlaff, & Tafarodi, 1992).

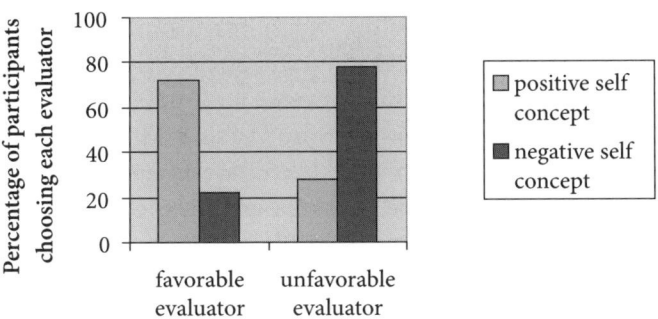

Figure 1. Preference for self-verifying interaction partner

The self-verification strivings of people with low self-esteem and depression are not masochistic, for rather than savoring unfavorable evaluations, they feel torn and ambivalent about them (Swann et al., 1992). For example, in choosing a negative evaluator, one person with low esteem noted that the positive evaluator "sounded good" but that the negative evaluator "seems to know more about me."

Direct evidence that the self-views of participants (rather than a covariate of self-views) drive their choice of interaction partner was offered by Swann, Hixon, Stein-Seroussi, and Gilbert (1990). They had participants choose an interaction partner while unable to access their self-views because the experimenter rushed their decision or had them decide while rehearsing a phone number. Those with positive and negative self-views alike displayed a preference for a positive partner. Only when people had available the mental resources to compare the fit between their self-views and the partners' evaluation did people with negative self-views display a preference for the negative evaluator.

And should people's efforts to find partners who verify their self-views fail and they wind up in relationships or in contexts in which their desire for self-verification is frustrated, a second strategy of self-verification may still ensure that they receive self-verifying reactions. Specifically, people may behave in ways that brings the other person's appraisal into line with their self-views.

Bringing others to see us as we see ourselves

Insofar as people use their self-views to guide their behavior, they may evoke self-verifying reactions. Also, insofar as people are motivated to bring others to verify their self-conceptions, they should *intensify* their efforts to elicit self-confirmatory reactions when they suspect that they are misconstrued. Swann and Read (1981) tested this proposition. The experimenter began by informing targets who perceived themselves as either likeable or dislikeable that they would be interacting with perceivers who had already formed impressions of them. Some targets learned that the perceiver had positive regard for them; some learned that the perceiver had negative regard for them; and still others learned nothing of the perceivers' evaluation of them. There was an overall tendency for targets to elicit reactions that confirmed their self-views (see also Curtis & Miller, 1986). In addition, this tendency was especially pronounced when targets suspected that perceivers' appraisals might disconfirm their self-conceptions. Targets who thought of themselves as likeable elicited particularly favorable reactions when they thought perceivers disliked them, and targets who thought of themselves as dislikeable elicited particularly unfavorable reactions when they suspected that perceivers liked them. In short, targets were especially inclined to elicit self-confirmatory feedback from perceivers when they suspected that perceivers' appraisals were incompatible with their self-views.

Swann and Hill (1982) obtained a similar pattern of results, using a different procedural paradigm and dimension of the self-concept (dominance). Targets began by playing a game with a confederate in which each player alternately assumed the dominant "leader" role or the submissive "assistant" role. During a break in the game, the experimenter asked the players to decide who should be the leader for the next set of games. This was the confederate's cue to deliver feedback to the participant. In some conditions, the confederate said that the participant seemed dominant; in other conditions, the confederate asserted that the participant seemed submissive. If the feedback confirmed targets' self-conceptions, they seemed to passively accept the confederate's appraisal. If the feedback *discon*firmed their self-conceptions, however, targets vehemently resisted the feedback and sought to demonstrate that they were not the persons the confederate made them out to be.

Of course, in both of the foregoing studies, some people behaviorally resisted the discrepant feedback more than others. Swann and Ely (1984) speculated that increments in self-concept certainty would be associated with heightened investment in verifying such views, which would in turn lead to greater resistance in the face of disconfirmation. To test this hypothesis, they first led perceivers to develop an expectancy about targets that was either high or low in certainty. In all cases, the expectancy was discrepant with the self-conceived extraversion of targets. Perceivers then interviewed targets who happened to be either certain or uncertain of their self-conceived extraversion. This situation created a potential "battle of wills," with perceivers' experimentally manipulated beliefs vying against targets' chronic self-views.

Consistent with earlier research (Snyder, 1984), perceivers acted on their expectancies by soliciting responses that would confirm their own expectancies but *dis*confirm targets' self-conceptions. For example, perceivers who believed that the target was an extravert often asked questions such as "Do you like to go to lively parties?" Targets who were low in self-certainty generally answered in ways that confirmed perceivers' expectancies (but disconfirmed their own self-conceptions) when perceivers were highly certain of their expectancies. In contrast, targets who were high in self-certainty actively resisted the questions (regardless of the perceivers' level of certainty), thereby bringing perceivers' expectancies into harmony with their self-views. Thus, as long as targets were high in self-certainty, self-verification "won" over behavioral confirmation in the battle of wills.

Other research suggests that the tendency for self-verification to triumph over behavioral confirmation generalizes to naturally occurring settings. For example, McNulty and Swann (1994) followed a group of college students over a semester. They discovered that, over the course of the semester, students tended to bring their roommates to see them as they saw themselves. In addition, this self-verification pattern was stronger than the corresponding tendency for students to bring their self-views into agreement with their roommates' initial impressions of them. Similarly, in a semester long investigation of MBA students in study groups, Swann, Milton, and Polzer (2000) found that the tendency of individual members of each group to bring the appraisals of other group members into agreement with their self-views prevailed over the countervailing tendency for the group members to shape the self-views of individuals in the group.

And what happens if people somehow wind up in relationships in which their partners refuse to bring their appraisals into line with the self-views of targets? In the next section, I suggest that targets will attempt to rectify the situation by withdrawing from the relationship, either psychologically or by terminating the relationship.

Fleeing contexts in which self-verification is not forthcoming

Several investigators have now examined how people react when they wind up in marriages in which their spouses perceive them more (or less) favorably than they perceive themselves. They have found repeatedly that people are less intimate and satisfied in relationships in which they are perceived incongruently (Burke & Stets, 1999; De La Ronde & Swann, 1998; Katz, Beach, & Anderson, 1996; Ritts & Stein, 1995; Schafer, Wickrama, & Keith, 1996; Swann, De La Ronde, & Hixon, 1994). Moreover, one study found that spouses in non-verifying relationships were especially inclined to opt for separation or divorce (Cast & Burke, 2002). Similarly, when college students with firmly held self-views find that their current roommate perceives them more or less favorably than they perceive themselves, they make plans to find a new roommate (Swann & Pelham, 2002).

As impressive as this evidence of self-verification strivings may be, a recent study by Schroeder, Josephs, and Swann (2004) is especially compelling. The question they asked was this: would people with low (but not high) self-esteem remain in jobs in which their wage trend was flat or declining, and quit jobs in which their wage trend increased. In light of evidence that people are more inclined to seek confirmatory evaluations insofar as the evaluator is highly credible (Hixon & Swann, 1993), they predicted that the longer people were employed, the stronger their preference for self-confirmatory feedback would be. That is, people with low self-esteem might initially tolerate positive performance feedback (increasing pay), but become increasingly less tolerant of such positivity as their employer acquired more evidence on which to base an evaluation of them.

To test these ideas, they measured the self-esteem of 7758 male and female college students using Tafarodi and Swann's (1995) self-esteem measure. Ten questions tap social worth (feeling valued and respected by others), and ten questions tap agency (feeling strong and capable due to one's knowledge of what one can do). Conceivably, both forms of self-esteem (social worth and agency) might be related to turnover. That is, perceived social worth might predict persistence in a job because salary might be understood as reflecting how much people are valued by their supervisors and co-workers, and perceived agency might be influential insofar as people use self-perceived competence as a yardstick for assessing their "market value."

We obtained employment information for participants between 1994 and 1999. This allowed us to determine how much each participant earned from any given employer in any given calendar quarter. The criterion variable was the employment longevity of participants with their original employer, adjusted for the time-on-the-job of those still with their employer at the end of the study.

The predictors of the employment lifetime variable were self-esteem (summed over social worth and agency), wage trend, and the interaction of these two. The results showed that self-esteem and wage trend began to interactively predict turnover after 24 months of employment. Most strikingly, those with low self-esteem preferred remaining in jobs in which they received no raises and preferred *leaving* jobs with increasing wage. In contrast, those with high self-esteem were more apt to remain with the original employer if their wages increased. Apparently, when faced with a choice between their negative self-views or high salaries, people with low social worth chose to retain their negative self-views.

A potential alternative interpretation of our findings is that people with low self-esteem were genuinely incompetent and they were either fired or resigned because they were embarrassed or felt overwhelmed. Contrary to this rival hypothesis, when we controlled for self-perceived ability (which has been shown to be related to measures of actual ability) the self-verification pattern remained.

Interestingly, the preference for self-verifying wages emerged only after a substantial period of time (two years) elapsed. The latter finding presumably reflects a tendency for perceived over- or under-payment to produce discomfort only when the employer is well acquainted with one's performance. Apparently, after two years, participants felt that their employer should have known them better than to pay them amounts that their self-views told them were too high. This finding is reminiscent of Swann et al.'s (1994) evidence of self-verification strivings among married but not dating persons. Whereas dating couples were intimate with positive but not negative partners, married couples were most intimate with partners who evaluated them in self-verifying manner, even if their self-views were negative. As in the present data, self-discrepant evaluations were troubling only when they came from credible evaluators.

Our findings challenge recent contentions that self-esteem is a mere product of social interaction that has no impact on significant social phenomena (e.g., Baumeister, Campbell, Krueger, & Vohs, 2003; Dawes, 1994; London, 1997). That is, it appears that people's self-views encourage them to systematically gravitate toward contexts that will reinforce their conceptions of themselves, even if these conceptions happen to be negative. Having said this, I should emphasize here that however paradoxical or self-defeating our participants' behaviors may appear to the outside observer, they may be adaptive within the frame of reference of the participants themselves. That is, by avoiding employment opportunities that are financially beneficial, participants with low self-esteem are avoiding situations that are likely to be discordant with their deep seated beliefs about themselves and therefore psychologically stressful. The responses of low self-esteem participants may thus be members of a larger class of responses that are designed to ensure that their worlds seem safe, predictable and congruent with previous experiences rather than dangerous, unpredictable, and incongruent with previous experiences.

Consequences of self-verification processes

The tendency for people to gravitate toward self-verifying relationship partners and employment settings has several distinct consequences. For example, by engaging in such activities, people may enlist accomplices who will assist them in their efforts to create self-verifying worlds that stabilize their self-views. Evidence for this possibility comes from research by Swann and Predmore (1985). These researchers brought couples into the laboratory, separated them, and asked spouses to rate their partner on several personality attributes. This enabled the researchers to differentiate partners who saw targets as they saw themselves ("congruent partners") from those that did not ("incongruent partners"). Targets were then joined by either their partner or a stranger. Shortly thereafter, the experimenter returned with a bogus evaluation of the "target" that an independent source had ostensibly generated. The evaluation was designed to be inconsistent with the target's self-views. After examining the evaluation, targets rated themselves. When targets examined the self-discrepant evaluation in the presence of a congruent partner, they displayed less self-concept change than when they examined it in the presence of an incongruent partner or stranger. Such evidence suggests that when people establish relationships with partners who see them congruently, they will enjoy stable self-views.

Self-verification processes may also influence group processes. Recall Swann et al.'s (2000) study of MBA students. At the middle of the semester, they assessed the extent to which participants brought the other members of their study groups to see them as they saw themselves. Then, toward the end of the semester, they assessed participants' feelings of connection to the group (i.e., group identification, social integration, and emotional conflict) as well as performance on creative tasks (e.g., tasks that benefit from divergent perspectives, such as devising a marketing plan for a new product or determining how to increase the productivity of a failing corporation). They discovered that self-verification effects fostered both feelings of connection and creative task performance, and this pattern emerged for negative as well as positive self-views. Moreover, in addition to the direct link between verification and performance on creative tasks, there was also evidence that feelings of connection to the group partially mediated the relation between verification and performance on creative tasks. Apparently, when group members had their unique attributes and perspectives verified they felt recognized and understood. Such feelings emboldened them to offer creative ideas and insights that they might otherwise have been inhibited to share. In addition, feeling known and understood by the group may have increased motivation to cooperate with one another by making members feel more identified with the group.

Polzer et al. (2002) extended these ideas even further by examining the implications of the self-verification process for the "value in diversity" hypothesis (e.g., Jehn, Northcraft, & Neale, 1999) — the notion that contact between workers from diverse backgrounds will lead to the development of novel solutions to the tasks at hand. Although intuitively appealing, the value in diversity hypothesis has received mixed support. In fact, in some research, diversity actually seems to foster dissension within groups (for a review, see Williams & O'Reilly, 1998).

Why might diversity sow dissension within groups? Some researchers (Pelled, Eisenhardt, & Xin, 1999; Tsui, Egan, & O'Reilly, 1992) have proposed that identifying individual group members with distinct groups (i.e., "out-groups") may disrupt group dynamics. Consistent with this, research on self-categorization theory has shown that out-group members evoke more disliking, distrust, and competition than in-group members (e.g., Brewer, 1979; Hogg, Cooper-Shaw, & Holzworth, 1993; Hogg & Hardie, 1991, 1992). Such processes may conspire to make diverse groups a fertile breeding ground for misunderstanding and discord.

To address these issues, Polzer et al. (2002) began by defining diversity as the amount of inter-individual variability across several demographic and functional categories (e.g., sex, race, previous job function, area of concentration in the MBA program). They reasoned that the identity negotiation processes through which group members come to see one another as they see themselves might offset the tendency for categorical differences between group members to disrupt group processes. In particular, they predicted that verification of self-views might encourage diverse group members to apply their differences in knowledge, experiences, and perspectives to the tasks at hand (e.g., Ely and Thomas, 2001) and that this would help them translate their diverse qualities into exceptional performance on creative tasks. Consistent with this, they found that self-verification achieved within the first ten minutes of interaction moderated the impact of demographic diversity on performance. Specifically, among groups that achieved high levels of self-verification, diversity facilitated performance. In contrast, among groups that failed to achieve substantial self-verification, diversity undermined performance. Thus, group members who quickly recognized the unique qualities of their fellow group members were optimally positioned to capitalize on the diversity in their group. In short, Polzer et al.'s evidence of links between self-verification, diversity, and performance suggest that the failure of previous researchers to consider self-verification processes may explain why they obtained mixed support for the value in diversity hypothesis.

Self-verification, identity negotiation, and making minds

The research considered here builds on past evidence that the expectations of perceivers shape the activities of targets (Snyder & Klein, this volume) by showing that targets do not merely passively assimilate the expectations of others. Instead, research on self-verification processes shows that people gravitate toward self-confirming relationship partners and jobs, even when doing so ensures that they will receive support for their negative self-views. Moreover, people's success in bringing others to validate their self-views is highly consequential. Witness that people are drawn to relationship partners and group members who offer them validation. Moreover, these feelings may, in turn, influence the extent to which they feel connected to the group as well as their actual performance. This research therefore suggests that the "making of minds" is properly understood as an interactive process in which both perceivers and targets shape the minds of one another through a process of identity negotiation.

In the spirit of my contention that identity negotiation is a two-way street, it is important to acknowledge that targets are not always successful in shaping the perceptions of perceivers. Indeed, several of the studies discussed here point to conditions under which the expectations of perceivers are apt to shape the self-views of targets. At least two key principles govern the outcome of the identity negotiation process (cf. Swann, Rentfrow, & Guinn, 2003).

The investment principle suggests that as investment in expectancies increases, those expectancies (whether they are entertained by perceivers or targets) are more apt to prevail in the identity negotiation process. For example, Swann and Ely (1984) demonstrated that targets tend to behaviorally confirm the expectancies of perceivers when perceiver's expectancies are high in certainly and target's self-views are low in certainty. Similarly, Swann & Pelham (2002) reported that targets were more committed to self-verifying roommates when their self-views were high in certainty and importance. In the language of making minds, the extent to which people feel that they know their own minds will determine the extent to which they work to bring the minds of others into harmony with their own views.

The accessibility principle states that for people to strive to verify an expectancy, they must possess the mental resources and motivation required to access that expectancy. Swann et al. (1990), for example, showed that people who were prevented from accessing their self-views (by depriving them of cognitive resources) failed to choose self-verifying interaction partners. Motivational factors, such as the nature of the relationship, may also influence how likely people are to access their self-views and translate them into behavior. For example, Swann et al. (1994) discovered that dating partners were most intimate with partners who viewed them favorably but married people were most intimate with spouses who saw them as they saw themselves. Presumably, the nature of the relationship determined whether or not people accessed their self-views and used these views to guide their responses to their partners.

Such research on the boundary conditions of self-verification and rival processes is important because it helps illuminate the nature of these processes. More generally, this work offers important insight into the making of minds. Indeed, understanding the interplay between people's self-views and their expectancies about one another seems to represent a key step in developing a comprehensive theory of the making of minds.

Acknowledgement

This research was supported by a grant from the National Institutes of Mental Health MH57455-01A2 to William B. Swann, Jr.

Note

1. Self-verification theory is related to, but distinct from, Freud's (1920) concept of repetition compulsion as well as later cognitive consistency and balance theories (e.g., Festinger, 1957; Heider, 1946). Whereas all such formulations argue that people strive for the familiar and avoid psychological inconsistency, they fail to specify the functional significance of inconsistency. Self-verification theory argues that people work to maintain their self-views because such self-views are a critically important source of psychological and interpersonal integrity and stability.

References

Baumeister, R. F., Campbell, J. D., Krueger, J. I., & Vohs, K. D. (2003). *Psychological Science in the Public Interest 4*, 1–44.

Brewer, M. B. (1979). In-group bias in the minimal intergroup situation: A cognitive-motivational analysis. *Psychological Bulletin, 86*, 307–324.

Burke, P. J., & Stets, J. E. (1999). Trust and commitment through self-verification. *Social Psychology Quarterly, 62*, 347–360.

Cast, A. D., & Burke, P. D. (2002). A theory of self-esteem. *Social Forces, 80*, 1041–1068.

Clark, G. L. (1954). *Elements of ecology.* New York: Wiley.

Cooley, C. S. (1902). *Human nature and the social order.* New York: Scribner's.

Curtis, R. C., & Miller, K. (1986). Believing another likes or dislikes you: Behavior making the beliefs come true. *Journal of Personality and Social Psychology, 51*, 284–290.

Dawes, R. M. (1994). *House of cards: Psychology and psychotherapy built on myth.* New York: Free Press.

De La Ronde, C., & Swann, W. B., Jr. (1998). Partner verification: Restoring shattered images of our intimates. *Journal of Personality and Social Psychology, 75*, 374–382.

Ely, R. J., & Thomas, D. A. (2001). Cultural diversity at work: The effects of diversity perspectives on work group processes and outcomes. *Administrative Science Quarterly, 46*, 229–273.

Giesler, R. B., Josephs, R. A., & Swann, W. B., Jr. (1996). Self-verification in clinical depression: The desire for negative evaluation. *Journal of Abnormal Psychology, 105*, 358–368.

Hixon, J. G., & Swann, W. B. Jr. (1993). When does introspection bear fruit? Self-reflection, self-insight, and interpersonal choices. *Journal of Personality and Social Psychology, 64*, 35–43.

Hogg, M. A., & Hardie, E. A. (1991). Social attraction, personal attraction, and self categorization: A field study. *Personality & Social Psychology Bulletin, 17*, 175–180.

Hogg, M. A. & Hardie, E. A. (1992). Prototypicality, conformity and depersonalized attraction: A self-categorization analysis of group cohesiveness. *British Journal of Social Psychology, 31*, 41–56.

Hogg, M. A., Cooper-Shaw, L., & Holzworth, D. W. (1993). Studies of group prototypicality and depersonalized attraction in small interactive groups. *Personality and Social Psychology Bulletin, 19*, 452–465.

Jehn, K. A., Northcraft, G. B., & Neale, M. A. (1999). Why some differences make a difference: A field study of diversity, conflict, and performance in workgroups. *Administrative Science Quarterly, 44*, 741–763.

Jones, S. C., & Panitch, D. (1971). The self-fulfilling prophecy and interpersonal attraction. *Journal of Experimental Social Psychology, 7*, 356–366.

Katz, J., Beach, S. R. H, & Anderson, P. (1996). Self-enhancement versus self-verification: Does spousal support always help? *Cognitive Therapy and Research, 20*, 345–360.

Kelley, H. H., & Stahelski, A. J. (1970). The social interaction basis of cooperators' and competitors' beliefs about others. *Journal of Personality and Social Psychology, 16*, 66–91.

Lecky, P. (1945). *Self-consistency: A theory of personality.* New York: Island Press.

London, T. P. (1997). The case against self-esteem: Alternate philosophies toward self that would raise the probability of pleasurable and productive living. *Journal of Rational-Emotive & Cognitive Behavior Therapy, 15*, 19–29.

McCall, G. J., & Simmons, J.L. (1966). *Identities and interactions: An examination of human associations in everyday life.* New York: Free Press.

McNulty, S. E., & Swann, W. B., Jr. (1994). Identity negotiation in roommate relationships: The self as architect and consequence of social reality. *Journal of Personality and Social Psychology, 67*, 1012–1023.

Mead, G. H. (1934). *Mind, self and society.* Chicago: University of Chicago Press.

O'Reilly, C. A., Caldwell, D. F., & Barnett, W. P. (1989). Work group demography, social integration, and turnover. *Administrative Science Quarterly, 34*, 21–37.

Pelham, B. W., & Swann, W. B., Jr. (1994). The juncture of intrapersonal and interpersonal knowledge: Self-certainty and interpersonal congruence. *Personality and Social Psychology Bulletin, 20*, 349–357.

Pelled, L. H., Eisenhardt, K. M., & Xin, K. R. (1999). Exploring the Black Box: An analysis of work group diversity, conflict and performance. *Administrative Science Quarterly, 44*, 1–28.

Polzer, J. T., Milton, L. P. & Swann, W. B., Jr. (2002). Capitalizing on Diversity: Interpersonal Congruence in Small Work Groups. *Administrative Science Quarterly, 47*, 296–324.

Ritts, V., & Stein, J. R. (1995). Verification and commitment in marital relationships: An exploration of self-verification theory in community college students. *Psychological Reports, 76*, 383–386.

Robinson, D. T., & Smith-Lovin, L. (1992). Selective interaction as a strategy for identity maintenance: An affect control model. *Social Psychology Quarterly, 55*, 12–28.

Rosenthal, R., & Jacobson, L. (1968). *Pygmalion in the classroom: Teacher expectations and pupils' intellectual development.* New York: Holt, Rinehart & Winston.

Sacks, O. (1985). *The man who mistook his wife for a hat and other clinical tales.* New York: Simon & Shuster.

Schafer, R. B., Wickrama, K. A. S., & Keith, P. M. (1996). Self-concept disconfirmation, psychological distress, and marital happiness. *Journal of Marriage and the Family, 58,* 167–177.

Schroeder, D., Josephs, R., & Swann, W. B., Jr. (2004). Foregoing *lucrative employment to preserve low self-esteem.* Unpublished manuscript.

Secord, P. F., & Backman, C. W. (1965). An interpersonal approach to personality. In B. Maher (Ed.), *Progress in experimental personality research,* (Vol. 2, pp. 91–125). New York: Academic Press.

Snyder, M. (1984). When belief creates reality. In L. Berkowitz (Ed.), *Advances in experimental social psychology* (Vol. 16, pp. 248–305). New York: Academic Press.

Snyder, M., & Klein, O. (this volume). Construing and constructing others: On the reality and generality of the behavioral confirmation scenario.

Swann, W. B., Jr. & Pelham, B. W. (2002). Who wants out when the going gets good? Psychological investment and preference for self-verifying college roommates. *Journal of Self and Identity, 1,* 219–233.

Swann, W. B., Jr. 1996. *Self-traps: The elusive quest for higher self-esteem.* Freeman: New York.

Swann, W. B., Jr., & Predmore, S. C. (1985). Intimates as agents of social support: Sources of consolation or despair? *Journal of Personality and Social Psychology, 49,* 1609–1617.

Swann, W. B., Jr., De La Ronde, C., & Hixon, J. G. (1994). Authenticity and positivity strivings in marriage and courtship. *Journal of Personality and Social Psychology, 66,* 857–869.

Swann, W. B., Jr., De La Ronde, C., & Hixon, J. G. (1994). Authenticity and positivity strivings in marriage and courtship. *Journal of Personality and Social Psychology, 66,* 857–869.

Swann, W. B., Jr., Hixon, J. G., Stein-Seroussi, A., & Gilbert, D. T. (1990). The fleeting gleam of praise: Behavioral reactions to self-relevant feedback. *Journal of Personality and Social Psychology, 59,* 17–26.

Swann, W. B., Jr., Milton, L. P., & Polzer, J. T. (2000). Should we create a niche or fall in line? Identity negotiation and small group effectiveness. *Journal of Personality and Social Psychology, 79,* 238–250.

Swann, W. B., Jr. & Pelham, B. W. (2002). Who wants out when the going gets good? Psychological investment and preference for self-verifying college roommates. *Journal of Self and Identity, 1,* 219–233.

Swann, W. B., Jr., Pelham, B. W., & Chidester, T. (1988). Change through paradox: Using self-verification to alter beliefs. *Journal of Personality and Social Psychology, 54,* 268–273.

Swann, W. B., Jr., Pelham, B. W., & Krull, D. S. (1989). Agreeable fancy or disagreeable truth? Reconciling self-enhancement and self-verification. *Journal of Personality and Social Psychology, 57,* 782–791.

Swann, W. B., Jr., Stein-Seroussi, A. & Giesler, B. (1992). Why people self-verify. *Journal of Personality and Social Psychology, 62,* 392–401.

Swann, W. B., Jr., Wenzlaff, R. M., & Tafarodi, R. W. (1992). Depression and the search for negative evaluations: More evidence of the role of self-verification strivings. *Journal of Abnormal Psychology, 101,* 314–371.

Swann, W. B., Jr. Milton, L. & Polzer, J. (2000). Creating a niche or falling in line: Identity negotiation and small group effectiveness. *Journal of Personality and Social Psychology, 79,* 238–250.

Swann, W. B., Jr. (1983). Self-verification: Bringing social reality into harmony with the self. In J. Suls & A. G. Greenwald (Eds.), *Social psychological perspectives on the self* (Vol. 2, pp. 33–66). Hillsdale, NJ: Erlbaum.

Swann, W. B., Jr. (1984). Quest for accuracy in person perception: A matter of pragmatics. *Psychological Review, 91,* 457–477.

Swann, W. B., Jr., & Ely, R. J. (1984). A battle of wills: Self-verification versus behavioral confirmation. *Journal of Personality and Social Psychology, 46,* 1287–1302.

Swann, W. B., Jr., & Hill, C. A. (1982). When our identities are mistaken: Reaffirming self-conceptions through social interaction. *Journal of Personality and Social Psychology, 43,* 59–66.

Swann, W. B., Jr., & Read, S. J. (1981). Self-verification processes: How we sustain our self-conceptions. *Journal of Experimental Social Psychology, 17,* 351–372.

Swann, W. B., Jr., Rentfrow, P. J., & Guinn, J. (2002). Self-verification: The search for coherence. In M. Leary and J. Tagney, *Handbook of self and identity* (pp. 367–383). Guilford: New York.

Tafarodi, R. W., & Swann, W. B., Jr. (1995). Self-liking and self-competence as dimensions of global self-esteem: Initial validation of a measure. *Journal of Personality Assessment, 65,* 322–342.

Tsui, A. S., Egan, T. D., & O'Reilly, C. A. (1992). Being different: Relational demography and organizational attachment. *Administrative Science Quarterly, 37,* 549–579.

Williams, K. Y., & O'Reilly, C. A. (1998). Demography and diversity in Organizations: A review of 40 years of research. *Organizational Behavior, 20,* 77–14.

Social reality makes the social mind

Self-fulfilling prophecy, stereotypes, bias, and accuracy

Lee Jussim[1], Kent D. Harber[2], Jarret T. Crawford[1],
Thomas R. Cain[1] and Florette Cohen[1]
[1]Rutgers University / [2]Rutgers University at Newark

This paper contests social psychology's emphasis on the biased, erroneous, and constructed nature of social cognition by: (1) showing how the extent of bias and error in classic research is overstated; (2) summarizing research regarding the accuracy of social beliefs; and (3) describing how social stereotypes sometimes improve person perception accuracy. A Goodness of Judgment Index is also presented to extract evidence regarding accuracy from research focusing on bias. We conclude that accuracy is necessary for understanding social cognition.

How are social beliefs related to social reality? Are people's social beliefs typically uninformed by social reality? Do people routinely change their behavior to fit others' expectations? Or do social beliefs primarily result from, rather than cause, social reality? These are fundamental questions, and their answers respectively define humans as socially confounded, living in social worlds of their own (or others') invention, or as socially astute, negotiating the social world as it is.

This paper reviews evidence showing that the mind typically reflects rather than produces social reality. There are exceptions, and constructivist phenomena, such as self-fulfilling prophecy and expectancy-confirming bias, occur. But such phenomena are often small and fleeting, whereas accuracy and responsiveness to social reality tend to be substantial and enduring. The paper is divided into three sections that demonstrate how social perception reflects more than it creates social reality: (1) a review of the expectancy-confirming bias and self-fulfilling prophecy research that reveals the limited power of these effects; (2) a review of research demonstrating accuracy in social perception; and (3) a reinterpretation emphasizing accuracy of research widely regarded as evidence of error and bias.

The limited power of expectancy-confirming biases

Expectancy-confirming biases occur when people's expectations cause them to perceive other people's behavior, accomplishments, or attributes in a manner that confirms these expectations.

This includes, but is not restricted to, stereotype-based expectations. For example, people evaluated a fourth grader's performance on a test more favorably when they believed she was from a middle class background than when they believed she was from a lower class background (Darley & Gross, 1983). Similarly, teachers sometimes more positively evaluate students for whom they have high (rather than low) expectations, even after controlling for actual performance (Jussim, 1989; Williams, 1976).

The power of expectancies to bias perception is one basis for the common social psychological emphasis on the power of beliefs to construct social reality. For example: "… people often see what they expect to see: they select evidence that confirms their stereotypes and ignore anomalies" (Jones, 1986, p. 42; for similar claims see, e.g., Fiske & Taylor, 1991; Jost & Kruglanski, 2002).

Table 1. Meta-analyses of expectancy-confirmation studies

Meta-analysis	Topic/Research question	Number of studies	Average expectancy effect
Swim et al., 1989	Do sex stereotypes bias evaluations of work?	119	.04
Stangor & McMillan, 1992	Do expectations bias memory?	65	.03
Sweeney & Haney, 1992	Does race bias criminal sentencing?	19	.09
Mazella & Feingold, 1994	Are mock jurors' verdicts affected by defendant:		
	Attractiveness	25	.10
	Race	29	.01
	Social class	4	.08
	Sex	21	.04
Kunda & Thagard, 1996	Do stereotypes bias judgments of targets:		
	Without individuating information?	7	.25
	With individuating information?	40	.19

Effect sizes are correlations (r's), between expectation and outcome. All meta-analyses focused on experimental research. Positive effects represent stronger expectancy-confirming biases and favoring the more privileged or high status groups (men, Whites, the rich, the attractive).

However, the accumulated evidence indicates that expectancies do not greatly bias social perception. Table 1 presents the results from meta-analyses of studies assessing expectancy-confirmation in many contexts. It shows that the effects of expectancies, averaged over hundreds of experiments, range only from 0 to .25.

The simple arithmetic mean of the effect sizes is .10, which is an overestimate, because the meta-analyses with more studies yielded systematically *lower* effect sizes ($r = -.43$ between effect size and number of studies). The few naturalistic studies of expectancy-confirming judgmental biases have yielded similarly small effects (e.g., Clarke & Campbell, 1955; Jussim, 1989; Williams, 1976). An overall effect of .10 means that expectancies substantially influence social perceptions about 5% of the time (as per Rosenthal's (1984) binomial effect size display). This means they *do not* influence perceptions 95% of the time.

The limited power of self-fulfilling prophecies

Self-fulfilling prophecies occur when one person's erroneous expectations for a second person cause that second person to behaviorally confirm the originally erroneous expectation (Jussim, 1991; Merton, 1948). Self-fulfilling prophecies constitute a second basis for the common social psychological emphasis on the power of belief to create reality. For example: "The thrust of dozens of experiments on the self-fulfilling prophecy and expectancy-confirmation processes, for example, is that erroneous impressions tend to be perpetuated rather than supplanted because of the impressive extent to which people see what they want to see and act as others want them to act …" (Jost & Kruglanski, 2002, pp. 172-173). Although such testaments to the power of self-fulfilling prophecies are common (see Jussim, 1991; Jussim & Harber, 2005, for reviews), they are not supported by the general pattern of results obtained in naturalistic or experimental studies.

Naturalistic studies. Table 2 summarizes results obtained in naturalistic studies that were capable of assessing both the accuracy and self-fulfillment of teacher expectations. These studies employed structural equation techniques to determine whether teacher expectations earlier in the school year predicted changes in student achievement (typically, by controlling for earlier student achievement) by the end of the school year (or later). The self-fulfilling effects of teacher expectations ranged from nonexistent to moderate, and, on average, were small (about .15). Other naturalistic studies of teacher expectations yield the same pattern of small effects averaging .1 to .2 (Jussim & Harber, 2005. Naturalistic studies of self-fulfilling prophecies in therapy, among college roommates, and among small working groups of MBAs yield a similar pattern (Berman, 1979; McNulty & Swann, 1994; Swann, Milton, & Polizer, 2000).

Table 2. Teacher expectations: Self-fulfilling prophecies and accuracy in naturalistic studies

Study	Correlation between teacher expectation and student achievement	Self-fulfilling prophecy effects[a]	Accuracy (correlation minus self-fulfilling prophecy)
Williams, 1976	.47 – .72	.00 – .13	.42 – .72
Brattesani et al., 1984	.74	.26	.48
Jussim, 1989	.36 – .57	−.03 – .18	.36 – .41
Jussim & Eccles, 1992	.50 – .55	.10 – .16	.36 – .49
Trouilloud et al., 2002	.79	.28	.51

[a]These are standardized regression coefficients. Ranges are presented when studies had multiple outcomes.

Experiments. Meta-analyses of experimental studies also show that self-fulfilling effects of perceivers' expectations are generally modest, averaging about .2 and, except in military contexts, range from 0 to about .3 (McNatt, 2000; Raudenbush, 1984; Rosenthal & Rubin, 1978). A self-fulfilling prophecy effect of .2 means that expectations substantially change the behavior of about 10% of the targets and that they do not substantially change about 90% of targets (see Jussim & Harber, 2005, for a detailed example). It is much more common for expectancies to have no effect than to become self-fulfilling.

Accuracy

What is social perceptual accuracy?

Although accuracy has long been controversial within social psychology (Jussim, 2005), it is conceptually a very simple phenomenon. Social perceptual accuracy refers to the correspondence between perceivers' beliefs about targets and what targets are actually like, independent of the perceivers' influence on them (Funder, 1995; Jussim, 2005).

The accuracy of teacher expectations

A simple way to distinguish self-fulfilling prophecies from accuracy under naturalistic conditions is to determine the difference between: (1) simple correlations between teacher expectations and student achievement, and (2) self-fulfilling effects of teacher expectations on student achievement. For example, the correlation between teacher expectations early in the year and student achievement at the end of the school year represents the overall predictive validity of teacher expectations. Predictive validity can come from only two sources, which are both mutually exclusive and exhaustive: (1) teacher expectations cause student achievement (e.g., through self-fulfilling prophecies); and (2) teacher expectations predict, but do not cause, student achievement. Prediction without causation represents accuracy.

The extent to which accuracy dominates self-fulfilling prophecies can be seen in Table 2. Accuracy accounts for about 75% of the correlation between teacher expectations and student achievement; self-fulfilling prophecy, about 25%. In general, teacher expectations predict student achievement primarily because they are accurate, even though there is also reliable evidence that self-fulfilling prophecies occur.

The accuracy of social stereotypes

Definition of stereotype. Stereotypes were once routinely defined as irrational and inaccurate (e.g., Allport, 1954; Brigham, 1971). Such definitions, however, included a tautology that limited their utility. If all stereotypes are inaccurate by definition, then only inaccurate beliefs about groups can be considered stereotypes. What term, then, denotes *accurate* beliefs about groups? Because of these and similar concerns, widespread disagreement emerged regarding whether stereotypes should be considered inaccurate by definition (Ashmore & Del Boca, 1981).

These problems have been eliminated by contemporary definitions of stereotypes, which are more value neutral and non-tautological. Thus, Ashmore and Del Boca (1981) define stereotypes as beliefs about the attributes of groups and their individual members (see e.g., Fiske & Taylor, 1991; McCauley, Stitt, & Segal, 1980; Ryan, 2002 for similarly neutral definitions). These definitions allow the accuracy of stereotypes to be evaluated in the same manner as schemas, beliefs, and category judgments.

We adopt Ashmore and Del Boca's (1981) agnostic definition. By doing so, the accuracy of any particular belief about a group becomes an empirical question. We do not assume that all stereotypes are accurate; people hold inaccurate beliefs about groups and these can be profoundly damaging. But the existence of some inaccurate beliefs about groups does not, in itself, negate the potential for other stereotypes to be accurate. Just as a scientific hypothesis of an association between two variables does not require a perfect ($r = 1.0$) correlation to be confirmed, neither does a lay belief. In the same spirit as that governing science, people's beliefs about race and sex differences, while not perfect, are often highly valid. We review evidence of such accuracy next.

Group differences are sometimes broadly consistent with stereotypes. Around the world, on average, males are more aggressive than females (Brannon, 1999). In the U.S., Jews are wealthier than other ethnic groups; African-Americans are more likely to be both perpetrators and victims of crime than are others; Asian-Americans are more likely to complete college than are others; and people with lower incomes are less well-educated than are people with higher incomes (Marger, 1994; www.census.gov, 2004). These are all verified group differences, and people who believe in them hold more accurate stereotypes than those who do not.

Stereotypes of African-Americans. McCauley and Stitt (1978) provided the first rigorous examination of the accuracy of people's beliefs about differences between African-Americans and other Americans. These beliefs included the percentage of African-Americans and other Americans who were: high school graduates, born illegitimately, unemployed last month, crime victims, on welfare, parents of four or more children, and in a household headed by a female. Their results provided clear evidence of stereotyping: of 42 possible comparisons, 37 showed that participants perceived Blacks as different from other Americans. Were these perceived differences correct? In all 37 cases of stereotyping, the direction of the perceived difference was identical to the direction of the actual difference; 20 of the perceived differences were similar in magnitude to the actual differences; and in the remaining 17 cases, participants *underestimated* the extent of actual differences between Blacks and other Americans. Overall, the correlation of the mean perceived difference with the Census difference was .87.

We are aware of only two other studies that have empirically assessed the validity of racial stereotypes (Ryan, 1996; Wolsko, Park, Judd, & Wittenbrink, 2000). These studies used a very different methodology. In both, self-reports of randomly surveyed African-Americans and Whites constituted the criterion, and accuracy was assessed using discrepancy scores (between stereotypes and the target group's self-report). Both found that Whites' stereotypes were quite accurate (although Ryan, 1996, found that African-Americans generally exaggerated the extent to which both Whites and African-Americans fit their group's stereotypes). Wolsko et al. (2000) also found that when people were urged to take group differences seriously (i.e., adopt a "multicultural" perspective rather than a "color-blind" perspective), both their stereotyping *and* their accuracy increased.

Sex stereotypes. Several studies have demonstrated accuracy in people's beliefs about sex differences. Swim (1994) performed two of the first, in which she: (1) assessed college students' beliefs about the size of sex differences on 17 attributes (aggressiveness, helpfulness, SAT scores, etc.); (2) located every meta-analysis assessing the difference between men and women on these 17 attributes; and then (3) compared the students' gender beliefs to the meta-analyses. Across two studies, the mean perceived sex difference correlated almost .8 with the size of the sex differences revealed in the meta-analyses. Other research also converges on the conclusion that people often have moderately to highly accurate perceptions of sex differences (Diekman, Eagly, & Kulesa, 2002; Hall & Carter, 1999). Research finding pervasive inaccuracy (Allen, 1995) is unusual.

Stereotypes, bias, and accuracy in person perception

Accuracy in judging differences between individuals from different groups. People may often hold beliefs about differences between groups of individuals that they know personally. For example, perceivers making claims about the differences between the Dutch and British football (soccer) players on their teams, or between the boys and girls in their math classes, are making claims about differences between small groups. This level of analysis addresses the role of stereotypes in causing systematic inaccuracy in perceivers' judgments about individuals they know personally. Many researchers have emphasized the idea that stereotypes often lead to inaccurate and unjustified judgments of individual targets (e.g., Fiske, 1998; Stangor, 1995). Support for this claim would be obtained by showing that group stereotypes bias judgments of individuals. For example, if sex stereotypes bias coaches' judgments of players' skill, coaches should perceive the skill of the boys as exceeding the skill of the girls by considerably more than is justified by the real skill differences, if any.

Alternatively, the perspective being presented here — that the content of social beliefs largely reflects social reality — suggests a different hypothesis: accuracy in perceivers' judgments of differences between small groups of individuals they know personally should be moderate to high, and bias should be small. Only a handful of studies, however, have addressed the accuracy of people's perceptions of differences and similarities between small groups they know personally. Those studies are reviewed next.

Madon et al. (1998) examined the accuracy of 7th grade teachers' perceptions of their students' performance, talent, and effort at math about one month into the school year. They assessed accuracy by performing the following analyses. First they identified perceived group differences by correlating teachers' perceptions of individual students with students' race, sex, and social class. This assessed whether teachers' systematically evaluated individuals from one group more favorably than individuals from another group. Next, Madon et al. assessed actual group differences in performance, talent, and effort by correlating individual students' final grades from the prior year (before the teachers knew the students), standardized test scores, and self-reported motivation and effort with students' race, sex, and social class. Accuracy was assessed by correlating perceived differences with actual differences.

Madon et al. found that teachers were mostly accurate. The correlation between teachers' perceived group differences and actual group differences was $r = .71$. The teachers' perceptions of sex differences in effort, however, were highly inaccurate — they believed girls exerted more effort than boys, but there was no sex difference in self-reported motivation and effort. When this one outlier was removed, the correlation between perceived and actual group differences increased to $r = .96$.

We are aware of only two other studies that have addressed whether people systematically and unjustifiably favor or disparage individuals belonging to certain groups (Clarke & Campbell, 1955; Jussim, Eccles, & Madon, 1996). Both yielded evidence of accuracy accompanied by small bias. All three studies (including Madon et al., 1998), however, were conducted in educational contexts — Jussim et al. (1996) addressed teachers' perceptions of students, and Clarke and Campbell (1955) addressed students' perceptions of one another. It remains an open, empirical question whether this pattern of accuracy and small bias in perceptions of demographic differences between individuals with whom one has extended contact is unique to classrooms, or characterizes social perception more broadly.

Does relying on stereotypes increase or reduce the accuracy of social judgment? Much of the social psychological scholarship on stereotypes and person perception has been written as if any effect of target category constitutes a source of inaccuracy and error in judgment (e.g., Fiske, 1998; Jones, 1986). If the stereotype is inaccurate, then using it to judge others will reduce accuracy (as Madon et al. (1998) demonstrated regarding sex stereotypes and teachers' perceptions of students' effort). Both common sense and normative models of decision-making (Kahneman & Tversky, 1973) indicate that reliance on an inaccurate expectation, stereotype, or base-rate should reduce accuracy. We are not contesting this conclusion.

The suggestion that any reliance on stereotypes constitutes a source of inaccuracy, however, is not justified. Judgments under uncertainty are properly influenced by base-rates (e.g., Kahneman & Tversky, 1973). Stereotypes are frequently viewed as subjective base-rates (e.g., McCauley et al. 1980; Wolsko et al., 2000). This suggests that when the stereotype is accurate, and when individuating information does not provide complete information relevant to the judgment, perceivers will be more accurate if they use rather than ignore base-rates. Only a handful of studies, however, have addressed this issue, and they are discussed next.

The utility of an accurate stereotype was demonstrated by Brodt and Ross (1998). College students made predictions about the behaviors and preferences of other college students who lived in one of two dormitories. The students in the "preppie" dorm were widely seen as politically conservative, wealthy, and conventional. The students in the "hippie" dorm were widely seen as politically leftwing with unconventional practices and preferences. Perceivers (other students who did not live in either dorm) viewed photographs of individual targets, were informed of each target's dorm, and then made predictions about each target's behaviors and attitudes. Perceivers' predictions were then compared to the targets' self-reports on these same preferences and attitudes.

When perceivers predicted targets to be consistent with their dorm (for a preppie dorm resident to have preppie attributes or for a hippie dorm resident to have hippie attributes), 66% of their predictions were correct (they matched the targets' self-reports). When perceivers jettisoned their dorm stereotypes, and predicted targets to be inconsistent with their dorm, 43% of their predictions were correct. Relying on the preppie/hippie dorm stereotypes enhanced the accuracy of person perception predictions. Three other studies found that, except when the stereotype was manifestly false, relying on a stereotype increased rather than reduced accuracy (Cohen, 1981, experiment two; Jussim, et al. 1996; Madon et al., 1998).

Individuating information. There are limits to the utility of even accurate stereotypes. Individuating information gleaned over time should produce a more accurate impression than will stereotypes. People seem to know this, and usually base their judgments far more on individuating characteristics, when such information is available, than on stereotypes (see, e.g., Kunda & Thagard's (1996) meta-analysis).

Reinterpreting studies of bias: The goodness of judgment index

Deviation from perfection versus improvement over uselessness

In most studies of judgment and decision-making, inaccuracy or bias is defined as deviation from perfection (whether perfection means zero difference between experimental groups or deviation from predictions of a normative model — e.g., Darley & Gross, 1983; Kahneman & Tversky, 1973). Yet perfection is so high a standard that researchers rarely apply it when testing their own theories and hypotheses. In social psychology, effect sizes rarely exceed r's of about .3 (Richard, Bond, & Stokes-Zoota, 2003). Nonetheless, researchers routinely (and justifiably) interpret such effects as validating their hypotheses.

The goal of establishing how well a model performs, rather than determining whether it significantly deviates from perfection, is explicit in several goodness-of-fit indices used to test structural equation models. One of the earliest tests of model quality was the chi-square, which evaluated whether the hypothesized model significantly deviated from perfection (an exact accounting of all covariances). With large samples, the chi-square was usually significant, which led to rejection of highly valid models and measures. To correct this problem, researchers developed measures of fit, such as the *Normed Fit Index* (Bentler & Bonett, 1980), that indicate how much explanatory power a model achieves, rather than whether the model significantly deviates from perfection.

The Goodness of Judgment Index

In the same spirit, Jussim (2004) proposed a *Goodness of Judgment Index* (GJI) for studies of error and bias. The GJI is simply:

$$\frac{\text{maximum possible imperfection} - \text{actual degree of imperfection}}{\text{maximum possible imperfection}}$$

"Maximum possible imperfection" is the most anyone could possibly be wrong under the circumstances. "Actual degree of imperfection" is how wrong the participants actually were.

Imperfection can be operationally defined as errors, discrepancies from predicted values, disagreements among perceivers, and so forth.

The GJI is simple to use and indicates the proportion of improvement of social judgment compared to complete error or bias. Scores above .5 mean that the judgment is closer to complete accuracy or agreement; scores below .5 mean that the judgment is closer to complete error or disagreement.

Reinterpretation of Rosenhan (1973)

The value of assessing accuracy via the GJI is apparent when applied to Rosenhan's 1973 "On Being Sane in Insane Places" study, which has long been cited as a classic example of the power of labels and expectations to bias judgment. Eight pseudo-patients (confederates who had no history of mental illness) were admitted to psychiatric hospitals after (falsely) complaining of auditory hallucinations. Upon admission, they immediately ceased complaining of symptoms of mental illness.

Pseudo-patients were kept from 7 to 52 days, with a mean length of stay of 19 days. None were diagnosed as sane. All were released with a diagnosis of schizophrenia "in remission". Furthermore, staff sometimes interpreted reasonable behavior as symptomatic of pathology (e.g., pacing halls from boredom as anxiety). Rosenhan (1973, p. 257) believed he had shown that "… we cannot distinguish insanity from sanity."

Although these data are not subject to re-interpretation by the GJI, they do provide more evidence of reasonableness than typically acknowledged. First, *the pseudo-patients were admitted complaining of auditory hallucinations.* If the pseudo-patients had not been lying, such complaints would suggest something seriously wrong. Second, most were released in about two weeks (excluding the 52 day outlier). Given that the pseudo-patients had been admitted presenting a psychopathic episode complete with hallucinations, this stay does not seem excessive.

The GJI can, however, help reinterpret a follow-up study Rosenhan (1973) conducted. Rosenhan identified a hospital whose staff doubted that they would misdiagnose patients' sanity. He then informed them that pseudo-patients would attempt to gain admission to their hospital during the upcoming three months. Psychiatrists were asked to rate the 193 new patients admitted during this period. Rosenhan (1973, p. 252) described his results this way: "Twenty-three [pseudo-patients] were considered suspect by at least one psychiatrist." There were, however, *no* pseudo-patients.

To compute the GJI, we gave Rosenhan the benefit of the doubt, and assumed that *all* of the psychiatrists wrongly identified the 23 authentic patients as confederates. To keep the math simple, we have assumed that there was only one psychiatrist (this produces the same GJI as assuming two of two, three of three, etc. identified the 23 patients as pseudo).

The GJI then becomes:

$$\frac{(193 \text{ possible errors} - 23 \text{ actual errors})}{193 \text{ possible errors}} = .88 \text{ accuracy}$$

The psychiatrists were right 88% of the time, based on our starting assumptions favoring bias and error. If we assume that only half, rather than all, of the psychiatrists identified these 23 patients as pseudo, the GJI goes up to .94. The conclusion that the sane are *sometimes* indistinguishable from the insane is justified by Rosenhan's studies. However, neither Rosenhan's conclusion that the insane are indistinguishable from the sane, nor the longstanding interpretation of this study as a testament to the constructive power of labels, are justified. When applied to other influential classics (e.g., Hastorf & Cantril, 1954), and to more recent research (Monin & Norton, 2003), the GJI has yielded values over .6 every time — and often yields values of about .9.

Conclusions

Why accuracy matters

Because accuracy research can advance behavioral science and address important social problems, it serves two central social psychological goals:

Scientific generativity. Potentially rich areas for future research involve identifying the situational and individual factors that determine when people will display greater or lesser social acuity in their perceptions of groups and individuals (as some have already begun to do — Hall & Carter, 1999; Kenny, 1994; Wolsko et al., 2000). Furthermore, fundamental questions about social perceptual processes can be addressed at the intersections between social psychology and other domains in which accuracy has long played an important role, such as perception and memory (Koriat, Goldsmith, & Panksy, 2000).

Identifying and correcting inaccurate stereotypes. Inaccurate stereotypes cause damage (Fiske, 1998). However, identifying inaccurate beliefs about groups requires distinguishing them from accurate beliefs about groups. Furthermore, the success of interventions intended to correct inaccurate stereotypes can only be determined by assessing the accuracy of the social beliefs that follow such interventions.

Making the social mind: Social reality as the major source of social beliefs

Whether social cognition is fundamentally rational and accurate or fundamentally inaccurate and biased has been controversial for decades. Perspectives emphasizing error, bias, and the ways in which social beliefs create social reality have dominated the literature on social cognition (e.g., Fiske, 1998; Jones, 1986; Kahneman & Tversky, 1973; Nisbett & Ross, 1980; Snyder, 1984). These views have created an image of a social perceiver whose misbegotten beliefs and flawed processes construct not only illusions of social reality in the perceiver's own mind, but actual social reality through processes such as self-fulfilling prophecies. In this bleak view, the mind becomes primarily a product of cognitive shortcomings and distorted social interactions.

This view is not justified by the data. Although people undoubtedly commit errors and biases, and are rarely perfectly accurate, almost none of the literature routinely cited as testaments to the power and prevalence of error and bias actually tests for accuracy. Consequently, despite the manner in which it is cited, that literature provides little direct information about accuracy. Furthermore, meta-analyses show that much of the literature routinely cited as demonstrating powerful self-fulfilling prophecies and expectancy-maintaining biases actually demonstrate effects that are best characterized as weak or modest.

Space did not permit us to review many programs of research demonstrating accuracy (e.g., Funder, 1995; Kenny, 1994). We intentionally focused on areas that have long been renowned for supposedly demonstrating the power of error, bias, and social and cognitive constructivism precisely because *even those areas* typically provide far more evidence of reasonableness and accuracy than they do of error, bias and constructivism.

The content of the human mind is undoubtedly socially constructed to some degree, and in ways not addressed in this paper or by much social psychology generally (upbringing, socialization, culture, etc.). But it is also evident that, if the criterion is the actual results of social psychological research (and not necessarily how those results have been discussed), social reality influences the content of the mind far more than the content of the mind constructs or creates social reality.

Acknowledgement

We thank Petra Hauf, Wolfgang Prinz, and Friedrich Försterling for organizing the Making Minds Conference and for comments that enhanced this paper.

References

Allen, B.P. (1995). Gender stereotypes are not accurate: A replication of Martin (1987) using diagnostic vs. self-report and behavioral criteria. *Sex Roles, 32,* 583–600.

Allport, G.W. (1954). *The nature of prejudice.* Reading, MA: Addison-Wesley.

Ashmore, R.D., & Del Boca, F.K. (1981). Conceptual approaches to stereotypes and stereotyping. In D.L. Hamilton (Ed.), *Cognitive processes in stereotyping and intergroup behavior* (pp. 1–35). Hillsdale, NJ: Erlbaum.

Bentler, P.M., & Bonett, D.G. (1980). Significance tests and goodness of fit in the analysis of covariance structures. *Psychological Bulletin 88,* 588–606.

Berman, J.S. (1979). Social bases of psychotherapy: Expectancy, attraction, and the outcome of treatment. *Dissertation Abstracts International, 40,* 5800B.

Brannon, L. (1999). *Gender: Psychological perspectives.* Boston: Allyn & Bacon.

Brattesani, K.A., Weinstein, R.S., & Marshall, H.H. (1984). Student perceptions of differential teacher treatment as moderators of teacher expectation effects. *Journal of Educational Psychology, 76,* 236-247.

Brigham, John C. (1971). Ethnic stereotypes. *Psychological Bulletin. 76, 15–38.*

Brodt, S.E., & Ross, L.D. (1998). The role of stereotyping in overconfident social prediction. *Social Cognition, 16,* 225–252.

Clarke, R.B., & Campbell, D.T. (1955). A demonstration of bias in estimates of Negro ability. *Journal of Abnormal and Social Psychology, 51,* 585–588.

Cohen, C.E. (1981). Personal categories and social perception: Testing some boundaries of the processing effects of prior knowledge. *Journal of Personality and Social Psychology, 40,* 441–452.

Darley, J.M., & Gross, P.H. (1983). A hypothesis-confirming bias in labeling effects. *Journal of Personality and Social Psychology, 44,* 20–33.

Diekman, A. B., Eagly, A. H., & Kulesa, P. (2002). Accuracy and bias in stereotypes about the social and political attitudes of women and men. *Journal of Experimental Social Psychology, 38*, 268–282.

Fiske, S. T. (1998). Stereotyping, prejudice, and discrimination. In D. Gilbert, S. T. Fiske, & G. Lindzey (Eds.), *The handbook of social psychology* (4th ed., Vol. 2, pp. 357–411). New York: McGraw-Hill.

Fiske, S. T., & Taylor, S. E. (1991). *Social Cognition* (second edition). New York: McGraw-Hill.

Funder, D. C. (1995). On the accuracy of personality judgment: A realistic approach. *Psychological Review, 102*, 652–670.

Hall, J. A., & Carter, J. D. (1999). Gender-stereotype accuracy as an individual difference. *Journal of Personality and Social Psychology, 77*, 350–359.

Hastorf, A. H., & Cantril, H. (1954). They saw a game: A case study. *Journal of Abnormal and Social Psychology, 47*, 129–143.

Jones, E. E. (1986). Interpreting interpersonal behavior: The effects of expectancies. *Science, 234*, 41–46.

Jost, J. T., & Kruglanski, A. W. (2002). The estrangement of social constructionism and experimental social psychology: History of the rift and prospects for reconciliation. *Personality and Social Psychology Review, 6*, 168–187.

Jussim, L. (1989). Teacher expectations: Self-fulfilling prophecies, perceptual biases, and accuracy. *Journal of Personality and Social Psychology, 57*, 469–480.

Jussim, L. (1991). Social perception and social reality: A reflection-construction model. *Psychological Review, 98*, 54–73.

Jussim, L. (2004). The goodness of judgment index. *Behavioral and Brain Sciences, 27*, 344–345.

Jussim, L. (2005). Accuracy: Criticisms, controversies, criteria, components and cognitive processes. *Advances in Experimental Social Psychology, 37*, 1–93.

Jussim, L., & Eccles, J. (1992). Teacher expectations II: Reflection and construction of student achievement. *Journal of Personality and Social Psychology, 63*, 947–961.

Jussim, L., Eccles, J., & Madon, S. J. (1996). Social perception, social stereotypes, and teacher expectations: Accuracy and the quest for the powerful self-fulfilling prophecy. *Advances in Experimental Social Psychology, 29*, 281–388.

Jussim, L., & Harber, K. D. (2005). Teacher expectations and self-fulfilling prophecies: Knowns and unknowns, resolved and unresolved controversies. *Personality and Social Psychology Review, 9*, 131–155.

Kahneman, D., & Tversky, A. (1973). On the psychology of prediction. *Psychological Review, 80*, 237–251.

Kenny, D. A. (1994). *Interpersonal perception: A social relations analysis*. New York: Guilford.

Koriat, A., Goldsmith, M., & Panksy, A. (2000). Toward a psychology of memory accuracy. *Annual Review of Psychology, 51*, 481–537.

Kunda, Z., & Thagard, P. (1996). Forming impressions from stereotypes, traits, and behaviors: A parallel-constraint-satisfaction theory. *Psychological Review, 103*, 284–308.

Madon, S. J., Jussim, L., Keiper, S., Eccles, J., Smith, A., & Palumbo, P. (1998). The accuracy and power of sex, social class and ethnic stereotypes: Naturalistic studies in person perception. *Personality and Social Psychology Bulletin, 24*, 1304–1318.

Marger, M. (1994). *Race and ethnic relations* (third edition). Belmont, CA: Wadsworth.

Mazella, R., & Feingold, A. (1994). The effects of physical attractiveness, race, socioeconomic status, and gender of defendants and victims on judgments of mock jurors: A meta-analysis. *Journal of Applied Social Psychology, 24,* 1315–1344.

McCauley, C., & Stitt, C. L. (1978). An individual and quantitative measure of stereotypes. *Journal of Personality and Social Psychology, 36,* 929–940.

McCauley, C., Stitt, C. L., & Segal, M. (1980). Stereotyping: From prejudice to prediction. *Psychological Bulletin, 87,* 195–208.

McNatt, D. B. (2000). Ancient Pygmalion joins contemporary management: A meta-analysis of the result. *Journal of Applied Psychology, 85,* 314–322.

McNulty, S. E., & Swann, W. B. Jr. (1994). Identity negotiation in roommate relationships: The self as architect and consequence of social reality. *Journal of Personality and Social Psychology, 67,* 1012–1023.

Merton, R. K. (1948). The self-fulfilling prophecy. *Antioch Review, 8,* 193–210.

Monin, B., & Norton, M. I. (2003). Perceptions of a fluid consensus: Uniqueness bias, false consensus, false polarization, and pluralistic ignorance in a water conservation crisis. *Personality and Social Psychology Bulletin, 29,* 559–67.

Nisbett, R. E., & Ross, L. (1980). *Human inference: Strategies and shortcomings of social judgment.* Englewood Cliffs, NJ: Prentice-Hall.

Raudenbush, S. W. (1984). Magnitude of teacher expectancy effects on pupil IQ as a function of the credibility of expectancy inductions: A synthesis of findings from 18 experiments. *Journal of Educational Psychology, 76,* 85–97.

Richard, F. D., Bond, C. F. Jr., & Stokes-Zoota, J. J. (2003). One hundred years of social psychology quantitatively described. *Review of General Psychology, 7,* 331–363.

Rosenhan, D. L. (1973). On being sane in insane places. *Science, 179,* 250–258.

Rosenthal, R. (1984). *Meta-analytic procedures for social research.* Beverly Hills, CA: Sage.

Rosenthal R., & Rubin, D. B. (1978). Interpersonal expectancy effects: The first 345 studies. *Behavioral and Brain Sciences, 3,* 377–386.

Ryan, C. S. (1996). Accuracy of black and white college students' in-group and out-group stereotypes. *Personality and Social Psychology Bulletin, 22,* 1114–1127.

Ryan, C. S. (2002). Stereotype accuracy. *European Review of Social Psychology, 13,* 75–109.

Snyder, M. (1984). When belief creates reality. *Advances in experimental social psychology, 18,* 47–305.

Stangor, C. (1995). Content and application inaccuracy in social stereotyping. In Y. T. Lee, L. Jussim, & C. R. McCauley (Eds.), *Stereotype accuracy: Toward appreciating group differences* (pp. 275–292). Washington, D. C.: American Psychological Association.

Stangor, C., & McMillan, D. (1992). Memory for expectancy-congruent and expectancy-incongruent information: A review of the social and social developmental literatures. *Psychological Bulletin, 111,* 42–61.

Swann, W. B. Jr., Milton, L. P., & Polizer, J. T. (2000). Should we create a niche or fall in line? Identity negotiation and small group effectiveness. *Journal of Personality and Social Psychology, 79,* 238–250.

Sweeney, L. T., & Haney, C. (1992). The influence of race on sentencing: A meta-analytic review of experimental studies. *Behavioral Sciences and the Law, 10,* 179–195.

Swim, J. K. (1994). Perceived versus meta-analytic effect sizes: An assessment of the accuracy of gender stereotypes. *Journal of Personality and Social Psychology, 66,* 21–36.

Swim, J., Borgida, E., Maruyama, G., & Myers, D.G. (1989). Joan McKay vs. John McKay: Do gender stereotypes bias evaluations? *Psychological Bulletin, 105,* 409–429.

Trouilloud, D., Sarrazin, P., Martinek, T., & Guillet, E. (2002). The influence of teacher expectations on students' achievement in physical education classes: Pygmalion revisited. *European Journal of Social Psychology, 32,* 1–17.

U.S. Census (2004). *www.census.gov.*

Williams, T. (1976). Teacher prophecies and the inheritance of inequality. *Sociology of Education, 49,* 223–236.

Wolsko, C., Park, B., Judd, C.M., & Wittenbrink, B. (2000). Framing interethnic ideology: Effects of multicultural and color-blind perspectives on judgments of groups and individuals. *Journal of Personality and Social Psychology, 78,* 635–654.

How to do things with logical expressions

Creating collective value
through co-ordinated reasoning

Denis Hilton, Gaëlle Villejoubert and Jean-François Bonnefon
University of Toulouse

We argue that logical expressions in human language enable speakers to perform particular acts as well as stating propositions which may be true or false. We present a conversational action planning model of co-ordinated reasoning, which we use to predict choice of logical expressions in situations in which two people co-operate in the face of risk and uncertainty. We first show how this model predicts preferences for formulations of conditional directives where a principal instructs an agent on how to behave in a hypothetical situation. Second, we show how this model accounts for choices of quantity and probability expressions that express risk, in situations where a professional advises a client on her options. We conclude that the pragmatic signals encoded in human logical vocabulary can facilitate the co-ordination of social interaction through aiding mutual recognition of intentions on joint projects where collaboration is likely to create value.

In 1776, the eminent economist and philosopher Adam Smith pointed out the importance of the division of labour for modern society: Without humans' capacity for specialising in tasks and collaborating with strangers, humankind would not enjoy anything near the success that it does. Somehow, without any explicit direction or centralised planning, human societies seem to be able to self-organise and re-organise into ever more successful economic and social arrangements (Seabright, 2004). Human societies thus seem to be able to make "collective minds" that maximise collective benefits for groups and enable them to prosper. How are such co-ordinated actions possible when many of the agents involved have never met in a face-to-face encounter?

As well as famously invoking the action of an "invisible hand" to regulate markets, Smith argued that this achievement depends on use of language, coupled with the human inclination to exchange goods (in Smith's words, their tendency "to truck and to barter"). Contemporary comparative psychology indeed paints a picture which is broadly in the spirit of Smith's speculation. Thus Tomasello et al. (2005) argue that humans, when compared to chimpanzees, have a tendency to enjoy sharing with others, which applies to both goods and information. Dessalles (2000) agrees that the human species has a unique disposition to give information to others — but argues that this is mainly because individuals wish to signal their worth as a coalition partner to others.

Overall and perhaps unsurprisingly, these arguments suggest that language and communication play a central role in the creation of collective value. More strikingly, the seemingly least bartering-laden use of language, the language of wisdom itself, plays a role in achieving the social co-ordination of intentions. In this article, we show that *logical* expressions such as conditionals, quantifiers and probability words serve important social functions that facilitate co-ordinated reasoning and action.

In particular, we demonstrate that logical vocabulary is impregnated with pragmatic signals — i.e. meanings that express the speaker's intentions and beliefs in the particular contexts in which they are uttered — which facilitate communication and collective planning to deal with risk and uncertainty. From this pragmatic perspective, logical vocabulary obeys a logic of goal satisfaction (cf. Kenny, 1966) which is quite different to the truth-functional criteria used to judge the correctness of a logical expression. Consider the proposition "if you see a leopard, then you run for your life." This is a logical proposition of the form "if p then q." From a truth-functional perspective, this is a true statement unless there are protagonists in some implied reference group (e.g. a tribe in Kenya) who choose not to run for their life (not-q) even though they see a leopard (p). Yet suppose this statement is uttered by a safari guide to inexperienced tourists in Kenya. In such a context, it is manifest that the safari guide does more than merely express a proposition that may be true or false of a given reference class of people (or animals); rather, he wants to make his listeners behave in a certain way should a certain situation arise. Such pragmatic functions are governed by social rationality, and the their quality is measured by the effectiveness with which they induce successful co-ordination through getting hearers to fulfil the speaker's intentions, e.g. by indeed running away when they have spotted a leopard.

We will illustrate our thesis with respect to empirical studies that consider two kinds of work situation requiring co-ordinated social interactions. The first study, on conditional instructions, examines an oft-observed case of co-ordination of activity (in work situations but also, e.g., in parent-child relationships): a principal directs an agent on how to behave as she desires in hypothetical situations. The second study, on quantifiers and probability expressions, examines situations of relationship equality, where an expert professional has to give useful advice to a client who has the ultimate power of decision. We present a conversational action planning model that predicts ways of formulating *felicitous* conditional instructions and advice using quantifiers and probability expressions; that is, instructions and advice which adequately communicate the intentions of the speakers and produce the appropriate effect on the listener.

Co-ordinated planning and social control in the face of risk

Human reasoning and rationality is embedded in — and may have emerged from — successful social communication. Other primates communicate and recognise intentions successfully, as when a dominant animal intimidates an inferior, and in this sense satisfy Gricean criteria for intentional communication (Grice, 1975), in that they can manifest information to others in order to get them to recognize their desires and do what they want (Strawson, 1964). But, if both humans and primates are able to understand others as intentional agents, only humans appear to have the motivation and cognitive skills to *share intentions*. Whereas primates do not manifest or recognize communicative intentions, such as the providing of information that is not immediately related to any perceivable goal of the "speaker", humans, by contrast, engage in collaborative interactions where a goal is shared and actions are co-ordinated in the pursuit of this goal. Thus, humans seem to have a unique disposition to read others' intentional states, and to share information and attention in a way that close primate relatives like chimpanzees do not (Tomasello et al., 2005).

In addition, the ability of language-trained chimpanzees to understand conditional expressions has only been demonstrated in an instrumental domain, where their keeper tells them (through a visual symbol system) that if they perform a certain action they will get a reward (Premack, 1976). From the chimpanzee's point of view the conditional rule could be regarded as a kind of indication from the keeper that allows her to form a plan to obtain a reward. Consequently, we need to better understand the goal-directed functions of logical expressions (e.g. instructions, advice, promises, and threats) and their use in co-ordinating planning in order to identify both continuities and differences between humans and other primates.

If pragmatics (intentional communication) of the kind shared with other primates is first, and semantics (truth-functionality) is second, logic and probability words (e.g., *if, because, some, few, possible, unlikely*) may be expected to have social functions built into their everyday use, besides their truth-functional definition. Specifically, we argue that the logical vocabulary of natural language has its origins in the necessity of achieving successful co-ordination of social interactions through communication, and is very well adapted to communicating perceptions of risk, danger and opportunity. From this perspective, sentences using logic expressions can be conceived as utterances aiming to get the hearer to do things, called *performative* utterances, rather than as statements merely describing states of affairs, called *constative* statements (cf. Austin, 1962).

These performative functions of logic words may be primary. Consider the following statements:

(1)   If there are *few wolves* in the West valley then don't hunt there.
(2)   If there are *a few wolves* in the West valley then don't hunt there.

The difference in meanings between (1) and (2) cannot be explained by the truth conditions of their respective antecedents: they describe similar proportions and are thus identical in this regard (Moxey & Sanford, 1993a, 1993b). Instead, such a difference can easily be apprehended by considering the different utilities the speaker attaches to the presence of wolves (wolves as meat, i.e., positive utility, vs. wolves as predators, i.e. negative utility). Such utilities will serve as a *reason* for the recommended course of action.

Rationality is defined here in terms of successful social co-ordination, which entails the correct perception and execution of the other's intentions. This definition contrasts with the verificationist criterion of being a correct description of an objective reality. Our concept of social rationality is also different to the two kinds of rationality defined by Evans and Over (1996). These authors define individual rationality in terms of reasoning according to formal principles (e.g., Bayes' theorem) or in terms of satisfying instrumental goals. Social rationality is not concerned with formal principles, although socially rational judgments can overlap with formally correct judgments. Neither is social rationality to be identified with instrumental rationality, which can be quite asocial, as the fulfilling of one's instrumental goals may not need any understanding of, or co-ordinating with, the goals of others.

We have argued that successful social co-ordination is necessary for collectives to achieve their goals. In order to illustrate this claim, we will begin by examining the case of conditional directives whereby a principal directs an agent on how to behave in a hypothetical situation. We will then extend our analysis of conversational action planning to quantifiers and uncertainty expressions.

A goal-based approach to performative conditionals

"If you see a leopard, run for your life." "If someone cannot show you a VIP pass, throw him out the VIP lounge." Conditional directives are *performatives* in that, should a hypothetical situation arise, their aim is to bring about a change in the world, a change that is desired by a principal and executed by an agent. In contrast, most work on the psychology of reasoning has examined *constative* conditionals (in the sense of Austin, 1962) such as indicatives and counterfactuals (see Evans & Over, 2004, for an overview), which take truth-values as more-or-less true descriptions of the world.

To this aim, we propose a simple conversational action planning (CAP) model whereby a principal (speaker) communicates his or her preferences to an agent (hearer) about what to do in a particular situation. In the language of signal detection theory, the model suggests that different formulations of the conditional relation (e.g., *If event then action, If and only if event then action, If not-event then not action, Action only if event*) will be used as a function of the relative costs of misses (MS: not taking the action when it is rational to do so) and false alarms (FA: taking the action when it is not rational to do so), as each conditional formulation implicitly conveys the preference of the speaker (principal).

For example, consider the following three instructions:

(3)   If there is suspect baggage, then take it out and search it.
(4)   [If and] Only if there is suspect baggage, then search it.
(5)   If there is no suspect baggage, then do not search it.

The CAP model predicts that a principal in the position of an airport security chief whose primary concern is to stop life-threatening baggage getting through security checks, will prefer to issue the instruction (3) to airport security agents. If, however, his main concern is not to make passengers wait too long, he should prefer to utter (4) or (5). Results supporting this prediction are reported in Hilton, Kemmelmeier, and Bonnefon (2001).

Hilton et al. (2001) also present evidence that agents (hearers) are quite capable of inferring what they are expected to do from the conditional instruction alone, even when the context is neutral about what the desirable action to take is. For example, in one scenario participants were asked to imagine that they were shop assistants whose boss had told them either: *If a customer is touching some clothes, offer him your help, If and only if a customer is touching some clothes, offer him your help, Offer a customer your help only if he is touching some clothes*, and *If a customer is not touching any clothes, do not offer him your help*. For any given formulation, participants were asked either to suppose P (The customer is touching the clothes) or to suppose not-P (the customer is not touching the clothes) and indicated their understanding with regard to Q (offer help) by choosing one of the three following answers: "I must do Q," "I must not do Q," "I am free to decide what to do."

Although nothing was said explicitly in the scenario to this effect, the shop assistant may infer that her boss may either be concerned about the cost of missing the opportunity to close sales with interested customers (through not offering help when a customer is touching the clothes, avoid-MS), or the cost of false alarms which frighten customers away by being too pushy (through offering help when it is not desired, avoid-FA).

Each conditional formulation appears to be informative with respect to what is required of the agent. Thus the dominant pattern elicited by *if P then Q* is that one must do Q when P is the case, but is free to decide what to do when P is not the case. Hence, this formulation succeeds in avoiding MSs, yet leaves opened the possibility of a FA. The dominant pattern elicited by *if and only if P then Q* is that one must do Q when P is the case, and one must not do Q when P is not the case. This formulation is thus interpreted in a way which prevents both MSs and FAs. The dominant pattern elicited by *if notP then notQ* is that one is free to decide what to do when P is the case, but one must not do Q when P is not the case. This formulation thus prevents FAs but leaves opened the possibility of a MS. Finally, the formulation *Q only if P* elicits both patterns attached to *if notP then notQ* and *if and only if P then Q*. Thus, this formulation always prevents FAs but only sometimes prevents MSs.

These results thus showed that conditional directives can be varied to express the principal's preferences about what an agent should do should a hypothetical situation arise. We may speculate that speakers will choose one logically equivalent formulation of a causal conditional over another as a function of the speaker's goals. For example, two people may share a causal model in which serving high quality products is a recipe for customer satisfaction in restaurants. But momentary changes in context-determined utilities (e.g., in the kinds of clients that are expected that evening) may require that this shared recipe be significantly nuanced in its application: a chef instructing a buyer will say *If the meat is 80% lean then buy it* when he is most concerned with the attaining a desirable goal (serving excellent food in a restaurant), but say *If the meat is 20% fat then don't buy it* when most concerned with the costs of a mistake (serving substandard food in a restaurant). So even though both conditionals have the same truth-values, we argue that they will have different performative functions because they express different preferences.

Note that it would be anomalous to express the principal's preferences probabilistically, for example by saying *If the customer is touching clothes, then probably offer him your help*. It is the principal's responsibility and not the agent's to assume the risk that the instruction may backfire. On the other hand, it seems that the principal could readily use probabilistic qualifications with constative conditionals in these kinds of situation: for example, the statement *If the customer is touching clothes, then he would probably like your help* does not sound anomalous. Intuitively, where the boss accepts that it is the assistant's right to decide what to do in this case (and take responsibility for the outcome), such a formulation could readily be used as a piece of indirect advice. More generally, it seems to us that probabilistic advice can be appropriately given when the speaker wishes to help the hearer make the correct decision, but does not want to impose a solution directly. Below, we turn to a consideration of a study of how the conversational action planning model can be applied to advice using quantifiers and probability expressions.

Advice on what to do under uncertainty: Pragmatic functions of quantifiers and probability words

Everyday experts and novices alike use words and phrases to characterize quantities and uncertainty. A reservation clerk may tell his clients that few seats are left on the plane they wish to take or alternatively that there are a few seats left; a doctor may tell his patients that recovery is highly likely or alternatively, that it is not certain that they will recover. What will determine the professional adviser's choice of word? What inferences may the recipient of the advice draw on the basis of this choice?

Research aiming at understanding how people select and understand quantifiers was based on the assumption that they denote vague numerical quantities (Hakel, 1969; Pepper & Prytulak, 1974) and that probability phrases denote vague numerical probabilities (Beyth-Marom, 1982; Lichtenstein & Newman, 1967), often formalised as membership functions (Wallsten, Budescu, Rapoport, Zwick, & Forsyth, 1986). Leaving aside general problems with the membership function approach (Weber & Hilton, 1990), we concentrate our attention here on what might lead a speaker to select one word over another which denotes the same vague quantity.

Advice-giving and the choice of quantity and uncertainty phrases

Consider a scenario (Villejoubert and Hilton, 2004) in which a travel agent wishes to help her client take the best decision about whether to book a ticket quickly (with the risk of taking a less-than-ideal flight) or to take his time about his decision (with the risk of booking too late to get a seat). Depending on the experimental

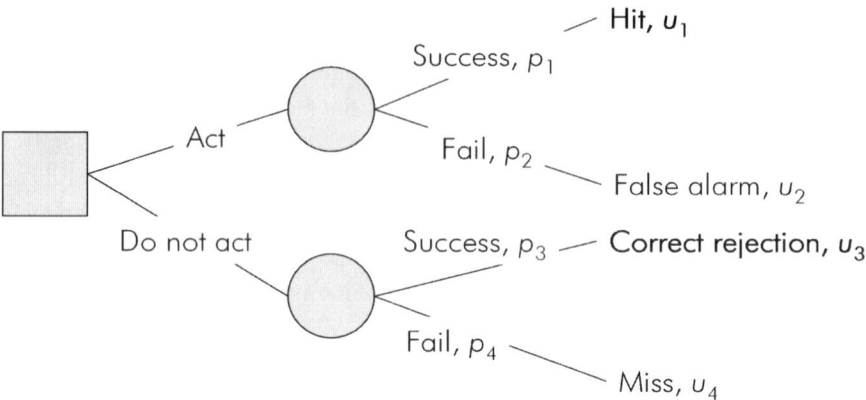

Figure 1. Formal representation of the decision to act.

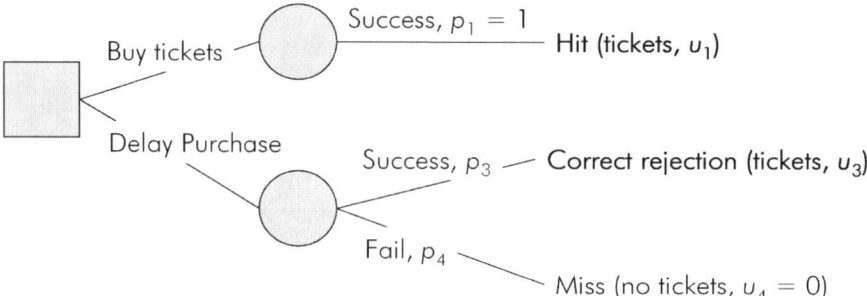

Figure 2. Formal representation of the Airlines scenario context.

condition, the clerk disposes of two pieces of information that can influence her choice of quantifier; the knowledge that there are 15 or 45 seats left on a 120-seat plane, and that these seats will normally be sold out in 2 or 14 days. The airlines scenario represents a particular case of the general decisional context presented in Figure 1.

Here, the action consists in buying the plane tickets straight away and the status quo consists in delaying the purchase. If the tickets are bought straight away, the probability p_1 of success is 1 (i.e., there is no longer a risk of losing the seats and $p_2 = 0$), the outcome corresponds to the tickets bought, which bears utility u_1. If the purchase is delayed, the customer may or may not be able to buy tickets and has to bear the costs of a miss. In case of a correct rejection, the delay of the purchase is followed by the possibility of buying tickets, with the probability p_3 where $0 \leq p_3 < 1$. The tickets bought at a later time have utility u_3 and $u_3 > u_1$ (i.e., the adviser knows that the customer prefers to delay his purchase). But, in the case of a miss, the delay of the purchase may also be followed by the impossibility of buying the tickets, with a probability p_4 where $0 \leq p_4 < 1$, and no associated utility $(u_4 = 0)$. Figure 2 summarizes this context.

An experiment was conducted in which participants were presented with a choice between two pieces of advice. The first piece of advice was a warning against the consequences of the status quo: "Be careful, it is possible that you won't have time to make a decision because there are … seats available." The second piece of advice encouraged the client to delay his decision: "Don't worry, you have time to make your decision because there are … seats available." Results showed that the time left to decide (14 days vs. 2 days) had a strong effect on a measure of the perceived risk that the seats would be sold out. In line with this, it was found that when clients had 14 days to decide, the number of seats left influenced the polarity of the quantifier word chosen. When there were 45 seats left, participants were more likely to use positive polarity words to encourage their clients to take their time because there were *a few, quite a few*, or *many* seats left. However, when clients had only 2 days to decide, participants almost exclusively used negative polarity words and warned them to decide quickly because there were *few, very few*, or *not many* seats left, regardless of whether the actual number was 15 or 45. In our view, these results illustrate our thesis that quantifiers in these situations are principally selected on the basis of their pragmatic function (encouraging vs. discouraging a putative course of action) rather than in terms of how well they describe some objectively given quantity.

These results were replicated with a more complex scenario involving a doctor advising his patient on whether or not to undertake a surgical operation. Participants were about three and a half times as likely to choose a negative probability phrase when the miss outcome (i.e., the negative consequence following the absence of action) was more severe than the false-alarm outcome (i.e., the negative consequence following the action). These results provide substantial support for our claim that the choice of polarity words is driven by the perceived utility of the action outcome, and that this utility is itself determined by comparison to the utility of the status quo, which serves as a reference point.

Receiving advice: Felicity and emotional response

The preceding results concerned the analysis of the speaker's use of quantifiers and probability words. The CAP model, however, also has implications for the understanding of the hearer's interpretation of these words. Consider once more the example of the airlines clerk who warns her client that he should make his booking sooner rather than later because there are *few* seats left on the plane he wishes to take. From a semantic perspective, one would merely expect that the client would assign a vague quantity to the number of seats left based on his personal membership function for the quantifier "a few." By contrast, we characterised good advice as a successful coordination between the speaker and the hearer. From this perspective, we can also assume that a given piece of advice will give rise to specific non-numerical expectations from the hearer. Thus, in the airlines example, the client should draw specific implicatures about the context within which this advice is taking place.

We hypothesized that the extent to which such expectations are later fulfilled should in turn affect the client's degree of satisfaction and emotional response both to the outcome of his decision and to the clerk's advice. Thus, if the advice is felicitous (i.e., if it recommends the best action to satisfy the hearer's goal in a given context), hearers should feel happier and more satisfied, independently of the type of the decision outcome (i.e., correct rejection or hit). Conversely, non-felicitous pieces of advice should entail lesser degrees of happiness and satisfaction as they will lead to either a miss or a false alarm outcome.

Another experiment was conducted in order to test these predictions. The experiment again used the airlines and surgeon scenarios, but this time participants had to take the role of the recipient of the advice. Half the participants were told the clerk indicated there were *few* seats left. They were then asked to imagine that they bought the plane ticket straight away and realised two days later that there were no seats left (i.e., that the advice was felicitous) or that there were still seats left (i.e., that the advice was not felicitous). The other half were told that the clerk indicated there were *a few* seats left on the plane and were asked to imagine that they subsequently delayed the purchase of their ticket. Here again the felicity of this advice was manipulated by telling participants either that there were seats available two days later (felicitous advice) or that there were not (infelicitous advice).

The estimated proportions of seats left on the plane were independent of the quantifier used in the advice. However, as in the previous experiment, the perceived risk of losing a seat was significantly higher when participants were told that they were "few seats" left (as opposed to "a few seats"). All participants were then asked to indicate their emotional state and their satisfaction following the realisation that there were (or not) seats available two days later. Results showed that people felt happiest, most satisfied, and least regretful when the advice was felicitous, independently of the actual advice (i.e., encouraged or warned against delay). Participants felt significantly less happy, less satisfied, and more regretful when they were encouraged to buy without delay but were then told that there were still tickets available two days later. However, they were least happy, least satisfied, and most regretful when they were encouraged to delay their purchase only to realise that there were no seats left two days later. Felicity of the advice also determined their emotions towards the reservation clerk. They felt happy towards the clerk as long as her advice was felicitous (independently of whether he advised to act or to delay action). Conversely, participants felt significantly less happy towards the clerk when her advice was not felicitous.

These results thus provide additional support for the social rationality hypothesis. Namely, when choosing to frame her advice with a positive or negative quantifier, the speaker is eliciting certain expectations in the recipient of this advice. The successful fulfilment of these expectations leads to goal satisfaction and in turn mediates the recipient's degree of happiness, satisfaction and his perceived regret as well as his emotional response to his advisor.

Conclusion

Many would point to the unique human mastery of logic and mathematics as a major explanation of the success of the species. But without wishing to minimise the importance of the representational power of abstract symbolic systems for human engineering and computer science, we believe that logical vocabulary has pragmatic functions that make it essential to co-operation and planning in the face of uncertainty. The prevalence of these pragmatic nuances, and their nuisance value for those who wish to use these words to signify abstract logical and mathematical operations, suggests to us that natural human reasoning emerges from these kinds of co-operative interactions.

The encouragement/discouragement perspective we have presented for conditional instructions and advice using quantifiers and probability expressions is quite general. For example, it could predict patterns of conditional advice: When the costs of misses are high we predict advice of the kind *If you have this operation you should preserve your sight* whereas if the costs of false alarms are high we predict advice of the kind *If you don't have this operation you may lose your sight.* Observation of such patterns of response will show equivalence between ways of expressing uncertainty and conditionals: They are fundamentally causal *arguments* for or against a course of action, and their expressed strength and direction reside in the degree to which the speaker wishes to encourage or discourage the action in question.

We have introduced a specific kind of instrumental rationality — that of successful co-ordination of social interactions. We have argued that for intersubjective conditionals a rational choice of a conditional formulation from the speaker's perspective will normally be one that promotes her interests by getting the hearer to understand what she wants. For a hearer, a rational interpretation will normally be one that best represents the speaker's intention (whether the hearer decides to do as the speaker wishes or not). Rationality comes to be defined here in terms of successful social co-ordination, and justified in terms of collective benefits (cf. Sperber, 2001).

Recognizing the social rationality of conditionals allows a new perspective to be taken on their development and adaptive functions. It seems that *performative* conditional directives of the kind that we have studied emerge early in social interaction between caregivers and children (Luria, 1959). Children may in turn internalise external speech (Vygotsky, 1962) and appropriate it to regulate their own activity (Luria & la Yudovich, 1956). This perspective would seem to support Sperber's (2001) argument that: "It is generally taken for granted that the logical and inferential vocabulary is — and presumably emerged — as tools for reflection and reasoning. From an evolutionary point of view, this is not particularly plausible. The hypothesis that they emerged as tools of persuasion may be easier to defend."

Although evolutionary psychologists find it implausible that the human mind would have evolved some domain-general reasoning ability (e.g. Cosmides, 1989; Gigerenzer & Hug, 1992), it does seem to us that one plausible evolved general ability would be conversational skills that for speakers are needed to get others to see the point, and for hearers are needed to see what the speaker wishes them to do and to do it. Indeed, if these skills are integrated with general goal-based planning and reasoning strategies, then it would not be surprising that people reason especially well about propositions when they can see the point of them.

Indeed, there is no doubt that, although there are many social animals, humans are among the most social. Many characteristics of the human mind may thus have evolved to facilitate social interaction and cooperation, for such interactions and cooperation enhanced the survival prospects of early humans. Hence, the capacity for logic may have emerged as a social phenomenon long before it became a scientific one. While truth-values constitute the building bricks of the logical mind, shared viewpoints do seem to provide the cement for building collective minds.

References

Austin, J. L. (1962). *How to do things with words*. Oxford: Clarendon Press.

Beyth-Marom, R. (1982). How probable is probable: A numerical translation of verbal probability expressions. *Journal of Forecasting, 1*, 257–269.

Cosmides, L. (1989). The logic of social exchange: Has natural selection shaped how we reason? Studies with the Wason selection task. *Cognition, 31*, 187–276.

Dessalles, J-L. (2000). *Aux origines de la parole: Une histoire naturelle de la parole.* Paris: Hermes.

Evans, J. St. B. T., & Over, D. E. (1996). *Rationality and reasoning.* Hove: Psychology Press.

Evans, J. St. B., & Over, D. E. (2004). *If.* Oxford: Oxford University Press.

Gigerenzer, G., & Hug, K. (1992). Domain specific reasoning, social contracts, and perspective change. *Cognition, 43,* 127–171.

Grice, H. P. (1975). Logic and conversation. In P. Cole & J. L. Morgan (Eds.), *Syntax and Semantic 3: Speech Acts* (pp. 41–58). New York: Academic Press.

Hakel, M. D. (1969). How often is often? *American Psychologist, 23,* 27–44.

Hilton, D. J., Bonnefon, J-F., & Kemmelmeier, M. (2001). Pragmatics at work: Formulation and interpretation of conditional instructions. In J. D. Moore, & K. Stenning (Eds), *Proceedings of the 23rd Annual Conference of the Cognitive Science Society,* Edinburgh, Scotland, August 1–4. Hillsdale: Lawrence Erlbaum.

Kenny, A. (1966). Practical inference. *Analysis, 26,* 65–75.

Lichtenstein, S., & Newman, J. R. (1967) Empirical scaling of common verbal phrases associated with numerical probabilities. *Psychonomic Science, 9,* 563–564.

Luria, A. R. (1959). The directive function of speech in development and dissolution, part I. *Word, 15,* 341–352.

Luria, A. R., & la Yudovich, F. I. (1956). *Speech and the development of mental processes in the child.* Harmondsworth: Penguin.

Moxey, L. M., & Sanford, A. J. (1993a). *Communicating quantities: A psychological perspective.* Hove, UK: Lawrence Erlbaum Associates.

Moxey, L. M., & Sanford, A. J. (1993b). Prior expectation and the interpretation of natural language quantifiers. *European Journal of Cognitive Psychology, 5,* 73–91.

Pepper, S., & Prytulak, L. S. (1974). Sometimes frequently means seldom: Context effects in the interpretations of quantitative expressions. *Journal of Research in Personality, 8,* 95–101.

Premack, D. (1976). *Intelligence in ape and man.* Hillsdale, NJ: Lawrence Erlbaum Associates.

Seabright, P. (2004). *The company of strangers: A natural history of economic life.* Princeton: Princeton University Press.

Smith, A. (1776/1991). *An inquiry into the nature and causes of the wealth of nations.* New York: Prometheus Books.

Sperber, D. (2001). An evolutionary perspective on testimony and argumentation. *Philosophical Topics, 29,* 401–413.

Strawson, P. F. (1964). Intention and convention in speech acts. *Philosophical Review, 73,* 439–60.

Tomasello, M., Carpenter, M., Call, J., Behne, T., & Moll, H. (2005). Understanding and sharing intentions: The origins of cultural cognition. *Behavioral and Brain Sciences, 28,* 675–735.

Villejoubert, G., & Hilton, D. (2004). *The pragmatics of quantifiers.* Paper presented at the Fifth International Conference on Thinking, Leuven, July 2004.

Vygotsky, L. S. (1962). *Thought and Language.* Cambridge: MIT Press.

Wallsten, T. S., Budescu, D. V., Rapoport, A., Zwick, R., & Forsyth, B. (1986). Measuring the vague meanings of probability terms. *Journal of Experimental Psychology: General, 115,* 348–365.

Weber, E. U., & Hilton, D. J. (1990). Contextual effects in the interpretation of probability words: Perceived base-rate and severity of events. *Journal of Experimental Psychology: Human Perception and Performance, 16,* 781–789.

Attributions and peer harassment

Sandra Graham
Department of Education, University of California Los Angeles

Attribution theory is used as a conceptual framework for examining how causal beliefs about peer harassment influence how victims think and feel about themselves. Evidence is presented that victims who make characterological self-blaming attributions ("it must be *me*") are particularly at risk of negative self-views. Also examined is the influence of social context, particularly the ethnic composition of schools and classrooms. It was found that students who were both victims of harassment and members of the majority ethnic group were more vulnerable to self-blaming attributions. In contrast, greater ethnic diversity, that is, classrooms where no one group was in the majority, tended to ward off self-blaming tendencies. Studies of peer harassment are a good context for examining one of the main themes of this volume, which is how the social context (e.g., peer groups, ethnic groups) influences the way individuals think and feel about themselves.

As authors of the articles in this volume, one question we were asked to address is how individuals' thoughts, feelings, and behavior are shaped by the ways in which they are perceived and treated by others. The study of peer harassment is an excellent context for addressing that question. I define peer harassment as the types of bullying, taunting, name calling, and intimidation that take place in and around school, especially when adult supervision is minimal. Survey data indicates that anywhere from 40 percent to 80 percent of American youth report that they personally have experienced victimization from others, ranging from relatively minor instances of verbal abuse and intimidation to more serious forms of victimization, including assault, property damage, and theft (e.g., Nansel et al., 2001). School bullying has now been recognized as a major public health concern, as the perpetrators of such abuse are becoming more violent and the targets of their abuse are feeling more vulnerable. Research in European and Asian countries documents that peer harassment is a universal school problem that transcends geographic, national, and cultural divides.

In this article, I describe recent research that my colleagues and I have undertaken to examine how children think, feel, and behave when they are victims of others' harassment. The theoretical framework that guides my research is attribution theory. Attributions are answers to "why" questions: such as "Why did I fail this exam?" or "Why doesn't anyone like me?" In earlier research, I examined the perceived causes of success and failure in both the academic and social domains, and how those attributions influence subsequent motivation (e.g., Graham, 1997). Here I apply attributional analyses to examine how victims construe the reasons for their plight and how particular causal perceptions influence adjustment. I have a particular focus on ethnic group membership as a social context variable and the role that it might play in understanding the psychological consequences of peer victimization. I hope to make a case for the importance of causal beliefs as a theoretical scaffold and ethnicity as a social context variable, both of which can aid our understanding of the dynamics of peer harassment.

The research presented in this article is compatible with the work of several other contributors to this volume. For example, social ostracism can be a type of peer harassment and it will be seen that the psychological and emotional consequences of ostracism that Williams describes resemble the reactions of youth who blame themselves for peer harassment. Once children come to see themselves as victims, they may inadvertently seek out experiences to confirm that self view, similar to self-verification processes described by Klein and Swann, or behave in ways to confirm their reputations as victims, similar to self-fulfilling prophesies as portrayed by Jussim. What all of our contributions share in common is a focus on the social context (e.g., peer groups, work groups, teacher-student dyads, or unseen competitors) as a major determinant of the way individuals think and feel about themselves.

Attributions about peer harassment

A growing empirical literature has documented the negative psychological, social, and academic consequences of being a victim of peer harassment (see Juvonen & Graham, 2001). Victims tend to have low self-esteem and to feel more lonely, anxious, unhappy, depressed, and insecure than their non-victimized peers. Acknowledging these known relationships, as an attribution theorist, I was especially interested in *why*. That is, what processes or mediating mechanisms might explain why some victimized youth might feel lonely, anxious, and have negative self-views?

One such mechanism might relate to how victims construe the reason for their plight. For example, a history of peer abuse and the perception of being singled out for such harassment might lead a victim to ask "Why *me*?" In the absence of disconfirming evidence, some victims might come to blame themselves for their peer relationship problems. Such an adolescent might conclude for example that, "I'm the kind of kid who deserves to be picked on." Self-blame and accompanying negative affect can then lead to many negative outcomes, including low self-esteem, loneliness, anxiety, and depression.

Relevant to this focus, Janoff-Bulman (1979) has made a distinction between behavioral and characterological self-blame for coping with rape (another obvious form of victimization). Janoff-Bulman described the two types of self-blame as follows:

> "Behavioral self-blame is control related, involves attributions to a modifiable source (one's behavior), and is associated with a belief in the future avoidability of a negative outcome. Characterological self-blame is esteem related, involves attributions to a relatively nonmodifiable source (one's character), and is associated with a belief in personal deservingness for past negative outcomes." (Janoff-Bulman, 1979, p. 1978)

In attributional language, behavioral self-blame is *internal* ('it's me"), *unstable* ("things can change"), and *controllable* ("I can do something about it"). That self-ascription resembles lack of effort as a cause of failure in the achievement domain (Weiner, 1986). In contrast, characterological self-blame is also *internal* ('it's me"), but *stable* ("things will always be that way"), and *uncontrollable* ("there's nothing I can do to change it"). That attribution is more akin to low aptitude as a cause of achievement failure. The maladaptive consequences of low aptitude compared to lack of effort in the achievement domain are well documented (see Weiner, 1986). In a similar vein, a number of researchers have documented that individuals who make characterological self-attributions for negative social outcomes cope more poorly, feel worse about themselves, and are more depressed than individuals who make behavioral self-attributions (see review in Anderson et al., 1994).

In our first study on peer harassment in a middle school, my colleagues and I adopted the distinction between characterological and behavioral self-blame to examine the attributions that young adolescents endorse to explain harassment from their peers (Graham & Juvonen, 1998). We recruited a sample of about 400 6th graders from 18 classrooms in a multi-ethnic middle school located in a working class community in Los Angeles, California. Mirroring the ethnic breakdown of the school, our sample was approximately 30% African American, 30% Latino, with the remaining 40% comprised about equally of four ethnic groups: Whites, Persian/Middle Easterners, Asian/Pacific Islanders, and Biracial youth.

All data were gathered via questionnaires that participants filled out during their homeroom period. The first part of the questionnaire consisted of self-report and peer nomination measures of victimization. For example, we asked participants to rate the extent to which they felt like "someone who gets picked on a lot" and we asked peers to nominate classmates who fit various behavioral descriptions that portrayed victimization (e.g., "Name three classmates who get put down or made fun of by others"). Those self-report and reputational measures were combined and used to classify respondents into victim subgroups (see Graham & Juvonen, 1998 for details about classification procedures). In the second part of the questionnaire that assessed psychological adjustment, respondents completed well-validated and widely used measures of self-esteem, loneliness, and social anxiety. To assess attributions for harassment in the third part of the questionnaire, participants were asked to imagine that they had experienced two types of victimization at school (being humiliated in the locker room, being physically threatened in the restroom). They then rated how much they agreed with 32 statements that captured their causal thoughts and feelings about the victimizing incident. The thoughts included attributions designed to tap characterological self-blame (e.g., "This sort of thing is more likely to happen to me than to other kids"; "Why do I always get into these situations?") and behavioral self-blame (e.g., "I should have been more careful this time"), as well as external attributions pertaining to others.

Based on self-reports and peer-reports of victimization, we identified the subgroup in our sample who could appropriately be classified as chronic victims ($n = 40$, about 10% of the sample). We compared their ratings on the two self-blame measures and the three adjustment indices to the subgroup who did not perceive themselves as victims and did not have that reputation among their peers ($n = 165$, about 40% of the sample). The results showed that victims, compared to non-victims, endorsed significantly more characterological self-blaming attributions for imagined peer harassment. There were no differences between the groups on the theoretically less maladaptive behavioral self-blame attributions, suggesting that all of the young adolescents in this study to some degree blamed their own (controllable) behavior when explaining peer harassment. Consistent with much of the research literature, victims were also lonelier, more socially anxious, and lower in self-esteem than their non-victimized classmates.

From an attributional perspective, we hypothesized that the relationship between peer victimization and psychological maladjustment might be mediated by attributions that implicate one's character. The results of a path analysis supported that mediational hypothesis. That is, much of the relation between self-reports of being a victim and maladjustment were explained by characterological self-blaming attributions. It is as if the victim is saying to himself/herself: "It's something about *me*, things will always be that way, and there is nothing I can do to change it." Those causal thoughts are then predicted to result in greater psychological distress.

Bringing ethnicity to the analysis

Thus far I have not said anything about ethnicity, despite the fact that our sample was multi-ethnic. I can say at the outset that there were no ethnic differences in the attributions that individuals endorsed for imagined peer harassment or in the relations between attributions and adjustment. That should not be surprising. There is no theoretical or empirical rationale for hypothesizing that attributions should vary as a function of victim ethnicity per se.

I do believe that ethnic variation and ethnicity of victim are important variables for understanding causal beliefs about victimization and their psychological consequences. But rather than focus on ethnicity per se, I want to make a case for examining ethnicity within a particular school or classroom context, where that context varies by ethnic composition. To illustrate, let me turn to what we know about the contextual antecedents of peer victimization.

According to Olweus (1994) victimization is most likely to occur in settings where there is an imbalance of power between perpetrator and victim. Such asymmetric power relationships can take many forms, as when the strong bully the weak or when older kids harass younger targets. Building on Olweus' ideas about power relationships, it also is possible that the ethnic makeup of a setting can signal an imbalance of power and can therefore function as an antecedent of victimization. That is, in a racially diverse school setting, one might hypothesize that students whose ethnic group is the statistical minority (i.e., less powerful in the numerical sense) would be more vulnerable to victimization. On the other hand, statistical majority groups (i.e., more powerful in the numerical sense) would be expected to have more perpetrators than targets of peer harassment.

We tested the relations between victim status and majority/minority ethnic group composition in our multiethnic middle school sample described above (Graham & Juvonen, 2002). Recall the ethnic composition of that sample. At 30% each, African Americans and Latinos were the two majority groups. At about 10% each, Whites, Persians, Asians, and Biracial youth were the four minority groups. Within each of those ethnic groups, we examined how many youth had reputations as victims versus aggressors based on peer nominations. As predicted, we found that the two groups who were the numerical majorities (African Americans and Latinos) had more members perceived as aggressive and fewer members perceived as victims than what would be expected by chance. In contrast, for the groups who were the numerical minorities (Whites, Persians, Asians, Biracial) we found a pattern of over-nominating peers from these groups as victims and under-nominating peers from these same groups as aggressive. Similar findings with other ethnic groups who were numerical minorities in their school have been reported in both

American (Hanish & Guerra, 2000) and European research (Verkuyten & Thijs, 2002). All of these studies therefore suggest that individuals' ethnic representation within context may be more important than their specific ethnic group in predicting their vulnerability to peer harassment.

Now what about the youth in these ethnic groups who do indeed have reputations as victims? In terms of the kind of adjustment variables that we have been examining, does it make a difference whether you are a victim in the majority or minority ethnic group? On the one hand, one could argue that ethnic minority victims would be the most vulnerable to loneliness, anxiety, low self-esteem, and self-blaming tendencies. That would be consistent with the way we think about an imbalance of power and the reality that minority group victims may have fewer same-ethnicity friends to either ward off potential harassers or buffer the consequences of victimization.

On the other hand, consider what it must be like to be a victim *and* a member of a numerical majority group. Being a victim when your ethnic group holds the numerical balance of power and has a stronger reputation as aggressive might be especially debilitating because you deviate from what is perceived as normative for your group. Wright, Giammarino, and Parad (1986) adopted the label *social misfit* to describe children whose problem social behavior deviated from group norms. Other social psychologists in the adult literature have studied derogation by ingroup members of ingroup deviants, a phenomenon that has been labeled the *black sheep* effect (e.g., Marques, Abrams, & Serodio, 2001).

How do such findings relate back to our attributional analyses of how victims construe the reasons for their plight? I propose as a working hypothesis that early adolescent victims who have characteristics that deviate from group norms will be particularly vulnerable to characterological self-blaming attributions ("it must be *me*"). I also believe that the process of vulnerability to characterological self-blame for non-normative behavior should generalize across different ethnic groups who hold the numerical balance of power in different contexts. In the section I turn to such tests of generality.

Ethnicity and peer harassment in context: Multi-level effects

The data for our next analysis come from the first wave (fall of 6th grade) of an ongoing longitudinal study of peer harassment across middle school (Bellmore, Witkow, Graham, & Juvonen, 2004). The demographics of the sample for this study improve upon many of the shortcomings of the sample that was studied in Graham and Juvonen (1998). Rather than 400 multi-ethnic sixth graders selected from 18 classrooms in one Los Angeles middle school, we recruited about 2000 sixth graders selected from 99 classrooms in 11 middle schools located throughout the city. The schools (and classrooms) were carefully selected to vary in ethnic composition. That selection strategy yielded a very ethnically diverse sample comprised of about 45% Latino youth, 25% African American, and about 10% each of Caucasian, Asian, and multi-racial youth. With this much larger and more diverse sample, we set out to test the influence of majority/minority ethnic status on the relations between peer victimization and psychological adjustment. As in the prior study, we had reputational (peer nomination) measures of peer victimization as well as self-report measures of loneliness, social anxiety, and self-blaming attributions for imagined peer harassment.

We also created two new measures of ethnic diversity, one at the individual level and one at the classroom level. For each participant, we created an individual level variable that we labeled percent same ethnicity. That variable described the proportion of peers in an individual's classroom who shared his or her ethnicity. The larger the proportion, the more likely an individual student is to be a member of the ethnic majority group. Thus the variable allowed us to examine the effects of being in a classroom with mostly same-ethnicity classmates (numerical majority status) in contrast to being a numerical minority.

The second measure of diversity that we created was at the classroom level. Here we devised a measure that took into account both the number of ethnic groups and the relative proportion of each within that classroom. Controlling for classroom level diversity permitted us to approach the kind of generality we wanted — that is, to examine the role of majority/minority status on victimization-adjustment relations, independent of one's specific ethnic group and independent of the variability associated with being in one type of classroom with a particular ethnic mix versus residing in another classroom with a different ethnic configuration. To assess ethnic diversity at the classroom level, we adapted a measure first used in the ethology literature, known as Simpson's index of diversity (Simpson, 1949). Possible values range from 0 to 1, where higher values (probabilities) indicate greater diversity.

Given the nested structure of our data (individual students of different ethnicities nested in classrooms that vary in diversity), we used hierarchical linear modeling (HLM) as our main analytic tool. That is, we examined whether the relationship between victim reputation and psychological adjustment was influenced by ethnic majority/minority status (i.e., percent same ethnicity) when controlling for the variability associated with classroom diversity.

The HLM analysis showed that victimization was related to more loneliness and social anxiety. More importantly for our purposes, that relationship was significantly moderated by ethnic majority–minority group status. Figure 1 shows the nature of that moderation for each adjustment outcome. Plotted here are the regression slopes predicting loneliness and social anxiety at high and low levels of victim reputation (one standard deviation above and below the mean) for students who were high and low in the proportion of classmates who shared their ethnicity. Consistent with our predictions, the regression slopes describing the relations between victim reputation and both outcomes were steeper for 6th graders who shared their classroom with a larger percentage of same-ethnicity classmates (i.e., the numerical ethnic majority). In other words, and in agreement with a social misfit analysis, loneliness and social anxiety were greatest for victims who were members of the ethnic majority group.

What about the moderating role of characterological self-blame? We conducted the same HLM analysis with both types of self-blame as dependent variables. Victimization predicted characterological self-blame but not behavioral self-blame, as in our previous research (Graham & Juvonen, 1998). At Wave 1 in the fall, the moderating role of percent same ethnicity only approached significance

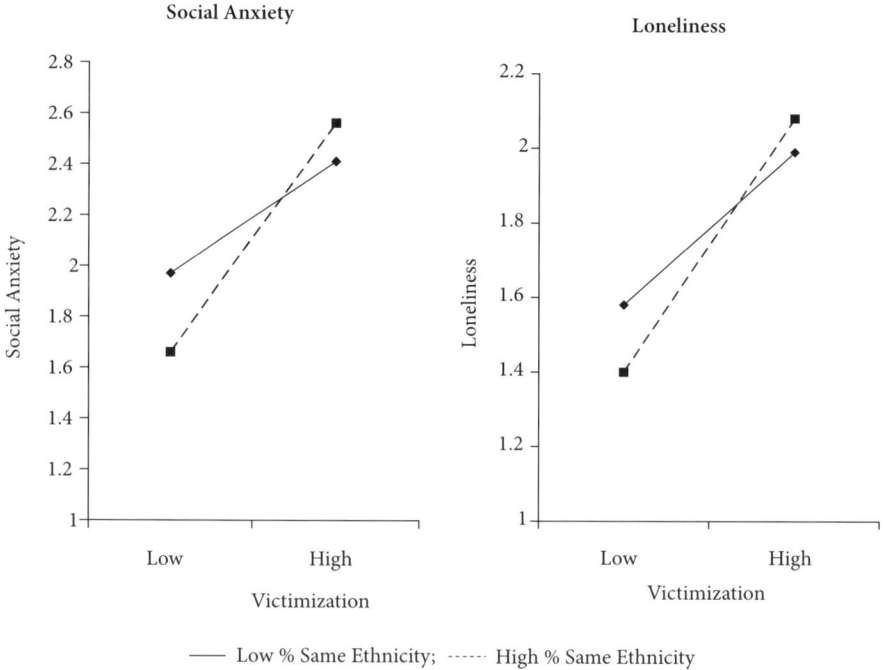

Figure 1. The relationship between victimization and adjustment as a function of ethnic majority/minority status (percent same ethnicity).

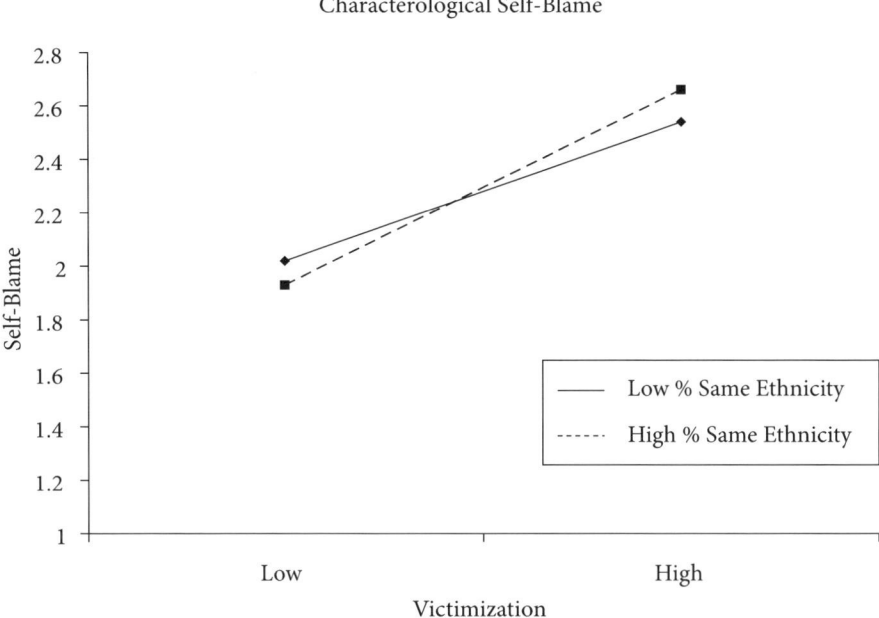

Figure 2. The relationship between victimization and characterological self-blame as a function of ethnic majority/minority status (percent same ethnicity).

($p < .07$). However, by the spring of the school year (Wave 2), that effect was significant and consistent with the findings for loneliness and social anxiety. As Figure 2 shows, victimization was a stronger predictor of characterological self-blame for students whose classmates shared their ethnicity. These short-term longitudinal analyses suggest that being a victim and a majority group member does influence self-blaming attributions, but that causal construals emerge gradually over time. In addition, more classroom diversity also predicted less characterological self-blame. There is something about membership in a more ethnically diverse classroom that promotes more positive self-views for all of the class members, independent of their victim reputation, ethnic group, or majority/minority status.

Conclusions

The analyses presented here lead me to the following conclusions:

First, ethnicity is an important context variable for understanding the experiences of early adolescents who are harassed by their peers. But it is not so much ethnic group *per se* as it is ethnicity within a particular school context. I do not think that it is productive to expect any particular ethnic group to be more or less at risk from being the target of peer abuse. Rather, I suspect that the critical variable is whether any one ethnic group does or does not hold the numerical balance of power. Numerical ethnic minority group members may be more vulnerable to experiencing harassment.

Second, being a victim and a member of the ethnic majority group has its own unique vulnerability. Like *social misfits* (Wright et al., 1986) or *black sheep* (Marques et al., 2001), when victims deviate from what is perceived as normative for their group they are more likely to feel lonely and socially anxious. In addition, their causal construals about the reasons for harassment are more likely to implicate the self.

Third, ethnic diversity in context — where no one group holds the numerical balance of power — may have particular psychological benefits. Independent of victim reputation and ethnic group membership, we found that students in classrooms that were more ethnically balanced felt less lonely, less socially anxious and over time were less likely to endorse characterological self-blaming attributions. I suggest as a guiding hypothesis that ethnic diversity creates enough attributional ambiguity to ward off self-blaming tendencies. Greater diversity among ethnic groups who share the balance of power discourages attributions for failure to the self ("it must be *me*") while allowing for attributions to external factors that protect self-esteem ("it could be *them*"). There is a vast empirical literature in adult social psychology on the self-protective functions of attributions to external causes among stigmatized groups (see Crocker, Major, & Steele, 1998). The time seems right to bring that literature to developmental social psychology and to studies of coping with the social stigma of chronic harassment by peers. Such an integration of developmental psychology and social psychology, with attributional analyses as the theoretical scaffold, can tell us a great deal about the social construction of self in response to the perceptions and reactions of others.

References

Anderson, C., Miller, R., Riger, A., Dill, J., & Sedikides, C. (1994). Behavioral and characterological attributional styles as predictors of depression and loneliness: Review, refinement, and test. *Journal of Personality and Social Psychology, 66,* 549–558.

Bellmore, A., Witkow, M., Graham, S., & Juvonen, J. (2004). Beyond the individual: The impact of ethnic context and classroom behavioral norms on victims' adjustment. *Developmental Psychology, 40,* 1159–1172.

Crocker, J., Major, B., & Steele, C. (1998). Social stigma. In D. Gilbert, S. Fiske, & G. Lindzey (Eds.), *The handbook of social psychology* (Vol. II, 4th edition). Boston: McGraw-Hill (pp. 504–553).

Graham, S. (1997). Using attribution theory to understand academic and social motivation in African American youth. *Educational Psychologist, 31*, 167–180.

Graham, S., & Juvonen J. (1998). Self-blame and peer victimization in middle school: An attributional analysis. *Developmental Psychology, 34*, 587–599.

Graham, S., & Juvonen, J. (2002). Ethnicity, peer harassment, and adjustment in middle school: An exploratory study. *Journal of Early Adolescence, 22*, 173–199.

Hanish, L. D., & Guerra, N. G. (2000). The roles of ethnicity and school context in predicting children's victimization by peers. *American Journal of Community Psychology, 28*, 201–223.

Janoff-Bulman, R. (1979). Characterological and behavioral self-blame: Inquiries into depression and rape. *Journal of Personality and Social Psychology, 37*, 1798–1809.

Juvonen, J., & Graham, S. (2001). *Peer harassment in school: The plight of the vulnerable and victimized.* New York: Guilford.

Marques, J., Abrams, D., & Serodio, R. (2001). Being better by being right: Subjective group dynamics and derogation of in-group deviants when generic norms are undermined. *Journal of Personality and Social Psychology, 81*, 436–447.

Nansel, T., Overpeck, M., Pilla, R., Ruan, W., & Simons-Morton, B. (2001). Bullying behaviors among US youth: Prevalence and association with psychosocial adjustment. *Journal of the American Medical Association, 285*, 2094–2100.

Olweus, D. (1994). Annotation: Bullying at school: Basic facts and effects of a school-based intervention program. *Journal of Child Psychology and Psychiatry, 35*, 1171–1190.

Simpson, E. H. (1949). Measurement of diversity. *Nature, 163*, 688.

Verkuyten, M., & Thijs, J. (2002). Racist victimization among children in The Netherlands: The effect of ethnic group and school. *Ethnic and Racial Studies, 25*,310–331.

Weiner, B. (1986). An *attributional theory of motivation and emotion.* New York: Springer-Verlag.

Wright, J. C., Giammarino, M., & Parad, H. W. (1986). Social status in small groups: Individual-group similarity and the social "misfit." *Journal of Personality and Social Psychology, 50*, 523–536.

The shaping of individuals' mental structures and dispositions by others

Findings from research on expressed emotion

Kurt Hahlweg

Institut für Psychologie, Technische Universität Braunschweig

Expressed emotion (EE) is a measure of the family environment that has been demonstrated to be a reliable, cross-culturally valid psychosocial predictor of relapse in patients with schizophrenia, mood disorders, and other — also somatic — illnesses. Assessed during the Camberwell Family Interview CFI, relatives are classified as being high in EE if they make more than a specified threshold number of critical comments or show any signs of hostility or marked emotional overinvolvement. In schizophrenia, the median relapse rate for patients returning after hospital discharge to a high EE environment is 48%, compared with 21% in a low EE-environment. In this article, the history of EE research will be outlined, and the evidence for the association between family EE and the course of schizophrenia and mood disorders will be presented. Conclusions about the treatment of major mental disorders are discussed as well as the directions of future studies.

The central question of this volume is how the shaping of individuals' mental structures and dispositions is determined by the way they perceive themselves and/or are treated by others. Related questions are: How deep does the impact of social context go and what are the mechanisms responsible for that impact? Does social context just scratch the surface of dispositions or does it go deep enough to affect the basic make up of the individual's mental machinery?

Schizophrenia is an example for a very deep impact on the individuals' basic mechanisms, changing in many cases the course of their lives. There is growing evidence that social factors contribute significantly to the course and outcome in schizophrenia. In particular, the relationship between high "Expressed Emotion" (EE) and schizophrenic relapse has been documented by many investigators.

1.   Schizophrenia: Symptoms, epidemiology, and treatment

Schizophrenia is the world's most serious and disabling mental disorder. It is costly beyond understanding — both in fiscal terms and in the price paid with human suffering and despair — for patients and relatives. The essential features of Schizophrenia are a mixture of characteristic positive and negative symptoms, which have to be present continuously for 6 months (APA, 1994).

Positive symptoms reflect an excess of normal functioning: Schizophrenia is recognized because of certain unusual features of thought, behaviour and mood. Most striking perhaps, and most puzzling to inexperienced people, are the disorders of thought, which result in delusions, hallucinations and abnormalities of speech. The patient may hold demonstrably false ideas with unshakeable conviction, may hear voices which no one else can hear and may speak incomprehensibly or use words or expressions which other people do not understand. The behavioural disturbances may be directly linked to the thought disorder, as when patients act upon a delusional belief, or in response to orders from hallucinatory voices. They may talk out loud to themselves or behave in an unpredictable or odd manner which demonstrates their difficulty in thinking straight. They may be overactive and even, occasionally, violent.

Another very common behavioural abnormality, however, can be summarized under the heading of 'social withdrawal' or 'negative symptoms'. The patient becomes slow, underactive, uncommunicative, lacking in energy or initiative, self-neglectful and seemingly self-absorbed. The abnormalities of mood include exaltation, depression, irritability and anxiety. Most common is an appearance of flattening of mood. The patient's facial expression is wooden, he does not use gesture or posture or variation in tone of voice to help verbal communication and he tends to react as though his emotions were blunted. He may be amused by situations which other people would find sad.

All these symptoms may be present singly, or in combination, or one following another, and they may range in severity from barely detectable to extremely obvious. The occurrence of these symptoms results in marked social and occupational dysfunction. The lifetime prevalence rate is about 1% and is similar throughout the world. The median onset is in the early to mid-20s for men and in the late 20s for women. The course is very variable; about 25% of patients show remission after one episode, about 50% experience several episodes and about 25% remain chronically ill.

Long-term neuroleptic treatment has been shown to be effective in preventing relapse, but even with continuous medication about 40% of patients relapse during the first year of discharge from the hospital compared with about 70% of patients taking placebo. The high rate of relapse has stimulated research on contributing factors: apart from medication non-compliance, social stressors, in particular life events and/or a family environment high on "Expressed Emotion" (EE, Leff & Vaughn, 1985) seem to be important.

2.   Expressed Emotion

2.1 How is Expressed Emotion (EE) assessed?

The measure for EE developed out of a series of studies carried out at the Social Psychiatry Unit in London (Maudsley Hospital) during the 1950s and 1960s (Brown, Birley & Wing, 1972). These studies investigated the relationship between clinical outcome in psychiatric patients and the quality of the relationship between patients and their close family members. Schizophrenic patients were more likely to relapse if they returned to live with parents or partners than if they went to live in lodgings or to live with siblings. In the following years Brown and his co-workers developed an interview and reliable rating scales to assess the relative's attitudes towards the patient. Expressed emotion is coded from the individual audio-taped Camberwell Family Interview (CFI; Vaughn & Leff, 1976) with a relative of the psychiatric patient. The CFI is a standardized interview, typically taking 1–2 hours to carry out, which is audiotaped for later coding. The ratings are based on statements made by the relative about the patient. Brown was not interested in measuring the effects of deeply disturbed relationships, but in developing scales that could extract the commonplace and usual range of feelings and emotions to be found in normal family life. More than 30 variables were investigated and only the following remained, showing high predictive validity over several studies.

The number of *critical comments* (statements of irritation, dislike, or resentment about the patient's behaviour or personality, usually expressed with corresponding voice tone) in the interview are counted. The degree of *emotional overinvolvement* (markedly overconcerned, overprotective, or self-sacrificing attitudes and behaviour) is rated on a 6-point scale for the whole interview. Relatives are classified as high EE (HEE) if they show evidence of excessive criticism or emotional overinvolvement. Otherwise, relatives are categorized as low EE (LEE). Generally, this interview is administered while the patient is hospitalized for an index episode of the disorder, and it is assumed that the EE rating reflects the type of family environment that the patient will encounter after discharge.

2.2 Does EE predict course of illness?

The predictive validity of the EE rating has been investigated in about 27 studies worldwide resulting in a found relapse rate nine months after discharge of 52% for patients living with a HEE relative in contrast to 22% for patients living in a LEE family (Butzlaff & Hooley, 1998; Kavanagh, 1992).

Of the 27 studies published, 24 showed a positive association between EE and relapse, with higher levels of EE in families being associated with greater rates of relapse in patients. The mean effect size was 0.31. This effect size is quite impressive when e.g. compared with data from medical studies: In the Physicians Health Study the effect of Aspirin on the prevention of heart attacks was clearly established. However, the effect size for Aspirin in that study was 0.034.

In a well-controlled study, Subotnik, Nuechterlein and Ventura (2002) investigated the predictors of the early course of schizophrenic and schizo-affective patients. Patients were treated with fluphenazine, individual case management, skills-focused group therapy, and family education. During a period of ongoing antipsychotic medication and psychosocial intervention, discrete stressful life events and highly critical or emotionally overinvolved attitudes towards patients and a higher symptom level were highly significant predictors of the chances of getting a psychotic relapse. The predictive role of these psychosocial stress variables is not accounted for by factors expected to index genetic factors (family history, neuro-cognitive vulnerability factors), suggesting that these environmental stress variables operate through separate processes.

The results of the Butzlaff and Hooley (1998) meta-analysis confirm that EE is a reliable, valid and robust predictor of relapse in schizophrenic patients. There are only little cultural differences with regard to the association between EE and relapse. There is, however, a great variety with regard to the prevalence of HEE, showing higher rates in families in industrialized, in contrast to under-developed, countries (e.g. Europe/USA: 60% of families are HEE; India/Mexico: 35%).

2.3. Is EE schizophrenia specific?

Expressed Emotion is clearly not a schizophrenia specific construct. Studies have shown that the EE measure is relevant not only for predicting relapse in Schizophrenia but also in Depression (effect size ES = 0.39; Butzlaff & Hooley, 1998), Eating Disorders (anorexia nervosa, obesity; ES = 0.51; Butzlaff & Hooley, 1998) recent-onset Mania (Miklowitz & Goldstein, 1997) and other illnesses in adults (e.g. Post Traumatic Stress Disorder PTSD, Alcohol Abuse), or in children (e.g. Depression, Conduct Disorder, Diabetes, Asthma and Epilepsy) (see Wearden, Tarrier, Barrowclough, Zastowny & Rahill, 2000).

2.4 Construct validity of EE

How far does the impact of social context go and what are the mechanisms responsible for that impact? This question is related to the construct validity of EE. What are the mechanisms underlying the correlation between family attitudes and the return of symptoms and what are the interactional correlates of EE?

2.4.1 Social psychophysiology

Vulnerability-stress models of schizophrenia assume that persons at risk to develop schizophrenia are characterized by vulnerability factors, e.g. autonomic hyperarousal when exposed to social stressors. Brown et al. (1972) reasoned that one consequence of the HEE-attitudes was to over-stimulate the schizophrenic patient, causing elevated levels of physiological arousal and an overload on the patient's ability to cope. Several studies (see Tarrier & Turpin, 1992) have assessed the effects of relatives' EE on the psychophysiological reactions of adult schizophrenics. The best measure to discriminate between patients living with HEE vs. LEE relatives was the number of spontaneous fluctuations (SFs) in skin conductance. It was hypothesised that the patients would display more autonomic nervous system activity when interacting face-to-face with a HEE-relative.

Tarrier, Vaughn, Lader and Leff (1979) were able to demonstrate that when a LEE-relative entered the room in the family's household and interacted with the patient, those patients habituated. This is in contrast to patients with HEE-relatives, who did not habituate over a 15-minute period. These findings were replicated in several other studies (see Tarrier & Turpin, 1992).

Therefore, the above mentioned hypothesis was confirmed. However, an overall question was left unanswered: Are the patient's electrodermal responses directly related to a specific characteristic of the relative, e.g. being critical of the patient during the interaction?

2.4.2 What are the interactional correlates of EE?

The EE-concept essentially measures the key relative's attitudes towards the patient, but since the CFI interview is only conducted with that relative alone, most often in the clinic, it is not clear whether or not HEE-relatives actually emit negative behaviour in real life interaction with the patient, e.g. at home. X, the patient, is exposed indirectly by inferring A, B, C's beliefs from their actions (implicit attributions). Put as a hypothesis: Relatives of schizophrenic patients differ in their interactional behaviour as a function of their EE-status.

In several studies, the research group of the late Michael Goldstein at UCLA (see Strachan et al., 1986) were able to show that a critical attitude of the relative toward the patient correlated with critical interactional behaviour when the family, including the patient, was asked to discuss a family problem in the video laboratory. As these studies only investigated the behaviour of the relatives, the contribution of the patient to the quality of the interaction remained unclear.

Therefore Hahlweg et al. (1989) applied another coding system to the interactional data, the Kategoriensystem fuer Partnerschaftliche Interaktion KPI (Category System for Partner and Family Interaction, Hahlweg, 2004). The KPI codes both verbal and nonverbal behaviour and the behaviour of relatives and patient. Because previous studies had aggregated the relatives' data over the whole interaction and had not considered the patient's behaviour, it was not possible to study the processes of family interaction as they emerged over time. Using the KPI, it was therefore possible to apply techniques of sequential analysis to the data to measure the relative contributions of patients and relatives to the observable family processes and to document whether patterns of interaction discriminate high EE from low EE families.

Forty-three families with a schizophrenic patient from the Los Angeles area were included in the study. The task was to express their wishes and feelings toward the problem and try to solve the conflict. High-EE critical relatives were characterized by a negative interactional style in that they showed more negative nonverbal affect, more criticism, and more negative solution proposals than either low EE or high EE-overinvolved relatives when discussing an emotionally loaded family problem. Both of the latter groups not only showed a lower rate of negative behaviours but also a higher rate of positive and supportive statements than the high EE-critical relatives. Patients who had high EE-critical relatives showed more negative nonverbal affect and more self-justifying statements than patients with either low EE or high EE-overinvolved relatives. Patients living with high-EE members, irrespective of subgroup, expressed more disagreements than patients living with low EE relatives. Using an identical methodology, Müller et al. (1992) were able to replicate these findings in a sample of 42 German families from Munich with a schizophrenic member.

These results point to the bidirectional influences in families, which are more clearly depicted when sequential analysis is used, because base rate analysis of family communication does not allow the investigation of the structure of the familial communication process. Here, the best method is to look for probability rules using sequential analysis. To analyse the data sequentially, the K-Gramm method (Hahlweg, 2004) was used. This method computes the conditional probability of a particular behaviour as a function of the behavioural sequence that precedes it.

The responses of both parents were combined. Because the number of observations per family is rather small, data was summarized across families in each EE-group. Unfortunately, when analysing longer sequences with any form of sequential analysis, statistical evaluations of the differences between groups are not possible because of the aggregation. The results must be therefore interpreted descriptively.

In the following, negative escalation patterns are defined as a sequence of negative non-verbal communication (e.g. angry facial expression, cold tone of voice, showing inattention). In Figure 1 the interactional behaviour of HEE- and LEE-families from Los Angeles and Munich are depicted. The conditional probability is given on the ordinate and the sequence length is shown on the abscissa. Sequence length 1 represents the base rate of negative behaviour. About 31% of all nonverbal behaviour by HEE-critical families was negative. In contrast, about 13% (US-sample) and 19% (German sample) of the behaviour of LEE-families was negative. To explain the figure further, the behaviour of the HEE-US Families will be described. If person A (e.g. the mother) shows negative behaviour (probability 31%), the conditional probability that person B, the patient, will respond negatively is 60% (sequence length 2). Given that person B responds in that way, the conditional probability is 80% that person A will again be negative (sequence length 3) and 81% that person B will again reciprocate (sequence length 4). This pattern of negative escalation continues and ends at a sequence length of 20 due to lack of further occurrences. In contrast, LEE-families escalate only briefly up to a sequence length of 5. The escalation process stops because of the lack of data; that is, person B then emits either a positive or a neutral behaviour. It made no difference whether the patient or the parents started a negative sequence. In both instances, the same interaction pattern resulted.

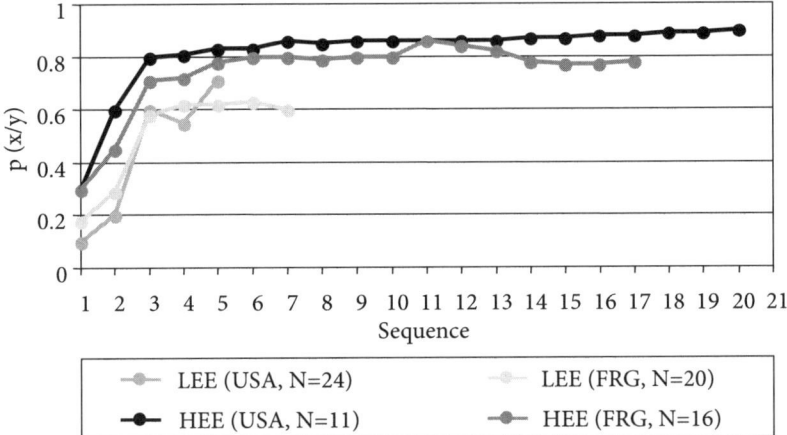

Figure 1. EE-dependent nonverbal negative interaction in families with a schizophrenic patient: Cross-cultural comparison between USA and Germany (from Hahlweg et al., 1989; Müller et al., 1992).

At least two consequences emerge from these results: (a) The findings clearly indicate the active role of the patient in establishing a positive or negative family atmosphere and argue against a tendency to blame the relatives for being responsible for a relapse (see Hatfield et al., 1987; Mintz et al., 1987). (b) In order to be able to modify the behaviour of all family members simultaneously, the patient should be included in family management.

2.5 Why do relatives express Expressed Emotion?

2.5.1 *Attribution theory*

Several authors speculated that high EE-attitudes may be caused by attributional processes (e.g. Brewin, McCarthy, Duda & Vaughn, 1991; Hooley, 1998). Relatives of psychiatric patients may attribute the causes of behaviour differently, e.g. those who hold patients (a) *accountable* for symptoms believed under volitional control (e.g. negative symptoms like apathy or self-neglect) or (b) *blame* the illness rather than the patient for symptoms that do not appear to have a volitional component (e.g. delusions, hallucinations).

Weiner's Attribution Theory (1986) lead to the following hypotheses: *Anger* toward another person is experienced when a negative outcome is attributed to a cause controllable by that person (resulting in HEE-criticism). *Pity* arises from seeing another person as experiencing negative outcomes caused by external and uncontrollable factors (resulting in LEE and in particular H-EOI). Attributions may be influenced by the patient's age (greater age = more controllability) and chronicity (longer illness = more stable attributions).

Brewin et al. (1991) studied the spontaneously expressed causal beliefs about the illness from relatives of schizophrenic patients. Perceiving the causes of the patient's behaviour as more personal and controllable by the patient was related to greater relative criticism and hostility, thus confirming the above hypothesis.

2.5.2 *Coercion process*

Coercion Theory was put forward by Patterson and Reid (1970) to explain the problematic interaction patterns that are found both among families of aggressive children and among distressed couples. In a coercive process, one person controls another person's behaviour through aversive stimulation in an attempt to change the behaviour of that person. In order to change the behaviour of person B, person A emits an aversive behaviour to which person B yields. Person A's behaviour is reinforced by person B's yielding and person B's behaviour is negatively reinforced by the cessation of A's aversive behaviour.

In the case of schizophrenic or depressed patients the HEE-relatives hold the patient accountable for symptoms he/she believes are under volitional control while they are actually not, like the negative symptoms of apathy or self-neglect. Trying to change the patient's behaviour by using aversive stimulation will only be successful in a few occasions, when the patient gives in and changes his/her behaviour for a short time. However, the intermittent reinforcement will stabilize the use of aversive stimulation by the relative. Unfortunately, in a family conflict the patient also will try to change the relatives' behaviour — using the described tactics. This will result in lengthy exchanges of aversive behaviour both by the relatives and the patient, as seen in the negative escalation curves in Figure 1.

These fruitless conflicts are accompanied by heightened autonomic arousal and diminished information processing, leading to feelings of helplessness and an inability to solve problems, with the result of a family climate characterized by high tension.

3.   Can EE be changed?

Till the end of the seventies explanations of psychopathology could readily be described as either interpersonal (subsuming environmental and behavioural accounts of psychopathology) or intrapersonal (e.g. pure psychodynamic or bio-medical models). Both models are inappropriate. Today, vulnerability-stress-models are used, incorporating biological and psychosocial variables to explain the onset and course of schizophrenia. The results cited above emphasize the impact of family interaction on the course of the schizophrenic disorder, and fit well in recent heuristic vulnerability-stress-models (Nuechterlein & Dawson, 1984; Zubin & Spring, 1977). Several consequences for prevention of relapse with schizophrenic patients ensue from this model and from the results of EE research. Neuroleptic medication seems to be necessary to control positive symptoms of the disorder, probably by lowering autonomic hyperarousal, while psychosocial intervention, to modify unfavourable familial factors, seems to be indispensable for effective prevention of relapse.

3.1 Psychoeducational Family Management

Several Anglo-American intervention programs based on the vulnerability-stress model have been developed, which combine family intervention and neuroleptic medication as a means of preventing relapse in schizophrenia (Falloon et al., 1984; Goldstein et al., 1978; Hogarty et al., 1988; Leff et al., 1985; Tarrier et al., 1989).

Although the individual concepts differ in their procedures, there are several common components: (a) Patients are on neuroleptic medication. (b) The intervention is relatively brief (15–25 sessions in the first year) and starts with informational sessions on psychosis and neuroleptic medication. (c) The main focus is on lowering EE variables like criticism and over-involvement. (d) The aim is to resolve current areas of conflict in the family, with the goal of minimizing social stress. (e) Therapy is not only directed at the problems of the patient, but also aims to alleviate the whole family's burden.

The results from these different studies are consistent in showing a marked reduction in relapse for patients in family treatment when compared with patients in standard psychiatric care. Relapse rates in the first year varied from 44% to 53% (mean: 49%) in the control groups, in contrast to 6% and 23% (mean: 13%) in patients with family intervention. After two years the mean relapse rates were 72% in the control groups and 31% in the experimental groups. Furthermore, these interventions, in particular the Behavioural Family Management (BFM) approach by Falloon et al. (1984), seem to increase the level of social competence of the patient, decrease the subjective burden of relatives, change the communication patterns in the family, and are cost-effective in comparison with routine psychiatric treatment. Psychoeducational approaches seem also to be effective in other cultural backgrounds. In a study conducted in China, Xiong et al. (1994) found that family intervention was significantly more effective than standard care in terms of rates and duration of hospitalization. In one own study we replicated the above cited findings in Germany (Hahlweg, Dürr & Müller, 1995).

4. Discussion: Implications and future research

The central question of this volume is how the shaping of individuals' mental structures and dispositions is determined by the way they perceive themselves and/or are treated by others, and whether the social context just scratches the surface of dispositions or affects the individual's mental machinery deeply.

Major mental disorders, in particular schizophrenia or depression, are examples for a very deep impact on the individual's basic mechanisms, changing in many cases the course of his/her life and those of their families. The EE-research provides impressive — and often replicated — evidence, that social factors contribute significantly to the course and outcome of mental and somatic disorder. In particular, the relationship between high EE and schizophrenic relapse has been documented by many investigators.

One has to keep in mind that the relative's emotion, which contributes to a higher relapse rate, is highly specific. Only criticism/hostility correlates with relapse, not emotions like helplessness or grief, nor warmth or love, which could also overstimulate the patient. Critical behaviour is very commonplace in social interaction especially in intimate relationships. And it is therefore not surprising that the same interactional patterns found in high or low EE families with a schizophrenic patient can also be found when investigating distressed and non-distressed couples (Hahlweg, 1996; 2003). Attributional theories and the coercion model are also the basis for explaining the interactional behaviours of marital partners.

What are specific though are the person's *vulnerabilities*, which have to be present to stimulate a relapse. These vulnerability factors are different for the various mental disorders investigated. Taking the personal and social factors and their bi-directionality into account, it is possible to change the HEE-risk factors and significantly lower the relapse rates in schizophrenia and affective disorders. HEE is not unchangeable and the EE-concepts are now a basis for psychosocial approaches in treating schizophrenic patients. EE certainly brought about a very impressive shift in the treatment of schizophrenia which is nowadays firmly rooted in the vulnerability-stress-model.

This is the good news. However, we still do not fully understand what EE is really about. Looking at the modest effect-sizes of the validity studies it is evident that not all low and high EE-families show the respective physiological or interactional patterns or attribute in the same way. A great deal of variability exists within each group of families and substantial overlap occurs between groups. Furthermore, the predictive utility of these interactional measures for identifying relapse-prone cases deserves exploration in future research. One way would be to leave the laboratory behind and observe families more closely in their home environment to study the build-up of tension over time.

References

American Psychiatric Association APA. (1994). *Diagnostic and statistical manual of mental disorders DSM IV*. Washington DC: APA.

Brown, G. W., Birley, J. L. T., & Wing, J. K. (1972). Influence of family life on the course of schizophrenic disorders: A replication. *British Journal of Psychiatry, 121,* 241-258.

Butzlaff, R. L., & Hooley, J. M. (1998). Expressed emotion and psychiatric relapse: A meta-analysis. *Archives of General Psychiatry, 55,* 547–552.

Falloon, I. R. H., Boyd, J. L., & McGill, C. W. (1984). *Family care of schizophrenia*. New York: Guilford.

Goldstein, M. J., Rodnick, E. H., Evans, J. R., May, P. R. A., & Steinberg, M. R. (1978). Drug and family therapy in the aftercare of acute schizophrenics. *Archives of General Psychiatry, 35,* 1169–1177.

Hahlweg, K. (1996). Interaktionelle Aspekte psychischer Störungen. In A. Ehlers & K. Hahlweg (Hg.), *Grundlagen der Klinischen Psychologie. Enzyklopädie der Psychologie, Serie II: Klinische Psychologie, Band 1* (S. 585–648). Göttingen: Hogrefe.

Hahlweg, K. (2003). Beziehungs — und Interaktionstörungen. In H. Reinecker (Hrsg.), *Lehrbuch Klinische Psychologie/Psychotherapie.* (4. vollständig neubearbeitete Auflage). Göttingen: Hogrefe.

Hahlweg, K. (2004). Kategoriensystem für Partnerschaftliche Interaktion (KPI): Interactional Coding System (ICS). In P. K. Kerig & D. H. Baucom (Eds.), *Couple observational coding systems* (pp. 127–142). Mahwah, NJ: Lawrence Erlbaum.

Hahlweg, K., Dürr, H., & Müller, U. (1995). *Familienbetreuung schizophrener Patienten. Ein verhaltenstherapeutischer Ansatz zur Rückfallprophylaxe.* Weinheim: Beltz Psychologie Verlags Union.

Hahlweg, K., Goldstein, M. J., Nuechterlein, K. H., Magana, A. B., Mintz, J., Doane, J. A., Miklowitz, D. J., & Snyder, K. S. (1989). Expressed emotion and patient-relative interaction in families of recent onset schizophrenics. *Journal of Consulting and Clinical Psychology, 57,* 11–18.

Hahlweg, K., & Wiedemann, G. (1999). Principles and results of family therapy in schizophrenia. *European Archive of Psychiatry and Clinical Neuroscience, 249,* Suppl.4 IV/108–115.

Hatfield, A. B., Spaniol, L., & Zipple, A. M. (1987). Expressed Emotion: A family perspective. *Schizophrenia Bulletin, 13,* 221–226.

Hogarty, G. E., McEvoy, J. P., Munetz, M., DiBarry, A. L., Bartone, P., Cather, R., Cooley, S. J., Ulrich, R. J., Carter, M., Madonia, M. J., & Environmental/Personal Indicators in the Course of Schizophrenia Research Group. (1988). Dose of fluphenazine, familial expressed emotion, and outcome in schizophrenia. Results of a two-year controlled study. *Archives of General Psychiatry, 45,* 797-805.

Hooley, J. M. (1998). Expressed emotion and psychiatric illness: From empirical data to clinical practice. *Behavior Therapy, 29,* 631–646.

Kavanagh, D. J. (1992). Recent developments in expressed emotion and schizophrenia. *British Journal of Psychiatry, 160,* 601-620.

Leff, J. P., Kuipers, L., Berkowitz, R., & Sturgeon, D. (1985). A controlled trial of social intervention in the families of schizophrenic patients: two year follow-up. *British Journal of Psychiatry, 146,* 594–600.

Leff, J. P., & Vaughn, C. E. (1985). *Expressed emotion in families.* New York: Guilford.

Miklowitz, D., & Goldstein, M. J. (1997). *Bipolar disorder. A family-focused treatment approach.* New York, Guilford.

Mintz, L. I., Liberman, R. P., Miklowitz, D. J., & Mintz, J. (1987). Expressed Emotion: A call for partnership among relatives, patients, and professionals. *Schizophrenia Bulletin, 13,* 227–235.

Müller, U., Hahlweg, K., Feinstein, E., Hank, G., Wiedemann, G., & Dose, M. (1992). Familienklima (Expressed Emotion) und Interaktionsprozesse in Familien mit einem schizophrenen Mitglied. *Zeitschrift für Klinische Psychologie, 21,* 332-351.

Nuechterlein, K. H. & Dawson, M. E. (1984). A heuristic vulnerability/stress model of schizophrenic episodes. *Schizophrenia Bulletin, 10,* 300–312.

Patterson, G. R. & Reid, J. B. (1970). Reciprocity and coercion: Two facets of social system. In C. Neuringer & J. L. Michael (Eds.), *Behavior modification in clinical psychology* (pp.133–177). New York: Appleton.

Strachan, A. M., Goldstein, M. J., & Miklowitz, D. J. (1986). Do relatives express expressed emotion? In M. J. Goldstein, I. Hand & K. Hahlweg (eds.), *Treatment of schizophrenia. Family assessment and intervention* (p. 51–58). Heidelberg: Springer.

Subotnik, K. L., Nuechterlein, K. H., & Ventura, J. (2002). Predictors of relapse in recent-onset schizophrenia. In A. Schaub (ed.), *New family interventions and associated research in psychiatric disorders* (pp.117–134). Wien, New York: Springer.

Tarrier, N., Barrowclough, C., Vaughn, C., Bamrah, J. S., Porceddu, K., Watts, S., & Freeman, H. (1989). Community management of schizophrenia. A two-year follow-up of a behavioral intervention with families. *British Journal of Psychiatry, 154,* 625-628.

Tarrier, N. & Turpin, G. (1992). Psychosocial factors, arousal and schizophrenic relapse. The psychophysiological data. *British Journal of Psychiatry, 161,* 3-11.

Tarrier, N., Vaughn, C. E., Lader, M. H., & Leff, J. P. (1979). Bodily reactions to people and events in schizophrenia. *Archives of General Psychiatry, 36,* 311–315.

Wearden, A. J., Tarrier, N., Barrowclough, C., Zastowny, T. R. & Rahill, A. A. (2000). A review of expressed emotion research in health care. *Clinical Psychology Review, 20,* 633–666.

Weiner, B. (1995). *Judgements of responsibility: A foundation for a theory of social conduct.* New York: Guilford.

Xiong, W., Phillips, M. R., Hu, X., et al. (1994). Family based intervention for schizophrenia patients in China: A randomised controlled trial. *British Journal of Psychiatry, 165,* 239–247.

Zubin, J., & Spring, B. (1977). Vulnerability — a new view of schizophrenia. *Journal of Abnormal Psychology, 86,* 103–126.

Ostracism

The making of the ignored and excluded mind

Kipling D. Williams and Jonathan Gerber
Purdue University / Macquarie University

This chapter explores the powerful consequences of ostracism — being ignored and excluded — at the neurophysiological, emotional, cognitive and behavioral levels. Once ostracized, individuals first recoil in pain, then perceive and respond to their social environments differently, leading them to interpret and attend to particular information that may help them be re-included or that may perpetuate their state of exclusion. We will discuss the nature and antecedents of adaptive and maladaptive reactions to ostracism. Finally, we will report several experiments aimed at explicating the links between ostracism and pro-social or anti-social behavior.

Ostracism: Its consequences on self and social exchange

"…solitude and silence closed round Willems: the cruel solitude of one abandoned by men…the silence unbroken by the slightest whisper of hope; an immense and impenetrable silence that swallows up without echo the murmur of regret and the cry of revolt." (Conrad, 1951/1896, p. 224).

To ostracize is to ignore and exclude an individual or a group. Ostracism is a universal experience, and has been observed across different cultures, times and species (Williams, 1997; 2001). The English language has many terms for ostracism, such as shunning, exile, to send to Coventry, to freeze out, the silent treatment and the cold shoulder. In each of these experiences, a person or group of people is ignored and excluded by others. The aim of this paper is to examine the impact of ostracism, especially as it relates to shaping the mind of the target of ostracism. First, we illustrate the ubiquity of ostracism and discuss our approach to studying it. Then, we present a model that guides our research. This model suggests that ostracism powerfully threatens the desired levels of four fundamental needs. In the short-term, reactions to ostracism follow a two-stage process: an immediate indiscriminate reflexive stage that is characterized by a painful response, and a reflective stage that is aimed at fortifying the most thwarted needs. This fortification results in a desire to recoup optimal self-relevant need levels that can direct individuals towards one of two general paths of social exchange: one that involves a heightened concern and detection of social information that will assist in correcting the self in order to be reconnected to and liked by others, or one that involves lashing out and retaliation.

The ubiquity of ostracism

Ostracism can be observed from an early age, and continues throughout the lifecycle. Children ostracize other children in the playground, choosing carefully who they wish to play with. Adults ostracize other adults, such as marriage partners using the silent treatment. The silent treatment is used by most people, with up to 75% of US adults admitting to using and receiving the silent treatment (Faulkner, 1997).

Although ostracism occurs most frequently at the dyadic or small group level, ostracism can also occur at the collective level, and across various contexts. At the dyadic level, ostracism may take the form of the silent treatment, or a parent punishing a child by giving them time out. At the collective level, different institutions have different forms of ostracism. Governments may ostracize a person by banishing them; a tribe might ostracize a member by employing social death. A religious organisation's use of excommunication, the military practice of silencing deviant members, the educational system's use of time-out as a punishment mechanism, or the use of solitary confinement in prisons are examples of institutionalised ostracism. Ostracism in the form of "still face" can be used as a therapeutic technique to direct autistic and Down's syndrome children to be more socially attentive (Nadel, this volume). In short, ostracism is a pervasive element of the human experience.

However, ostracism is not just limited to the human species, but is also observed across many other species, particularly the social animals. As discussed in Gruter and Masters (1984), observational accounts of ostracism in a variety of species have been noted, including lions, Bonobo chimps (see Call, this volume) and other primates, wolves, and even bees (Cheng, personal communication).

Multi-method approach

We have used a multi-method approach to examine the impact of ostracism, on those who use it as well as those it is used on. This approach has allowed us to look at converging and diverging evidence from a variety of perspectives. We have used many research paradigms, including experiments (physical ball-tossing, conversation, computer programs, chat room, cell phone/text-messaging, field experiments, physiological/social cognitive neuroscience, virtual reality), role-plays and simulations (Williams, Bernieri, Faulkner, Grahe, & Gada-Jain, 2000; Zadro, Williams, & Richardson, 2004), qualitative approaches (narratives, structured interviews), and surveys and diaries (the S-O-R: Sydney Ostracism Record, an event contingent record; Williams, Nezlek, Wheeler, & Govan, 2004; Williams, Wheeler, & Harvey, 2001).

One of the experimental techniques we have used in recent years is Cyberball. Because many of the studies summarized in this article used the Cyberball paradigm, we will describe its essential aspects here. This paradigm, developed by Williams, Cheung, and Choi (2000) uses a computer-based program in which three or four players take turns tossing a ball to each other on the screen by pressing keys. Participants are led to believe that they are playing a computer game with two or three other people via the Internet. They are asked to visualize the other players, and are told the experiment is examining mental visualisation. The other players in the game are actually computer-controlled, and the researcher determines the schedule of throws the participant receives. The experimenter can determine whether the participant will be included, ostracized, or will receive more throws. The experimenter can also vary between periods of inclusion and periods of ostracism.

Ostracism thwarts desired levels of four fundamental needs

A model of ostracism was proposed by Williams (1997; 2001) and guides our research into the perception and impact of ostracism. Whereas the model discusses a variety of factors that pertain to the complexity of ostracism (for instance, that there are different types of and motives for ostracism), here we will concentrate on the core and peripheral aspects of the model. At the core is the proposition that ostracism threatens or thwarts the desired levels of four fundamental needs: belonging, self-esteem, control, and meaningful existence.

These needs have been postulated as fundamental in separate research programs. Belonging, or the need to belong, is the drive that people exhibit to have frequent caring interactions with others (Baumeister & Leary, 1995). The need for control reflects the strong urge people have to have some perception of control over their environment and relationships (Skinner, 1996). Meaningful existence is the need to feel that our lives are in some way worthwhile, as particularly emphasised by terror management theory (Solomon, Greenberg, & Pyszczynski, 1991; see also Case & Williams, 2004). Self-esteem, or the desire to feel worthy, is one of the more robust psychological traits, although it is possible to view it as a mechanism to help achieve belongingness or meaningful existence (Leary, Tambor, Terdal, & Downs, 1995; Wisman & Koole, 2003).

The uniqueness of ostracism in affecting these four needs can be ascertained by contrasting ostracism with a dyadic argument (Zadro, Williams, & Richardson, 2005). In an argument, both people feel they belong, as there is interaction, whereas in ostracism the target does not belong as they are being excluded. During an argument, both parties have some control due to the fact that either party can influence the course of the argument, but in ostracism there is no opportunity for the target to gain control by having an interaction. The control lies in the hand of the source of ostracism. Similarly, a target's need for meaningful existence is not threatened in an argument, as they are seen to be worthy enough to fight with, while ostracized targets may feel they are not worthy of notice. This is not true for all cases of ostracism, as in punitive ostracism the target may feel that they are significant enough to be punished, and therefore may still retain a sense of meaningful existence. Lastly, self-esteem is lowered in an argument due to interpersonal criticism, but this effect is heightened in ostracism, as the person may be given no reason for the ostracism. This can lead a target of ostracism to conduct their own appraisal of what is causing the ostracism, resulting in generating many more reasons for ostracism than in actuality, and hence lowering their self-esteem more.

Stages of responses to ostracism

Responses to brief episodes of ostracism proceed through two distinct stages (responses to continuous or repeated episodes over a life time form a third stage of responses that will not be discussed in this paper; but see Williams, 2001 for a full discussion of this stage). The immediate reaction to ostracism is indiscriminate and painful; with depletion in need satisfaction levels. This is followed in the medium-term by coping responses, where moderating variables affect a person's ability to regain lost satisfaction. In the long-term, repeated ostracism can cause people to accept their ostracism, leading to helplessness and depression.

Stage 1 — Immediate reactions to ostracism — reflexively indiscriminate and painful

When targets are ostracized, the immediate effects are indiscriminate and painful, with people experiencing reductions in the satisfaction of needs, along with negative affect and anxiety. The pain of ostracism is felt at both the psychological and neurophysiological levels.

Neurophysiologically, a recent study by Eisenberger, Lieberman, and Williams (2003) demonstrated that the social pain of ostracism is similar to physical pain at the neurophysiological level. Participants were placed in an MRI scanner, and were led to believe they were playing Cyberball with two other participants in similar fMRI scanners in different labs. Blood flow activity was recorded at baseline, and then at the beginning of the game when they participants were told that the game was already in progress but their own computer was not yet hooked up to the other two players' computers (this would be unintentional ostracism). Then their computers were connected and participants were included, followed by an episode of seemingly intentional ostracism. The exclusion of participants led to increased activity in their anterior cingulate cortex (ACC), and the right ventral prefrontal cortex (RVPFC). The ACC is the same region active during physical pain, suggesting that ostracism taps primal reactions of hurt. Self-reports of distress were highly correlated with ACC activity. The activity in the RVPFC moderated feelings of distress for the intentional (but not intentional) ostracism, suggesting that this regulates the ACC activity.

Statistically, the effects of ostracism are powerful, yielding large effect sizes of between 1.0 and 2.0, and often only requiring only three participants per condition to achieve reliable effects. Even minimal instances of ostracism are capable of producing effects rapidly; many experiments have demonstrated powerful self-report, physiological, and behavioral effects with only 4 minutes of ostracism.

The sheer power of ostracism has led us to examine it under the most minimal and degraded circumstances, in order to determine what exactly is necessary for people to perceive and react negatively to ostracism. Is there a point at which ostracism become so minimal that no detrimental effects are observed? Are there conditions under which ostracism will not matter?

It would seem reasonable that ostracism would require human rejection, or else people will easily dismiss the ostracism. However, using Cyberball, even when subjects are explicitly told a computer program is interacting with them, there is a negative impact on the four needs, and lower mood (Zadro, Williams, & Richardson, 2004). There are no differences between human and computer ostracism, except that people are angrier if ostracized by a computer, as this violates their sense of fairness. For ostracism to have an effect, a perceived intention to ostracize might be necessary. If the target believes there is no intention to ostracize, this may eliminate the effect. However, telling participants that they are being ostracized as a random assignment (i. e., telling them it is scripted), still leads to decreases in needs satisfaction (Zadro, et al., 2004, Study 2).

Are there instances in which we would not mind being ostracized (or maybe even prefer being ostracized) because we have no attraction to those who are ostracizing us? For instance, suppose an individual was ostracized by a group he or she despised? Surely that would not be experienced as negative. Or so one might surmise. In a study by Gonsalkorale and Williams (2003), subjects were ostracized by either an ingroup (others who lean toward the same political party), a respected outgroup (those who lean toward the rival political party) or a despised outgroup (the KKK). The findings were startling. There were no differences in reported levels of need satisfaction for individuals who were ostracized by the ingroup, rival outgroup members, or a despised outgroup. All instances of ostracism resulted in substantially lower levels of feelings of belonging, self-esteem, control, and meaningful existence.

Perhaps the reason for the ostracism would matter. Gifted children often complain that their worse obstacle is dealing with being ostracized by the other children in their classroom. But, they at least have the satisfaction of knowing they are intellectually superior to the others. Being ostracized because one is inferior to others is doubly demeaning. However, our examination of immediate effects of ostracism on individuals who were convinced they performed significantly better (tall poppies) or worse (small poppies) indicated they both experienced the ostracism negatively, despite the fact that our tall poppies actually performed better on a subsequent task (Kosasih & Williams, 2004).

Nor does it look like ostracism is moderated by other variables such as individualism or mood. Self-report measures of collective/individualism are not correlated with the effects of ostracism. Mood also fails to moderate the effects of ostracism. Although ostracism lowers mood and raises anger, neither of these effects mediate the behavioral consequences of ostracism.

Finally, we (Gerber & Williams) are currently examining the impact of relational devaluation (Leary, 2005) as it applies to Cyberball ostracism. Specifically, usually all participants are thrown the ball once or twice, and then half are ostracized while the other half continue to be included. Leary would suggest that because they were first included, the reason ostracism is so painful is that it signals relational devaluation. That is, they were once liked (or included), and now (for some reason), they are no longer liked (or included). If relational devaluation is at the core of ostracism's unpleasantness, then we would expect less or no pain and unpleasantness if participants were ostracized for the entire time. There would be no chance for devaluation because they would have no evidence of valuation in the first place. Our preliminary results suggest that this is not the case. Including participants for longer at the beginning does not heighten the effects of ostracism. Furthermore, it appears the effects might be most severe for those who are ostracised from the beginning, and progressively decrease the more a person is included at the start, when controlling for the length of exclusion. However, of the four needs, self-esteem may not follow this general pattern. Preliminary results suggest self-esteem may decrease further if a participant is included more at the start of Cyberball. This lends mild support to the relational devaluation theory.

In summary, the minimal necessary conditions for ostracism to have a negative impact are not yet known. It looks as if the perception of ostracism automatically triggers reductions in satisfaction of the four needs. The immediate reaction to perceived ostracism is seemingly immune to cognitive intervention. Regardless of why it is occurring, who is doing it, or to whom it is being done, ostracism is immediately registered as painful and unpleasant.

Stage 2 — Coping with ostracism

After the immediate reduction in people's needs satisfaction levels, people move on to a coping stage, where they use available cognitive, emotional, physiological, and behavioral resources to *regain* levels of needs satisfaction. Whereas the first stage of ostracism is immediately painful, there are several moderators to coping during the second phase.

The first moderating variable is the attributions a person makes as to why they are being ostracized. The target may alleviate the feelings associated with ostracism by taking into account the source's motives. The target may believe the source was mistaken, or that the source was ostracising due to a role prescribed to them, such as a CEO ignoring a junior employee. The target may believe the source ostracized defensively as they were afraid of being ostracized themselves. These attributions may defuse the situation and help the target to increase their level of needs satisfaction.

The target may also think about discounting factors such as whether they were ostracized by an outgroup, or ostracized unintentionally. The existence of such factors can alleviate the sense of threat that it proposes to the people themselves.

It is possible that some augmenting factors could help ostracism be viewed in a positive light. If a person perceives they were ostracized for being superior (e.g. a tall poppy) they can easily discount the ostracism.

Individual differences in optimal levels for the four needs and related traits may also impact on coping responses to ostracism. For example, Zadro, Boland, and Richardson (2004) found that both normal individuals and people high in social phobia reacted with the same level of distress at the immediate reflexive stage after Cyberball ostracism. After a 45-minute waiting period, the normals returned to high need satisfaction levels, whereas those high in social phobia were still distressed and had shown only partial recuperation.

Does ostracism lead to pro-social or anti-social behaviors?

Ostracism has consequences upon future cognitive and behavioral reactions, indicating that individual differences and situational constraints interact with the social minds of ostracized targets. One particularly intriguing controversy in the existing literature on ostracism, social exclusion, and rejection is the impact that these similarly aversive social behaviors have on the tendency for targeted individuals to display pro- versus anti-social responses.

On the one hand, ostracism can cause adaptive pro-social responses, which may help the target to be reincluded. In a study by Williams et al. (2000), participants were ostracized using Cyberball by minimal ingroup or outgroup members (PC vs. Mac users), and subsequently performed a perceptual comparison task with a new set of participants. Ostracized individuals conformed more to a unanimously incorrect group decision than included participants. However, this only occurred as long as there were at least some ingroup members doing the ostracism.

There are many other adaptive responses to ostracism. People are more likely to join a new group after being ostracized, regardless of the attractiveness and desirability of the prospective group (Wheaton, 2001), work harder on a collective task (Williams & Sommer, 1997), are more likely to mimic a good organizational citizen (Ouwerkerk, Van Lange, Gallucci, & Kerr, 2005), and are more likely to engage in unconscious mimicry, especially with ingroup members (Lakin & Chartrand, 2003; 2005). Further to this, there is a vast literature on the effectiveness of 'time-out' disciplinary procedures, a procedure designed to procure pro-social compliance through the use of ostracism.

However, sometimes the response to ostracism can be maladaptive. The target may react in ways that reinforce their exclusion. Exclusion and rejection can increase anti-social behaviours (Twenge, Baumeister, Tice, & Stucke, 2001), decrease pro-social behaviours (Tice, Bratslavsky, & Baumeister, 2001), make people less intelligent on thoughtful problems (Baumeister & DeWall, 2005), and can lead to generalized aggression toward group members similar to ostracism sources, as in mass violence (Gaertner, et al., 2004). An analysis of accounts of US school shootings suggests that ostracism has precipitated thirteen of the fifteen incidents in recent years (Leary, Kowalski, Smith, & Phillips, 2003).

There are at least two possible explanations for these apparently contradictory results: the nature of the needs threatened, and the transparency of the response set.

The first possibility might depend on which needs are most threatened. A threat to a person's feeling of belonging and self-esteem may lead to pro-social behavior because the best way to fortify the thwarted need is to make oneself more socially adept and attractive. However, a threat to feelings of control and meaningful existence may be fortified best by an anti-social response. Anti-social behavior have often used Twenge and Baumeister's "Life alone" paradigm. This paradigm implies permanent exclusion in future life, which may more strongly threaten control and meaningful existence than Cyberball. After all, an individual can expect the usual social bonds following a Cyberball experiment.

Williams and Warburton (2003) provide some evidence to support the thesis that loss of control leads to aggression. In this study, inclusion or ostracism were induced using the Cyberball paradigm. This was followed by either a controllable or uncontrollable noise blast. Subjects were then asked to allocate an amount of hot sauce to a new third person. The amount of hot sauce allocated was a measure of aggression. Aggression increased only for those participants who were both ostracized and also had no control over the noise blasts.

The second explanation for the differences causing pro and anti-social responses is that the response chosen may depend on the transparency of the response set. Explicit and transparent response sets may lead to pro-social behavior, in an attempt at impression management. Disguised responses, on the other hand, may allow subjects to vent their anger & frustration via an anti-social response. This thesis was tested by Govan, Case, and Williams (2002; see also, Williams & Govan, 2004), using explicit and implicit measures of prejudice. Ostracism has effects on measures of explicit and implicit prejudice. An explicit measure of prejudice was constructed, combining explicit and obvious measures of prejudice against Aboriginal Australians (from Pedersen & Walker, 1997). An implicit association task (IAT; Greenwald, McGhee, & Schwartz, 1998) was used as the implicit measure, in which Aboriginal- and European-named suburbs (e.g. Booragul, Koolewong for Aboriginal suburbs, Pymble, Asquith for European suburbs) were paired with Pleasant and Unpleasant words (eg. love, sickness). Whereas both included and ostracized participants portrayed themselves as open-minded and unprejudiced in the explicit measures, ostracized individuals showed higher levels of implicit prejudice than included participants.

Future directions and summary

The future direction of our ostracism research takes us in a variety of directions, and to new paradigms. Advances in immersive environment technologies have attracted our interest in using virtual reality as a working paradigm for ostracism. In addition to the added control offered by programming the social environment, we suspect that we can very quickly instill the feeling of invisibility in our participants. Early indications suggest that we can palpably induce a feeling of oblivious ostracism in participants who are wandering around a virtual cocktail party, in which the others appear not to even recognize the participant's existence. This is particularly true when participants challenge the virtual avatars and try to block their progress as they walk across the room. Nothing suggests invisibility better than being walked through!

At this point, we feel we have fairly well established the immediate indiscriminate painful experience of being ostracized. Nevertheless, there is still a little unpacking to do at this initial level. We have always intentionally defined ostracism as a naturally occurring compound of being ignored *and* excluded. However, there has been no attempt to determine whether both ignoring and excluding are necessary to cause the perception and experience of ostracism. Earlier work by Williams, Shore, and Grahe (1998) provided evidence that when people thought of the silent treatment, silence was not the top behavioral index; it was lack of eye contact. This suggested to us that lack of eye contact might be crucial to indicate being ignored. Exclusion, on the other hand, suggests the absence of inclusion in behavioral interactions of the others. Thus, in the context of the ball-tossing paradigm, we might be able to disentangle ignoring from exclusion by the orthogonal manipulations of being looked at or not with being thrown the ball or not. Current work in our virtual reality lab by Kate Wallbank attempts to disentangle the two concepts in this manner. Participants who have donned head-mounted displays play a 3-dimensional beach ball game with two others (on a virtual beach) who do or do not look at the participant and who include or exclude the participant in the ball tossing. Our hunch is that perceptions of ostracism may either be an additive process of ignoring and exclusion, or a necessary combination of the two.

Furthermore, with respect to the issue of under what conditions ostracism leads to anti-social behavior, we are hypothesizing that ignoring may be particularly frustrating, and would therefore be more connected with a feeling of loss of control. This, we think, would be more likely to lead to an aggressive response. Exclusion, however, is more related to belonging and the perception that others do not like the participant. Therefore we think that reactions to these two threats may lead to behavior that is more pro-, rather than anti-, social. After the ostracism experience, participants will enter Chicken World (inspired by Cohen, Nisbett, Bowdle, & Schwartz, 1996), where they will see a person walking down a narrow corridor towards them. The participant can move out of the person's way, and this will measure aggression, allowing us to further investigate anti-social responses to ostracism.

Finally, we (Gerber & Williams, 2004) are currently examining the impact of relational devaluation (Leary, Springer, Negel, Ansell, & Evans, 1998) as it applies to Cyberball ostracism. Specifically, usually all participants are thrown the ball once or twice, and then half are ostracized while the other half continue to be included. Leary would suggest that because they were first included, the reason ostracism is so painful is that it signals relational devaluation. That is, they were once liked (or included), and now (for some reason), they are no longer liked (or included). If relational devaluation is at the core of ostracism's unpleasantness, then we would expect less or no pain and unpleasantness if participants were ostracized for the entire time. There would be no chance for devaluation because they would have no evidence of valuation in the first place. Our preliminary results suggest that this is not the case. Including participants for longer at the beginning does not heighten the effects of ostracism. Furthermore, it appears the effects might be most severe for those who are ostracised from the beginning, and progressively decrease the more a person is included at the start, when controlling for the length of exclusion. However, of the four needs, self-esteem may not follow this general pattern. Preliminary results suggest self-esteem may decrease further if a participant is included more at the start of Cyberball. This lends mild support to the relational devaluation theory.

At the other end of the continuum, our research program looks beyond the immediate stage and concentrates more on the Stage 2 (coping) phase. Here is where we should see an interaction between the individual and the environment in terms of different reactions to ostracism. Once the individual has experienced the pain, the question becomes how to cope with it. Individual differences should play an important role, so we will be looking at ones that should have a direct relation on disparate perceptions and reactions to ostracism, such as attachment style, rejection sensitivity, desire for control, self-esteem, and others. In a similar vein, attributions for the motives behind the ostracism, once considered and reflected upon, ought to either diminish or augment the impact of ostracism. Thus, unintentional ostracism (as in the case of one's computer not being hooked up to the others for Cyberball) or ostracism by despised others (like the KKK) ought to be easily dismissed with enough time to cognitively evaluate the meaning of the ostracism incident. To assess the combination of these individual and situational factors, we need to examine ostracized individuals after some period of time has allowed them to consider the meaning behind the ostracism. Existing research suggests that this could occur in less than 45-minutes (Zadro, Bowland, & Richardson, 2004), and perhaps it even occurs faster than that.

In summary, it appears that the detection of ostracism is *hard-wired*. It sounds an alarm, much like physical pain, that the organism needs to *do* something or risk survival. Immediate reactions are indiscriminate: they defy logic, the impact of discounting factors, and individual differences. Subsequent reactions to ostracism are not hard-wired, but are acquired through experience and are also a function of personality. These strategies could be pro-social in orientation, increasing the inclusionary status of the individual in subsequent interactions. However, total obsequiousness is probably not terribly healthy or functional. They could also lead to anti-social, retaliative, lashing out responses. While affording the individual control and a sense of being recognized as existing, it perpetuates further ostracism, and is therefore, also unhealthy and dysfunctional. Future research should be directed more towards examining Stage 2 — the reflective coping stage. Moving beyond demonstrating the painful immediate pre-cognitive responses, we expect that with time for reflective consideration and a desire to fortify the most thwarted needs, the experience of ostracism will *make minds* react differently to people and social situations.

Acknowledgment

This research was supported in part by a grant from the Australian Research Council to the first author.

References

Baumeister, R. F., & DeWall, C. N. (2005). The inner dimension of social exclusion: Intelligent thought and self-regulation among rejected persons. In K. D. Williams, J. P. Forgas, & W. von Hippel (Eds.), *The social outcast: Ostracism, social exclusion, rejection, and bullying* (pp. 53–73). New York: The Psychology Press.

Baumeister, R. F., & Leary, M. R. (1995). The need to belong: Desire for interpersonal attachments as a fundamental human motivation. *Psychological Bulletin, 117,* 497–529.

Case, T. I., & Williams, K. D. (2004). Ostracism: A metaphor for death. In J. Greenberg, S. L. Koole, & T. Pyszczynski (Eds.), *Handbook of experimental existential psychology* (pp. 336–351). New York: Guilford Press.

Cheng, K. (November 1999). Personal communication about bees and ostracism. Macquarie University, Sydney.

Cohen, D., Nisbett, R. E., Bowdle, B. F., & Schwarz, N. (1996). Insult, aggression, and the southern culture of honor: An "experimental ethnography." *Journal of Personality and Social Psychology, 70,* 945–960.

Conrad, J. (1951/1896). *An outcast of the islands.* London: Ernest Benn.

Eisenberger, N. I., Lieberman, M. D., & Williams, K. D. (2003). Does Rejection Hurt? An fMRI study of social exclusion. *Science, 302,* 290–292.

Faulkner, S., Williams, K, D., Sherman, B., & Williams, E. (1997). The *"silent treatment": Its incidence and impact.* Paper presented at the 69th annual meeting of the Midwestern Psychological Association, Chicago.

Gaertner, L., & Iuzzini, J. (2005). Rejection and entitativity: A synergistic model of mass violence. In K. D. Williams, J. P. Forgas, & W. von Hippel (Eds.), *The social outcast: Ostracism, social exclusion, rejection, and bullying* (pp. 307–320). New York: The Psychology Press.

Gerber, J., & Williams, K. D. (2004). Separating relational devaluation from ostracism. Unpublished manuscript. Macquarie University, Sydney.

Gonsalkorale, K., & Williams, K. D. (2003, September). *The KKK won't let me play: Ostracism hurts even by despised outgroups.* Paper presented at the Brisbane Social Identity Conference, Brisbane, Australia.

Govan, C. L., Case, T. I., & Williams, K. D. (2002, April). *Implicit and explicit responses to ostracism: Social judgment of Aboriginal and White Australians.* Paper presented at the 31st Annual meeting of the Society of Australasian Social Psychologists, Adelaide, South Australia.

Greenwald, A. G., McGhee, D. E., & Schwartz, J. L. K. (1998). Measuring individual differences in implicit cognition: The implicit association test. *Journal of Personality and Social Psychology, 74,* 1022–1038.

Gruter, M., & Masters, R.D. (1984). *Ostracism: A Social and Biological Phenomenon.* Elsevier: New York.

James, W. (1890). *The principles of psychology (Vol. 1).* New York: Dover.

Kastenbaum, R. (1992). *The psychology of death (2nd Ed.).* New York: Springer.

Kosasih, M., & Williams, K. D. (2004). Ostracism of small and tall poppies. Unpublished manuscript. Macquarie University, Sydney.

Lakin, J. L., & Chartrand, T. L. (2003). Using nonconscious behavioral mimicry to create affiliation and rapport. *Psychological Science, 14,* 334–339.

Lakin, J. L., & Chartrand, T. L. (2005). Exclusion and nonconscious behavioral mimicry. In K. D. Williams, J. P. Forgas, & W. von Hippel (Eds.) *The social outcast: Ostracism, Social exclusion, rejection, and bullying* (pp. 279–296). New York: The Psychology Press.

Leary, M. R. (2005). Varieties of rejection. In K. D. Williams, J. P. Forgas, & W. von Hippel (Eds.), *The social outcast: Ostracism, Social exclusion, rejection, and bullying* (pp. 35–52). New York: The Psychology Press.

Leary, M. R., & Downs, D. L. (1995). Interpersonal functions of the self-esteem motive: The self-esteem system as a sociometer. In M. H. Kernis (Ed.), *Efficacy, agency, and self-esteem Plenum series in social/clinical psychology* (pp 123–144). CITY: Plenum Press.

Leary, M., Kowalski, R. M., Smith, L., & Phillips, S. (2003). Teasing, rejection, and violence: Case studies of the school shootings. *Aggressive Behavior, 29,* 202–214.

Leary, M. R., Springer, C., Negel, L., Ansell, E., & Evans, K. (1998). The causes, phenomenology, and consequences of hurt feelings. *Journal of Personality and Social Psychology, 74,* 1225–1237.

Leary, M. R., Tambor, E. S., Terdal, S. K., & Downs, D. L. (1995). Self-esteem as an interpersonal monitor: The sociometer hypothesis. *Journal of Personality and Social Psychology, 68,* 518–530.

Ouwerkerk, J. W., Van Lange, P. A. M., Gallucci, M., & Kerr, N. L. (2005). Avoiding the social death penalty: Ostracism and cooperation in social dilemmas. In K. D. Williams, J. P. Forgas, & W. von Hippel (Eds.), *The social outcast: Ostracism, social exclusion, rejection, and bullying* (pp. 321–332). New York: The Psychology Press.

Rosenberg, M. (1989). *Society and the adolescent self-image.* Princeton, NJ: Princeton University Press.

Seligman, M. (1975). *Helplessness: On depression, development, and death.* San Francisco: Freeman.

Skinner, E. A. (1996). A guide to constructs of control. *Journal of Personality and Social Psychology, 71,* 549–570.

Smith, A., & Williams, K. D. (2004). R U There? Ostracism by cell phone text messages. *Group Dynamics: Theory, Research, & Practice,8(4),* 291–301.

Solomon, S., Greenberg, J., & Pyszczynski, T. (1991). Terror management theory of self-esteem. In C. R. Snyder & D. R. Forsyth (Eds.), *Handbook of social and clinical psychology: The health perspective* (pp 21–40). New York: Pergamon Press.

Tice, D. M., Bratslavsky, E., & Baumeister, R. F. (2001). Emotional distress regulation takes precedence over impulse control: If you feel bad, do it! *Journal of Personality and Social Psychology, 80,* 53–67.

Twenge, J. M., Baumeister, R. F., Tice, D. M., & Stucke, T. S. (2001). If you can't join them, beat them: Effects of social exclusion on aggressive behavior. *Journal of Personality and Social Psychology, 81,* 1058–1069.

Warburton, W. A., & Williams, K. D. (2004). Ostracism: When competing motivations collide. In J. P. Forgas, K. D. Williams, & S. M. Laham (Eds.), *Social motivation: Conscious and unconscious processes* (pp. 294–313). NY: Cambridge University Press.

Wheaton, A. (2001). *Ostracism and susceptibility to the overtures of socially deviant groups and individuals.* Unpublished Honours Thesis, Macquarie University, Sydney.

Williams, K.D. (1997). Social ostracism. In R. M. Kowalski (Ed.), *Aversive interpersonal behaviors* (pp. 133–170). New York: Plenum.

Williams, K. D. (2001). *Ostracism: The power of silence.* New York: Guilford Press.

Williams, K. D., Bernieri, F., Faulkner, S., Grahe, J., & Gada-Jain, N. (2000). The Scarlet Letter Study: Five days of social ostracism. *Journal of Personal and Interpersonal Loss, 5,* 19–63.

Williams, K. D., & Govan, C. L. (2004). Reacting to ostracism: Retaliation or reconciliation? In D. Abrams, J. Marques, & M. Hogg. (Eds.). *The social psychology of inclusion and exclusion* (pp. 47–62). Philadelphia: The Psychology Press.

Williams, K. D., Nezlek, J., Wheeler, L., & Govan, C. L. (2004, January). *Everyday ostracism.* Presented at the Society for Personality and Social Psychology, Austin, Texas.

Williams, K. D., Shore, W. J., & Grahe, J. E. (1998). The silent treatment: Perceptions of its behaviors and associated feelings. *Group Processes and Intergroup Relations, 1,* 117–141.

Williams, K. D., & Sommer, K. L. (1997). Social ostracism by coworkers: Does rejection lead to loafing or compensation? *Personality and Social Psychology Bulletin, 23,* 693–706.

Williams, K. D., & Warburton, W. A. (2003). Ostracism: A form of indirect aggression that can result in aggression. *International Review of Social Psychology, 16,* 101–126.

Williams, K. D., Wheeler, L., & Harvey, J. (2001). Inside the social mind of the ostracizer. In J. P. Forgas, K. D. Williams, & L. Wheeler (Eds.), *The social mind: Cognitive and motivational aspects of interpersonal behavior* (pp. 294- 320). New York: Cambridge University Press.

Williams, K. D., & Zadro, L. (2001). Ostracism: On being ignored, excluded and rejected. In M. R. Leary (Ed.), *Interpersonal rejection* (pp. 21–53). New York: Oxford University Press.

Williams, K. D., Cheung, C. K., & Choi, W. (2000). CyberOstracism: Effects of being ignored over the Internet. *Journal of Personality and Social Psychology, 79,* 748–762.

Wisman, A., & Koole, S. L. (2003). Hiding in the crowd: Can mortality salience promote affiliation with others who oppose one's worldviews? *Journal of Personality and Social Psychology, 84,* 511–526.

Zadro, L., Boland, C., & Richardson, R. (2004). *How long does it last? The immediate and delayed effects of ostracism and the moderating influence of social anxiety.* Unpublished manuscript, University of New South Wales, Sydney.

Zadro, L., & Williams, K. D. (2001, February). *Effects of short-term ostracism on sources and targets.* Paper presented at the Annual Meeting of the Society for Personality and Social Psychology, San Antonio, TX.

Zadro, L., Williams, K. D., & Richardson, R. (2004). How low can you go? Ostracism by a computer lowers belonging, control, self-esteem, and meaningful existence. *Journal of Experimental Social Psychology. 40*, 560–567.

Zadro, L., Williams, K. D., & Richardson, R. (2004). *Interviews with long-term targets and sources of the silent treatment.* Unpublished manuscript, University of New South Wales, Sydney.

Zadro, L., Williams, K. D., & Richardson, R. (2005). Riding the "O" Train: Comparing the effects of ostracism and verbal dispute on targets and sources. *Group Processes and Interpersonal Relations, 8*, 125–143.

Self processes in interdependent relationships

Partner affirmation and the Michelangelo phenomenon

Caryl E. Rusbult[1], Madoka Kumashiro[2], Shevaun L. Stocker[3],
Jeffrey L. Kirchner[4], Eli J. Finkel[5] and Michael K. Coolsen[6]
[1]Vrije Universiteit Amsterdam / [2]University of Hamburg / [3]University of
Wisconsin / [4]University of North Carolina at Chapel Hill / [5]Northwestern
University / [6]Shippensburg University

This essay reviews theory and research regarding the "Michelangelo phenomenon," which describes the manner in which close partners shape one another's
dispositions, values, and behavioral tendencies. Individuals are more likely to
exhibit movement toward their ideal selves to the degree that their partners
exhibit affirming perception and behavior, exhibiting confidence in the self's
capacity and enacting behaviors that elicit key features of the self's ideal. In turn,
movement towards the ideal self yields enhanced personal well-being *and* couple
well-being. We review empirical evidence regarding this phenomenon and discuss self and partner variables that contribute to the process.

The research reviewed in this essay examines an interaction process that bridges
the gap between *intra*personal psychology and *inter*personal psychology. In brief,
our research explores the ways in which interpersonal experience shapes the self,
including personal dispositions, values, and behavioral tendencies.[1] Our work rests
on the assumption that the self does not spring full-blown from a vacuum — rather,
the self is fashioned at least in part by interpersonal experience. The interpersonal
agents who exert the most powerful effects on the self are those with whom we are
most strongly interdependent — friends, family, and romantic partners. Such influence can be very positive or very negative: Some partners bring out the best in one
another, whereas others either fail to do so or bring out the worst in one another.

This essay presents theory and research regarding an interaction process
termed the Michelangelo phenomenon. We begin by addressing three theoretical traditions that form the basis for our work — the behavioral confirmation,

interdependence, and self-discrepancy traditions. Then we introduce the Michel-angelo phenomenon and its consequences, introducing the concepts of partner affirmation and movement toward the ideal self. After outlining empirical find-ings relevant to key predictions, we distinguish this phenomenon from related in-teraction processes, including partner affirmation, partner verification, self-other merger, and the Pygmalion phenomenon. We close with a review of specific self and partner processes in the Michelangelo phenomenon.

Theoretical background

Behavioral confirmation processes

Our theoretical analysis begins with the concept of *behavioral confirmation*, de-fined as the means by which an interaction partner's expectations about the self become reality by eliciting behaviors from the self that confirm the partner's ex-pectations (Darley & Fazio, 1980; Snyder, Tanke, & Berscheid, 1977; also see Klein, this volume). How does this process unfold? Interaction partners develop beliefs about the self's strengths and limitations, preferences and disinclinations. During interaction, partners tend to act in accord with their beliefs about the self. In so doing, partners create opportunities for the self to display some behaviors, con-strain interaction in such a manner as to inhibit the display of other behaviors, and thereby elicit a subset of the self's full repertoire of possible behaviors (e.g., Harris & Rosenthal, 1985).

Self-discrepancy processes

Is behavioral confirmation likely to be a good thing or a bad thing? And impor-tantly, how should we conceptualize "good thing" versus "bad thing?" Is behav-ioral confirmation "good" when it is enhancing, or elicits normatively desirable behaviors from the self? Is it "good" when it is verifying, or elicits behaviors that are compatible with the individual's self-conception? Our answer begins as a meta-phor, and rests on the manner in which sculpting was envisioned by its greatest practitioner: "Michelangelo conceived his figures as lying hidden in the block of marble... The task he set himself as a sculptor was merely to extract the ideal form... to remove the stone that covered [the ideal]" (Gombrich, 1995, p. 313). As such, the creative process and the artist's tools are aspects of salvation, in that by chipping away at the stone, the figure slumbering in the block is allowed to emerge. In Michelangelo's vision, the slumbering figure was something heroic, vi-brant, and divine — the "ideal form."

Like blocks of stone, humans, too, possess ideal forms. The human equivalent of Michelangelo's slumbering form is a possible self to which the individual aspires (Higgins, 1987, 1996; Markus & Nurius, 1986). In particular, humans can be said to possess an *ideal self*, defined as the constellation of dispositions, motives, and behavioral tendencies an individual ideally wishes to acquire. People experience distress when they perceive discrepancies between the ideal self and the *actual self*, defined as the dispositions, motives, and behavioral tendencies an individual believes he or she actually possesses. The distress associated with actual-self/ideal-self discrepancies is motivating — people seek to bring the actual self into alignment with the ideal self (e.g., Moretti & Higgins, 1990).

Interdependence processes

Among the many interpersonal forces that shape the self, few sculptors are likely to exert effects as powerful as those of our close partners. How so? To begin with, extended interdependence involves adaptation — over time in a relationship, interacting individuals adjust to one another by selectively developing some aspects of the self and eliminating others (Kelley & Thibaut, 1978; Rusbult & Van Lange, 2003; also see Vallacher, this volume). Moreover, strong interdependence provides particularly good opportunities for mutual influence and adaptation, in that strong interdependence entails frequent and powerful influence across diverse types of activity. Over the course of repeated interaction in the context of strong interdependence, each person's interaction-specific adaptations eventually become embodied in stable dispositions, values, and behavioral tendencies: Each person's self is sculpted by the partner; each person's dispositions, values, and behavioral tendencies come to reflect the particular conditions of interdependence experienced with the partner.

The Michelangelo phenomenon and its consequences

Partner affirmation versus disaffirmation

The concept of partner affirmation describes the manner in which a partner sculpts the self, or the degree to which the partner is an ally (vs. foe) in the self's goal pursuits. *Partner perceptual affirmation* describes the degree to which a partner believes that the self can acquire ideal-congruent qualities: Does Mary "see the best in what John might be?" As illustrated in Figure 1, we suggest that partner perceptual affirmation promotes *partner behavioral affirmation*, which describes the degree to which a partner behaves toward the self in such a manner as to

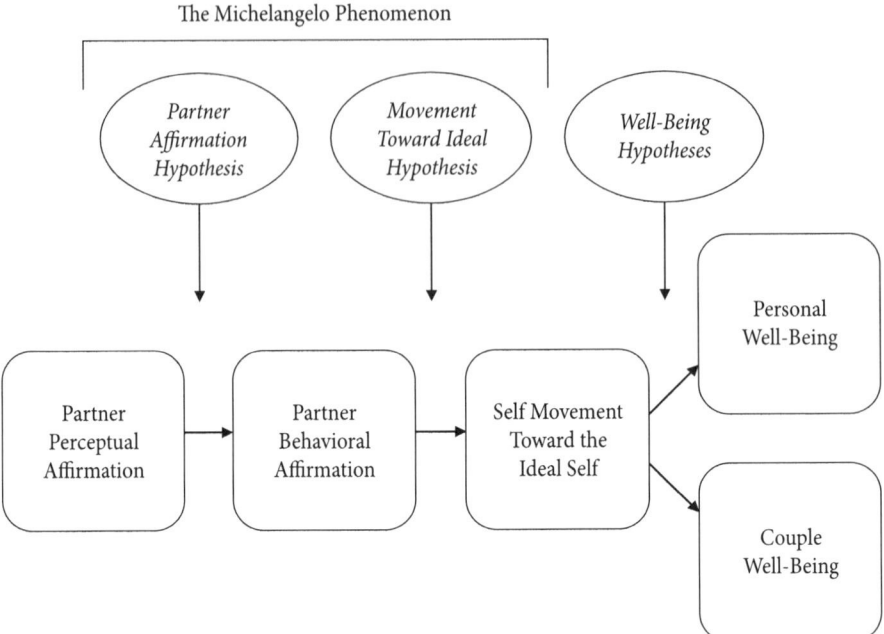

Figure 1. The Michelangelo phenomenon, personal well-being, and couple well-being.

elicit ideal-congruent qualities: Does Mary "draw out the best in John?" In turn, behavioral affirmation yields *self movement toward the ideal* self: John becomes a reflection of that which he ideally wishes to be. This three-step process is the Michelangelo phenomenon (Drigotas, Rusbult, Wieselquist, & Whitton, 1999).

Thus, the Michelangelo metaphor describes a beneficent unfolding of the confirmation process. For instance, imagine that John wants to become a warmer and more affable person. If Mary's perceptions of John are congruent with his ideal self — if she thinks he has the capacity to become a warmer and more affable person — she is likely to "sculpt" toward that ideal, eliciting behaviors that are consistent with John's ideal self. For instance, at a nerve-racking dinner with John's new boss, Mary may direct conversation in such a manner as to elicit a convivial story from John, putting him at ease and helping him display his best self. Over the course of frequent interactions during which Mary helps John display his best self, John will flourish, moving closer to the genuinely genial person that he wishes to become.

Of course, partner sculpting may bring out the best *or* the worst in the self. The concept of affirmation is a continuum, ranging from affirmation at the upper end of the continuum, through failure to affirm, to disaffirmation at the lower end of the continuum. There are two ways in which the process may go awry. First, a partner's perceptions and behavior may be antithetical to the self's ideal. In truth,

Mary may believe that John is socially inept. On the basis of this belief, she may inadvertently (or deliberately) create situations in which John appears inept. John may find it difficult to behave in a friendly and forthcoming manner when Mary is present, and may become increasingly socially awkward. Eventually, John may recognize that he is not at his best around Mary, and may feel dismayed that her opinion of him is antithetical to his ideal self.

Second, a partner's perceptions and behavior may be oriented toward goals that are irrelevant to the self's ideal. For instance, Mary may "love John for the wrong reasons" — she may love him for his strength and instrumental abilities. Mary may praise John for being hardnosed, or may exert effort in support of his professional advancement. John may value Mary's admiration, and may even become a stronger and more instrumental person. However, if strength is not a central component of John's ideal self, then Mary's actions — however positive and well-intentioned — must be seen as irrelevant to that which he holds most dear. Mary will play no role in promoting John's central goals and aspirations, and eventually, John may recognize that Mary has rather thoroughly "missed the boat" about him.

Personal well-being and couple well-being

As illustrated in Figure 1, we suggest that the Michelangelo phenomenon has important consequences for both personal well-being and couple well-being. Why might this phenomenon promote personal well-being? Many social scientists have proposed such an association, arguing that growth striving is a primary human motive. For instance, Freud (1923) argued for such a motive in his discussion of ego ideal, Rogers (1961) and Maslow (1962) described such a motive in terms of self-actualization, and Bowlby (1969) addressed growth striving in his concept of exploration. Contemporary motivation theories, too, emphasize the importance of self-determination and personal growth (Deci & Ryan, 2000; Emmons, 2003). To the extent that striving for personal growth is indeed a primary motive, when people move closer to their ideal selves, this motive is gratified. Thus, movement toward the ideal self should be associated with a wide range of personal benefits, including enhanced life satisfaction and superior psychological adjustment; movement away from the ideal self is likely to yield decrements in personal well-being, in the form of dejection and depression (Higgins, 1987).

Why might this phenomenon promote couple well-being? To begin with, a partner who perceptually affirms the self demonstrates empathic understanding, which in turn should enhance feelings of love ("you see me as I ideally want to be"; Ickes, Stinson, Bissonnette, & Garcia, 1990). In addition, behavioral affirmation promotes outcome correspondence and ease of coordination, in that the behaviors of self and partner are synchronized (rather than at odds) in their orientation to the self ("we act in harmony, toward shared goals"; Rusbult & Van Lange, 2003). And finally, assuming that movement toward the ideal self is gratifying in itself, partners who yield such gratifications are likely to be highly valued ("I'm a better person when I'm with you"; Deci & Ryan, 2000; Emmons, 2003).

Thus, we suggest that individuals grow and relationships flourish *not* so much as a simple consequence of partner enhancement (Mary elicits an idealized image of John; Murray, Holmes, & Griffin, 1996) or partner verification (Mary elicits qualities that are congruent with John's self-perception; Swann, DeLaRonde, & Hixon, 1994) or self-other merger (Mary and John acquire one another's dispositions; Aron & Aron, 2000). Rather, we suggest that individuals and relationships are most likely to flourish when partners effectively elicit and nurture one another's ideal selves; individuals and relationships stagnate and languish when partners block or inhibit one another's movement toward the ideal self.

Empirical evidence regarding the Michelangelo phenomenon

We have observed consistent support for model predictions using both experimental and nonexperimental methods, employing both obtrusive and unobtrusive measures, in the context of a wide range of relationships. For example, in one study we asked each participant to bring a friend to the research session; we obtained descriptions of participants and their partners via both self-report (from participants) and peer report (from friends; Drigotas et al., 1999). Importantly, we observed good support for predictions in analyses examining the association of participant-reported criteria with friend-reported predictors: Friends' descriptions of the participant's partner (does the partner elicit the participant's ideal self?) were predictive of participant descriptions of their own movement toward the ideal self, as well as whether, three months later, the relationship had persisted versus ended.

In other studies we asked couples to discuss each person's pursuit of an important personal goal (Rusbult et al., 2004a, 2004b). We used videotapes of these conversations to develop two types of behavioral measure: (a) participants later reviewed their conversation, providing on-line ratings of both their own and the partner's behavior; and (b) we developed a coding scheme to tap relevant variables, and trained research assistants to rate both target and agent behaviors (e.g., "partner criticized target's goal pursuits," "target expressed determination about goal pursuits"). Independent of this conversation, participants completed measures of personal well-being and couple well-being. Analyses examining both types of behavioral measure revealed that when partners were judged to display more insightful and affirming behaviors, selves exhibited greater confidence about their ideals, selves reported greater subjective well-being, and relationships scored higher in adjustment.

And finally, we have obtained experimental support for model predictions. For example, in a "getting acquainted" study, participants received information about a target person's first impressions — information about traits the target believed they possessed (Kumashiro, Wolf, Coolsen, & Rusbult, 2004). This information centered on qualities the participant had earlier identified as part of his or her ideal self, indifferent self, or feared self. Participants were asked to predict their interaction experiences with the target. In comparison to the feared-self and indifferent-self conditions, in the ideal-self condition — where the target thought the participant possessed ideal-self attributes — participants anticipated that they would like the target more, and predicted that interaction with the target would be more pleasant.

Before moving on, two additional findings should be noted: First, mediation analyses routinely reveal support for our model of direct and indirect causal effects, demonstrating that (a) partner behavioral affirmation significantly (and fully) mediates the association of perceptual affirmation with self movement toward ideal, and (b) self movement toward ideal significantly (yet partially) mediates the association of behavioral affirmation with both personal well-being and couple well-being (Drigotas et al., 1999; Rusbult et al., 2004a, 2004b). (Interestingly, in several studies we have found that [c] in predicting couple well-being, behavioral affirmation may be as important as [or more important than] self movement toward ideal.) Second, analyses of longitudinal data reveal that (a) earlier partner affirmation predicts change over time in movement toward the ideal self, and (b) earlier affirmation *and* movement toward ideal predict change over time in personal well-being and couple well-being (Drigotas et al., 1999; Rusbult et al., 2004a, 2004b). And importantly, such associations are evident even when we statistically control for a variety of potential confounds, including self-esteem, depression, and socially desirable response tendencies (Drigotas et al., 1999; Kumashiro, Rusbult, & Estrada, 2004; Rusbult, 2004a, 2004b).

How the Michelangelo phenomenon differs from other self-relevant interaction processes

Of course, our model is not the only extant theory that addresses self processes in ongoing relationships. Accordingly, it is important to distinguish the Michelangelo phenomenon from related interpersonal processes — processes to which it bears some similarity, or with which it may share some common themes. In the following paragraphs we consider how partner affirmation relates to alternative self-relevant processes.

Partner affirmation and partner enhancement

How does partner affirmation differ from *partner enhancement*, or partner behavior that is exceptionally positive with regard to the self (i.e., idealization, positive illusion)? Many studies have revealed that partner enhancement yields good consequences, demonstrating that selves whose partners view them favorably not only are more satisfied with their relationships, but also develop increasingly positive self-images (e.g., Murray et al., 1996). Empirically, enhancement and affirmation are likely to be positively associated, in that when partners exhibit affirming behavior, their actions are also likely to be experienced as quite positive, or enhancing. To "unconfound" these variables, we must define enhancement in terms of *normative desirability*, or the degree to which an elicited trait is "desirable for people of your age and sex." For example, in the experiment in which participants received false feedback about a target person's first impressions, this information concerned the participant's ideal self, indifferent self, or feared self, *and* was high, medium, or low in normative desirability (Kumashiro et al., 2004b). Analyses performed on key criteria — including liking for the target and anticipated pleasantness of interaction — revealed reliable effects of affirmation, along with weak or nonsignificant effects of enhancement. Thus, in the final analysis, people prefer that their partners elicit behaviors that are positive *and* congruent with their ideal selves, rather than eliciting behaviors that are merely normatively desirable.[2]

Partner affirmation and partner verification

How does partner affirmation relate to *partner verification*, or behavior that elicits the actual self (or the self's *beliefs* about the actual self)? Many studies have revealed that people value feedback that confirms their preexisting self-conceptions. For example, positive partner regard is valued and enhances intimacy among people with high self-esteem, whereas positive partner regard is unpleasant for those with low self-esteem (Swann et al., 1994; also see Swann, this volume). How can we reconcile such findings with work regarding the benefits of partner affirmation? First, we suggest that to competently affirm the self's ideal, partners must accurately perceive the block of stone they seek to sculpt (e.g., what possibilities are inherent in the block, what flaws must be circumvented?) — that is, to affirm John,

Mary must possess a reasonably accurate (implicit or explicit) understanding of his actual self. Second, we suggest that although selves may appreciate partners who accurately perceive their strengths *and* limitations, they also want to be loved despite their limitations, and hope that the partner will behave in such a manner as to help translate the actual self into the ideal self. We have conducted several studies to examine the simultaneous effects of affirmation and verification, and have found that (a) partner affirmation consistently accounts for unique variance in key criteria beyond partner verification, (b) partner verification frequently accounts for unique variance beyond partner affirmation, and (c) the associations among Michelangelo model variables typically are not moderated by the self's level of self-esteem (Drigotas et al., 1999; Kumashiro et al., 2004a; Rusbult et al., 2004a, 2004b). Thus, it is well and good to have a partner "let you be the real you," but it is equally important that the partner "help you become the ideal you." Moreover, there is no necessary inconsistency between eliciting another's actual self and eliciting his or her ideal self. These variables sometimes operate in concert, such that both tendencies contribute to personal growth and couple vitality.

Partner affirmation and self-other merger

How does the Michelangelo phenomenon differ from self-other merger (Aron & Aron, 2000)? Humans arguably are motivated by the need for *self-expansion* — for greater physical and social influence, cognitive complexity, and social identity. Some research suggests that close involvement provides a means of self-expansion, in that strong interdependence involves *inclusion of other in the self*, or incorporating a partner's attributes and resources (Aron & Aron, 2000). However, it is unclear whether the benefits of self-other merger are attributable to the full panoply of acquired partner attributes, or whether such benefits are mainly attributable to the acquisition of desirable partner attributes. We suggest that it is not straightforward self-expansion, but ideal-self-expansion — or expansion toward the ideal self — that promotes personal well-being and couple vitality. That is, including Mary in his self should benefit John mainly when such inclusion promotes John's movement toward his ideal self; embracing Mary's less-than-ideal dispositions is unlikely to be helpful. Moreover, we suggest that beneficial self-other merger may come about in part because a partner possesses key components of the self's ideal. In two studies examining this line of reasoning, mediation analyses demonstrated that: (a) Michelangelo model variables partially to wholly mediate the associations of self-other merger with key criteria; (b) partner possession of the self's ideal partially mediates the associations of Michelangelo model variables with key criteria; and (c) partner possession of the self's ideal partially to wholly accounts for the associations of self-other merger with key criteria (Rusbult et al., 2004a, 2004b). Thus, self-other merger is particularly beneficial when it entails acquiring partner qualities that are components of one's ideal self. Moreover, when a partner possesses qualities that are important components of one's ideal, the partner is better able to affirm the self's ideal (encouraging and challenging the self) and the self is better able to use the partner as a model and inspiration for movement toward the ideal.

Partner affirmation and the Pygmalion phenomenon

How does the Michelangelo phenomenon differ from the *Pygmalion phenomenon*? Whereas the Michelangelo phenomenon describes a partner who sculpts toward the *self's* ideal, the Pygmalion phenomenon describes a partner who sculpts toward the *partner's* ideal. Of course, if the self's ideal and the partner's ideal are compatible, this issue becomes moot. However, in two longitudinal studies, we have found that when self ideals and partner ideals for the self are incompatible, a partner's inclination to "foist his or her own ideals onto the self" yields negative consequences (Rusbult et al., 2004a, 2004b). Thus, not all sculpting is beneficial. When partners sculpt one another toward their own ideals rather than the self's ideals — even when such sculpting is masterful and yields a lovely product — the consequences are maladaptive for both selves and couples.

Self processes and partner processes in the Michelangelo phenomenon

Self processes: The block of stone and the slumbering figure

Our work emphasizes internally-defined ideals — the goals the self genuinely wishes to achieve, not the goals that parents, colleagues, friends, or lovers think the self *ought* to achieve. In distinguishing between the *ideal self* and the *ought self*, it has been argued that: (a) pursuit of the ideal self centers on aspirations, whereas pursuit of the ought self centers on obligations; (b) movement toward the ideal self yields exhilaration, whereas movement toward the ought self yields comfort; and (c) disparities from the ideal self induce dejection, whereas disparities from the ought self induce anxiety (Higgins, 1987, 1996). As such, pursuit of the ideal self is at the core of personal growth strivings. Of course, the emergence of the ideal self is not necessarily a solitary activity — selves may embrace ideals with interpersonal origins. For instance, John's desire to acquire greater warmth may be shaped by the fact that he adored his Aunt Rosemary, an easy-going woman with a talent for putting others at ease. Or for instance, Mary may seek to become an art history expert in part because John introduced her to the world of art during their travels in Italy.

We suggest that the emergence and evolution of the ideal self may best be described as an incremental process — that is: (a) although ideals may sometimes emerge full-blown in a flash of insight, they may just as often (perhaps even typically) develop in a gradual, step-by-step manner; (b) the emergence and modification of ideals may entail systematic or automatic cognitive processes — the ideal self may comprise carefully articulated goals or vaguely conceived yearnings, it may be a salient component of the self's everyday activities or may exist largely at an unconscious level; and (c) the ideal self is not a static construct — ideals typically evolve over time. Moreover, we suggest that motivation to realize one's ideal self is relatively constant across the lifespan. Although the character of the ideal self may vary over the life course — centering on industry or professional achievement at one life stage, centering on intimacy at another stage, and centering on generativity or ego integrity at yet other stages (Erikson, 1950) — we assume that the desire to realize one's ideals (whatever their character) is a relatively abiding human concern.

What qualities of the self are relevant to understanding movement toward one's ideal? In ongoing work we are examining three classes of variable that are relevant to understanding the Michelangelo phenomenon — to variables resting on the self's insight, ability, and motivation. First, movement toward the ideal self should be more probable to the extent that individuals possess greater *insight*, or greater clarity in their actual and ideal selves. Second, movement toward the ideal self should be more probable to the extent that an individual possesses adequate *ability*, including goal-relevant skills, control over relevant resources, the ability to develop strategies for goal attainment, and a sense of efficacy with respect to the goal at hand. And third, movement toward the ideal self should be more probable to the extent that *motivation* is greater, including commitment to the goal, the inclination to delay gratification, high self-esteem and self-confidence, and strong promotion orientation.

Of course, although some ideals are pursued and attained chiefly as a result of the self's actions, selves frequently benefit from the backing of insightful, able, and motivated sculptors. In ongoing work, we are also addressing qualities of the self that *elicit* partner affirmation. Partner affirmation should be facilitated to the extent that an individual: (a) *elicits partner insight*, or clear understanding of the self's ideals (John must make his ideals "visible" to Mary, sharing his dreams and aspirations); (b) *elicits partner ability*, or calls forth the skills that are relevant to promoting the self's ideals (John must capably signal his needs and convey what types of assistance would be most helpful); and (c) *elicits partner motivation*, or genuine desire to promote the self's ideals (John must inspire Mary's commitment to his goals, and express gratitude for her efforts on his behalf).

Partner processes: The sculptor and the slumbering figure

By what mechanisms do partners "select" certain of the self's behaviors, motives, or dispositions? First, partners may engage in *retroactive selection*, wherein they reward (or punish) certain of the self's preferences or behaviors. For instance, when John enacts warm and friendly behaviors at a dinner party, Mary may reinforce such behavior by affectionately touching his arm. Second, partners may engage in *preemptive selection*, wherein they enact specific behaviors that elicit (or inhibit) certain preferences or behaviors on the part of the self. For instance, in a situation wherein John might normally feel self-conscious, Mary may call attention to a photograph of John's closest buddies, thereby introducing a signal that instigates a calm and caring mood. And third, partners may engage in *situation selection*, wherein they create situations in which certain of the self's preferences or behaviors become more probable (or less probable). For instance, at a nerve-racking dinner party, Mary may preemptively steer conversation in such a manner as to elicit John's warm and other-oriented behaviors.

Moreover, some forms of affirmation are active (steering the self toward situations in which the self will excel) whereas others are passive (providing unconditional support, a secure emotional environment); some forms are deliberate (offering information, instrumental support) whereas others are inadvertent (unconsciously serving as a model). And importantly, affirmation is not necessarily warm and gentle; sometimes affirming behavior is "tough." For instance, Mary may sometimes affirm John by crossly telling him to quit thinking about himself and instead put himself in others' shoes, imagining what would make others feel loved and valued. Also, effective affirmation is not necessarily consciously controlled (Bargh & Chartrand, 1999): On some occasions Mary may consciously seek to promote John's warm and caring behavior; on other occasions she may unconsciously and automatically exhibit affirming perception and behavior. For instance, if Mary believes that "kindness defines good manners," she may project her ideals onto John, unconsciously behaving toward him as she, herself, would most like to be treated.

In our ongoing work, we assume that the partner attributes promoting effective affirmation can also be characterized in terms of insight, ability, and motivation. First, effective affirmation should be facilitated by *partner insight*, or a clear understanding of the self's actual and ideal selves; accurate knowledge should be enhanced by variables such as empathy and perspective-taking. Second, effective affirmation should be enhanced by *partner ability*, or possession of the skills and resources relevant to promoting the self's ideals — proposing effective strategies, delivering the precise type of assistance that is needed (instrumental *and* social-emotional support), directly assisting the self, and actively participating in the self's goal pursuits. And third, effective affirmation should be facilitated by *partner motivation*, or genuine desire to promote the self's ideal — unconditional support, genuine enthusiasm for the self's goal pursuits, willingness to sometimes sacrifice personal interests to promote the self's goals (exerting effort, enduring costs), and an inclination to regard the self's pursuits as a "team effort."

Conclusions

Our work incorporates concepts from the behavioral confirmation, self-discrepancy, and interdependence traditions to identify processes that are central to understanding the self in its relational context. The Michelangelo phenomenon is a congenial pattern of interdependence in which close partners sculpt one another in such a manner as to bring each person closer to his or her ideal self. To date, empirical evidence suggests that key components of this phenomenon relate to one another in predicted ways. Recent findings also begin to identify the processes and mechanisms that underlie the Michelangelo phenomenon, including a variety of self and partner dispositions, motives, and behavioral tendencies. We hope that such findings may extend our understanding of the social nature of the self, highlighting one means by which adaptation to interdependence partners shapes human dispositions, values, and behavioral tendencies.

Acknowledgment

The research reviewed in this essay was supported by grants from the National Science Foundation (BCS–0132398), Fetzer Institute, and Templeton Foundation.

Notes

1. The two members of a dyad may act as both target and agent. Throughout this essay, we use "self" to describe the target, or the object of another's perception and behavior, and we use "partner" to describe the agent, or the person who directs behavior toward the target and influences the target's dispositions, values, and behavioral tendencies.

2. Of course, this issue frequently boils down to terminology, in that when researchers operationally define enhancement in terms of *what the self regards as positive* (e.g., as in Murray et al.,
1996), enhancement is tantamount to affirmation (and, perhaps, should be described as such).

References

Aron, A., & Aron, E. (2000). Self-expansion motivation and including other in the self. In W.
Ickes & S. Duck (Eds.), *The social psychology of personal relationships* (pp. 109–128). New
York: Wiley.

Bargh, J. A., & Chartrand, T. L. (1999). The unbearable automaticity of being. *American Psychologist, 54,* 462–479.

Bowlby, J. (1969). *Attachment and loss: Vol. 1, Attachment.* New York: Basic Books.

Darley, J. M., & Fazio, R. H. (1980). Expectancy confirmation processes arising in the social
interaction sequence. *American Psychologist, 35,* 867–881.

Deci, E. L., & Ryan, R. M. (2000). The "what" and "why" of goal pursuits: Human needs and the
self-determination of behavior. *Journal of Health and Social Behavior, 2,* 237–256.

Drigotas, S. M., Rusbult, C. E., Wieselquist, J., & Whitton, S. (1999). Close partner as sculptor of
the ideal self: Behavioral affirmation and the Michelangelo phenomenon. *Journal of Personality and Social Psychology, 77,* 293–323.

Emmons, R. A. (2003). Personal goals, life meaning, and virtue: Wellsprings of a positive life.
In C. L. Keyes & J. Haidt (Eds.), *Flourishing: Positive psychology and the life well-lived* (pp.
105–128). Washington: APA.

Erikson, E. (1950). *Childhood and society* (2nd Ed.; pp. 247–269). New York: W. W. Norton.

Freud, S. (1923). *The ego and the id.* New York: Norton.

Gombrich, E. H. (1995). *The story of art* (16th Ed.). London: Phaidon.

Gotlib, I. H., & Whiffen, V. E. (1991). The interpersonal context of depression: Implications for
theory and research. In W. H. Jones & D. Perlman (Eds.), *Advances in personal relationships*
(Vol. 3, pp. 177–206). London: Kingsley.

Harris, M. J., & Rosenthal, R. (1985). Mediation of interpersonal expectancy effects: 31 meta-
analyses. *Psychological Bulletin, 97,* 363–386.

Higgins, E. T. (1987). Self-discrepancy: A theory relating self and affect. *Psychological Review,
94,* 319–340.

Higgins, E. T. (1996). The "self digest": Self-knowledge serving self-regulatory functions. *Journal
of Personality and Social Psychology, 71,* 1062–1083.

Ickes, W., Stinson, L., Bissonnette, V., & Garcia, S. (1990). Naturalistic social cognition: Empathic accuracy in mixed-sex dyads. *Journal of Personality and Social Psychology, 59,* 730–742.

Kelley, H. H., & Thibaut, J. W. (1978). *Interpersonal relations: A theory of interdependence.* New
York: Wiley.

Kumashiro, M., Rusbult, C. E., & Estrada, M. J. (2004a). *The Michelangelo phenomenon in everyday life: An interaction record study of self and partner processes.* Unpublished manuscript,
University of North Carolina, Chapel Hill, NC.

Kumashiro, M., Wolf, S., Coolsen, M., & Rusbult, C. E. (2004b). *Partner affirmation, verification,
and enhancement as determinants of attraction to potential dates: Experimental evidence of
the unique effect of affirmation.* Unpublished manuscript, University of North Carolina,
Chapel Hill, NC.

Markus, H., & Nurius, P. (1986). Possible selves. *American Psychologist, 41*, 954–969.

Maslow, A. H. (1962). *Toward a psychology of being.* Princeton, NJ: Van Nostrand.

Moretti, M. M., & Higgins, E. T. (1990). Relating self-discrepancy to self-esteem: The contribution of discrepancy beyond actual-self ratings. *Journal of Experimental Social Psychology, 26*, 108–123.

Murray, S. L., Holmes, J. G., & Griffin, D. W. (1996). The self-fulfilling nature of positive illusions in romantic relationships: Love is not blind, but prescient. *Journal of Personality and Social Psychology, 71*, 1155–1180.

Rogers, C. R. (1961). *On becoming a person.* Boston: Houghton Mifflin.

Rusbult, C. E., Coolsen, M., Kirchner, J., Stocker, S., Kumashiro, M., Wolf, S., Estrada, M. J., & Clarke, J. (2004a). *Partner affirmation and self movement toward ideal in newly-committed relationships.* Unpublished manuscript, University of North Carolina, Chapel Hill, NC.

Rusbult, C. E., Kumashiro, M., Finkel, E., Kirchner, J., Coolsen, M., Stocker, S., & Clarke, J. (2004b). *A longitudinal study of the Michelangelo phenomenon in marital relationships.* Unpublished manuscript, University of North Carolina, Chapel Hill, NC.

Rusbult, C. E., & Van Lange, P. A. M. (2003). Interdependence, interaction, and relationships. *Annual Review of Psychology, 54*, 351–375.

Snyder, M., Tanke, E., & Berscheid, E. (1977). Social perception and interpersonal behavior: On the self-fulfilling nature of social stereotypes. *Journal of Personality and Social Psychology, 35*, 656–666.

Swann, W. B., Jr., DeLaRonde, C., & Hixon, J. G. (1994). Authenticity and positivity strivings in marriage and courtship. *Journal of Personality and Social Psychology, 66*, 857–869.

Constructing perspectives in the social making of minds

Jeremy I.M. Carpendale[1], Charlie Lewis[2], Ulrich Müller[3] and Timothy P. Racine[4]
[1]Simon Fraser University / [2]Lancaster University / [3]University of Victoria / [4]University of Manitoba

The ability to take others' perspectives on the self has important psychological implications. Yet the logically and developmentally prior question is how children develop the capacity to take others' perspectives. We discuss the development of joint attention in infancy as a rudimentary form of perspective taking and critique examples of biological and individualistic approaches to the development of joint attention. As an alternative, we present an activity-based relational perspective according to which infants develop the capacity to coordinate attention with others by differentiating the perspectives of self and other from shared activity. Joint attention is then closely related to language development, which makes further social development possible. We argue that the ability to take the perspective of others on the self gives rise to the possibility of language, rationality and culture.

Constructing perspectives in the social making of minds

How an awareness of others' perspectives on the self influences development is the complex and important question that this volume is organized around. Classic and recent developmental theories recognize that the ability to take the perspective of others toward the self contributes to the development of language (Tomasello, 2003), rationality (Mead, 1934; Piaget, 1977/1995; Vygotsky, 1934/1986), and morality (Piaget, 1932/1965; Kohlberg, 1981). In this article, we focus on the question of how the awareness of other perspectives arises in the first place. The origin of the perspective taking ability is logically and developmentally prior to the issue of how the awareness of other perspectives influences development. To explore the emergence of a rudimentary form of perspective taking we review research on the development of the infant's ability to share or coordinate attention with an adult in triadic interaction involving the self, other and the world. The ability to establish "joint attention" within such a triadic framework is considered to be an important milestone toward the awareness of other perspectives. We first briefly review research on the developmental course of joint attention. Next, we critique examples of nativist and individualistic theories that have been proposed to explain its development. We then present our relational, activity-based constructivist approach to the development of perspective taking, according to which infants first distinguish and then coordinate the perspectives of self and other. Finally, we discuss how the emergence of an initial form of perspective taking influences language development, which, in turn, makes more complex forms of perspective taking possible; forms which are currently discussed under the label of children's "theories of mind." In the end, we argue that perspective-taking, cognition and language are mutually constitutive of one another and are influenced by children's engagement in ever more complex social processes.

Joint attention

Joint attention occurs within many different forms of interaction (Tomasello, 1995). One form is gaze following, which is demonstrated when an adult establishes eye contact with an infant and then turns to look to one side and the infant follows the adult's direction of gaze. Pointing gestures constitute another type of joint attention. Pointing may be used for different purposes, but two of the main functions that have been described in the literature are making requests (proto-imperatives) and directing others' attention (protodeclaratives) (Bates, 1976). Parents understand the protoimperative as communicating, "Get that for me" or "I want that." Protodeclaratives serve to express interest or engage another person. Although these abilities seem prima facie to reflect some understanding of attention, what psychological hay to make of these activities is an area of considerable debate in the literature.

There is general agreement though that infants' capacity for joint attention is of "cosmic importance" (Bates, 1979, p. 33). For Tomasello (1999) this is a small but essential acquisition that makes human forms of cognition possible and there are grounds for assuming that the rest of social cognitive development is "icing on the cake" compared to the importance of joint attention. It is the foundation on which language, culture and history are built. Joint attention seems to be required for word learning (Baldwin, 1995) and opens the door to more sophisticated forms of social interaction. It is correlated with later social and language development measures (Carpenter, Nagell, & Tomasello, 1998). Also, difficulties with this form of interaction (especially pointing not to make requests but just to direct others' attention) often, but not always, indicate autism (Baron-Cohen, Allen, & Gillberg, 1992; Hobson, 2002). As far as we know we are the only life forms on the planet, indeed the only part of the universe, that is aware of itself. This is made possible through the ability to take the perspective of others on the self. Although there is general agreement about the importance of perspective taking for further social and cognitive development, controversies arise with respect to two closely intertwined issues: the age at which joint attention develops and the definition of joint attention.

When does joint attention arise?

Researchers disagree about the particular age at which joint attention emerges. This is due to the fact that some forms of gaze following appear as early as 3 or 4 months of age. Other more complex forms, however, do not emerge until children are about 12, 15, or even 18 months old. Part of this controversy hinges on the way gaze following is assessed and on the strictness of the scoring criteria that are applied — that is, what researchers count as successful gaze following. For example, 3-month-old infants have some ability to follow another person's gaze and to locate objects if the objects are close by within their visual field but they fail to follow gaze to objects that are further away. When presented with two objects in their visual field and the adult is looking at the one that is further away from the infant, six-month-old infants usually fail to locate the object the adult is looking at because they stop at the first interesting object they see on their scan path. By contrast, 12-month-old infants will go on to find the object that the adult is looking at (Butterworth, 2001). Such findings suggest that rather than an all-or-none phenomenon it may be more fertile to distinguish different levels in the development of gaze following (Müller & Carpendale, 2004).

There is some controversy about whether there are also different levels of complexity of pointing gestures. Infants generally begin pointing at 11 to 12 months, on average, but onset of pointing ranges from 8 to 13 months (Butterworth, 2001). Moore and D'Entremont (2001) reported that at 1 year of age infants' pointing did not depend on whether or not their parent had already seen the interesting sight. But at 2 years of age infants pointed more when their parent had not seen the interesting sight or was not looking at it, reflecting a more sophisticated understanding of the role of pointing in interaction. However, Liszkowski, Carpenter, Henning, Striano, and Tomasello (2004) report evidence supporting their claim that at 12 months infants point in order to direct others' attention because infants respond differently depending on the adult's response to their pointing gestures.

Defining joint attention

The controversy about *when* joint attention develops is related to exactly *what* is meant by joint attention. Furthermore, this is also related to what we think these forms of interaction involving joint attention reveal about infants' social understanding, and even whether we should group all forms of interaction involving joint attention together. In order to bring out this point, we need to discuss different definitions of joint attention.

A common definition of joint attention is, "Looking where someone else is looking" (Butterworth, 1998, p. 171). This captures an important aspect of the phenomenon, but we need to refine this definition because otherwise it would include cases of "passive joint attention", simple "on looking" (Bakeman & Adamson, 1984) or "simultaneous looking" (Tomasello, 1995). What is essential to joint attention is that "Two individuals know that they are attending to something in common" (Tomasello, 1995, p. 106). Joint attention is not just looking in the same place; it also involves being aware that one's attention is shared with someone else (Baldwin, 1906).

Because attention may be shared only from the observer's but not the infant's point of view, it is a difficult problem to establish clear-cut criteria for the occurrence of episodes of joint attention in infancy. The only indicator available to the researcher is the infant's behavior, and this behavior can be interpreted in a rich or lean way. Richly interpreted, joint attention interaction is assumed to reveal an "implicit theory of mind" (Bretherton, 1991). This rich interpretation has been referred to as the "commonsense view" (Moore & Corkum, 1994, p. 351), according to which it is assumed that the infant understands the psychological relation between the adult and what the adults sees, and that "the infant is able to represent both self and other as seeing objects."

One way to consider leaner interpretations is to look at research with chimpanzees. Chimpanzees can follow gaze, but a series of experiments conducted by Povinelli and Eddy (1996) suggests that they do not seem to fully understand the psychological significance of seeing. For example, chimpanzees are just as likely to beg from someone who clearly cannot see them because she has her eyes closed or even has a bucket over her head as they are to beg from someone who is looking directly at them. However, more recent research by Tomasello, Call, and Hare (2003) shows that in competitive situations subordinate chimpanzees attempt to get pieces of food that a dominant chimpanzee has not seen rather than pieces of food that the dominant chimpanzee has seen, suggesting an understanding of the behavioral implications of seeing. Povinelli, Bering, and Giambrone (2003) are also skeptical about chimpanzees' use of pointing gestures. However, Leavens, Hopkins, and Thomas (2004, p. 56) found that "captive chimpanzees exhibit referential communication through manual gesture with no explicit training to do so," perhaps because a problem situation they share with human infants is a "dependency on others to obtain otherwise unattainable objects." One lesson to draw from research with nonhuman primates is that a commonsense assumption that interaction involving joint attention necessarily reveals a full understanding of attention should be questioned. In gaze following, for example, it is not clear that an infant or chimpanzee knows they are attending to the same state of affairs as another. A lean interpretation should not, however, discount early abilities but rather distinguish them from later forms and provide a developmental account.

From a lean perspective, infants first engage in triadic interaction without any clear understanding of others' attention and they gradually develop such understanding within this interaction. The transition from unintentional communication to intentional (self-conscious) communication can be characterized in various ways such as shared versus joint attention, or "passive" versus "coordinated" joint attention (Bakeman & Adamson, 1984). For example, when young infants cry this communicates their hunger or distress to their parent — that is, this influences others' behavior but without any conscious awareness or intention (Chapman, 1991, p. 213). Later in development crying could become intentional communication (Chapman, 1991). The task is to explain how infants develop from the form of communication in the situation of a dog scratching at a door to be let in, versus a person knocking at a door. The dog has just learned to scratch at the door because it works, but the person comes to have some awareness of the meaning being conveyed.

Theories of infant social development

Different theories have been proposed to explain the origin of joint attention in infancy. We present exemplars of nativist and individualistic approaches to joint attention. We then contrast these approaches with out own relational, activity-based approach. From a nativist perspective, Baron-Cohen (1995, p. 12) claims that "mindreading has an innate, biological, modular basis." He draws on the idea from evolutionary psychology that the mind consists of a series of innate modules that have evolved to solve particular problems that were present in the ancestral environment. Some of these modules or mechanisms unfold to enable joint attention to be computed. One mechanism detects intentional action and a second detects eye direction. These mechanisms produce dyadic representations that link an agent to an object. A third mechanism coordinates this information to determine if self and other are both attending to the same thing, producing shared attention. The fourth mechanism is the theory of mind module.

There are a number of problems with this approach. For example, Tomasello (1999) has argued that there has not been enough evolutionary time to evolve a series of modules such as those proposed by Baron-Cohen (1995). Instead, Tomasello (1999) has proposed that we should be looking for a small adaptation that made a big difference for human cognition, and he suggested that the capacity for joint attention itself is a likely candidate. Secondly, Moore (1996, p. 25) pointed out that to begin with infants use head turns and not eye direction in gaze following. The use of eye direction only comes later. Thirdly, joint attention cannot be modular in the sense of being restricted to the domain of social cognition because gaze following and pointing require some understanding of space (Müller & Carpendale, 2004). Fourthly, it is one thing to explain the evolution of shared attention in the sense of looking in the same place. However, it is something entirely different to explain joint attention because the latter involves the understanding and conveying of meaning. It is not just a matter of looking in the same direction as another, but of also realizing that attention is being shared. Finally, to rely on a modular algorithm to compute even lower-order mental states like intentions, Baron-Cohen must assume that meanings are fixed. However, meaning is indexical, and algorithms cannot be (Racine, 2002). Pointing, as an example of joint attention, cannot be a fixed innate pattern because, like human language in general, it conveys different meaning in different sequences of interaction, and so it is unlike animal communication systems (for a discussion of this view of language see Turnbull, 2003).

However, humans have obviously evolved the capacity to develop joint attention and so it is important to think about the biological adaptations that allow human infants to develop the ability to engage in triadic interaction. To speculate from the perspective of a relational position, these adaptations would include factors such as the extended period of dependency in human infancy that ensures social interaction (Vygotsky, 1998). Portmann (1944/1990) has argued that human infants are born approximately one year earlier than other similar mammals. This period of dependency has a high cost and it must have a correspondingly high pay off. It means that a great deal of early development occurs within a social context rather than in the womb — a period of "social gestation." Also motivational factors, like an interest in faces and emotional engagement with others, would be important to ensure that infants are engaged in social interaction. Clearly the capacity to benefit from such experience is also essential. These are some of the ingredients needed in order for the infant to be engaged in the kind of interpersonal interaction in which they can develop social understanding.

We still have to account for how joint attention develops. In addition to modular perspectives there are also a number of theories meant to account for the *development* of joint attention. Many current approaches to this problem are individualistic in nature in the sense that they start from the perspective of the individual's self-knowledge, and stipulate that the knowledge of others' minds is derived from self-knowledge, usually through analogical reasoning. That is, infants are assumed to have knowledge of their own inner experience, they see others as "like me" and they reason by analogy that the other may have the same inner experience that goes along with the outer manifestation (Meltzoff, Gopnik, & Repacholi, 1999; Tomasello, 1995, 1999).

The analogical argument is old and has, in the past, drawn many criticisms. For example, it assumes that the infant first understands her own intentions. But for the infant to understand her own intentions would require the assumption that intentions are some sort of inner entity that could be introspected upon. Wittgenstein (1968), however, argued instead that intentions are aspects of activity. Adults can think about intentions because they have a language for talking about this aspect of human activity. Furthermore, a logical difficulty is that the argument already assumes what it is meant to explain. That is, it assumes an understanding of self and other for this sort of reasoning to work. Otherwise when the infant observes another person and uses the analogical argument to infer the other person's mental states, the logical conclusion of the argument would be, 'there goes another one of my mental states' (see Müller & Carpendale, 2004; Scheler, 1970; Soffer, 1999). Of course, analogical reasoning is possible once children have developed a self-other distinction, but it cannot be the source of that distinction.

A relational approach to social development

An alternative to the individualistic approach is a relational framework (Carpendale & Lewis, 2004, 2006; Jopling, 1993; Müller & Carpendale, 2004), which holds that there is initially a relative lack of differentiation between the perspectives of the infant and others. The starting point of an undifferentiated activity matrix has been described as "adualism" (Baldwin, 1906), or "great-we" (Vygotsky, 1998, p. 233), or "radical egocentrism", as if the infant "were the centre of the universe — but a centre that is unaware of itself" (Piaget, 1970/1972, p. 21), "undifferentiated group life" (Merleau-Ponty, 1964, p. 119), a "primordial sharing situation" (Werner & Kaplan, 1963), or a "primordial soup" (Hobson, 1993).

We should first deal with a possible objection to the relational perspective. It is sometimes claimed that Piaget and others assumed "that infants at first are unable to differentiate between stimuli belonging to the self versus the environment" (Gergely, 2002, p. 27). This interpretation of egocentrism and adualism encounters problems because there is evidence that young infants do respond differently to external and self-stimulation. For example, Rochat and Hespos (1997) reported that newborn and 4-week-old infants respond differentially to their own hand versus the experimenter's finger touching their cheek. Furthermore, Rochat and Striano (2002) found that by 4 months of age infants react differently to video images of themselves versus an experimenter mimicking them. However, infants' ability to respond differentially in different conditions reveals nothing about their understanding of self and other. Rochat and Striano (2002, p. 44) acknowledge that their finding does not mean that infants at this age "actually recognize themselves or express conceptual self-awareness." Secondly, and contrary to Gergely's interpretation of Piaget, an ability to distinguish self from other stimulation would be required in order to experience being an agent in the world, which is the foundation on which development is based for Piaget (Russell, 1996) and would be essential in the development of a self-other distinction.

From a relational approach, social understanding is grounded in interpersonal relatedness: "The infant must discover her own mind in interaction with others" (Müller & Runions, 2003, p. 47). From this perspective, "psychogenesis begins in a state where the child is unaware of himself and the other as different beings" (Merleau-Ponty, 1964, p. 119). From an observer's point of view we see the infant interacting with others and the world, but at first the infant has not developed these distinctions (Piaget, 1977/1995; Vygotsky, 1998). The distinctions between self and other are gradually constructed by the infant through activity.

We need to explain the transition from conveying meaning unintentionally, or without consciousness, such as the young infant or the trained chimpanzee extending an arm and index finger and having what they want given to them, to the older child conveying meaning intentionally or consciously. From a relational approach we begin with activity. The idea of 'attention' is an adult psychological concept but young infants first develop an awareness of others' attentiveness or activity being directed toward aspects of the world (Hobson, 2002). This is an understanding of the behavioral directedness of others toward objects independent of one's own directedness. From a relational approach, infants come to make distinctions between the perspectives of self and other through forming schemes for activity with caregivers, or sets of expectations about interaction. Such action schemes or expectations involving gaze following, pointing and other forms of interaction are gradually combined, resulting in more consolidated and flexible practical knowledge or sets of expectations about interacting with people. Such consolidation enables infants to interact with others in a form of interaction that involves coordinating attention — at first with more support from others and the environment, and slowly requiring less help.

The assumptions of the relational framework that self and other initially form a tightly interlocked, undifferentiated activity matrix, and that social development in the first years of life mainly consists of the increasing differentiation and integration of self- and other-directedness, provide the basis for a meaningful interpretation of behavioral changes in infants' social-emotional behavior. Let us illustrate the fertility of these assumptions for understanding changes in emotional responses, gaze following, and the understanding of pointing.

With respect to emotional development, it has been shown that young infants respond to distress behaviors by others by being distressed themselves (Bischof-Köhler, 1989; Hoffman, 1991; Piaget, 1945/1962, Obs. 2). Infants' responses are due to contagion (i.e., the distress cues from another person are confounded with unpleasant feelings that are aroused in the self; see Hoffman, 1991). Anybody who has visited a nursery in the hospital and seen, or heard, the powerful repercussions of one infant starting to cry will be familiar with this phenomenon. Contagion reflects a lack of differentiating between self and other; the relation between self and other is immediate, the infant resonates with another person but is not able to "distance" herself from another person (Vygotsky, 1978). By contrast, when infants are about 18 months old, they respond to the distress cues of another person by trying to console the other person (often in an egocentric manner by giving the other person their favorite toy; see Bischof-Köhler, 1989; Zahn-Waxler, Radke-Yarrow, Wagner, & Chapman, 1992). These empathic responses must be based on some rudimentary differentiation between the other person's emotional expression and infants' own emotions because the infants' responses are more appropriate to the other person's situation than to their own situation (Hoffman, 1991). In other words, the emergence of empathic responses indicates that the infant has differentiated herself from the other to such an extent that she is capable of understanding the other's emotion in relation to the other's situation (i.e., in a mediated way).

With respect to gaze following, it has been found that 7-month-old infants will look on successive trials in the same direction in which they encountered an interesting event on previous trials, regardless of the direction in which an adult turns her head and directs her gaze on these successive trials (Corkum & Moore, 1998). This perseverative looking behavior indicates that at this age infants do not yet understand that another person can establish spatial relations with objects that are independent of their own spatial relations.

The final illustration of the process of differentiation comes from infants' understanding of pointing. Before they follow the other person's point (i.e., around 12 to 13 months of age), infants frequently look at the hand of the person pointing, and not at the object referred to (Desrochers, Morrisette, & Ricard, 1995). Infants' difficulty with displacing the reference from the pointing finger to the object

pointed at indicates that they do not understand the other person as an independent agent who can establish spatial relations with an object that are independent
of the infants' own spatial relations.

The relational framework suggests that the self-other differentiation occurs in
the context of interactions between the infant and other persons. Specifically, the
coordination of actions in social practices (e.g., Piaget, 1936/1963, on the feeding
situation) leads to a mediation of the self-other relations by means of which the
infant becomes increasingly capable of distancing herself from the other person,
and, at the same time, of more deliberately and flexibly coordinating her actions
with the person. Situations in which the other person presents an obstacle to the
infant's projects, issues prohibitions, or violates expectations provide the germ
cell for recognizing that the other person is directed toward objects in a manner
that is independent from the infant. Initially, the other person's agency may just
be understood in an unspecific manner (e.g., interesting things happen when the
other person is around) or negatively (e.g., as a force that presents an obstacle, see
Piaget, 1936/1963). However, in the course of social interactions, infants learn to
understand the other as a person who is actively directed toward specific things
(e.g., understanding declarative gestures). In order to illuminate the process of
self-other differentiation and integration, it would be useful if future studies examined how social practices (and the disruption of social interactions) contribute
to this differentiation. Specifically, these studies should be longitudinal in design,
and they should combine natural observations (caregiver-child interaction) and
experimental procedures (e.g., controlled contexts for measuring gaze following,
comprehension and production of pointing, training studies testing effect of style
of parent-infant/child interaction on joint attention skill, etc.).

The role of language in the development of further forms of perspective taking

The ability to follow flexibly and direct others' attention is foundational for language. Language is essentially triadic in structure; it involves directing others' attention within a situation of shared attention (Tomasello, 2003). Language is then
a means for further development in taking others' perspectives in more complex
settings. Further levels of perspective taking require a more sophisticated understanding of the psychological world. How do children develop such an understanding of other minds? That is, given the level of social understanding involved
in joint attention interaction, which involves some appreciation of other perspectives, how do children take the next step into understanding other minds and the
psychological world of beliefs, desires and intentions? Most approaches under the
banner of 'theory-of-mind' share a focus upon the child as an individual, even

though they differ in their proposed answers. From the theory-theory perspective the child learns about minds by inference and forms a theory about beliefs, intentions and desires as causal inner entities. Other approaches assume that introspection on one's own beliefs and intentions is important. From the innate module perspective, German & Leslie (2004) state that the theory of mind mechanism is essential because it "allows the young brain to *attend* to ... mental states despite the fact that such states cannot be seen, heard, felt, or otherwise sensed" (emphasis original). What could it mean to have an innate ability to attend to something that can be "neither seen, heard not felt"? Something must be observable.

This way of setting up the problem that children must solve is the real issue and it may be partially due to our view of language. If we start from a conception of words as names for things then we tend to think of psychological terms as names for inner mental entities that are causally related to behavior. This view of the mind comes from a view of meaning as based on word-object relations, which is the target of Wittgenstein's private language argument (Carpendale & Lewis, 2004, 2006; Montgomery, 2002; Racine, 2004; Wittgenstein, 1968). Another way of pointing out the problems with this view of beliefs as inner mental entities is to consider the frame problems (Bickhard, 2001). The implication that Bickhard draws from this issue is that if we think of beliefs as mental entities then the number of beliefs we could be said to have is simply unbounded. For example, Bickhard points out that most of us believe that stepping in front of an oncoming truck is dangerous. But we also believe the same thing for blue trucks and red trucks and even pink and white striped trucks, and this list could go on and on. The point is that we could be said to have any number of beliefs, and therefore these cannot be any sort of a mental entity.

Instead, we argue that beliefs, intentions and desires are aspects of human activity. They are tied up with our way of acting in the world and children learn about them through learning to talk about this psychological world. In Malcolm's (1991, p. 46) words, all psychological terms "either redescribe or else presuppose ways of acting. ... It is these ways of acting that provide the foundation for the psychological concepts." From this approach, it is not that children learn about mental states through inference or introspection, but rather by learning about the circumstances linked to the use of mental state terms, that is, the public criteria for their use (Carpendale & Lewis, 2004, 2006).

Shared practices serve as the basis for children to learn such terms. Words like 'think' and 'know' are very complex and are used in many different language games, but children start with somewhat simpler words such as 'look' and 'see.' These are also psychological words because their use is tied up with a psychological understanding of the *implications* of seeing. Children might ordinarily learn to use these words within joint attention interactions, such as when pointing. Other basic psychological terms referring to emotions and desires may be added to the child's natural reactions (Malcolm, 1991).

Thus, psychological words derive their meaning from the role they play in patterns of everyday human activity. Such shared social interactions have universal roots in infants' natural reactions and in universal routines like those concerned with caring for infants (Canfield, 1993). But at more complex levels there would also be cultural differences introduced in conceptions of the psychological world. We suggest that beliefs, intentions and desires are aspects of human activity and are thus observable and this is how children learn about the psychological world. The ability to talk about the psychological world then provides the capacity to think about and reflect on this world. That is, the inner psychological world develops from the outer. This then allows for further development of the ability to take the perspectives of others on the self.

Current research on the relations between language and false belief understanding can be interpreted from the perspective we are proposing (see Carpendale & Lewis, 2004, 2004) and there are also implications for future research (Turnbull & Carpendale, 2001). From this perspective, it is important to study the ways in which children learn to talk about the psychological world by learning the circumstances that are linked with such words. Because children acquire the criteria for the use of words in a piecemeal fashion they are likely to use words such as mental state terms with an understanding that is different from adults. For example, Lillard's (1993) research shows that although young children use the word 'pretend' their understanding of it differs from that of adults. Furthermore, particular forms of parent-child talk may facilitate or hinder the child's understanding of the social situations related to talk about the psychological world (Racine, Carpendale, & Turnbull, 2003).

Conclusion

To conclude, we argue that taking others' perspectives seems to be uniquely human and makes language and culture possible and it is essential in the development of rationality and morality. This raises the question of how this essentially human capacity develops. We argue that the capacity to take others' perspectives cannot be an innate fixed action pattern but rather must develop within social interaction. We do, however, have to think about the biological adaptations that make this development possible. We have also argued that individualistic approaches are problematic because they rely on the analogical argument. As an alternative, we believe it is more fruitful to take a relational perspective, according to which infants begin from a point of relative lack of differentiation between the perspectives of self and other, and gradually develop these distinctions through engagement in social interaction. Infants must first distinguish and then coordinate their perspective with others within social interaction. At this point they can begin to use language, which depends on this triadic structure. Language then provides a means for further social development and the ability to think about the psychological world, which in turn allows for the ability to take others' perspectives in more complex situations. Children's ability to understand others' perspectives and to take the perspective of others on the self is foundational in the development of language, thinking and mind.

Acknowledgement

This research was supported in part by grants from the Social Sciences and Humanities Research Council of Canada.

References

Bakeman, R., & Adamson, L. B. (1984). Coordinating attention to people and objects in mother-infant interactions. *Child Development, 55*, 1278–1289.

Baldwin, D. A. (1995). Understanding the link between joint attention and language. In C. Moore & P. J. Dunham (Eds.), *Joint attention: Its origins and role in development* (pp. 131–158). Hillsdale, NJ: Erlbaum.

Baldwin, J. M. (1906). *Thoughts and things, Vol. 1: Functional logic.* New York: The MacMillan Company.

Baron-Cohen, S. (1995). *Mindblindness: An essay on autism and theory of mind.* Cambridge, MA: MIT Press.

Baron-Cohen, S., Allen, J., & Gillberg, C. (1992). Can autism be detected at 18 months? The needle, the haystack and the CHAT. *British Journal of Psychiatry, 161*, 839–842.

Bates, E. (1976). *Language and context.* New York: Academic Press.

Bates, E. (1979). *The emergence of symbols: Cognition and communication in infancy.* New York: Academic Press.

Bickhard, M. H. (2001). Why children don't have to solve the frame problems: Cognitive representations are not encodings. *Developmental Review, 21*, 224–262.

Bischof-Köhler, D. (1989). *Spiegelbild und Empathie* [Mirror image and empathy]. Bern: Huber.

Bretherton, I. (1991). Intentional communication and the development of an understanding of mind. In D. Frye & C. Moore (Eds.), *Children's theories of mind: Mental state and social understanding* (pp. 49–75). Hillsdale, NJ: Erlbaum.

Butterworth, G. (1998). What is special about pointing in babies? In F. Simion & G. Butterworth (Eds.), *The development of sensory, motor and cognitive capacities in early infancy: From perception to cognition* (pp. 171–190). Hove, UK: Psychology Press.

Butterworth, G. (2001). Joint visual attention in infancy. In G. Bremner & A. Fogel (Eds.), *Blackwell handbook of infant development* (pp. 213–240). Oxford: Blackwell.

Canfield, J. V. (1993). The living language: Wittgenstein and the empirical study of communication. *Language Sciences, 15,* 165–193.

Carpendale, J. I. M. & Lewis, C. (2004). Constructing an understanding of mind: The development of social understanding within social interaction. *Behavioral and Brain Sciences, 27*(1), 79–141.

Carpendale, J. I. M. & Lewis, C. (2006). *How children develop social understanding.* Oxford: Blackwell.

Carpenter, M., Nagell, K., & Tomasello, M. (1998). Social cognition, joint attention, and communicative competence from 9 to 15 months of age. *Monographs of the Society for Research in Child Development, 63* (Serial No. 255).

Chapman, M. (1991). The epistemic triangle: Operative and communicative components of cognitive development. In M. Chandler & M. Chapman (Eds.), *Criteria for competence: Controversies in the conceptualization and assessment of children's abilities* (pp. 209–228). Hillsdale, NJ: Erlbaum.

Corkum, V., & Moore, V. (1998). The origins of joint visual attention in infants. *Developmental Psychology, 34,* 28–38.

Desrochers, S., Morissette, P., & Ricard, M. (1995). Two perspectives on pointing in infancy. In C. Moore & P. J. Dunham (Eds.), *Joint attention: Its origins and role in development* (pp. 85–101). Hillsdale, NJ: Erlbaum.

Gergely, G. (2002). The development of understanding self and agency. In U. Goswami (Ed.), *Blackwell Handbook of childhood cognitive development* (pp. 26–46). Oxford: Blackwell

German, T. P., & Leslie, A. M. (2004). No (social) construction without (meta) representation: Modular mechanisms as a *basis* for the capacity to acquire an understanding of mind. *Behavioral and Brain Sciences.*

Hobson, R. P. (1993). *Autism and the development of mind.* Hove, UK: Erlbaum.

Hobson, R. P. (2002). *The cradle of thought: Explorations of the origins of thinking.* London: Macmillan.

Hoffman, M. L. (1991). Empathy, social cognition, and moral action. In W. M. Kurtines & J. L. Gewirtz (Eds.), *Handbook of moral behavior and development, Vol. 1: Theory* (pp. 275–301). Hillsdale, NJ: Lawrence Erlbaum Associates, Publishers.

Jopling, D. (1993). Cognitive science, other minds, and the philosophy of dialogue. In U. Neisser (Ed.), *The perceived self* (pp. 290–309). Cambridge, MA: MIT Press.

Kohlberg, L. (1981). *Essays in moral development: The philosophy of moral development* (Vol. 1). San Francisco: Harper & Row.

Leavens, D. A., Hopkins, W. D., & Thomas, R. K. (2004). Referential communication by chimpanzees (*Pan troglodytes*). *Journal of Comparative Psychology, 118,* 48–57.

Lillard, A. S. (1993). Young children's conceptualization of pretense: Action or mental representational state? *Child Development, 64,* 372–386.

Liszkowski, U., Carpenter, M., Henning, A., Striano, T., & Tomasello, M. (2004). Twelve-month-olds point to share attention and interest. *Developmental Science, 7,* 297–307.

Malcolm, N. (1991). The relation of language to instinctive behaviour. In J. Hyman (Ed.), *Investigating psychology: Sciences of the mind after Wittgenstein* (pp. 27–47). New York: Routledge.

Mead, G. H. (1934). *Mind, self and society*. Chicago: The University of Chicago Press.

Meltzoff, A. N., Gopnik, A., & Repacholi, B. M. (1999). Toddlers' understanding of intentions, desires, and emotions: Explorations of the dark ages. In P. D. Zelazo, J. W. Astington & D. R. Olson (Eds.), *Developing theories of intention* (pp. 17–41). Mahwah, NJ: Erlbaum.

Merleau-Ponty, M. (1964). The child's relations with others. In M. Merleau-Ponty, *The primacy of perception* (pp. 96–155). Evanston, IL: Northwestern Press. (Original work published 1960)

Montgomery, D. E. (2002). Mental verbs and semantic development. *Journal of Cognition and Development, 3*, 357–384.

Moore, C. (1996). Theories of mind in infancy. *British Journal of Developmental Psychology. 14*, 19–40.

Moore, C., & Corkum, V. (1994). Social understanding at the end of the first year of life. *Developmental Review, 14*, 349–372.

Moore, C., & D'Entremont, B. (2001). Developmental changes in pointing as a function of parent's attentional focus. *Journal of Cognition and Development, 2*, 109–129.

Müller, U., & Carpendale, J. I. M. (2004). From joint activity to joint attention: A relational approach to social development in infancy. In J. I. M. Carpendale & U. Müller (Eds.), *Social interaction and the development of knowledge* (pp. 215–238). Mahwah, NJ: Erlbaum.

Müller, U., & Runions. K. (2003). The origins of understanding of self and other: James Mark Baldwin's theory. *Developmental Review, 23*, 29–54.

Piaget, J. (1962). *Play, dreams and imitation in childhood*. New York: Norton. (Original work published 1945).

Piaget, J. (1963). *The origins of intelligence in children*. New York: W. W. Norton & Company, Inc. (Original work published in 1936).

Piaget, J. (1965). *The moral judgment of the child*. New York: The Free Press. (Original work published 1932).

Piaget, J. (1972). *The principles of genetic epistemology*. London: Routledge & Kegan Paul. (Original work published in 1970).

Piaget, J. (1995). *Sociological Studies*. London: Routledge. (Original work published 1977)

Portmann, A. (1990). *A zoologist looks at humankind*. New York: Columbia University Press. (Original work published 1944).

Povinelli, D. J., Bering, J. M., & Giambrone, S. (2003). Chimpanzees' "pointing: Another error of the argument by analogy? In S. Kita (Ed.), *Pointing: Where language, culture, and cognition meet* (pp. 35–68). Mahwah, NJ: Erlbaum.

Povinelli, D. J., & Eddy, T. J. (1996). What young chimpanzees know about seeing. *Monographs of the Society for Research in Child Development, 61* (Serial No. 247).

Racine, T. P. (2002). Computation, meaning and artificial intelligence: Some old problems, some new models. *Canadian Artificial Intelligence, 50*, 8–19.

Racine, T. P. (2004). Wittgenstein's internalistic logic and children's theories of mind. In J. I. M. Carpendale & U. Müller (Eds.), *Social interaction and the development of knowledge* (pp. 257–276). Mahwah, NJ: Erlbaum.

Racine, T. P., Carpendale, J. I. M., & Turnbull, W. (2003). *Parent-child talk about a picture book, perspectives and social understanding.* Paper presented at the 70th Biennial Convention of the Society for Research in Child Development, Tampa, FL.

Rochat, P., & Hespos, S. J. (1997). Differential rooting response by neonates: Evidence for an early sense of self. *Early Development & Parenting, 6,* 105–112.

Rochat, P., & Striano, T. (2002). Who's in the mirror? Self-other discrimination in specular images by four- and nine-month-old infants. *Child Development, 73,* 35–46.

Russell, J. (1996). *Agency: Its role in mental development.* Hove, UK: Erlbaum (UK) Taylor & Francis.

Scheler, M. (1954). *The nature of sympathy* (translated by P. Heath). Hamden, CT: Archon Books. (Original work published 1913).

Soffer, G. (1999). The other as alter ego: A genetic approach. *Husserl Studies, 15,* 151–166.

Tomasello, M. (1995). Joint attention as social cognition. In C. Moore & P. J. Dunham (Eds.), *Joint attention: Its origins and role in development* (pp. 103–130). Hillsdale, NJ: Erlbaum.

Tomasello, M. (1999). *The cultural origins of human cognition.* Cambridge, MA: Harvard University Press.

Tomasello, M. (2003). *Constructing a language: A usage-based theory of language acquisition.* Cambridge, MA: Harvard University Press.

Tomasello, M., Call, J., & Hare, B. (2003). Chimpanzees understand psychological states — the question is which ones and to what extent. *Trends in Cognitive Sciences, 7,* 153–156.

Turnbull, W. (2003). *Language in action: Psychological models of conversation.* Hove, UK: Psychology Press.

Turnbull, W., & Carpendale, J. I. M. (2001). Talk and social understanding. *Early Education and Development, 12,* 455–477.

Vygotsky, L. S. (1978). *Mind in society: The development of higher psychological processes.* Cambridge, MA: Harvard University Press.

Vygotsky, L. (1986). *Thought and language.* Cambridge: MIT. (Original work published 1934).

Vygotsky, L. S. (1998). *The collected works of L. S. Vygotsky, Vol. 5, child psychology.* New York: Plenum Press.

Werner, H., & Kaplan, B. (1963). *Symbol formation.* New York: Wiley.

Wittgenstein, L. (1968). *Philosophical investigations.* Oxford: Blackwell.

Zahn-Waxler, C., Radke-Yarrow, M., Wagner, E., & Chapman, M. (1992). Development of concern for others. *Developmental Psychology, 28,* 126–136.

The shaping of animals' minds

Lucie H. Salwiczek[1,2] and Wolfgang Wickler[2]
[1]Department of Experimental Psychology, University of Cambridge / [2]Max Planck Institute of Behavioural Physiology, Seewiesen

Mind is seen as a collection of abilities to take decisions in biologically relevant situations. Mind shaping means to form habits and decision rules of how to proceed in a given situation. Problem-specific decision rules constitute a modular mind; adaptive mind-shaping is likely to be module-specific. We present examples from different behaviour 'faculties' throughout the animal kingdom, grouped according to important mind-shaping factors to illustrate three basically different mind-shaping processes: (I) external stimuli guide the differentiation of a nervous structure that controls a given behaviour; (II) information comes in to direct a fixed behaviour pattern to its biological goal, or to complete an inherited behaviour program; (III) specific stimuli activate or inactivate a pre-programmed behaviour. Mind-shaping phenomena found in the animal kingdom are suggested as 'null-hypotheses' when looking at how human minds might be shaped.

Human psychologists use the term mind for a collection of faculties, or mental capacities, involved in perceiving, remembering, evaluating, and deciding. To not just describe, but understand how the human mind is structured and why it is structured that way, an evolutionary view is necessary. Therefore we will have to consider non-human animals' minds. One may then wish to know more precisely what a mind is. Saidel (2002) convincingly argues that one should use a functional definition by postulating an ability that a mind has and ask if particular organisms have that ability. We here postulate as crucial for mind the ability to make biologically meaningful decisions (McFarland, 1977). They in turn have to be inferred from some overt behaviour that is then taken as a behavioural marker of mind. In non-human animals, meaningful decisions are mostly involved in solving problems of ecological relevance to a given species' environment. In order to be understood as mind-related, a behaviour should then be relevant for helping an organism to survive and reproduce.

We will scrutinize this mind concept by presenting selected examples from different animals to stress the fact that perceiving, remembering and evaluating capacities necessary for making decisions may be correlated to events not only in a brain, but also in less centralized, functionally equivalent nervous systems of so-called lower animals.

Mind shaping may include some form of learning, be it trial-and-error-learning or social learning. Trial-and-error-learning requires that the learner exploits the feed-back of results achieved by his own goal-directed actions. Social learning needs some type of interaction with model individuals who in some way or another provide relevant information (Heyes, 1994). Learning is operationally defined as a change in an animal's behaviour that is caused by a specific experience, which is stored as information in long-term memory. But long-term mind-shaping is often accomplished without learning, based on other physiological mechanisms. Imprinting for instance, defined as a long-term effect triggered in a sensitive phase, may either be related to learning (cognitive imprinting) or result from other physiological processes (physiological imprinting; see below). While genetic programs offer similar problem-solving programs to individuals that belong to the same species and the same sex, individual experiences and learning enable an individual to find its own solutions to problems; the respective mental capacities may then well differ between conspecific individuals.

We do not intend a review paper but want to provide a guideline for comparing mind-shaping processes in animals. For the present purpose we will distinguish three different mind-shaping processes:

(I) special stimuli direct, early in ontogeny, the structural differentiation of parts of the central nervous system that control a given behaviour;

(II) information is added to complete or supersede a given behaviour program later in ontogeny;

(III) defined stimuli activate or modulate an already pre-programmed behaviour; this may happen at any time during life.

(I) Parts of the nervous system are structurally differentiated by external stimuli

Mental capacities may develop under tight genetic guidance. Some genetically pre-programmed properties will always be a factor in an individual's perception and decision making. In animals without genetic sex determination, environmental stimuli may determine the sex of the developing embryo, i.e. the development of its male or female morphology, physiology and sex-related behaviour, including the corresponding processes of perception, memory and decision making.

For some turtles, lizards and crocodiles incubation temperature is the decisive environmental stimulus for sex determination (Bull, 1980; Gans, 1988).

Of all reptile brains the crocodile brain is the most highly developed (Mertens, 1960), as is the sex-specific differentiation of behaviour. Female crocodiles build nests to shelter the eggs and remain close to the nest for several months to protect the eggs from predators. The female estuarine crocodile (*Crocodylus porosus*) builds a mound of mud and decaying plant material, in the centre of which are the eggs. With her tail she splashes water onto the nest, thus promoting the heat-generating process of vegetative decay. When ready to emerge, the young utter squeaking sounds whereupon the mother removes the debris and gently picks up the young with her powerful jaws and carries them in her mouth to near water. Male crocodiles on the contrary fight heavily for territories but catch and swallow baby crocodiles, even their own ones. The very different sexual behaviour repertoires of adult crocodiles are not determined in the egg, but develop according to the breeding temperature.

The same applies to some other reptiles. On top of this, breeding temperature may also decide upon more subtle sex role characteristics. In the leopard gecko (*Eublepharis macularius*) males are produced at temperatures between 30° and 32.5°C. Males that developed under a higher temperature are more aggressive and less sexually active than males that developed under a lower temperature. Furthermore, incubation temperature even influences behavioural plasticity in adulthood: heterosexual social experiences increase territorial behaviour (scent marking) and courtship behaviour (tail vibrations) in low-temperature but not in high-temperature males. These character differences arise during embryogenesis when temperature influences the differentiation of brain nuclei which are the neural mechanisms underlying aggressive and sexual behaviour (Coomber et al., 1997; Sakata & Crews, 2003).

In mammals a similar phenomenon can be found, mediated not by temperature but by hormones. In several rodents (house mice *Mus*, Mongolian gerbils *Meriones*, red-backed voles *Clethrionomys*) an individual's intra-uterine position between either two brother (2M) or two sister (2F) embryos profoundly affects the individual's subsequent behaviour and reproductive life history (Zielinski & Vandenbergh, 1991). This is caused by a prenatal susceptibility to wombmates' hormones (Clark & Galef, 1994, 1995). 2M female house mice become more aggressive, less sexually active, have lower life-time fecundity but larger home ranges than 2F females. In *Meriones* gerbils 2M females will, as mothers, produce litters containing more sons than daughters. So their female embryos will also more likely have two male neighbours, to the same after-effect. That means, females acquire from their brothers, through a prenatal endocrine mechanism, a male-biased sex-ratio among their offspring; and those females' brothers enhance the production of their own nephews by an effect on their sisters (Vandenbergh, 1993; Vandenbergh

& Huggett, 1994). An epigenetic mind-shaping effect on an individual's gender role behaviour can thus even be transferred into subsequent generations.

(II)   External information complements an inherited behaviour program

In many animals various epigenetical — environmental and social — influences act at some point in ontogeny to shape an individual's mental capabilities. Genetic and epigenetic mind-shaping processes will then complement each other. The information required to complete a given behaviour program may concern the perception or the execution part of a behaviour; that is, it may be needed either (1) to correctly identify the target of a given behaviour, or (2) to develop a specific behaviour performance to perfection; and (3) some behaviours need improvement of both perception and execution.

(1) Target identification

a.   Physiological imprinting on food types

'Imprinting' is an aspect of passive experience during a sensitive period, usually in the early stages of an animal's life. It provides an alternative to an innate recognition of important objects and has long-term effects on social relationships, food or habitat selection.

Some insect mothers deposit their eggs on a special substrate that serves as food for their developing larvae; a plant leaf in the case of some butterflies, a living caterpillar in the case of *ichneumonid* wasps. After pupation the emerging adult still remembers the substrate on which it developed and, if a female, will prefer that same type of substrate for her own egg deposition (Thorpe, 1956), thereby determining the same process for the next generation and potentially starting a new food tradition. The information acquired in the feeding context is transferred into the adult reproductive behaviour, directing egg-laying to its biologically meaningful target substrate. To do so, this information obtained by the larva has to survive the profound reorganization (Breidbach, 1988) of the bodily structures during pupation of the larva into a flying insect.

b.   Cognitive imprinting on social companion

Imprinting often serves to recognize species-specific characteristics. Individuals of various precocious bird species acquire the ability to identify a fellow-member of their species by an early posthatch exposure to the parent. This is proven by the fact that the young, if artificially misimprinted on an individual of a foreign species, will keep contact and consistently follow that pseudo-parent. A misimprinted male duckling will later in his life consort and try to mate with members of the wrong species (Lorenz, 1935), while in geese the misdirected preference is maintained only as long as the young need parental care.

A sensitive period for imprinting may also arise in relevant situations later in life. Instead of offspring becoming imprinted on their parents, in some cichlid fishes parents become imprinted on their offspring. If one replaces the very first brood of *Hemichromis* parents by that of a foreign species the parents will raise those foreign young. But thereafter the *Hemichromis* parents will care for young of that foreign species only and will swallow young that hatch from their own eggs (Myrberg, 1964).

c.   Social learning about enemies

Cultural transmission of enemy recognition has been analysed in detail by Curio (1988). He showed that adult birds' conspicuous mobbing behaviour towards a visible predator attracts inexperienced individuals and serves to socially transmit recognition of local predators to them. In this critical experiment, naïve European blackbirds (*Turdus merula*) were exposed to some neutral object, for instance a multicoloured plastic bottle, while an experienced bird was tricked into mobbing a resting owl that was shielded from view of the naïve birds. So the naïve birds connected the predator harassment to the neutral object and from then on habitually mobbed this object. The pupil birds eventually turned into tutor birds passing this mistaken information on to their own offspring.

d.   Social learning about food

Cross-generational transfer of food preferences, which has a long-term influence on the offspring's later food choice, can take place in different ways. Spiny mice (*Acomys*), for example, adopt maternal food preferences via nose-mouth contact with a feeding mother: the mother holds still with the mouth slightly open in a stereotypic posture (McFadyn-Ketchum & Porter, 1989) which may be interpreted as an initial step towards teaching. Weanling rats learn to prefer food eaten by their true as well as by foster-mothers, indicating that the preference transfer is non-genetic (Bronstein et al., 1975). Infant primates, too, tend to synchronize their feeding bouts with those of their mothers and feed on the same food items as their mothers (Hauser, 1994). Likewise, cultural transmission of new feeding techniques by observational learning has been observed in free living vervet monkeys (*Cercopithecus aethiops*) and chacma baboons (*Papio ursinus*) (Cambefort, 1981).

Rabbit embryos adopt their mother's food preferences even prenatally via odours associated with mother's diet. This process, that could well be interpreted as a case of imprinting, leads to enhanced, stimulus-specific sensitivity of the basic sensory mechanism, illustrating mind-shaping via an epigenetic social influence on a perception apparatus (Hudson & Distel, 1999).

Some free living birds establish feeding traditions not by becoming passively imprinted but by active social learning (Diamond, 1987). A young bird may closely follow its parents, intently observing their feeding and then trying to eat from the same spot. To become efficient foragers, the young of some finch species need more than one year of training about where to look for what kind of food (Werner & Sherry, 1987).

(2) Performance improvement

Examples in the preceding paragraph illustrate cases where information has to be acquired to direct a genetically fixed behaviour pattern to a biologically meaningful target object. On the other hand, information about the target object may be genetically provided while the corresponding behaviour pattern needs functional improvement.

a.   Trial-and-error learning about food acquisition

The Galápagos woodpecker finch *Cactospiza pallida* is famous for using twigs or cactus spines which it holds in its beak to push, stab or lever arthropods out of tree holes and crevices. The bird varies the technique according to the particular task and modifies its tools by shortening too long ones and breaking off twig-lets that would prevent insertion (Eibl-Eibesfeldt, 1961). All young woodpecker finches pick up and playfully manipulate twig-like objects and try to probe with them into holes. In areas with few holes but with otherwise easily accessible prey, individuals soon loose interest in twigs and will as adults not even try to use tools. Neither young nor adults learn from observing other birds using tools. However, young birds that start their lives in an environment with ample opportunity to find holes and insects in them, will by trial-and-error learning soon become skilled tool-users regardless of whether they had tool-using or non-tool-using parents. Effective tool-use thus has an innate component but also requires complementation by learned components from adequate interaction with specific environmental features (Tebbich et al., 2001) to establish tool-using behaviour and to develop the necessary fine-tuned motor coordination, presumably by enhanced cerebellar synaptogenesis (Byers & Walker, 1995).

b.   Social learning of birdsong

When they learn how to sing, most songbirds listen to adult tutors, keeping the songs in mind as acoustic templates, and then assimilate (emulate) their own vocalizations to the model sounds memorized from the first months of their lives. This "training phase" seems to be comparable to the babbling phase of human children (Marler, 1973). Song learning is the nearest known functional and evolutionary parallel to human language in the animal kingdom, encompassing the cultural tradition of the structure, semantic and syntax of vocal elements as a communication system (Salwiczek & Wickler, 2004), including the corresponding mind-shaping processes.

Strains of socially learned vocalizations tend to diverge due to cultural drift and give rise to local song dialects. Communication between representatives of the diverging strains may become increasingly difficult, rendering mating ever less likely. Where dialects in this way limit gene flow, genetic evolution becomes constrained by tradition, and culture starts to keep genes on a leash. Traditive (i.e. not genetically transmitted) elements, that shape minds accordingly and determine partner choice, may thus even direct ongoing genetic evolution (Salwiczek, 2001).

(3) Goal identification plus behaviour improvement

In some animal species, the growing individuals still need both information about important objects and about specific performances.

a.   Social learning about both new food and feeding techniques

A well known example recorded since 1930 from several tit species in many parts of England is the habit to pierce the covers of milk bottles (Fisher & Hinde, 1949). Milk is not a normal source of food for these birds, but in some localities a few birds discovered how to drink milk from bottles delivered to doorsteps. Watching a companion feeding from a bottle raises interest in others who then try by themselves. They thereby learn to recognise milk bottles as a potential supply of food and then attack the bottles within a few minutes of their being left at the door. Some parties of tits even used to follow the milkman's cart down the street, removing the caps from bottles in the cart.

In addition to socially learning about this new food and where to locate it, each individual bird has to find out by trial and error how to open a bottle. Accordingly, the method of opening varies greatly, and each individual may employ several techniques. A cap of metal foil can first be punctured by hammering with the beak and then the thin strips of metal can be torn off. Cardboard taps may be removed in total, or torn off layer by layer, or a small hole can be made in it. People of course tried to cover the tops of the bottles; but the birds even removed a flat stone from the top of a bottle or reached the milk in spite of a tea cloth spread over the bottle. It may thus take persistent attempts to reach the milk even though the top of a bottle is no longer visible (Fisher & Hinde, 1949).

A continuous cultural evolution of feeding techniques was reported by the late Eugène Marais (1971): *Chacma* baboons in South Africa in the midst of the nineteenth century discovered that milk could be found in the stomach of sheep lambs.

They caught the lambs, tore open their entrails and ate the curdled milk. Within 80 years this habit spread and became a regular habit in the Central Cape Province. Next the baboons began to eat the flesh of the slaughtered lambs and to capture lambs for no other purpose. They also changed the killing method; originally they just tore open the entrails, but later they would stretch the lamb on its back, bite both jugular veins and leave the lamb until it was dead. Then the flesh was torn from the body and eaten. In the end the baboons began to slaughter large sheep too.

b.   Social learning that establishes complex (proto-)cultures

Behavioural traditions play a vital role in primates, who in nature depend heavily on learning from conspecifics various details about their technical and social world. To achieve this they exploit past experiences of elders and pass on to their offspring skills and information that would be dangerous or arduous for them to acquire on their own (Tomasello & Call, 1997). Various traditive traits in chimpanzee behaviour have recently been summed up as 'chimpanzee cultures'; they include tool usage, nest-building, grooming and courtship behaviour, gestural communication, and knowledge about medicinal plants and their usage (Wrangham et al., 1994; Whiten et al., 1999). Clearly chimpanzees' and other primates' minds are shaped like human minds by associative learning, active curiosity and social copying.

Socially transmitted packages of information that control behaviour are called 'memes' (Dawkins, 1989). They are mind shaping by definition, influencing decision-making evaluations, and overt behaviour in various ways. Socially acquired preferences may guide food preferences, nest site selection, communication style, mate choice, etc. Memes not only shape minds but can install complete new behaviour programs already in animals. In humans memes form the set of cultural instructions people carry in their brains; memes are evidenced as ideas (neural codes) as well as associated overt behaviour patterns, language included. There are cases of important coevolution of memetic and genetic traits in humans (Durham, 1991) and birds (Salwiczek, 2001). But because there is no reason why successfully spreading memes should be connected to an individual's genetic success, memes can as well function like parasites in the hosting human or non-human organism (Dawkins, 1982; and see the next section).

(III) External stimuli switch on or off a pre-existing inherited program

Overt perception, memory as well as evaluation, and in turn decision making may be inclusively manipulated by external stimuli which selectively block or activate complete behaviour programs.

(1) gender role activation

Individuals of various animal species have their genetic sexual predisposition epigenetically modulated by social stimuli which can act on different physiological levels. Social sex determination and social mind shaping in the sexual context (expressed in partner choice, memory for social interactions in dominance situations, evaluating options for successful reproduction, and deciding between alternative behaviours) are found in sequential hermaphrodites, who undergo change of sex and gender role as adults, either once and for good, or repeatedly.

Some labrid fish species are peculiar in that they have three types of sexuals: initial females and initial males, both genetically determined, and supermales who arise either from sex change in an initial female, or from role change in an initial male (reviewed by Grober, 1998). In *Thalassoma bifasciatum* initial males and females are of similar yellow colouration, while supermales have blue heads, a black-white-black banding behind the head, and green bodies. Supermales are highly aggressive and defend breeding sites where they gain exclusive access to females and may mate with up to 100 females per day. Initial males do not defend breeding sites, are less aggressive and mate in large aggregations of about 50 males per female; they also try to sneak mate with a supermale/female pair. Should the supermale from a social group disappear, the largest initial stage individual, either male or female, will within minutes increase aggression towards similar-sized individuals and direct courtship towards females. It thereby gains social dominance at once, while gonadal sex change needs 7–10 days. The physiological background of these changes in behaviour and responsiveness is as follows: Sex reversal is blocked in individuals by the presence of a dominant male. Decreases in the amount of aggressive behaviour received by the largest individual result in rapid changes in brain peptid expression, allowing for higher rates of male-typical behaviour. This triggers changes in the hypothalamic-pituitary-gonadal system, in coloration, endocrinoloy, gonad anatomy and physiology, and in overt behaviour (Grober, 1998).

Social dominance, which in turn depends upon differences in relative body size between group members or pair mates, is the key factor in the inhibition of sex or role changes in subordinate individuals, in vertebrates and invertebrates. This is most apparent in species whose individuals can change sex more than once. While in the labrid fish *Thalassoma* sex change is irreversible, the closely related cleaner fish *Labroides dimidiatus* may change sex repeatedly: If a male is kept together with a larger female both will change sex (Kawamura et al., 2002).

Neither *Thalassoma* nor *Labroides* care for the brood. But the mind-shaping effects of socially-mediated sex reversal become particularly obvious in complex behaviour changes of species with brood care. In the gobiid fish *Trimma okinawae*

(Sunobe & Nakazono, 1993) males occupy a spawning site in a hole or under a rock which they defend aggressively against other males. Towards a female they show a specific courtship behaviour, hopping towards her, swimming round her, and leading her to the spawning site. After spawning the male cares for the eggs until they hatch. Female-typical behaviour is limited to visiting the territories of nearby males, thereby starting male courtship, and then attaching the eggs to the ceiling of a male's home. As in *Labroides*, individuals can change from one sex role to the other and back; their overt behaviour repertoire changes as does the corresponding specific attention to social and environmental stimuli, including those coming from their own eggs.

Similarly, sex and behaviour can change in the marine polychete worm *Ophryotrocha diadema*, which forms stable monogamous pairs, one individual acting as male, the other as female. During synchronizing courtship both engage in extensive rubbing of their bodies against each other and form a mucous tunnel, in which one lays eggs and the other fertilizes. The egg cocoon is cared for by the partners taking turns. Either parent may leave the tunnel for some time and then come back to the eggs. Interestingly, both partners in a pair tend to simultaneously change sex after one, or a few, spawnings, and they repeat this regularly every 3–4 days. The reason is that some 80% of the physiological reproductive effort is allocated to the female functions and females therefore are soon drained of resources. They then change to the less costly male role, and males thus become more apt to function as females. Furthermore, male reproductive success drops with increasing size because females prefer to mate with small males to avoid a costly conflict over sex (Premoli & Sella, 1995).

The fish species mentioned are called sequential hermaphrodites because their complete physiological (including gonadal) sex and sex role reversal takes some time (up to 10 days). The *Ophryotrocha* worm can change sex roles between successive spawnings within 3 days. While sequential hermaphrodites can only act either as male or as female at any one time, simultaneous hermaphrodites are constantly ready for both gender roles. Simultaneous hermaphrodites are common among many lower animals (worms, snails, and seastars) but also occur among fishes. Here social stimuli determine an individual's sex for just a momentary social interaction. Consequently, pair mates have to arrange who is male and who is female at a given moment. Such opportunistic switching between roles requires persistent decision-making; it may be understood as 'open-mindedness', as opposed to a shaped mind which should keep its shape for some sizeable time span.

As an example we mention the black Hamlet *Hypoplectrus nigricans*, a serranid coral reef fish. A pair could finish spawning within a few minutes if at first one partner ejected all its eggs, the other fertilized them, and then both changed roles.

However eggs are costly in production, while an individual has enough sperm to fertilize the eggs of several mating partners. The fertilizing individual of a pair therefore, instead of offering its own eggs in return, might withhold its eggs and leave to search for other egglayers. Understandably any individual will prefer the male part for reproduction which in turn leads to subtle behavioural negotiations and so-called egg-trading between mating individuals. As a counter measure, the egglaying individual of a mating pair will only offer a small portion of their available eggs for fertilization and will then wait for the partner to reciprocate (Fischer, 1981). Under egg parcelling a cheater could win only a small portion of eggs 'unpaid', and the partner would still have enough eggs to remain a preferred mating partner. This, together with an estimate of costs for cheating (how long it takes to find a new partner, with how many eggs) keeps the action going, though over a seemingly unnecessary long time (Friedmann & Hammerstein, 1991).

(2) Heteronomous mind-shaping

Many animals have some of their own genetically pre-determined species-specific behaviour programs untimely unlocked, and their minds 'mis-shaped', from modulating influences from foreign species. Mind-shaping parasites of all types can, to their own benefit, manipulate the decisions, and activate specific behaviours, of their hosts to the benefit of the parasite. This is an often neglected factor that shapes the minds of host animals. The rabies virus for instance causes foxes to stop caring for their family and instead roam about to bite, rather indiscriminately, other animals (including humans). This behaviour clearly is detrimental for the fox but beneficial for the virus who rides in fox saliva into new hosts. Some parasites castrate their host and stop its interest in sexual rivalry and costly reproductive behaviour, thus enhancing the chance for the host to survive as a resource for the parasite (Baudoin, 1975). Other parasites as larvae turn an intermediate host's negative phototaxis into a positive one such that the host, instead of hiding from predators, presents itself in the open and falls easy prey to a predatory animal which in fact is the parasite's final host. A more intricate mind-shaping is executed by the larva of the liver fluke *Dicrocoelium*. When adult it lives in sheep and related ruminants. Fluke eggs, dispersed in the host's faeces, are finally eaten by ants. Inside the ant, a fluke's metacercaria larva enters a specific area of the ant's lower oesophageal ganglion. From there it changes — as a 'brain-worm' — the ant's sleeping behaviour to the effect that the ant, at night, no longer returns to the subterranean ant colony but instead climbs a grass stem and spends the night firmly bitten to a grass tip. Early in the morning when the ant hangs numb, grazing ruminants will swallow it and become infected with the liver fluke (Hohorst & Sprengel, 1972). We need not expand further on that topic. A breathtaking survey of parasites' tricks is given by Zimmer (2000).

Conclusions

Zoologists invited to give a lecture at a Making Mind conference will invariably compare human and non-human animals. The benefits of such cross-taxa comparison are gratefully acknowledged in medicine, but when it comes to comparing cognitive abilities there is a strong tendency to view animals as separate, special, creations and man even more separate and more special, or even to make humans incomparably unique by definition. We think the uniqueness of any species must not just be conceived but has to be shown to exist, and this can only be done by thorough comparisons. Mind-shaping phenomena found in the animal kingdom could, on the other hand, be used as 'null-hypotheses' when looking at how human minds might be shaped.

We understand 'mind' as some abstract organ which is involved in perceiving, remembering, evaluating, and making biologically relevant decisions. Under the premise that decision-making has to be inferred from an individual's overt behaviour, the mind-concept can in a meaningful way be applied to non-human animals. Mind shaping then means to form habits and decision rules about how to proceed in a given situation; it commits the individual to follow a decision rule for that situation. The re-appearance of that situation is mandatory for us to identify a decision rule. On the other hand, it is only in the case of a re-occurring situation that it pays for the individual to form a decision rule at all. The 'shape' in question, then, should outlive the time span necessary for repeated appearances of that situation.

Mind shaping concerns different behaviour 'faculties' in animals. The need to solve problems of different kinds will require different special-purpose programs, each with its own situation-specific decision rules. Those different programs or abilities would constitute a modular mind (Barkow et al., 1992), and an adaptive mind shaping then is likely to be module-specific: A migratory bird will be genetically determined to decide when and where to fly, may be imprinted to recognize conspecifics and enemies, will socially learn how to communicate, and will by trial-and error acquire specific feeding techniques. Complex cultural traditions will be similarly based on quite different mind-shaping processes.

So far no thorough studies are available that show how many behaviour faculties can be influenced by mind shaping in a single species. It may well be that humans are peculiar in the range of mind-shaping effects upon all levels of behaviour organization. On the other hand, because the ability to take decisions has to be inferred from functional behaviour, one has to take interrelated functions into consideration when looking for a corresponding mind module that may have been shaped. If a female mouse uses a larger home range, is less sexually active, but is a more effective mother compared to other females, she — while still in her mother's uterus — may have just a mind module shaped that is responsible for agonistic decisions, perhaps based on a critical threshold for attacking or avoiding conspecifics.

Depending on the species, various influences of environmental or social origin may be involved in forming habits and decision rules. Whether to behave in a female or male way is environmentally determined via breeding temperature in reptiles, but is socially determined by dominance situations in some worm and fish species. Knowledge about where to lay the eggs is ecologically mediated via larval feeding substrate in some insects. Social transmission of knowledge about what to eat can take very different ways: it is mediated in bees by their dancing communication system, in some rodents by physiological imprinting, and in baboons by imitative learning.

Learning is a well-known process in habit formation, be it by trial-and-error learning, where an individual itself strives to solve a problem, or by social learning, where the key information to solve the problem is taken from a tutor individual. Both processes require an active interest from the learner individual. When learning by trial-and-error, the individual displays an amazing perseverance despite a series of failures; a goal-directed fervour prevents it from being discouraged and giving up after initial fruitless efforts. During social learning the individual exhibits a special curiosity in others' actions (e.g. thoroughly watching its feeding parents; Werner & Sherry 1987) and may even solicit lessons from a tutor; young songbirds for instance during the song-learning phase may prod an adult male to sing.

On the other hand, we selected examples from throughout the animal kingdom to point out that learning need not be involved in epigenetic mind shaping in animals. Instead an individual's mind can be passively (and unavoidably) shaped by external stimuli. This happens in reptiles whose brain nuclei, responsible for activities in social situations, become sex-specifically organized by the incubation temperature, and some rodents undergo an intra-uterine establishment of food preferences and hormonally induced gender-role expression. These processes may be called 'physiological imprinting', as opposed to 'cognitive imprinting' — as a case of (in principle avoidable) borderline-learning — which would apply to those situations where the learner has to join another individual's activities to become imprinted, for instance on the biologically correct social companions, as in the following reaction in waterfowl, on locally important enemies, as in mobbing behaviour, or on maternal food preferences, as in synchronously feeding near the mother's mouth.

Our examples illustrate different mind-shaping processes: An external stimulus may guide the basic differentiation of a nervous structure that controls a given behaviour. In various vertebrates brain areas differ in size and anatomical structure between sexes and in the behavioural consequences of brain sex (Gahr, 1994, 1996). These brain differences develop under the influence of hormones. Hormone functions in their turn are often genetically determined, but can also be causally related to epigenetic factors, as exemplified by the intra-uterine influences on rodent females' expression of social behaviour. Environmental factors like breeding temperature can yield the same result as described for the differentiation of brain nuclei underlying the behavioural plasticity of the male gecko.

Another type of mind-shaping compensates for a lack of information. Gathering information by trial-and-error-learning is decisive for the woodpecker finch to develop and improve basic behaviour elements into functional tool-use. Socially provided information may be needed to direct a fixed behaviour pattern to its biological goal if the individual is, for instance, inherently able to eat, walk or be aggressive or fearful, but needs information about what to eat, and whom to follow or treat as a predator. Baboons need information about both new behaviour tactics and the targets for special ways of foraging. Likewise chimpanzees, in order to acquire a cultural habit, need information about which things to handle as well as tactics about how to handle them.

And finally, mind-shaping may operate via specific stimuli to activate or inactivate a pre-programmed behaviour. In cases of long-term or short-term sex reversal a male or female set of reproductive activities is triggered mainly via a change in relative social dominance.

All mind-shaping parasites, too, activate part of the host-specific behaviour repertoire. The liver fluke larva elicits a sleeping behaviour characteristic for solitary *hymenoptera* (Kaiser, 1995), the ants' phylogenetic ancestors. Although no longer shown by socially living ants, they still harbour the dormant program. A host whose life is driven by a parasite will not show part of the parasite's behaviour. And instead of prying into the intricate physiology of a complex host organism it will be more economic for a parasite to exploit the host's own decision-making, by manipulating the evaluation functions by way of disinformation (from the host's point of view). A parasite for instance, that needs a longlived caterpillar to live in, may reinforce the production of some kind of juvenile hormone, thereby persistently 'convincing' the host that he is still too young for pupation into a flying insect and consequently he continues growing with ever more moulting cycles. Thus a host's mind, which is manipulated by a parasite, still makes meaningful decisions, though biologically meaningful for the parasite. Needless to say that this is the same way how memes can influence an individual's mind.

All things considered, an individual's learning history may only to some degree explain the making of its mind. In humans, too, mind-shaping ranges from the foetus being passively influenced (or even imprinted), e.g. by hearing specific voices (Kolata, 1984), to perinatal food-related chemosensations and childhood eating experiences that establish culture-typical foods, up to curiosity-driven learning and incorporating culturally transmitted assumptions about the existence and particular — even counter-intuitive — causal powers of supernatural entities and agencies. We suggest using mind-shaping phenomena found in the animal kingdom as a 'null-hypotheses' when looking at how human minds might be shaped.

Acknowledgment

The Max Planck Society finances Dr. Salwiczek's research.

References

Barkow, J. H., Cosmides, L., & Tooby, J. (1992). *The adapted mind*. Oxford: Oxford University Press.

Baudoin, M. (1975). Host castration as a parasitic strategy. *Evolution, 29*, 335–352.

Breidbach, O. (1988). *Die Verpuppung des Gehirns*. Köln: Universitätsverlag.

Bronstein, P. M., Levine, M. J., & Marcus, M. (1975). A rat's first bite: the nongenetic, cross-generational transfer of information. *Journal of comparative and physiological psychology, 89*, 295–298.

Bull, J.J. (1980). Sex determination in reptiles. *Quarterly Review of Biology, 55*, 3–21.

Byers, J.A., & Walker, C. (1995). Refining the motor training hypothesis for the evolution of play. *American Naturalist, 146*, 25–40.

Cambefort, J. P. (1981). A comparative study of culturally transmitted patterns of feeding habits in the chacma baboon Papio ursinus and the vervet monkey Cercopithecus aethiops. *Folia Primatologica, 36*, 243–263.

Clark, M. M., & Galef, B. G. (1994). A male gerbil's intrauterine position affects female response to his scent marks. *Physiology and Behavior, 55*, 1137–1139.

Clark, M. M., & Galef, B. G. (1995). Prenatal influences on reproductive life history strategies. *Trends in Ecology and Evolution, 10*, 151–153.

Coomber, P., Crews, D., & Gonzalez-Lima, F. (1997). Independent effects of incubation temperature and gonadal sex on the volume and metabolic capacity of brain nuclei in the leopard gecko (Eublepharis macularius), a lizard with temperature-dependent sex determination. *Journal of Comparative Neurology, 380*, 409–421.

Curio, E. (1988). Cultural transmission of enemy recognition by birds. In T. Zentall, T. & B.G. Galef, B. G. (Eds.), *Social learning: psychological and biological perspectives* (pp. 75–97). Hillsdale, New Jersey: Lawrence Erlbaum Associates.

Dawkins, R. (1982). *The extended phenotype: the gene as the unit of selection*. New York: W. H. Freeman.

Dawkins, R. (1989). *The selfish gene (new edition)*. Oxford: Oxford University Press.

Diamond, J. M. (1987). Learned specializations of birds. *Nature, 330*, 16–17.

Durham, W.H. (1991). *Coevolution*. Stanford California: Stanford University Press.

Eibl-Eibesfeldt, I. (1961). Über den Werkzeuggebrauch des Spechtfinken Camarhynchus pallidus (Slater und Slavin). *Zeitschrift für Tierpsychologie, 18*, 343–346.

Fischer, E. A. (1981). Sexual allocation in a simultaneously hermaphroditic coral reef fish. *American Naturalist, 117*, 64–82.

Fisher, J., & Hinde, R. A. (1949). The opening of milk bottles by birds. *British Birds, 42*, 347–357.

Friedman, J.W., & Hammerstein, P. (1991). To trade or not to trade; that is the question. In R.Selten (Ed.), *Game equilibrium models. I. Evolution and game dynamics* (pp. 257–275). Berlin: Springer Verlag.

Gahr, M. (1994). Brain structure: causes and consequences of brain sex. In R.V. Short & E. Balaban (Eds.), *The Differences between the Sexes* (pp. 273–299). Cambridge: Cambridge University Press.

Gahr, M. (1996). Die sexuelle Differenzierung von Gehirn und Verhalten. *Habilitationsschrift*. München: LMU.

Gans, C. (Ed.) (1988). *Biology of reptilia. vol. 18, Ecology B*. New York: Alan R. Liss.

Grober, M. S. (1998). Socially controlled sex change: integrating ultimate and proximate levels of analysis. *Acta ethologica, 1*, 3–17.

Hauser, M. D. (1994). The transition to foraging independence in free-ranging vervet monkeys. In B. G. Galef, M. Mainardi & P. Valsecchi (Eds.), *Behavioural aspects of feeding* (pp. 165–202). Chur, Switzerland: Harwood Academic Publishers.

Heyes, C. M. (1994). Social learning in animals: categories and mechanisms. *Biological Reviews, 69*, 207–231.

Hohorst, W., & Sprengel, T. (1972). Entwicklungszyklus des Kleinen Leberegels (Dicrocoelium dendriticum). *Publikationen zu wissenschaftlichen Filmen*, Film D 1081. Göttingen: Institut für den Wissenschaftlichen Film.

Hudson, R., & Distel, H. (1999). The flavor of life: Perinatal development of odor and taste preferences. *Schweizerische Medizinische Wochenschrift, 129*, 176–181.

Kaiser, W. (1995). Rest at night in some solitary bees — a comparison with the sleep state of honey bees. *Apidologie, 26*, 213–230.

Kawamura, T., Tanaka, N., Nakashima, Y., Karino, K., & Sakai, Y. (2002). Reversed sex-change in the protogynous reef fish Labroides dimidiatus. *Ethology, 108*, 443–450.

Kolata, G. (1984). Studying learning in the womb. *Science, 225*, 302–303.

Lorenz, K. (1935). Der Kumpan in der Umwelt des Vogels. *Journal für Ornithologie, 83*, 137–413.

Marais, E. N. (1971). *My friends the baboons*. London: Anthony Blond Ltd.

Marler, P. (1973). Speech development and bird song: are there any parallels? In G. A. Miller (Ed.), *Communication, language, and meaning* (pp. 73–83). New York: Basic Books, Inc..

McFadyn-Ketchum, S. A., & Porter, R. H. (1989). Transmission of food preferences in spiny mice (Acomys cahirinus) via nose-mouth interaction between mothers and weanlings. *Behavioral Ecology and Sociobiology, 24*, 59–62.

McFarland, D. J. (1977). Decision making in animals. *Nature, 269*, 15–21.

Mertens, R. (1960). *The world of amphibians and reptiles*. New York: McGraw-Hill.

Myrberg, A. A. (1964). An analysis of preferential care of eggs and young by adult cichlid fishes. *Zeitschrift für Tierpsychologie, 21*, 53–98.

Premoli, M. C., & Sella, G. (1995). Sex economy in benthic polychaetes. *Ethology Ecology & Evolution, 7*, 27–48.

Saidel, E. (2002). Animal minds, human minds. In M. Bekoff, C. Allen, & M. Burghardt (Eds.), *The cognitive animal* (pp. 53–57). Cambridge Mass./ London: The MIT Press.

Sakata, J. T., & Crews, D. (2003). Embryonic temperature shapes behavioural change following social experience in male leopard geckos, Eublepharis macularius. *Animal Behaviour, 66*, 839–846.

Salwiczek, L. (2001). Grundzüge der Memtheorie. In W. Wickler & L. Salwiczek (Eds.). *Wie wir die Welt erkennen. Erkenntnisweisen im interdisziplinären Diskurs* (pp. 119–201). Freiburg / München: Verlag Karl Alber.

Salwiczek, L. H., & Wickler, W. (2004). Bird song: an evolutionary parallel to human language. *Semiotika, 151*, 163–182.

Sunobe, T., & Nakazono, A. (1993). Sex change in both directions by alteration of social dominance in Trimma okinawae (Pisces: Gobiidae). *Ethology, 94*, 339–345.

Tebbich, S., Taborsky, M., Fessl, B., & Blomqvist, D. (2001). Do woodpecker finches acquire tool-use by social learning? *Proceedings of the Royal Society London B, 268*, 2189–2193.

Thorpe, W. H. (1956). *Learning and instinct in animals*. London: Methuen & Co.

Tomasello, M., & Call, J. (1997). *Primate cognition*. New York/Oxford: Oxford University Press.

Vandenbergh, J. G. (1993). And brother begat nephew. *Nature, 364*, 671–672.

Vandenbergh, J. G., & Huggett, C. L. (1994). Mothers' prior intrauterine position affects the sex ratio of her offspring in house mice. *Proceedings of the National Academy of Science, 91*, 11055–11059.

Werner, T. K., & Sherry, T. W. (1987). Behavioral feeding specialization in Pinaroloxias inornata, the "Darwin's Finch" of Cocos Island, Costa Rica. *Proceedings of the National Academy of Science USA, 84*, 5506–5510.

Whiten, A., Goodall, J., McGrew, W. C., Nishida, T., Reynolds, V., Sugiyama, Y., Tutin, C. E. G., Wrangham, R. W., & Boesch, C. (1999). Cultures in chimpanzees. *Nature, 399*, 682–685.

Wickler, W., & Salwiczek, L. H. (2003). Foreign-language phenomena in birds: means to understand the evolution of high level acoustic communication. In R. Ahrens (Ed.), *Europäische Sprachenpolitik / International Language Policy* (pp. 395–412). Heidelberg: Universitätsverlag Winter.

Wrangham, R. W., McGrew, W. C., de Waal, F. B. M., & Heltne, P. G. (1994). *Chimpanzee cultures*. Cambridge, Mass. / London: Harvard University Press.

Zielinski, W. J., & Vandenbergh, J. G. (1991). Effect of intrauterine position and social density on age of first reproduction in wild-type female house mice (Mus musculus). *Journal of comparative Psychology, 105*, 134–139.

Zimmer, C. (2000). *Parasite rex*. New York: The Free Press.

Chimpanzees are sensitive to some of the psychological states of others

Josep Call

Max Planck Institute for Evolutionary Anthropology, Leipzig

Animals react and adjust to the behavior of their conspecifics. Much less is known about whether animals also react and adjust to the psychological states of others. Recent evidence suggests that chimpanzees (*Pan troglodytes*) follow the gaze of others around barriers, past distracters, and check back if they find nothing. Chimpanzees can gauge the motives of a human experimenter and distinguish his intentional from accidental actions. These results suggest that chimpanzees interpret the perceptions and actions of others from a psychological perspective -they seem to know what others can and cannot see and what goals others pursue. It is hypothesized that the co-operation of (1) the ability to operate on psychological states and (2) the motivation to share emotions and experiences with others are key ingredients in the making of human minds.

Recent advances on the study of infant cognition have revealed a number of sophisticated skills in various domains. Young infants reason about various physical properties of objects and events (Baillargeon, 1995), they have some appreciation of numbers (Wynn, 1998), and learn language in ways not known before (Tomasello, 2003). The study of social cognition in infants has also experienced considerable progress. By six months of age infants are sensitive to biological motion (Bertenthal, 1996), have expectations about human actions (Woodward, 1999), and follow the gaze of others (D'Entremont, Hains & Muir, 1997). Between 9 and 12 months of age infants perceive actions as goal directed (Gergely, Nádasdy, Csibra & Bíró, 1995), follow gaze around barriers and past distractors (Butterworth & Jarred, 1991; Moll & Tomasello, 2004), and begin to engage in joint attention with adults (Carpenter, Nagell & Tomasello, 1998). By 14 months they distinguish intentional and accidental actions (Carpenter, Akhtar & Tomasello, 1998), interpret unfulfilled actions appropriately (Meltzoff, 1995), understand that others are selecting action plans (Gergely, Bekkering & Kiraly, 2002), and understand that others may attend selectively to certain aspects of the environment (Caron, Kiel, Dayton & Butler,

2002; Tomasello & Haberl, 2003). After these initial developments in the areas of intention and attention, children in their second year of life begin to use epistemic states such as pretense, knowledge, and belief that will culminate around fifth birthdays with the ability to pass formal false belief attribution tasks.

Much less is known about the development of nonhuman social minds, including those of our closest relatives. In this paper I will make a case for the existence of social minds in the chimpanzee and other great apes. My goal is not to convince the reader that chimpanzee minds are exactly like human minds, but to show that there are important similarities that extend beyond observable behavior into the psychological realm. Thus, a main thesis of this paper is that at least chimpanzees not only perceive the behavior of others, they also interpret it. This proposal will probably strike a familiar cord with many developmentally-oriented researchers who have thought about similar issues in relation to human development. This is no coincidence. Perhaps more than ever, the areas of developmental and comparative cognition are following paths with multiple points of common interest.

To make the case for social minds in chimpanzees, I will present some recent data on the ability of chimpanzees (and other great apes when it is available) to understand perceptions and actions of others, which correspond to the psychological states of attention and intention, respectively. A series of studies on gaze following will illustrate the area of attention whereas studies on goal detection and distinguishing intentional from accidental actions will illustrate the area of intention. Both data sets share in common that similar studies have been conducted with human infants so that a direct comparison is possible. In the final part of the paper I will discuss the implications of this research for theory of mind, and highlight a possible important difference that may have made human and ape minds so close in so many respects, and so different in others.

The perceptions of others

One of the perhaps most influential developments in social cognition is that of joint attention. Joint attention, which emerges between 9 to 12 months of age in humans (Carpenter et al., 1998), consists of two individuals attending to the same third entity (be it an object or another social entity) and to each other. Thus, joint attention is not simply looking at the same object simultaneously, but alternating gaze between the object of interest and the social partner. According to several theorists, joint attention is important because it allows infants to align their impressions of the external world with those of others by experiencing the same phenomena that others are experiencing. In fact, joint attention is regarded as a key component in the development of both language (Tomasello, 1999) and epistemic mental states (Baron-Cohen, 1995).

A key building block of joint attention is gaze following defined as using the gaze (or head) direction of a social partner toward a third external entity. Gaze following is a skill that develops progressively in human infants. Six month-old infants can follow gaze to targets that are visible within their visual field (D'Entremont et al., 1997). By 12 months of age infants can also follow gaze behind and around barriers (Moll & Tomasello, 2004), past distractors (Butterworth & Jarred, 1991) and to entities located behind them (Deák, Flom & Pick, 2000). At this age infants are also sensitive to the information provided by the eyes, and will follow gaze more often when the eyes are visible than when they are covered (Brooks & Meltzoff, 2002). Moreover, 14 month-old infants are more likely to follow gaze if the head and eyes point in the same direction than if they point in different directions (Caron, Butler & Brooks, 2002). Taken together these results suggest that infants are not just following cues such as head direction, but they also have an appreciation of what others can see. Given the central importance of gaze following for the development of social cognition in human infants, we could start our quest for other social minds by asking how widespread this ability is in other animals.

Several studies have shown that primates, dolphins, goats, seals, and dogs are capable of gaze following (Itakura, 1996; Tschudin, Call, Dunbar, Harris & van der Elst, 2001; Kaminski, Riedel, Call & Tomasello, 2005; Scheumann & Call, 2004; Miklósi, Polgárdi, Topál & Csányi, 1998). For instance, Tomasello, Call, and Hare (1998) presented five primate species with the following situation. A human experimenter located on an observation tower surveyed the group of individuals until he found two that were sitting facing each other and with one of them (the looker) facing the observation tower. Then, the experimenter showed a piece of food to the looker that induced her to look up at it, and they scored how the subject responded to the looker's orienting response. In the control condition, the experimenter presented the food in an identical manner in the absence of a looker. All five species reliably followed the looker's gaze direction to the food much more often in the experimental than in the control condition. Other studies have extended these findings by showing that primates can respond to the visual gaze direction of humans when the target is above and behind them (e.g., Itakura, 1996) or that chimpanzees also follow the gaze direction of human beings, and they can even do this on the basis of eye direction alone, independent of head direction (e.g., Povinelli & Eddy, 1996).

There are of course many interpretations of gaze following behavior. One possibility is that it simply reflects an automatic orienting response based on either a hard-wired mechanism or some acquired contingency. For instance, individuals may have learned that if the eyes (or head) of the partner turn to the left — look at the left side whereas if they go to the right — look at the right side (Emery, 2000). Note that this interpretation is silent regarding the reason for looking behavior, it is just about orientation. Another possibility is that gaze following, although based on an orienting response, also possesses a perspective-taking component. In particular, the observer may understand that when others look in a certain direction it is because they are seeing something interesting or unusual. Contrasting the orientation and the perspective-taking alternatives brings us face to face with the topic of this paper. Are animals like chimpanzees behavior-readers only or mind-readers too?

There are several studies to help us decide which one of these two alternatives is more accurate. First, chimpanzees follow the gaze direction of humans to a specific location even if they have to look past and ignore other novel objects along the way in order to fixate the target location. This would seem to indicate that they are not just turning in the same general direction as the looker and then searching randomly for something interesting; they are targeting the looker's perceptual activity (Tomasello, Hare, & Agnetta, 1999). Second, if adult chimpanzees track the gaze of another individual to a location and find nothing interesting there, they quite often look back to the individual's face and track her gaze direction a second time (Call, Hare & Tomasello, 1998). This "checking back" — which only adult chimpanzees do — is a key criterion used to assess human infants' understanding of the visual experience of others, since it would seem to indicate that the subject expects to find a target of the looker's perceptual orientation. Interestingly, if a looker looks repeatedly to a location with no salient target, adult (but again not juvenile) chimpanzees stop responding to that individual's looking behavior (Tomasello, Hare, & Fogleman, 2001), indicating acquired expectations about when it is likely that following the gaze direction of another is likely to lead to an interesting target.

But perhaps the most telling situation occurs when a human looks behind a barrier. Following a suggestive finding of Povinelli and Eddy (1996), Tomasello et al. (1999) had a human experimenter look around various types of barriers (or look straight ahead in a control condition). In this case, a simple gaze following response (turning head to look in the direction the experimenter is looking) would not be enough — that would simply lead to the subject fixating the barrier itself. To track the experimenter's gaze to its target subjects needed to move a few meters so as to attain the appropriate viewing angle to permit them to look behind the barrier. And this is just what they did (much more often than in the control condition) for all four of the barrier types investigated.

In summary, chimpanzees follow the gaze of others in flexible ways inconsistent with an automatic orienting response. When there is a distracter they ignore it; when there is a barrier they move themselves in order to see what the other is seeing; when they do not see anything novel in the absence of a barrier they check back and eventually stop looking if they repeatedly find nothing there. Thus, these results suggest that apes follow the gaze direction of others because they want to see what the other is seeing. The alternative is that individuals do not engage in perspective taking and have learned to react appropriately to each of these situations independently from each other.

The actions of others

If joint attention is a skill that allowed infants and adults to begin to coordinate their perceptions of the external world, understanding intentional action is a skill that allows infants to parse the complex streams of behavior displayed by adults (Baldwin, Baird, Sayler & Clark, 2001). By being attuned to the intentions and goals of others, infants can anticipate the behavior of others, can learn from others (even in the absence of the solution), and can explain the behavior of others more effectively. Given such a central role in the development of social cognition, it is not surprising that the study of intentional and goal directed action has received considerable attention in recent years. By 6 months of age, infants have expectations about human actions, but not about inanimate objects performing similar actions. Woodward (1999) interpreted these results as evidence that infants perceive actions as goal directed. By 9 months of age infants can distinguish the motives behind certain actions (Behne, Carpenter, Call & Tomasello, 2005), understand the actions of entities as goal-directed, and expect the use of efficient actions to achieve those goals (Gergely & Csibra, 2003). Starting at 14 months of age infants can distinguish accidental versus intentional actions (Carpenter et al., 1998), perceive that others chose plans of action that meet the requirements of the situation (Gergely et al., 2002), and can use unfulfilled actions on objects to produce the intended goal of a demonstrator (Meltzoff, 1995).

Although Premack and Woodruff's (1978) study on chimpanzee intentions signaled the starting point to the now vast literature on children's theory of mind, comparatively little progress has been made with nonhuman animals since then. There are only a handful of studies devoted to the study of intentions — and those represent a patchy collection of positive, negative, and unclear results. Here, I will concentrate on those paradigms that have produced data both for children and apes.

First, there is the behavioral re-enactment procedure developed by Meltzoff (1995) to assess infants' understanding of unfulfilled actions. In this task, infants witnessed a human model repeatedly trying to produce a result on an object but failing to achieve her goal (unfulfilled condition). For instance, trying to pull apart a dumbbell or trying to hang a rubber band on a peg. After children observed this demonstration, they were handed the object and the experimenter scored whether the infant reproduced the intended outcome. This condition was compared to other conditions in which the human model produced the desired outcome (full demonstration condition) and another in which the model manipulated the object without trying to produce the effect (manipulation condition). Eighteen-month-old infants reproduced the target action in both the full demonstration and unfulfilled conditions equally often, and significantly more often than in the manipulation condition.

Myowa-Yamakoshi and Matsuzawa (2000) adapted this procedure to test chimpanzees and also found no differences between full demonstration and unfulfilled conditions, but in this case the similarity was due to a very low successful performance in both conditions. Neither condition substantially improved the chimpanzees' performance. Similarly, Call, Carpenter and Tomasello (2005) also tested chimpanzees and found no significant differences between those conditions and the baseline condition in which subjects were given no information on how to manipulate the objects. Nevertheless, subjects in the unfulfilled condition seemed less likely to reproduce the result that the experimenter was trying. For instance, if the experimenter unsuccessfully tried to open a tube by breaking it in the center, subjects opened it by removing its bottom and top lids. Conversely if the human tried to remove the lids, subjects tended to break the tube in the center.

Second, we used another paradigm to test whether chimpanzees and orangutans (*Pongo pygmaeus*) understood the distinction between intentional and accidental actions. Although we could have adapted one of the paradigms based on imitation (e.g., Carpenter et al., 1998), we disregarded this possibility given the little inclination of apes to reproduce actions (see Call & Carpenter, 2003). Instead we opted for a paradigm in which a human offered cues to the ape about the location of hidden food. In particular, Call and Tomasello (1998) trained chimpanzees and orangutans to use a landmark placed on top of one of three opaque containers as an indicator of the location of hidden food. During training the apes never saw the human actually placing the marker on the container, but the marker was already on top of one of the containers when they were presented to the ape. On test trials a human experimenter then placed the marker on one of the containers intentionally, but either before or after this he let the marker fall accidentally onto one of the other containers. The marker was removed at the time of choice of the ape, so for test trials the ape was faced with a choice in which one bucket had been marked with the marker intentionally and the other accidentally. Apes as a group chose the container that was marked intentionally, although no individual except a language-trained orangutan was above chance on his own. The apes' performance was comparable to that of 2.5 year-old children presented with the same task and worse than that of 3-year-old children.

Third, we investigated whether chimpanzees can gauge the motives of a human experimenter; more specifically we tested whether in a food sharing situation they can distinguish between a human who is unwilling to give them food from one that is unable to do so. Thus, we presented chimpanzees with a situation in which a human gave them food through a hole in their cage. After the experimenter had passed a few grapes to the subject, he took another grape but did not pass it to the subject and we manipulated the reason for stopping the transfer. In some cases, he was unable because the hole was too small, it was occupied with other tasks, or did not see the food. In other cases, he was unwilling to give the food. In such trials he put the food close to the ape but would then pull it back, or left the food on the platform and stared at the ape for no apparent reason, or just ate the food. Overall, we presented three trios of unwilling and unable conditions. Each trio consisted of an unwilling condition paired with two unable conditions. Each trio shared some basic features such as the overall motions of the grape or the experimenter's gazing pattern.

The reason for having multiple conditions organized in trios was double. First, we wanted to get as many conditions as possible so that a potential difference could not be accounted for by a superficial difference between a single unwilling and a single unable condition. Second, organizing the conditions in trios allowed us to control to some extent the effect some variables had; such as the reward's motion patterns and the eye contact between the experimenter and the subject. For instance, if we had only had a single unwilling condition that involved eye contact between the experimenter and the subject and a single unable condition that did not, then one could argue that any differences between conditions are due to the presence of eye contact. Eye contact may have simply made subjects more nervous and that, not intention assessment, was the reason underlying the observed differences.

One important methodological consideration of this study is that we did not train subjects to respond in any way, they were not differentially reinforced for their responses, and we only administered two trials per condition. Instead we scored the natural reactions of the chimpanzees and assessed whether they behaved differentially across conditions. In particular we scored two variables: behaviors directed at the experimenter or the food (in most cases these were aimed at convincing the experimenter to transfer the food) and how long subjects remained at the testing station without receiving food. Chimpanzees reacted in different ways to unwilling and unable conditions. When the experimenter was unwilling, they gestured more and they left the testing station earlier than when the experimenter was unable to pass the food. This difference existed even though they were not differentially rewarded. One can postulate a different explanation for each difference across conditions or one can argue that the underlying principal is behind several of those conditions. Note that these findings were comparable to those found with 9- to 18-month-old infants (Behne et al., 2005).

In summary, chimpanzees distinguished between an experimenter that was unwilling and one who was unable to give them food. They also distinguished the intentional from the accidental actions of a human in a communicative situation. In contrast, there was little evidence that they benefited from witnessing unfulfilled actions in a social learning situation. Thus, these results suggest that apes go beyond the observable information and infer the goals of others. Again, the alternative, as was the case in the area of attention, is that individuals have learned to respond to each situation independently.

Parsimony and mental state attribution

In trying to make a case for the use of psychological states in apes, I chose to explore the most recent evidence on the understanding of perception and actions in others. Recent developments support earlier proposals regarding the mental attribution skills of the great apes (e.g., Whiten & Byrne, 1988). Chimpanzees (and other apes) can follow the gaze of others around barriers, past distracters, check back when they do not detect anything remarkable, and stop looking if they find nothing in repeated occasions. In regard to actions, chimpanzees and orangutans distinguish intentional from accidental actions and they can gauge the motives of a human passing them food. Taken together, these results suggest that apes have some understanding of attention and intention. Recently, Suddendorf and Whiten (2001) reached a similar conclusion after reviewing the available literature.

Against this conclusion, one can argue that there is no need to postulate anything beyond perceiving and reacting to behavioral cues (e.g., Povinelli & Vonk, 2003). Each particular condition within the various experiments can be explained as reacting to particular contingencies. Therefore, these results may tell us nothing about apes' ability to infer psychological states in others. After all, one could argue, individuals have to use observable behavior to react appropriately to their social partners in the first place, so there is no need to postulate anything else beyond analyzing behavior. Although it is clear that observable information has to be the basis for apes' reasoning about their social world, it does not necessarily have to remain at the behavioral level. In fact, there is ample evidence than many animals process information beyond perceptual inputs (e.g., Vauclair, 1996). Moreover, the strength of the argument based on observable information exclusively is weakened when one has to postulate different explanations for each phenomenon within a given domain such as attention. Tomasello and Call (2006) argued that the alternative to postulating some understanding of what others can or cannot see is no less than 12 different behavioral explanations for each of the known phenomena in this domain. Finally, another set of post-hoc behavior-based explanations is needed to accommodate the findings of another domain such as intention.

The alternative to multiplying explanations for each particular observation is to postulate that individuals do indeed go beyond behavioral cues thus making some inferences about the psychological states of others. Whiten (1994) used the notion of an intervening variable to make a case for mindreading in primates so that disparate behavioral acts may be based on the same mental state. Thus, the observations regarding perception and actions may correspond to the psychological states of attention and intention, respectively. If we accept this possibility, it is critical that we specify the nature of this psychological level. Although we have argued that the data available are not easily explained by invoking a purely behavioral dimension based on detecting behavioral cues, it is also true that there is no solid evidence to suggest that the understanding of epistemic states plays a fundamental role in the social cognition of apes. Instead, we have argued that these data reflects the operation of psychological states of attention and intention.

To be more specific, understanding attention in others refers to the ability to appreciate what others can or cannot see or so-called level I perspective taking (Flavell, 1992). Currently, it is unclear whether individuals also display level II perspective taking, that is, they appreciate how others will see certain events. This would involve imagining how a given object would look from a different angle, not just whether it would be visible or not. Likewise, Tomasello et al. (2005) have argued that intention of the kinds described for the apes and young infants may be based on perceiving goals, not necessarily imagining a plan for action. In other words, the available data can be explained by postulating that apes appreciate what others are trying to accomplish but there is no evidence suggesting that they can also imagine how a given individual is going to accomplish her goal. Note that this what-how distinction is common to attention and intention. Future research should help us specify the relation between what and how within and between domains such as attention and intention. More specifically, future research should move in at least two directions. First, investigate further those psychological states for which there is some evidence available, such as attention or intention, by trying to see if there is more than level I perspective taking (i.e., the what vs. how distinction). Second, explore whether other psychological constructs such as desires or even epistemic states such as knowledge and belief are part of the apes' suite of psychological states. Such a piecemeal approach reflects the need to treat the different psychological states separately because each informs about different aspects (Tomasello et al., 2003; Whiten, 1994). Although epistemic states such as knowledge or belief have attracted most research attention, and some authors argue that it is only with such states that children develop a coherent theory of mind (e.g., Baron-Cohen, 1995), it is worth noting that psychological states such as attention or intention are very likely to be more basic than epistemic states both from an ontogenetic and a phylogenetic perspective.

The motivation to share: No magic bullet but a key ingredient

So far I have presented a case for narrowing the gap between apes and humans with the regard to the sensitivity to some psychological states. After highlighting the similarities, the reader may wonder about the differences, because even if we share some psychological states with apes, our minds are still quite different. The easy way out would be to say that it is the epistemic states that distinguish us from them. Even though epistemic states play a fundamental role in the way our social cognition works, the differences between humans and apes can be seen even before epistemic states take center stage in children at around four years of age. Recently, we have proposed that the intrinsic motivation to share experiences with others may be critical (Tomasello et al., 2005). This aspect combined with the ability to reason about psychological states is what may make human minds. But before I develop that idea further let me say a word about the social cognition of other animals.

Breaking the human 'monopoly' on psychological states to bring the apes into the 'inner circle', may give the impression that only apes and humans make inferences about the psychological states of others. However, it is conceivable that other animals, even those that are distantly related to us, may also have some ability to appreciate the psychological states of others. Recent studies are beginning to show that various mammals and birds have sophisticated social cognitive skills (see papers in Rogers & Kaplan, 2004). For instance, dogs can follow gaze to locations behind themselves (Hare, Call & Tomasello, 1998; Miklósi et al., 1998), will not take forbidden food when humans are looking at them (Call, Bräuer, Kaminski & Tomasello, 2003), and can take the perspective of humans even when they cannot directly see them (Bräuer, Call & Tomasello, 2004). These results suggest that dogs have perspective-taking abilities comparable to those of chimpanzees. It would not be surprising to find comparable skills in other species as well once research is conducted.

Returning to the issue of human minds, Tomasello et al. (2005) argued that human cognition is grounded on two converging developments: the ability to infer psychological states and the motivation to share emotions and experiences. We have already indicated that humans and apes can infer some psychological states such as attention and intention. We have also indicated that there is no evidence that apes understand epistemic states or even certain levels of attention (e.g., level II perspective taking). These may be important differences between humans and apes but they only become evident after human infants' second or third birthdays.

Tomasello et al. (2005) argued that another important difference appears much earlier in time and from a different direction. Human infants, unlike apes, are intrinsically motivated to share emotions and experiences. Although apes can be said to engage in joint attention defined as looking at the same object and at the social partner, they do not direct the attention of others to interesting sights of their environment just to share that experience. It is true that they vocalize when they sight food or predators but in those situations the main target of interest is the sighted object, not the social partner. In contrast, human infants direct attention to outside entities just to share attention with their partners; the so-called declarative gestures. It is the social interaction that is critical, not the object per se. Interestingly, even though apes often use imperative gestures in various contexts such as play, sex, or feeding, unlike children, they very rarely engage in declarative gestures. It is hypothesized that this motivation to share experiences with others, has important repercussions on the development of social cognition in humans. In fact, one of the early indicators of developmental deficits in children with autism is the lack of declarative gestures (Baron-Cohen, 1995). Note that children with autism are also delayed in their ability to solve tasks of false belief attribution. This is not to say that the motivation to share is the key ingredient for developing human social cognition. It is better characterized as a key ingredient that together with the ability to infer psychological states may make the social minds displayed by typically-developing humans.

References

Baillargeon, R. (1995). Physical reasoning in infancy. In M.S. Gazzaniga (ed.), *The cognitive neurosciences* (pp. 181–204). Cambridge, MA: MIT Press.

Baldwin, D.A., Baird, J.A., Saylor, M.M., & Clark, M.A. (2001). Infants parse dynamic action. *Child Development, 72,* 708–717.

Baron-Cohen, S. (1995). *Mindblindness. An essay on autism and theory of mind.* Cambridge, MA: MIT Press.

Behne, T., Carpenter, M., Call, J., & Tomasello, M. (2005). Unwilling or unable? Infants' understanding of others' intentions. *Developmental Psychology, 41,* 328–337.

Bertenthal, B. (1996). Origins and early development of perception, action, and representation. *Annual Review of Psychology, 47,* 431–59.

Bräuer, J., Call, J., & Tomasello, M. (2004). Visual perspective taking in dogs (*Canis familiaris*) in the presence of barriers. *Applied Animal Behaviour Science* 88, 294–317.

Brooks, R., & Meltzoff, A.N. (2002). The importance of the eyes: How infants interpret adult looking behavior. *Developmental Psychology, 38,* 958–966.

Butterworth, G., & Jarred, N. (1991). What minds have in common is space: Spatial mechanisms serving joint visual attention in infancy. *British Journal of Developmental Psychology, 9,* 55–72.

Call, J., Bräuer, J., Kaminski, J., & Tomasello, M. (2003). Domestic dogs are sensitive to the attentional state of humans. *Journal of Comparative Psychology, 117,* 257–263.

Call, J., & Carpenter, M. (2003). On imitation in apes and children. *Infancia y Aprendizaje, 26,* 325–349.

Call, J., Carpenter, M., & Tomasello, M., (2005). Copying outcomes and copying actions in the process of social learning: Chimpanzees (*Pan troglodytes*) and human children (*Homo sapiens*). *Animal Cognition, 8,* 151–163.

Call, J., Hare, B., Carpenter, M., & Tomasello, M. (2004). Unwilling or unable: Chimpanzees' understanding of human intentional action. *Developmental Science, 7,* 488–498.

Call, J., Hare, B.H., & Tomasello, M., (1998). Chimpanzee gaze following in an object-choice task. Animal *Cognition, 1,* 89–99.

Call, J., & Tomasello, M. (1998). Distinguishing intentional from accidental actions in orangutans (*Pongo pygmaeus*), chimpanzees (*Pan troglodytes*) and human children (*Homo sapiens*). *Journal of Comparative Psychology, 112,* 192–206.

Caron, A. J., Butler, S. C. & Brooks, R. (2002). Gaze following at 12 and 14 months: do the eyes matter? *British Journal of Developmental Psychology, 20,* 225–239.

Caron, A. J., Kiel, E. J., Dayton, M., & Butler, S. C. (2002). Comprehension of the referential intent of looking and pointing between 12 and 15 months. *Journal of Cognition & Development, 3,* 445–464.

Carpenter, M., Akhtar, N., & Tomasello, M. (1998). Fourteen- through 18-month-old infants differentially imitate intentional and accidental actions. *Infant Behavior & Development, 21,* 315–330.

Carpenter, M., Nagell, K., & Tomasello, M. (1998). Social cognition, joint attention, and communicative competencies from 9 to 15 months of age. *Monographs of the Society of Research in Child Development, 63*(4).

Deak, G.O., Flom, R.A., & Pick, A.D. (2000). Effects of gesture and target on 12- and 18-month-olds' joint visual attention to objects in front of or behind them. *Developmental Psychology, 36,* 511–523.

D'Entremont, B., Hains, S. M. J., & Muir, D. W. (1997). A demonstration of gaze following in 3- to 6-month-olds. *Infant Behavior & Development, 20,* 569–572.

Emery, N. J. (2000). The eyes have it: The neuroethology, function and evolution of social gaze. *Neuroscience & Biobehavioral Reviews, 24*, 581–604.

Flavell, J.H. (1992). Perspectives on perspective taking. In H. Beilin & P.B. Pufall (Eds.). *Piaget's theory: Prospects and possibilities.* (pp. 107–139). Hillsdale, New Jersey: Lawrence Erlbaum Associates.

Gergely, G., Bekkering, H., & Király, I. (2002). Rational imitation in preverbal infants. *Nature, 415*, 755.

Gergely, G., & Csibra G. (2003). Teleological reasoning in infancy: the naïve theory of rational action. *Trends in Cognitive Sciences, 7*, 287–292.

Gergely, G., Nádasdy, Z., Csibra G., & Bíró S. (1995). Taking the intentional stance at 12 months of age. *Cognition 56*, 165–193.

Hare, B.H., Call, J., & Tomasello, M. (1998). Communication of food location between human and dog (*Canis familiaris*). *Evolution of Communication, 2*, 137–159.

Itakura, S. (1996). An exploratory study of gaze-monitoring in nonhuman primates. *Japanese Psychological Research, 38*, 174–180.

Kaminski, J., Riedel, J., Call, J., & Tomasello, M. (2005). Domestic goats (*Capra hircus*) follow gaze direction and use social cues in an object choice task. *Animal Behaviour 69*, 11–18.

Meltzoff, A. (1995). Understanding the intentions of others: Re-enactment of intended acts by 18-month-old children. *Developmental Psychology, 31*, 1–16.

Miklósi, A., Polgárdi, R., Topál, J., & Csányi, V. (1998). Use of experimenter-given cues in dogs. *Animal Cognition, 1*, 113–121.

Moll, H., & Tomasello, M. (2004). 12- and 18-month-old infants follow gaze to spaces behind barriers. *Developmental Science, 7*, F1-F9.

Myowa-Yamakoshi, M., & Matsuzawa, T. (2000). Imitation of intentional manipulatory actions in chimpanzees. *Journal of Comparative Psychology, 114*, 381–391.

Povinelli, D.J., & Eddy, T.J. (1996). Chimpanzees: Joint visual attention. *Psychological Science, 7*, 129–135.

Povinelli, D.J., & Vonk, J. (2003). Chimpanzee minds: Suspiciously human? *Trends in Cognitive Sciences, 7*, 157–160.

Premack, D., & Woodruff, G. (1978). Does the chimpanzee have a theory of mind? *Behavioral and Brain Sciences, 4*, 515–526.

Rogers, L., & Kaplan, G. (2004). *Comparative vertebrate cognition: Are primates special?* New York: Kluwer Academic.

Scheumann, M., & Call, J. (2004). The use of experimenter-given cues by South African fur seals (*Arctocephalus pusillus*). *Animal Cognition, 7*, 224–236.

Suddendorf, T., & Whiten, A. (2001). Mental evolution and development: Evidence for secondary representation in children, great apes, and other animals. *Psychological Bulletin, 127*, 629–650.

Tomasello, M. (1999). *The cultural origins of human cognition.* Cambridge: Harvard University Press.

Tomasello, M. (2003). *Constructing a language.* Cambridge: Harvard University Press.

Tomasello, M., & Call, J. (2006). Do chimpanzees know what others see — or only what they are looking at? In S. Hurley & M. Nudds (eds.). *Rational animals.* Oxford: Oxford University Press.

Tomasello, M., Call, J., & Hare, B. (1998). Five primate species follow the visual gaze of conspecifics. *Animal Behaviour, 55*, 1063–1069.

Tomasello, M., Call, J., & Hare, B. (2003). Chimpanzees understand psychological states — the question is which ones and to what extent. *Trends in Cognitive Sciences, 7,* 153–156.

Tomasello, M., Carpenter, M., Call, J., Behne, T., & Moll, H. (2005). Understanding and sharing intentions: The ontogeny and phylogeny of cultural cognition. *Behavioral and Brain Sciences, 28,* 675–735.

Tomasello, M., & Haberl, K. (2003). Understanding attention: 12- and 18-month-olds know what is new for other persons. *Developmental Psychology, 39,* 906–912.

Tomasello, M., Hare, B., & Agnetta, B. (1999). Chimpanzees, *Pan troglodytes,* follow gaze direction geometrically. *Animal Behaviour, 58,* 769–777.

Tomasello, M., Hare, B., & Fogleman, T. (2001). The ontogeny of gaze following in chimpanzees and rhesus macaques. *Animal Behaviour, 61,* 335–343.

Tschudin, A., Call, J., Dunbar, R.I.M., Harris, G., & van der Elst, C. (2001). Comprehension of signs by dolphins (*Tursiops truncatus*). *Journal of Comparative Psychology, 115,* 100–105.

Vauclair, J. (1996). *Animal cognition. An introduction to modern comparative cognition.* Cambridge, Massachusetts: Harvard University Press.

Whiten, A. (1994). Grades of mindreading. In Lewis, C. & Mitchell, P. (Eds.). *Children's early understanding of mind* (pp. 47–70). Hillsdale, New Jersey: Lawrence Erlbaum Associates.

Whiten, A., & Byrne, R. W. (1988). The manipulation of attention in primate tactical deception. In R. Byrne, & A. Whiten (Eds). *Machiavellian intelligence: Social expertise and the evolution of intellect in monkeys, apes, and humans* (pp 211–223). Oxford: Clarendon Press.

Woodward, A. (1999). Infants ability to distinguish between purposeful and non-purposeful behaviors. *Infant Behavior and Development 22,* 145–160.

Wynn, K. (1998). An evolved capacity for number. In Cummins, D.D. & Allen, C. (Eds.). *The evolution of mind.* (pp. 107–126). New York: Oxford University Press.

The understanding of own and others' actions during infancy

"You-like-Me" or "Me-like-You"?

Petra Hauf[1] and Wolfgang Prinz[2]
[1]St. Francis Xavier University, Antigonish / [2]Max Planck Institute for Human Cognitive and Brain Sciences, Leipzig

Developmental psychologists assume that infants understand other persons' actions *after and because* they understand their own ("Like-me" perspective). However, there is another possibility as well, namely that infants come to understand their own actions *after and because* they understand other persons' actions ("Like-you" perspective). We reviewed infant research on the influence of perceived actions on self-performed actions as well as the reverse. Furthermore, we investigated the interplay between both aspects of action understanding by means of a sequence variation. The results show the impact of agentive experience for action understanding, but not the reverse. The question whether infants' perceived and to-be-produced actions share common representations of the perceptual and the motor system is discussed in relation to its implications for the social making of minds.

Descartes claimed that all human beings have privileged access to themselves, whereas knowledge about other persons is always mediated and transformed via perception. Thus, developmental psychologists agree that mental structures and dispositions are shaped in early infancy. However, the issue of how these changes are modulated by the infants' social context is still a matter of controversy. On the one hand, some approaches restrict the influence of social context only to the extent of providing the information that is needed for the maturation of already predisposed mental structures. On the other hand, alternative approaches suggest that mental structures underlying the self are the product of social interaction. The same issue is discussed concerning the development of action understanding. The underlying question is like the hen-and-egg problem: Do infants come to understand other people's actions *after and because* they understand their own — or is the opposite the case, that they come to understand themselves *after and because* they understand others? The first account represents the prevailing position that underlies the majority of theories of agency and intentionality ("Like-me" perspective). According to the alternative position, infants first understand others as intentional agents and only then and thereby do they come to understand themselves that way ("Like-you" perspective).

The following review focuses on the development of action understanding in preverbal infants, especially on the interplay of action production and action perception. *Firstly*, we argue that the functional equivalence of self-performed actions and perceived actions performed by others is a useful idea not only for action understanding in adults but also in infants. *Secondly*, we bring together studies about the influence of action production on action perception (doing oneself to seeing others) with studies about the influence of action perception on action production (seeing others to doing oneself). These two aspects are only rarely connected in typical developmental approaches. *Thirdly*, we present data from our own studies which explicitly investigated the interplay of both aspects of action control, namely action perception and action production. Thereby, we discuss the developmental changes in action understanding during the first year of life. *Finally*, we conclude by highlighting the importance of early action understanding for the social making of minds.

1.   The functional equivalence of action perception and action production

The functional equivalence of self-performed actions and perceived actions performed by others is a useful idea for action understanding. One prominent theory that focuses on the understanding of the functional relationships between perception and action is the Common Coding Approach, introduced by Prinz (1990, 1997). The core assumption of this approach is that perceived and to-be-produced actions share common representational resources. This differs from the more traditional approaches which state (more or less) explicitly that perceptual codes and action codes are separate and incommensurate and therefore need some transformation or translation in order to explain how coordination between the perceptual system and the action system is achieved. The common coding account tells a much simpler story. Events and actions are represented in a common domain. As a consequence, codes of both types (perceived actions and to-be-produced actions) can communicate with each other directly and there is no need for a translation process to mediate between the perceptual system and the motor system. *Event codes* and *action codes* should be considered the functional basic of percepts and action plans, respectively. Percepts and acts both refer to events with comparable attributes, the only difference being that *percepts* refer to ongoing, actor-independent events and *acts* to to-be-generated, actor-dependent events. This implies that percept codes and action codes are formed in the same format. Therefore, it is assumed that they share the same representational domain and are commensurate. Empirical support for such a functional equivalence derives from rather different domains, for example, from studies on sensorimotor synchronization (e.g. Aschersleben & Prinz, 1995; Drewing & Aschersleben, 2003), on stimulus-response compatibility (e.g. Kunde, 2001; Müsseler & Hommel, 1997), and on action perception (Knoblich & Flach, 2001; for an overview see Hommel, Müsseler, Aschersleben, & Prinz, 2001). Two general conclusions can be derived from this work: (1) Certain products of perception on the one hand and certain antecedents of action on the other hand share a common representational domain. This is the so-called *common-coding principle*. (2) Actions are planned and controlled in terms of their anticipated effects; that is, that representations of action effects play an important role in both the planning and the control of those actions. This is the so-called *action-effect principle*.

The results of extensive investigations in adults showed that the common coding approach offers a powerful framework for the coherent interpretation of both action perception and action production. Furthermore, there is evidence for shared representations of self-performed actions and perceived actions performed by others from further research domains. Neuroscientists as well as experimental psychologists focus on the brain and the psychological mechanisms that connect the perception and the production of actions. "Mirror neurons" in the premotor cortex of the monkey brain fire both when an action is observed and when it is produced (e.g., Gallese, Fadiga, Fogassi, & Rizzolatti, 1996; Rizzolatti, Fadiga, Fogassi, & Gallese, 2002). Related findings in humans using PET and fMRI methods reveal common brain regions subserving both the perception and production of actions (e.g., Decety, 1996; Grèzes & Decety, 2001; Iacoboni et al., 1999; Decety & Sommerville, 2003).

Although, these are dramatic discoveries, research from a developmental perspective is still rare. The question of whether the principle of shared representations applies to infants' action perception and action production as well, is still an unsolved issue. Therefore, further elaborations about the developmental processes involved in acquiring the supposed common representations of perception and action are required.

2. The development of functional equivalence during infancy

The functional equivalence of perceived and to-be-produced actions is a useful idea for action understanding not only in adults but also in infants. Based on this common representation one could assume that even very young infants have an abstract representation of actions and this representation is used both by the perceptual system in order to perceive and understand actions of other persons and by the motor system in order to perform actions. First evidence for this was shown by Hauf and colleagues (2004) who found that infants at the age of 12 and 18 months represented modeled actions not only by the perceived actions per se, but also by the effects related to these actions.

The theory of common coding which derived from cognitive experiments with adults is now extended to developmental psychology with infants. Furthermore, the idea of common representations in this sense is also used by Meltzoff (2002). Thereby it is assumed that infant imitation involves "active intermodal mapping" (AIM). The idea is that infant imitation involves a goal-directed matching process. The goal or behavior (action) is visually specified. Infants' self-performed actions provide proprioceptive feedback that is compared to the representation of the observed action. AIM proposes that such comparison is possible because the perception and the production of actions are coded within a common framework, the so-called *supramodal act space*. Meltzoff (2002) argues that "exteroception (perception of others) and proprioception (perception of self) speak the same language" (p. 24). The idea of similarity between perception of others and perception of self is also reflected in the Common Coding Theory, which argues that percept codes and action codes are formed in the same format (Prinz, 1990, 1997).

The idea of functional equivalence between perceived and to-be-produced actions and its implication for the development of action understanding during infancy is obviously important. Nevertheless, the typical developmental approaches deal only with one part of the story. They either focus on the influence of action production on action perception (*from doing oneself to seeing others*) or they are interested in how action perception influences subsequent action production (*from seeing others to doing oneself*). Both research traditions exist in parallel, unfortunately having nearly no reference to each other.

From doing oneself to seeing others

The common contemporary view, the "Like-me" perspective, claims that human beings need agentive experiences to understand others as actors. Infants are able to perform actions, and their level of understanding is thus based on personal experience. It is only then that infants transfer this knowledge to the understanding of actions performed by other people. Even though this claim influenced developmental theories over decades, there are only a few studies addressing the question of how the infant's own previous action can influence his/her subsequent perception and understanding of others' actions. In contrast, recent experimental approaches focused on other aspects like the influence of agentive experience on object features, object exploration, or action memory. For example Needham, Barett, and Peterman (2002) enriched infants' object contact by giving experience earlier than they would normally acquire. These infants received multiple sessions wearing "sticky mittens" (mittens with palms that stuck to the edges of toys and allowed the infants to pick up the toys) to reach for and "grasp" objects. After these enrichment sessions, the experienced 3-month-old infants showed more object exploration and object-directed actions compared to inexperienced peers. Thus, the early experience of agentive acting on objects influenced their subsequent object exploration behavior. Furthermore, agentive experiences not only transmit knowledge about object features and influence object exploration, but also affect the performance of action sequences after a delay (Hayne, Barr, & Herbert, 2003).

The transfer of knowledge from self to others is also a basic issue in the developing understanding of other persons' goal-directed actions. For example, by means of habituation paradigms, infants watch others' actions without acting by themselves. Nevertheless, it is argued that infants can only understand others' actions, if they are able to perform them as well. Recent findings indicate that by 6 to 9 month of age, infants represent certain single actions as directed at goals, rather than purely physical trajectories through space (Jovanovic, Kiraly, Elsner, Geregely, Prinz, & Aschersleben, under review; Woodward, 1998, 1999). To illustrate, when infants were habituated to an event in which a person grasped an object, they subsequently demonstrated a strong novelty preference (longer looking time) to events which maintained the physical properties of the reach but disrupted the relation between the person and her goal, but showed no such response to events which varied the physical properties of the reach while maintaining the goal (Woodward, 1998). As these results were not found with mechanical devices (Jovanovic et al., under review; Woodward, 1998; but also see Hofer, Hauf, & Aschersleben, 2005) and with unfamiliar actions like a back-of-the hand movement (Woodward, 1999; but also see Jovanovic et al., under review) it was assumed that agentive experience plays a crucial role for the understanding of goal-directed actions performed by others. This is a core assumption in the literature, about the understanding of goal-directedness as well as on the understanding of intentional actions (Carpenter, Akthar, & Tomasello, 1998; Meltzoff, 1995). And in fact, a recent study of Sommerville, Woodward, and Needham (2005) showed that action experience facilitated action perception. Infants, as young as 3 months, who reached first for an object (with a "sticky" mitten) focused on the relation between the actor and her goal during a subsequent habituation task, whereas infants without this experience failed. Converging evidence is reported by Sommerville and Woodward (2005), using a means-end task: pulling a cloth to retrieve a toy. Twelve-month-olds understand that the initial step of the cloth-pulling sequence is directed toward the ultimate goal of attaining the toy. However, 10-month-olds only understood this goal during the visual task if they were able to solve a similar sequence by own action production. These findings indicate a developmental link between infants' goal-directed action production and their ability to detect such goals in the actions of others.

Taken together, agentive experiences evidently play a crucial role for action understanding during infancy. Nevertheless, studies have to control for the reverse. Couldn't it be that having early visual experience with actions — while perceiving other people acting — influences own action production as well? Infants have multiple possibilities to watch actions long before they are able to control their muscles in a way to perform these actions. Even though we have not yet empirically demonstrated this impact, it cannot be neglected and should be addressed in further research.

From seeing others to doing oneself

Contrary to the traditional view, the "Like-you" perspective would view humans starting out in life as observers. They perceive other persons' actions, understand them, and transfer this knowledge to their own subsequent self-performed actions. The question about the impact of perceived actions on produced actions is widely spread to the field of imitation. Children learn by watching adults. They often do as parents do instead of as parents say, suggesting that visual models exert a powerful influence on children's actions. Imitation plays an especially prominent role during infancy. In order to imitate, infants must watch others' actions, use the visual perception as a basis for an action plan, and execute the motor output. Thus, imitation taps perception, cross-modal coordination, and motor control. If imitation takes place after a delay, memory is involved as well (Mandler, 1990; Meltzoff & Moore, 1994). Furthermore, the ability to perform own actions and to recognize the effects of these actions in the environment is one important source for the developing self in infancy (Rochat & Striano, 2000). However, infants' learning about the consequences of self-produced actions is constrained by motor development. As infants have ample opportunity to observe other people, their actions, and the consequences of these actions in the environment, observational and imitative learning is an efficient alternative for acquiring knowledge about others' and own actions. Several authors have shown that from 6 to 9 months of age, infants start to understand other people's actions as goal-directed (e.g. Jovanovic et al., under review; Woodward, 1998, 1999). However, to understand the goals of observed actions is one thing, while to transfer this knowledge to one's own actions may be another. Whereas observational learning provides infants with action-effect knowledge, imitative learning requires not only this knowledge, but furthermore the transfer of the observed action-effect relations to own actions (Tomasello, 1999; Want & Harris, 2002). Research on infant imitation shows that imitative learning develops not before 6 to 9 months of age (Barr, Dowden, & Hayne, 1996; Heimann & Meltzoff, 1996; Meltzoff, 1988; Tomasello, 1999). Thereby, the range of behaviors that infants imitate expands with age from facial and body movements, to actions on objects, to intended actions and social goals (Meltzoff, 1995). Through watching others, infants learn about the action outcomes associated with a variety of acts. These action outcomes play a crucial role for both action understanding (Jovanovic, et al., under review) and action production (Hauf, Elsner, & Aschersleben, 2004). The study of Hauf and colleagues showed that 12- and 18-month-olds produced a target action that elicited an interesting action effect with shorter latency and more often than other actions which were not combined with such an interesting action effect. Thus, the observation of an action-effect relation led to selective production of different action steps. Elsner & Aschersleben (2003) demonstrated that 12 — 18, but not 9-month-old infants perform more target actions after having observed the model than when exploring the object on their own. Even though the infants benefit from watching others' actions, the transfer of specific action-effect relations to own behavior emerged later. Only from 15 months of age did infants perform more target actions when their own actions led to the same, instead of different, effects as the model's actions did. There is further evidence that infants learn efficiently and even flexibly by observation. By 14 months, infants reenact the final goal of a modeled action, but do not always reproduce the means (Gergely, Bekkering, & Kiraly, 2002), indicating that they recognized the final act as the ultimate goal.

Taken together, the reported findings indicate that the representations of human actions on objects can be formed by observation alone and that they persist over delays. Although Meltzoff (2002) suggests an innate observation/execution system, it is equally important that infants are not compelled to move immediately from perception to motor performance. For example, deferred imitation introduces memory and the representation of actions (Barr et al., 1996; Heimann & Meltzoff, 1996; Meltzoff, 1988). Thus, these representations are a sufficient basis for organizing own actions later on.

3. The interplay of action perception and action production during infancy

The review of developmental studies on infants' action understanding showed impressively that most of the studies focus on only one aspect of action understanding. They either deal with the influence of action production on action perception or with the reverse. However, both aspects are often at least implicitly included or discussed. For example, Meltzoff (2002) claims that infants gain an understanding of others by analogy to the self ("like me"). They use the knowledge of how they feel when they produce an expression to infer how somebody else feels. But, in real-world social interactions, learning is *bi-directional*. Infants learn about others by analogy to the self, but they also learn about themselves, their powers, and potential, through interactions with others.

Based upon this, we focused on the interplay of the two aspects of action understanding, namely action perception and action production. We investigated the developmental changes underlying action understanding during the first year of life. Therefore, we addressed the question of whether infants come to understand other people's actions *after and because* they understand their own actions — or whether it is the opposite and infants come to understand their own actions *after and because* they understand others' actions. At this point, we were some of the first researchers to investigate this interplay by means of the same experimental paradigm during the first year of life. The critical point in the conducted studies was the variation of the sequence between perception and production. In a so-called *self study* the infants first produced an action and subsequently perceived two adults acting on a toy. In the so-called *other study* the order was reversed. The infants first perceived two adults acting on a toy and subsequently acted on toys by themselves.

(A) From doing oneself to seeing others. With this series of experiments we investigated how self-produced actions influence infants' interest in actions performed by others. The infants started to act on a toy at a table (*doing oneself*). Then the infants were given the chance to watch two short video clips on two screens simultaneously (*seeing others*; Fig. 1, top). Both videos showed the same two adults sitting at a table and acting on a toy. In one video clip the two adults were acting on the same toy the infants had played with during the production phase. The other video showed the same two adults, but now acting on a different toy. Whereas the 7-month-olds showed no preference for one of the two videos, the 9- and 11-month-olds significantly preferred the video clip showing the two adults acting on the same toy (Hauf, Aschersleben, & Prinz, in press). Further experiments support the position that only self-performed actions influenced the subsequent perception of actions performed by others: (1) Thus, there was no

preference anymore, if not the infant herself but an experimenter in front of the infant was acting on the toy. (2) Furthermore, there was no preference anymore, if the videos showed the two adults only looking at the toy, without showing any action and if the videos showed only the toys, without acting persons, respectively. Apparently, the preference for the same-toy-video was clearly related to self-performed action on the one hand and to perceiving actions performed by others on the other hand. Infants at the age of 9- and 11-months are interested in learning about the use of objects and — given the chance — they like to compare their own actions with those of others.

(B) *From seeing others to doing oneself.* By means of the same experimental paradigm we investigated how action perception influences subsequent self-performed actions. Now the infants first watched a video clip on a screen which showed two adults acting on a toy by taking turns (*seeing others*). Following this the infants were seated at a table and two toys were presented within reach simultaneously (*doing oneself*; Figure 1, bottom). Thus, the infants had the chance to

Self-Study

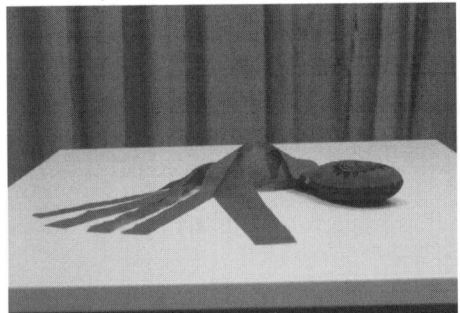 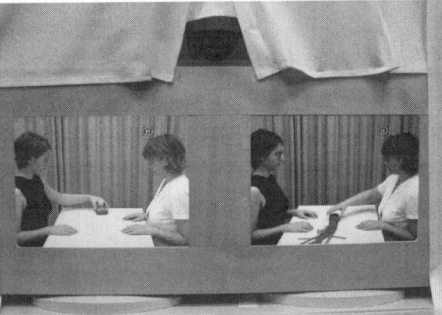

Other-Study

Figure 1. Experimental set up for the self and other studies. Whereas the self study started with action production followed by action perception (top), it was the reverse in the other study (bottom).

choose and to act either with the same toy they had just seen in the video, or with a different one. Neither the 7-, nor the 9- and 11-month-olds showed any differences. They all looked and acted equally long on both toys. Even though it is well known that infants at this age are able to imitate televised models (Barr & Hayne, 1999), previous action perception did not influence subsequent active action production in this setting (Hauf, subm.).

Interestingly, the different theoretical views would predict different result patterns for both studies: The "Like-me" perspective claims that human beings need agentive experience to understand others as actors. Thus, it would imply a preference for the same-toy-video in the self study (*from doing oneself to seeing others*), but not in the other study. Conversely, the "Like-you" perspective would see humans starting as observers. Therefore, it would assume a preference for the same toy in the other study (*from seeing others to doing oneself*), but not in the self study. At first glance, the reported results — preferences in the self study, but not in the other study — suggest converging evidence for the "Like-me" perspective at least in terms of infants' action understanding. But what about the 7-month old infants? If the starting point of action understanding is self-agentive action, than the 7-month-olds should show the same result pattern as the older age groups. This is especially true if we follow the argumentation of Meltzoff and Brooks (2001), who postulate an innate mechanism which enables infants to recognize equivalence between perceived and executed acts. "Because human acts are seen in others and performed by the self, the infant can represent the other as "like-me": I can act like the other and reciprocally the other acts like me" (p. 174). No doubt, the 7-month-olds are able to see the act in others as well as to perform this act by themselves. Nevertheless, they did not show any preference.

"You-like-me" or "Me-like-You"?

The crux with the postulation of the self-other equivalence is the following: If equivalence between perceived and to-be-produced actions is achieved then the "Like-me" perspective is just as true as the "Like-you" perspective, because the functional equivalence includes a bi-directional influence of action perception and action production by definition. To illustrate, the "Like-me" analogy is often used to explain imitation of intentional actions, even though the starting point in this case is the perception of demonstrated actions produced by others (Meltzoff, 1995; Carpenter, Akthar, & Tomasello, 1998). Meltzoff and Brooks (2001) argue that only the "sensitivity to human acts and ability to map equivalence between self and others provides leverage for understanding the beginning of social cognition" (p. 173). In this framework infants perform actions and watch others' actions.

Thus, infants can represent the other as "like-me" (both are acting) and therefore transfer their own mental states to others as well. But, evidently infants benefit from observing others' actions. A long time before they are able to relate observed actions to corresponding motor patterns, they are intensively observing other persons' actions. Later on, they match this knowledge to their own actions and start to imitate. Thus, infants can represent themselves as "like-you" (both are acting) as well. Taken together, there is no clear evidence for one of the two perspectives on infants' action understanding. Therefore, the question that still has to be addressed is whether the functional equivalence of perceived and to-be-produced actions is innate — as postulated by Meltzoff and Brooks — or whether it develops during the first months of life.

To answer this question, further research on the permanent exchange between action perception and action production is needed. A real-world social interaction is determined by bi-directional learning. This is especially true for actions. Infants learn about actions by an analogy to self-produced actions, but they also learn about themselves and their possibilities through observing others' actions. The studies by Hauf and colleagues showed that self-performed actions influence subsequent action perception, but not the reverse. Sommerville and colleagues (2005) demonstrated similar effects: action experience facilitated action perception, whereas action perception did not influence subsequent action production. Probably, one could find an influence of perceived actions on to-be-produced actions if a target action is shown that is not yet in the motor repertoire of the infant. In this case there is only perceptual information without any mapping to the motor system. Later on, one could investigate how the production of this target action develops in relation to different perceptual enrichment sessions.

Further information about the functional equivalence could be derived from studies about imitating and being imitated. Meltzoff (1990) tested whether infants recognize when another acts "like me". To study this, an adult imitated everything the infant did, while another adult imitated what another baby had done. Both adults were acting contingently in infantile ways, but the 14-month-old infants looked longer at the person who was imitating them and also smiled more often at that person. Evidently, infants recognized a deeper commonality between self and other. In this context, Nadel (2002) argues that imitation recognition will emerge much later than imitation. Converging evidence is reported by Agnetta and Rochat (2004) who showed that 9-month-old infants are already able to imitate as well as to discriminate between the mimicking and the contingent experimenter. But only 14- and 18-month-olds discriminate additionally between an experimenter mimicking the infants' actions and an object mimicking these actions (without being handled by a person!). Based upon this, it could be assumed that infants generate implicit awareness of being imitated and imitation. Thus, imitation and imitation recognition are tightly linked and show impressively the achieved functional equivalence of perceived and to-be-produced actions.

As already indicated, we are not able to answer the question addressed in the title at this point in time. Do infants come to understand other people's actions *after and because* they understand their own actions ("Like-me") or do they come to understand themselves *after and because* they understand others ("Like-you")? But we are able to say that at least at the age of 9 months infants have already achieved the functional equivalence. The representation of knowledge about one's *own* actions is similar to the representation of knowledge about *others'* actions (Prinz, 1990, 1997; Hommel et al, 2001). Now, further research has to show how mental representations develop very early in infancy and whether the establishing of these representations needs input from both perception and motor systems (von Hofsten, 2004).

4. Conclusions

Instead of summarizing the reported aspects of the paper, we wish to speculate about the impact of infants' action understanding on the social making of minds. Human beings act within and also interact with their social environment from the beginning. The newborn is already sensitive to temporal contingency between events and, after a few weeks, infants can form expectancies for social contingency (Nadel et al., 1999). Thus, it is not surprising that an extreme increase of learning about self and others takes place during the first year of life. Social interaction is by definition bi-directional. In this sense, early imitation provides a mechanism for infants' learning about other people, distinguishing them from things, and establishing empathy. For young infants persons are 'entities that can be imitated and also who imitate me' (Meltzoff & Gopnik, 1993). Accordingly, infants' behavior is shaped by observing others and agentive experience shapes their interest in others. If we assume that the understanding of own and others' actions is a precursor for the understanding of own and others' mental states, it should also be assumed that the mechanisms playing a role in action understanding are playing a similar role in mind understanding. Maybe we could not even develop a moral mind without an imitative mind. Social interaction plays a crucial role for both imitative behavior as well as moral behavior, and both are shaped through communication with others. The deep impact of social interaction is dramatically obvious in cases where this interplay is disturbed, in infants and children (see Nadel, 2005, this volume) as well as in adults (see Hahlweg, 2005; Williams & Gerber, 2005, this volume). Thus, there is no doubt about the social making of minds, a fact that highlights once more the absolute necessity of research on the developing mind.

References

Agnetta, B., & Rochat, P. (2004). Imitative games by 9-, 14-, and 18-month-old infants. *Infancy, 6(1)*, 1–36.

Aschersleben, G., & Prinz, W. (1995). Synchronizing actions with events: The role of sensory information. *Perception and Psychophysics, 57*, 305–317.

Barr, R., & Hayne, H. (1999). Developmental changes in imitation from television during infancy. *Child Development, 70*, 1067–1081.

Barr, R., Dowden, A., & Hayne, H. (1996). Developmental changes in deferred imitation by 6- to 24-month-old infants. *Infant Behavior and Development, 19*, 159–170.

Carpenter, M., Akthar, N., & Tomasello, M. (1998). Fourteen- through 18-month-old infants differentially imitate intentional and accidental actions. *Infant Behavior and Development, 21*, 315–330.

Decety, J. (1996). Do imagined and executed actions share the same neural substrate? *Cognitive Brain Research, 3*, 87–93.

Decety, J., & Sommerville, J. A. (2003). Shared representations between self and other : a social cognitive neuroscience view. *Trends in Cognitive Science, 7(12)*, 527–533.

Drewing, K., & Aschersleben, G. (2003). Reduced timing variability during bimanual coupling: A role for sensory information. *The Quarterly Journal of Experimental Psychology, 56A*, 329–350.

Elsner, B., & Aschersleben, G. (2003). Do I get what you get? Learning about the effects of self-performed and observed actions in infancy. *Consciousness & Cognition, 12*, 732–751.

Gallese, V., Fadiga, L., Fogassi, L., & Rizzolatti, G. (1996). Action recognition in the premotor cortex. *Brain, 119*, 593–609.

Gergely, G., Bekkering, H., & Kiraly, I. (2002). Rational imitation in preverbal infants. *Nature, 415*, 755.

Grèzes, J., & Decety, J. (2001). Functional anatomy of execution, mental simulation, observation, and verb generation of actions: A meta-analysis. *Human Brain Mapping, 12*, 1–19.

Hahlweg, K. (2005). The shaping of individuals' mental structures and dispositions by others: Findings from research on expressed emotions. *Interaction Studies, 6:1*, 131–144.

Hauf, P. (subm.). Baby see – Baby do! What infants learn from other persons' actions. *Manuscript submitted for publication.*

Hauf, P., Aschersleben, G., & Prinz, W. (in press). Baby do – Baby see! How action production influences action perception in infants. *Cognitive Development.*

Hauf, P., Elsner, B., & Aschersleben, A. (2004). The role of action effects in infants' action control. *Psychological Research, 68*, 115–125.

Hayne, H., Barr, R., & Herbert, J. (2003). The effect of prior practice on memory reactivation and generalization. *Child Development, 74(6)*, 1615–1627.

Heimann, M., & Meltzoff, A. (1996). Deferred imitation in 9- to 14-month-old infants: A longitudinal study of a Swedish sample. *British Journal of Developmental Psychology, 14*, 55–64.

Hofer, T., Hauf, P., & Aschersleben, G. (2005). Infant's perception of goal-directed actions performed by a mechanical device. *Infant Behavior and Development, 28(4)*, 466–480.

Hommel, B., Müsseler, J., Aschersleben, G., & Prinz, W. (2001). The theory of event coding: A framework for perception and action planning. *Behavioral and Brain Sciences, 24*, 849–937.

Iacoboni, M., Woods, R. P., Brass, M., Bekkering, H., Mazziotta, J. C., & Rizolatti, G. (1999). Cortical mechanisms of human imitation. *Science, 286*, 2526–2528.

Jovanovic, B., Kiraly, I., Elsner, B., Geregely, G., Prinz, W., & Aschersleben, G. (under review). The role of effects for infants' perception of action goals.

Knoblich, G., & Flach, R. (2001). Predicting the effects of actions: Interactions of perception and action. *Psychological Science, 12*, 467–472.

Kunde, W. (2001). Response-effect compatibility in manual choice reaction tasks. *Journal of Experimental Psychology: Human Perception and Performance, 27*, 387–394.

Mandler, J. M. (1990). Recall of events by preverbal children. In A. Diamond (Ed), *The development and neural basis of higher cognitive functions. Annals of the New York Academy of Sciences, 608*, 485–516.

Meltzoff, A. (1988). Infant imitation and memory: Nine-month-olds in immediate and deferred tests. *Child Development, 59*, 217–225.

Meltzoff, A. (1990). Foundations for developing a concept of self: The role of imitation in relating self to other and the value of social mirroring, social modeling, and self practice in infancy. In D. Cicchetti & M. Beeghly (Eds), *The self in transition: Infancy to childhood* (pp. 139–164). Chicago: University of Chicago Press.

Meltzoff, A. (1995). Understanding the intentions of others: Re-enactment of intended acts by 18-month-old children. *Developmental Psychology, 31*, 838–850.

Meltzoff, A. (2002). Elements of a developmental theory of imitation. In A. Meltzoff & W. Prinz (Eds), *The imitative mind. Development, evolution and brain bases* (pp. 19–41). New York: Cambridge University Press.

Meltzoff, A., & Brooks, R. (2001). "Like-me" as a building block for understanding other minds: Bodily acts, attention, and intention. In B. F. Malle, L. J. Moses, & D. A. Baldwin (Eds), *Intentions and intentionality: Foundations of social cognition* (pp. 125–148). Cambridge, MA: MIT Press.

Meltzoff, A., & Gopnik, A. (1993). The role of imitation in understanding persons and developing a theory of mind. In S. Baron-Cohen, H. Flusberg, & D. Cohen (Eds.), *Understanding other minds* (pp. 335–366). Oxford: Oxford University Press.

Meltzoff, A., & Moore, M. K. (1994). Imitation, memory, and the representation of persons. *Infant Behavior and Development, 17*, 83–99.

Müsseler, J., & Hommel, B. (1997). Blindness to response-compatible stimuli. *Journal of Experimental Psychology: Human Perception and Performance, 23(3)*, 861–872.

Nadel, J. (2005). Experiencing contingency and agency: first step toward self-understanding? *Interaction Studies, 6:3*, 447–462.

Nadel, J. (2002). Imitation and imitation recognition: Functional use in preverbal infants and nonverbal children with autism. In A. Meltzoff & W. Prinz (Eds), *The imitative mind. Development, evolution and brain bases* (pp. 42–62). New York: Cambridge University Press.

Nadel, J., Carchon, I., Cervella, C., Marcelli, D., & Réserbat-Plantey, D. (1999). Expectancies for social contingency in 2-month-olds. *Developmental Science, 2*, 164–174.

Needham, A., Barrett, T., & Peterman, K. (2002). A pick-me-up for infants' exploratory skills: Early simulated experiences reaching for objects using "sticky mittens" enhances young infants' object exploration skills. *Infant Behavior and Development, 25,* 279–295.

Prinz, W. (1990). A common coding approach to perception and action. In O. Neumann & W. Prinz (Eds.), *Relationships between perception and action* (pp. 167–201). Berlin: Springer-Verlag.

Prinz, W. (1997). Perception and action planning. *European Journal of Cognitive Psychology, 9(2),* 129–154.

Prinz, W. (2002). Experimental approaches to imitation. In A. Meltzoff & W. Prinz (Eds), *The imitative mind. Development, evolution and brain bases* (pp. 143–162). New York: Cambridge University Press.

Rochat, P., & Striano, T. (2000). Perceived self in infancy. *Infant behavior and development, 23,* 513–530.

Rizzolatti, G., Fadiga, L., Fogassi, L., & Gallese, V. (2002). From mirror neurons to imitation: Facts and speculations. In A. Meltzoff & W. Prinz (Eds), *The imitative mind. Development, evolution and brain bases* (pp. 247–266). New York: Cambridge University Press.

Sommerville, J. A., & Woodward, A. L. (2005). Pulling out the intentional structure of action: The relation between action processing and action production in infancy, *Cognition, 95(1),* 1–30.

Sommerville, J. A., Woodward, A. L., & Needham, A. (2005). Action experience alters 3-month-old infants' perception of others' actions. *Cognition 96(1),* B1–B11.

Tomasello, M. (1999). *The cultural origins of human cognition.* Cambridge, MA: Harvard University Press.

Von Hofsten, C. (2004). An action perspective on motor development. *Trends in Cognitive Sciences, 8(6),* 266–272.

Want, S. C., & Harris, P. L. (2002). How do children ape. Applying concepts from the study of non-human primates to the developmental study of 'imitation' in children. *Developmental Science, 5,* 1–13.

Williams, K., & Gerber, J. (2005). Ostracism: The making of the ignored and excluded mind. *Interaction Studies, 6:3,* 359–374.

Woodward, A. L. (1998). Infants selectively encode the goal of objects of an actor's reach. *Cognition, 69,* 1–34.

Woodward, A. L. (1999). Infants' ability to distinguish between purposeful and non-purposeful behaviors. *Infant Behavior and Development, 22,* 145–160.

Experiencing contingency and agency

First step toward self-understanding in making a mind?

Jacqueline Nadel[1], Ken Prepin[1] and Mako Okanda[2]
[1]UMR CNRS 7593 / [2]Kyoto University

Precursors of inferential capacities concerning self- and other- understanding may be found in the basic experience of social contingency and emotional sharing. The emergence of a sense of self- and other-agency receives special attention here, as a foundation for self-understanding. We propose that synchrony, an amodal parameter of contingent self-other relationships, should be especially involved in the development of a sense of agency. To explore this framework, we have manipulated synchrony in various ways, either by delaying mother's response to infant's behaviour, disorganizing mother's internal synchrony between face and voice, freezing the partner in a still attitude, or on the contrary maximizing synchrony through imitation. We report results obtained with healthy and clinical populations that are supposed to be at the beginning of basic experiences concerning the ownership of their actions: infants of 2 months and 6 months, low-functioning children with autism and MA matched young children with Down Syndrome. Our results support the idea of a two-step process linking understanding of self to understanding of other and leading on to form the concept of human beings as universally contingent entities.

Numerous studies using classical conditioning have shown that neonates do associate and anticipate events (Gewirtz, 1969). A few hours after birth, they already discriminate regularities such as: "just after A (= a finger pressing my forehead left/right), comes B (= a drop of water on lips left/right side)". They do not only turn their head in the appropriate direction, they also express distress when B no longer occurs (Blass *et al.*, 1994). Current research on social perception shows that the early capacity to perceive regularities, and to anticipate B from A, rapidly includes social events. In this case, the anticipated event is not a physiological gain, but rather a psychological benefit: what is gained is not a drop of water, but a glance, a smile, a word.

How can we explain such an early detection of social contingency? Gergely and Watson (1996; 1999) have proposed a theoretical framework that may provide a fruitful background for a complete exploration of infants' subtle capacity to associate and anticipate social events that are related to their current behaviour. Starting from Watson's demonstration that 2 month-olds not only can relate external events to their own behaviour, but also are keen with such events (Watson, 1972), Gergely and Watson (1996; 1999) postulate an innate module of contingency detection (DCM) that concerns social as well as physical events. DCM enables the infant to perceive causal relationships, to establish expectancies for contingency, thus acting as a determinant of social responsiveness. DCM is seen as composed of two independent mechanisms, one anticipating the probability of a future event as regard to present behaviour, and the second retrospectively searching for a link between a present event and past behaviour. Such properties of CDM are hypothesized to lead the infants to distinguish between the sensorial consequences of their motor behaviour, and external sources of perception. This clearly fits the important distinction proposed by Russell (1996) between external perception and perceptions that are at will, since they are caused by one's own actions: from this distinction will emerge a sense of ownership of one's own action, as opposed to and complemented by a sense of other-agency.

Given that the unique actions producing perfectly synchronous perceptions are our own ones, it follows that the detection of synchrony may be considered as a primitive basis for an early distinction between self and external world, a first milestone in making a mind. In particular, Rochat (2002) has underlined that self-imitation is a primary source of knowledge about the self and a basic process by which infants gain self-reflective abilities (p. 86). Results by Watson (1985), Rochat and Morgan (1995) and Schmuckler (1996) support the hypothesis of a developmental switch from an initial attention bias in favour of perfect synchrony between action and perception to a later attraction toward imperfect synchrony. In other words, the preference for perception of own actions soon gives place to a preference for behaviours that reflect, though imperfectly, the infant's behaviour. Computing temporal, spatial and intensity information, CDM takes account of the global degree of relationship between events. According to the prediction attached to the model, imitation of her behaviour should be the most attractive social response among all those that can be offered to a young infant, and a tight temporal contingency accompanied by an attuned comment of the infant's behaviour (Stern, 1985) will be preferred to simple temporal contingency.

Looking back to twenty years of research of our group, it is now obvious to us that we have been turning around the question processed by Gergely and Watson' model, without a clear awareness of such a convergence. In this paper we will stress the convergence and differences between the above mentioned theoretical model and our findings with young infants. As we will see, infants are able to detect a non-contingent behaviour of their mother earlier than predicted by Gergely and Watson's model. They do so more efficiently if the history of their relationship with their mother is a contingently stable one. We will next suggest that the model may need further specification of what is synchrony for older infants and propose an additional dynamical perspective. We will then refer to the second part of Gergely and Watson's model (1996; 1999), that emphasizes the role of parents' mirroring of their infant's action. We will show the relevance of this model to explain our findings with healthy young infants and low-functioning children with autism, and stress its convergence with a theoretical formalism designed by Gaussier and colleagues (Gaussier, Baccon, Prepin, Nadel & Hafemeister, 2004). Finally, we examine the relevance of the hypothesis of an impairment of CDM in autism. Watson (1994) and Gergely and Watson (1999) postulate that the shift of orientation from self-based perfect contingencies to environment-based contingencies occurring around two- to -three months in typically developing infants, does not take place strongly enough to supplant the search for perfect contingency. According to the authors this may explain stereotypies, that can be seen as a kind of self-imitation, and social avoidance. We will see that even low-functioning children with autism are highly sensitive to almost perfect contingency in imitative responses.

I. Early detection of non-contingent responses of mother

One of the first studies demonstrating the early sensitivity to social non-contingency was conducted by Tronick, Als, Adamson, Wise and Brazelton (1978). This study showed that 3-month-olds display negative reactions and finally disengage when their mothers pause with a still face, like infants of depressed mothers tend to do. Gusella, Muir and Tronick (1988) replicated the results at the same age via a televised face to face situation. However, several concerns were raised about the all-or-none nature of the still face paradigm. To test more convincingly infants' sensitivity to social non-contingency, Murray and Trevarthen (1985) organized a TV face-to-face interaction between mothers and 6-to-12 week-olds. After a pause, they replayed the episode which therefore was no more contingent with the current behaviour of the infant. Comparing the live and replayed episode, they found a strong negative effect of the replay on the infant's behavioural state, and concluded that young infants expect contingency and detect non-contingent behaviour. Rochat, Neisser and Marian (1998) did not replicate the findings and concluded that Murray and Trevarthen's results could be explained by a natural decline of interest for the TV interaction.

In a series of experiments with an updated design and procedure, we have tested the capacity of 2 month-old infants to detect and expect contingency via experimental violations of social contingency. In an initial experiment with 10 infants aged 2 months, (Nadel, Carchon, Kervella *et al.*, 1999), we have designed a live1-replay-live2 procedure, instead of the live-replay procedure used by Murray and Trevarthen (1985). We have used a double teleprompter device that allowed us to offer to mothers and infants a continuous image and voice of their partner and to present to the infants alternately 30 seconds of live and replay episodes of their mother's communication with a seamless shift. Results replicated Murray and Trevarthen's previous ones. In addition, they showed a recovery of infant's positive state during mother's second contingent communication for the seven infants who did not cry during replay. A recent experiment with fourteen 2-month-old infants of healthy mothers gave similar results (Nadel, Soussignan, Canet, Libert & Gérardin, 2005). When the 14 infants of healthy mothers were compared with 14 same-age infants of depressed mothers, results showed a linear decrease of smile in infants of depressed mothers contrasting with a curvilinear curve in infants of healthy mothers. They also demonstrate lower negative reactions to non-contingent maternal behaviour. These findings suggest the importance of a stable contingent relationship with the mother for the development of expectancies for contingency and extended use of the DCM. A third experiment was conducted with 50 infants aged 2 months, that were randomly assigned to two conditions (Soussignan, Nadel, Canet & Gérardin, 2006): One group was presented the live-replay-live condition and the other was presented a continuous live interaction (live1-live2-live3) with the mother. Results demonstrate that the second episode of 30 seconds is not processed similarly in the case of live interaction and in case of non-contingent interaction: only non-contingent interaction induces a change of infants' affect. Taken together, the findings of these experiments clearly establish that infants as young as 2 months detect and expect social contingency.

II. Six-month-olds' processing of partially contingent responses

Gergely and Watson's model of contingency predicts young infants' preference for high level of synchrony compared to lower levels. This prediction suggests that visual plus auditory contingent responses will be more attractive than a synchronic response in one modality only. This is what research demonstrates (Walker-Andrews, 1997; see Muir & Nadel, 1998, for a review). However, no prediction can be derived from the CDM model with regard to how young infants process the information coming from two sensory modalities, one contingent to her behaviour and the other non-contingent. Does the infant react differentially (and thus distinguish) when two distinct sources produce the two sensory messages and when there is only one source? Does she expect two modalities coming from the same source to be intrinsically synchronic?

One of us is currently developing a general model of coupling between dynamic systems exchanging energy (Prepin, 2003). Agents engaged in a TV face-to-face interaction can be considered as dynamic systems exchanging energy. Energy can be exchanged using two different flows through two different channels (see Figure 1): the visual channel where facial and bodily motor outputs of one system are visual inputs for the other(s), and the auditory channel, where vocal and verbal outputs of one system are auditory inputs for the other(s). The two flows of energy produced by a dynamic system can be related according to various combinations. Generally when different flows of energy co-occur, they are produced by a unique source, but they may co-occur although produced independently by two different systems.

Notice that the receptor can process and combine energy flows in a number of ways, independently or not from their real state of connection: the receptor can process each flow separately, select one flow and neglect the other, sum up the two flows, consider the two flows as competing, or extract their common properties, thus capturing their intrinsic coherence. This way of processing depends on the receptor's ability to determine if the energy flows it receives come from one source or two independent sources.

Our model predicts that the receptor will distinguish co-occurring flows of information from co-varying ones if it detects shared a-modal parameters, such as speed, rhythm, periodicity, and intensity of flows that reflect their inherent tight connections. When common properties are extracted from two flows of energy, the guess is that the two flows are expected to come from the same system. Conversely, two flows coming from the same system are expected to be tightly connected, not only co-occurring but also coherently responding. Is the young infant able to extract these common properties so as to distinguish between incoherent co-occurring information that comes from two independent sources and incoherent co-occurring information that comes from a unique source? To explore this question and evaluate the role of multimodal synchrony in contingency detection, our experimental design was updated so as to disconnect visual and auditory modalities. We can at will present to the infant a coherently contingent mother, a mother whose response to the infant is contingent for one modality (voice contingent, for instance) but non- contingent for the other (face replayed, for instance)

Figure 1. A model of coupling between dynamic systems
Given a system *Syst.1* which receives simultaneously information from different channels, how will this system process the two flows? We present here a schema of the situations that *Syst.1* can encounter:

Syst.1, *Syst.2* and *Syst.3* are dynamic systems exchanging energy (as shown by arrows) through different channels: the visual channel where facial and bodily motor outputs of one system are visual inputs for the other(s), and the auditory channel, where vocal and verbal outputs of one system are auditory inputs for the other(s). Those two channels are symbolised by red and blue colours. *Syst.1* receive flows of information from both channels. Two conditions can be distinguished:

a) The two information flows come from one source (*Syst.2*), which receives *Syst.1*'s outputs and is thus contingent with *Syst.1* (i.e. the *Live* conditions in our experiments).

b) The two information flows can come from two independent sources: *Syst.2* contingent with *Syst.1*, and *Syst.3* which does not receive any ouputs from *Syst.1* or *Syst.2* and which is thus non-contingent with *Syst.1* (i.e. the conditions *Contingent voice of the mother presented with non-contingent face of mother or of stranger*).

a.

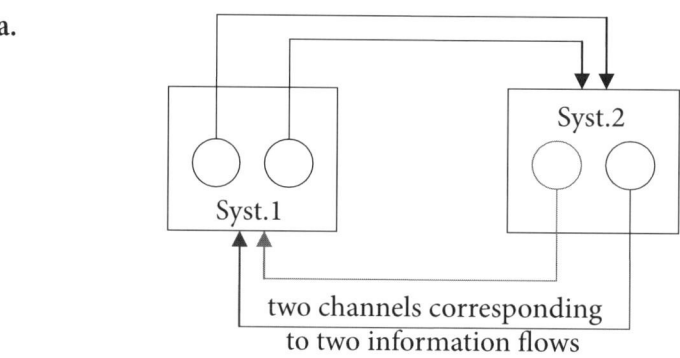

b.

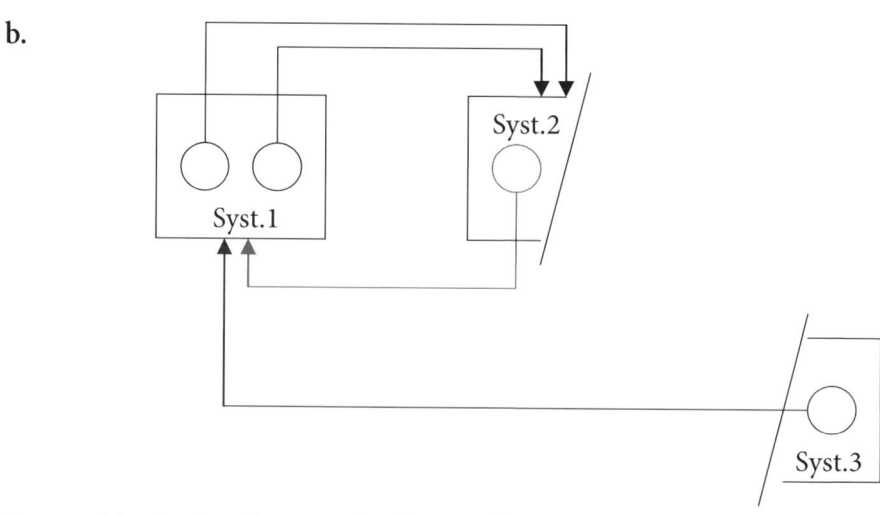

Figure 1. The visual-auditory coupling between dynamic systems.

or two modalities coming from two distinct sources (contingent mother's voice coupled with the non-contingent pre-recorded face of a stranger).

To test this model, two TV experiments were led with 6 month-old infants. In the first experiment (Prepin, Simon, Canet, Mahé, Soussignan & Nadel, submitted), 19 infants were presented three 30-second uninterrupted episodes of maternal interaction in the following order: mother's contingent face and voice (live 1), mother's contingent voice with non-contingent (replayed) face, and again mother's contingent face and voice (live2). The three episodes were presented with a seamless shift. The presence/absence of Gaze to the screen, Smile, Grimace and self-centred movements were coded each $40/100^{th}$ of a second for the three episodes. In the second experiment, 10 infants were presented three 30-second uninterrupted episodes of maternal interaction in the following order: mother's contingent face and voice (live 1), mother's contingent voice coupled with the non-contingent (pre-recorded) face of another mother responding to her infant, and again mother's contingent face and voice (live 2).

Comparing the results of the two experiments for the four indices, we found no significant difference during the first live interaction. The infants' response to the perturbation episode (episode 2) however, was significantly different for gaze: while infants withdraw from the image of the dysfunctioning mother, they maintained gaze at the screen in experiment 2, where the mother's voice was coupled with a non-contingent stranger's face [t $(27) = 2.13$, $p < .04$]. Infants showed also a significantly higher amount of self-centred movements in experiment 1 [t $(27) = 2.07$, $p < .05$] and a marginally significant higher level of grimacing for experiment 1.

Taken together, these findings are in agreement with the hypothesis that 6-month-old infants have formed the concept of mother as an intermodal entity whose sensorial outputs should cohere in a contingent bimodal response to the infant's behaviour, and clearly distinguish a dysfunctioning intermodal entity from co-occurring sensory messages originating from two different sources. To the CDM model, we propose to add the early distinction between contingency detection and detection of co-occurring messages that are not necessarily coherent and may be partially contingent only.

III. Social biofeedback and the effect of being imitated in young children and low-functioning children with autism

According to Gergely and Watson's model (1996; 1999), parents' mirroring of their infants behaviour acts as a social biofeedback. Considering that the internal changes of emotional states are beyond perceptual awareness, the model proposes that those states cannot be understood as such without an external feedback of what is felt. In other words, parents' mirroring of infants' facial expressions will play a role similar to the effect of a biofeedback documenting upon what is related to our internal experience: getting a perceptual knowledge of our blood pressure allows us to relate various internal states to various levels of blood pressure. Here the biofeedback is social and is provided through imitation.

Recently, a theoretical formalism designed by Gaussier and colleagues in an epigenetic robotic perspective (Gaussier, Baccon, Prepin, Nadel & Hafemeister, 2004) resulted in similar proposals. At the start, the conceived architecture can couple perception and action and is driven by a homeostatic principle according to which perception and action should be in accordance. It follows that any perception that perfectly fits the kinesthetic feedback of action reinforces the link between perception and action, and leads to a repetitive behaviour. Reversely, any deviation between perception and action is registered as a signal of error which leads the architecture to act next so as to correct the error via a mirroring of the perceived action: the architecture will thus act according to a process similar to that of social biofeedback. This formalism can describe very simply the distinction between perfect synchrony resulting in self-imitation (Rochat, 2002) and imitation of another's action. It can also describe the process by which facial expressions of internal states that are felt, but not seen, can gain an intermodal representation via a re-enactment of what is externally perceived and resemblance to what was felt: this clearly deals with the principle of social biofeedback. To illustrate the relevance of the formalism designed by Gaussier and colleagues (2004) and of the social biofeedback model, we will report previous findings with 2-year-old infants and recent research with 2-month-olds.

Young infants prefer imitative contingency

A preference for imitative contingency compared to other contingent responses is already to be found very early in development. Three month-olds react more to an imitative mother (Field, Guy & Umbel, 1985). Two-month-olds imitate more imitative than non-imitative mothers (Nadel, Revel, Andry & Gaussier, 2004). Infants gaze and smile more to an imitative adult than to an adult who is timely contingent only (Meltzoff, 1990), and this finding was replicated with 9 to 18 month-old infants (Agnetta & Rochat, 2004).

In ecologically valid settings, we have demonstrated the preference of 2-year-olds for a mirroring of their behaviour, compared to other contingent responses of peer-age partners (Nadel, 1986; Nadel & Fontaine, 1989). The same dyads of 30 month-olds were presented with two different settings with the same partner within 24 hours. Once they met in a setting that afforded synchronic imitation insofar as it was furnished with two identical sets of 10 objects, and another time they were presented with 20 different objects. When we compared the social indices in the two conditions, we found that attention to partner was significantly higher in the setting with two identical sets of objects, that imitation was the main social behaviour in this setting (70% of total time), and that verbalizations were equally rare in the two settings. Initiations of contact were more frequently successful (i.e. answered) when they took place during imitative actions; social signals such as smiles, and non verbal behaviours such as offering, occurred more frequently during the imitative sequences. There were seven times more laughs in the double setting than in the setting with single objects, although the objects proposed were equally attractive in the two settings. Another interesting finding confirmed the preference of young children for a combination of temporal, spatial and intensity signals of contingency. Children in the double setting monitored their temporal synchrony during the imitative sequence, the model waiting for the imitator, and the imitator rushing to imitate on time (Nadel-Brulfert & Baudonnière, 1982). As a consequence, actions with identical objects were in tight temporal connection, thus producing a high level of contingency between partners.

Verbal children switch to a preference for low contingency

A few months later, when children master verbal language, the preference for synchronic among other non-verbal means of interaction declines abruptly in dyads of 42–46 months meeting in similar conditions than 30 month-olds (Nadel, 1986; Nadel & Fontaine, 1989). After 4 years, hostility grows toward synchronic imitation now considered as mockery. This hostility is still present in adulthood and was expressed fully in the Platonic tradition, when synchronic imitation was considered as holding danger for individual identity and for self-consciousness. A way to complete the CDM model is to take account of this later switch toward low contingency and propose a three-step model of contingency.

IV. Autism: An impairment of the Contingency Detection Module?

Low-functioning children with autism may be so deeply involved in repetitive behaviour that they do not even notice their social environment. Except for these cases of extreme focus on self-produced behaviour, the majority of non verbal children with autism are attracted toward highly contingent responses to their behaviour. They show various levels of detection of being imitated, that parallel the levels described elsewhere for typical development (Nadel, 2002). A high level will consist in testing the intentionality of the imitator through strategies like changing the rhythm of activity, changing the object used, or stopping action, while gazing at the experimenter. Those who do not test the experimenter but reciprocate imitation, smile, approach the experimenter, or gaze fixedly at her, show an awareness of being imitated but probably do not understand the intentionality of the imitator. However, this basic response to being imitated is a first step toward an access to the attribution of intentionality to the imitator. This was shown in a collaborative study with Field and colleagues (Field, Field, Sanders & Nadel, 2002). In this study, repeated sessions of being imitated during one week proved to significantly generate awareness of being imitated, increase imitation, and enhance close proximity with the imitator. These findings were recently replicated by Heimann and colleagues who proposed three sessions of imitative interactions in a day instead of in a week (Heimann, Laberg, & Nordoen, in press). The burst of social awareness that these findings suggest is to be linked to the discovery of self-agency during imitative sessions. While acting, children discover the external consequence of their action mirrored by another person (a clear example of social biofeedback). They perceive not only that they are the author of their action but also that they are at the origin of the other's action, that they have a power over another person. Some of them will perceive next that this power is restricted to the other's will, since the person is an agent. This scenario was the bet of a pilot study led with the still face paradigm that we revisited for this purpose (Nadel, Croué, Mattlinger et al., 2000).

The Still Face paradigm pioneered by Tronick and colleagues (1978) has generated a large amount of robust data. Interestingly, it appears to also be a powerful tool to test other questions such as: When do children start forming a general concept of persons as contingent agents intending to interact? Do low-functioning children with autism form such a general concept? Do high levels of contingent behaviour favor the building of such concept? To address these questions, we substituted the 'interaction-still face-interaction' procedure with a 'still face-interaction-still face' procedure. And, instead of a familiar partner, we "froze" a stranger. If the children show negative reactions in front of a still adult that they have never met before, we will conclude that they expected him/her to share with them, thus that they had formed the concept of a person as a contingent agent. If they show concern only during the second still face, after a highly contingent interaction with the adult, we will conclude that they need prior imitative experience with a person, before they will form expectancies about her social behaviour and willingness to share.

Results showed a significant difference between behaviour displayed by the children during Still face 1 and Still face 2. During Still Face 1, they explored the new arrangement of their sport room and looked at or manipulated the objects displayed, all in two exemplars. During Still Face 2, after three minutes of having been imitated by the stranger, they appeared to have a unique focus: have the stranger be socially responsive. Their disappointment, their embarrassment, their surprise, their attempts to attract the stranger's attention show that they understand the still behaviour as being at will. They now react to the still face like people typically react to ostracism (see Williams and Gerber, this volume): it is an insult to their being there.

Infants with Down Syndrome matched on developmental age do not need a previous interaction with the still stranger to react as if ostracized: they immediately withdraw, take a distance and look wary. More precisely, when comparing the two clinical matched groups during still face 1, we found that children with Down Syndrome presented significantly more negative facial expressions ($U = 5$; $p < .001$), complained more ($U = 28$; $p < .05$), and had a lower amount of object manipulation ($U = 27$; $p < .05$.) than children with autism. During the second still face however, the only difference between groups concerned the higher amount of gaze to stranger in children with Down Syndrome ($U = 14,5$; $p < .01$), a result in conformity with established criterion of social gaze avoidance in children with autism. The equivalence of other social indices in the two groups document a clear-cut change in the social behaviour of children with autism after the imitative session. This change in children with autism reveals the importance of being imitated in the understanding of other's agency.

In another 'still face' experiment, we have tested the prediction that higher contingent behaviours are more efficient to awaken social awareness in children with autism. In this experiment, two matched groups of children with autism were presented with two different interactive conditions: a non imitative interaction versus an imitative interaction. Imitative interaction was proved to be a more powerful way of initiating positive emotional behaviours towards the stranger during the second still face than non imitative contingent interaction (Escalona, Field, Nadel & Lundy, 2002).

Concluding comments

How to make a mind is certainly a question that cannot be answered without the help of a developmental model of perception-action coupling (Prinz, 1990). Data concerning the early role of action on perception and of perception on action show that the precedence of one on the other is far from being demonstrated (Hauf, El-sner & Aschersleben, 2004; Hauf & Prinz, this volume; Sommerville & Woodward, 2005). All data however converge to underline the developmental role of action. A basic coupling of perception and action concerns imitation. Synchronic imita-tion of others and its reverse facet, sensitivity to being imitated, both contribute to exert the distinction between perceptions caused by self and perceptions caused by the external world, in a context of high contingency. Russell (1990) has highlight-ed the basic role of this distinction in understanding intentionality. The model of a Contingency Detection Module proposed by Gergely and Watson (1996; 1999), as well as the perception-action-based formalism developed by Gaussier and col-leagues (2004) provide inspiring frameworks for a systematic approach to study-ing the role of imitation in the development of agency and self-understanding in young infants and non verbal children with autism. This paper was aimed at providing developmental and psychopathological data that support and complete these frameworks, in an attempt to approach the basic conditions that make an imitative infant a developing mind.

Acknowledgements

More recent research presented in this paper was funded by ADAPT, UE contract, Vth Frame-work, IST- 2001–37173.

References

Agnetta, B., & Rochat, P. (2004). Imitative games by 9-, 14-, and 18-month-old infants. *Infancy*, 6, 1, 1–36.

Blass, E.M., Ganchrow, J.R., & Steiner, J.E. (1984). Classical conditioning in newborn humans 2- 48 hours of age. *Infant Behavior and Development, 7*, 223–35.

Escalona, A., Field, T., Nadel, J., & Lundy, B. (2002). Imitation effects on children with autism. *Journal of Autism and Developmental Disorders, 32*, 2, 141–144.

Field, T., Field, T., Sanders, C., & Nadel, J. (2001). Children display more social behaviors after repeated imitation sessions; *Autism, 5, 3*, 317–323.

Field, T., Guy, L., & Umbel, V. (1985). Infants' responses to mothers' imitative behaviors. *Infant Mental Health Journal, 6*, 40–44.

Gaussier, p., Baccon, J.C., Prepin, K., Nadel, J., & Hafemeister, L. (2004). Formalization of recog-nition, affordances and learning in isolated or interacting animats. *The Society for Adaptive Behavior SAB'04*: MIT Press.

Gergely, G., & Watson, J. (1996). The social biofeedback model of parental affect-mirroring. *International Journal of Psycho-Analysis, 77*, 1181, 1212.

Gergely, G., & Watson, J. (1999). Early social-emotional development: Contingency perception and the social biofeedback model. In P. Rochat (Ed.), *Early social cognition* (pp. 101–136). Hillsdale, NJ: Erlbaum.

Gewirtz, J. (1969). Mechanisms of social learning: some roles of stimulation and behaviour in early development. In D. Goslin (Ed.), *Handbook of socialization theory and research (pp. 57–212).* Chicago: Rand McNally.

Heimann, M., Laberg, K., & Nordoen, B. (2006). Imitative interaction increases social interest and elicited imitation in nonverbal children with autism. *Infant and Child Development, 15*, 297–309.

Hauf, P., & Prinz, W. (this volume). The understanding of own and others' actions during infancy.

Hauf, P., Elsner, B., & Aschersleben, G., (2004). The role of action effects in infants' action control. *Psychological Research, 6*, 115–125.

Meltzoff, A. (1990). Foundations for developing a concept of self: the role of imitation in relating self to other and the value of social mirroring, social modeling, and self practice in infancy. In D. Cicchetti & M. Beeghly (Eds.), *The self in transition: Infancy to childhood* (pp. 139–164). Chicago: University of Chicago Press.

Meltzoff, A., & Gopnik, A. (1993). The role of imitation in understanding persons and developing a theory of mind. In S. Baron-Cohen, H. Flusberg & D. Cohen (Eds.), *Understanding other minds* (pp. 335–366). Oxford: Oxford University Press.

Muir, D., & Nadel, J. (1998). Infant social perception. In A. Slater (Ed.), *Perceptual development* (pp.247–285). Hove, UK: Psychology Press Ltd.

Murray, L., & Trevarthen, C. (1985). Emotional regulation of interaction between two-month-olds and their mothers. In T.M. Field & N.A. Fox (Eds.), *Social perception in infants* (pp. 101–125). Norwood, NJ: Ablex.

Nadel, J. (1986). *Imitation et communication entre jeunes enfants.* Paris: Presses Universitaires de France.

Nadel-Brulfert, J., & Baudonnière, P. M. (1982). The social function of reciprocal imitation in 2-year-old peers. *International Journal of Behavioral Development, 5*, 95–109.

Nadel, J., Carchon, I., Kervella, C., Marcelli, D., & Réserbat-Plantey, D. (1999). Expectancies for social contingency in 2-month-olds. *Developmental Science, 2*, 2, 164–173.

Nadel, J., Croué, S., Mattlinger, M.-J., Canet, P., Hudelot, C., Lecuyer, C., & Martini, M. (2000). Do autistic children have expectancies about the social behaviour of unfamiliar people? A pilot study with the still face paradigm. *Autism, 2*, 133–145.

Nadel, J., & Fontaine, A.M. (1989). Communicating by imitation: a developmental and comparative approach to transitory social competence. In B. Schneider *et al.* (Eds.), *Social competence in developmental perspective* (pp.131–144). Dordrecht: Kluwer.

Nadel, J., Guérini, C., Pezé, A., & Rivet, C. (1999). The evolving nature of imitation as a format for communication. In J. Nadel & G. Butterworth (Eds.), *Imitation in infancy* (pp. 209–234). Cambridge: Cambridge University Press.

Nadel, J., & Muir, D. (Eds.) (2005). *Emotional Development.* Oxford, NY: Oxford University Press.

Nadel, J., Revel, A., Andry, P., & Gaussier, P. (2004). Toward communication: first imitations in infants, low-functioning children with autism and robots. *Interaction Studies: Social Behaviour and Communication in Biological and Artificial Systems, 5*, 1, 45–74.

Nadel, J., Soussignan, R., Canet, P., Libert, G., & Gérardin, P. (2005). Two-month-old infants of depressed mothers show mild, delayed and persistent change in emotional state after non-contingent interaction. *Infant Behavior and Development, 4*, 418–425.

Prepin, K. (2003). *Development of tools for the study and modelling of imitation games*. Post-master report, University of Cergy, 40 p.

Prepin, K., Simon, M., Canet, P., Mahé, A.S., Soussignan, R., & Nadel, J. (submitted). The effect of a mismatch between mother's voice and face on 6-month-old-infants interaction.

Prinz, W. (1990). A common coding approach to perception and action. In O. Neumann & W. Prinz (Eds.), *Relationships between perception and action* (pp.167–201). Berlin: Springer Verlag.

Rochat, P. (2002). Ego function of early imitation. In A. Meltzoff & W. Prinz (Eds.), *The imitative mind* (pp. 85–97). Cambridge, MA: Cambridge University Press.

Rochat, P., & Morgan, R. (1995). Spatial determinants in the perception of self-produced leg-movements in 3- to 5- month-old infants. *Developmental Psychology, 31*, 626–636.

Rochat, P., Neisser, U., & Marian, V. (1998). Are young infants sensitive to interpersonal contingency? *Infant Behavior and Development, 21* (2), 355–366.

Russell, J. (1996). *Agency*. Hove: Erlbaum (UK) Taylor and Francis Ltd.

Schmuckler, M.A. (1996). Visual-proprioceptive intermodal perception in infancy. *Infant Behavior and Development, 19*, 221–232.

Sommerville, J., & Woodward, A. (2005). Pulling out the intentional structure of action: the relation between action processing and action production in infancy. *Cognition, 95*, 1, 1–30.

Soussignan, R., Nadel, J., Canet, P., & Gérardin, P. (2006). Sensitivity to social contingency and positive emotion in 2-month-olds. *Infancy, 10*(2), 123–144.

Stern, D. (1985). *The interpersonal world of the infant*. New York: BasicBooks.

Tronick, E., Als, H., Adamson, L., Wise, S., & Brazelton, T. (1978). The infant's response to entrapment between contradictory messages in face-to-face interaction. *Journal of the American Academy of Child Psychiatry, 17*, 1–13.

Walker-Andrews, A. (1997). Infants' perception of expressive behaviors: differentiation of multimodal information. *Psychological Bulletin, 121*, 437–456.

Watson, J. (1972). Smiling, cooing and the "game". *Merrill-Palmer Quarterly, 18*, 323–339.

Watson, J. (1985). Contingency perception in early social development. In T. Field & N. Fox (Eds.), *Social perception in infants* (pp. 157–176). Norwood, NJ: Ablex.

Watson, J. (1994). Detection of self: the perfect algorithm. In S. Parker, R. Mitchell & M. Boccia (Eds.), *Self-awareness in animals and humans: Developmental perspectives* (p.131–148). Cambridge, MA: Cambridge University Press.

Williams, K., & Gerber, J. (this volume). The making of the ignored and excluded mind.

The social construction of the cultural mind

Imitative learning as a mechanism of human pedagogy

György Gergely and Gergely Csibra
Institute for Psychological Research, Hungarian Academy of Sciences,
Budapest / Centre for Brain and Cognitive Development,
Birkbeck College, London

How does cultural knowledge shape the development of human minds and, conversely, what kind of species-specific social-cognitive mechanisms have evolved to support the intergenerational reproduction of cultural knowledge? We critically examine current theories proposing a human-specific drive to *identify with* and *imitate* conspecifics as the evolutionary mechanism underlying cultural learning. We summarize new data demonstrating the *selective interpretive nature of imitative learning* in 14-month-olds and argue that the predictive scope of existing imitative learning models is either too broad or too narrow to account for these findings. We outline our alternative theory of a human-specific adaptation for 'pedagogy', a communicative system of mutual design specialized for the fast and efficient transfer of new and relevant cultural knowledge from knowledgeable to ignorant conspecifics. We show the central role that innately specified ostensive-communicative triggering cues and learner-directed manner of knowledge manifestations play in constraining and guiding selective imitation of relevant cultural knowledge that is both new and cognitively opaque to the naive learner.

Introduction: Imitative learning as a human-specific adaptation for cultural transmission

Minds construct culture and culture constructs minds. The ontogenetic development of the human mind is deeply influenced both by the characteristics of the multitude of cultural products it encounters, and by the relevant behaviours of their knowledgeable users that it observes. But the reverse, we shall argue, is also true: forms of human culture would not be able to spread and survive crossgenerationally had the mind of the human infant not been equipped with adapted cognitive resources specialized for the reception and transmission of relevant cultural knowledge. Therefore, one of the central issues raised by human culture concerns the nature of the social-cognitive mechanisms that mediate the reproduction, spread, and intergenerational transmission of cultural forms among members of the community.

The dominant candidate for such a mechanism has long been the special human capacity and inclination to *imitate* the actions of conspecifics. *Imitative learning* has been proposed as a human-specific adaptation for cultural learning (e. g., Meltzoff, 1996; Tomasello 1999; Tomasello et al., 1993; 2005) for several reasons. First, humans — more than most other species — are prolific and flexible imitators, who seem specially adapted to imitate a wide range of behaviors, often without direct reinforcement (Meltzoff, 1996). Second, while 'cultural' behavioral traditions (such as group-specific termite fishing or nut cracking techniques) also exist in non-human primates (Goodall, 1986; Whiten et al., 1999), it has been argued that such cultural skills are socially transmitted through observational learning mechanisms that do *not* involve imitation (such as stimulus enhancement, response facilitation, or trial-and-error emulation) (Heyes & Galef, 1996; Thorpe, 1963; Tomasello, 1996; Tomasello & Call, 1997).

In this paper we shall critically reexamine the dominant role attributed to imitative learning in the intergenerational transmission of human cultural knowledge. First, we shall consider two influential recent proposals (one by Andy Meltzoff (1996), the other by Mike Tomasello and colleagues (1993, 2005)) claiming that an identification-based drive to imitate the actions of conspecifics forms the central species-specific adaptation for cultural learning in humans. We shall evaluate these theories in the light of new evidence (Gergely, Bekkering, & Király, 2002; Király, Csibra, & Gergely, 2004) demonstrating the selective interpretive nature of imitative learning in human infants. It will be argued that the predictive scope of the two theories in question is either too broad (Meltzoff) or too narrow (Tomasello) to account for the relevance-based selectivity that characterizes young infants' imitative learning of novel means. We shall contrast these models with our own alternative proposal for a human-specific adaptation for 'pedagogy', a complex communicative system of mutual design specialized for the fast and efficient transmission of cultural knowledge (Csibra and Gergely, 2005; Gergely and Csibra, 2005a). We shall argue that imitation is not an adaptation for human cultural learning in its own right, but only a basic low-level capacity (available to many non-human species (Heyes, 1993)) that in humans have become recruited as a subcomponent of the system of pedagogical knowledge transfer. In closing, we shall show how the selective, relevance-guided nature of early imitative learning can be best accounted for as a result of the constraining effects of the built-in assumptions of the 'pedagogical stance' about the ways in which relevant cultural information is ostensively communicated by knowledgeable others for the sake of naive conspecifics. These assumptions function in humans to guide and constrain imitative learning by identifying the culturally relevant contents for the learner to be retained and fast learned.

Imitative learning as a human-specific drive to "act like" other humans

Based on their demonstrations of neonatal imitation, Meltzoff and Moore (1977, 1989, 1997) argued that (a) human infants have a prewired mechanism to map observed behavior of others onto the corresponding motor scheme of the self, (b) this mechanism allows infants to recognize others as conspecifics, as being "just-like-them", (c) infants have an innate predisposition to "identify" with others perceived as "just-like-them", and (d) they "have an inbuilt drive to "act like" their conspecifics" (Meltzoff, 1996, p. 363).

In a seminal study, Meltzoff (1988) has shown that this innate propensity to imitate humans also leads infants very early on to *imitatively learn novel means actions* from observing others. Fourteen-month-olds watched as a human model illuminated a magic light-box by leaning forward from waist and touching its top panel with her forehead. A week later, 67% of the infants re-enacted the novel 'head-action', while none performed it in a base-line control group that had not seen the action demonstrated. This illustrates how, in Meltzoff's theory, the infant's innate drive for identification, and the consequent tendency to imitate other humans, also provide the basic mechanism for cultural learning.

Imitation and mindreading: "Insightful" imitation as a precondition for cultural learning

Imitative learning also plays a crucial role in Tomasello's (1999; Tomasello et al., 1993, 2005) theory of cultural learning. Similarly to Meltzoff, Tomasello (1999) suggests that "Imitative learning… relies fundamentally on infants' tendency to *identify* with adults" (p. 82). Tomasello et al. (2005) argue, however, that simple "bodily identification" as evidenced by neonatal imitation is not sufficient to support the kind of imitative learning that makes human cultural learning possible. For Tomasello, 'true' imitative learning *qua* cultural learning also necessitates the understanding of the *intentions* behind the other's action. "True imitative learning…involves the infant's reproducing the adult's actual behavioral strategies in their appropriate functional contexts, which implies an understanding of the intentional state underlying the behavior" (Tomasello et al., 1993, p. 497). Apart from this strong cognitive requirement for imitative learning, Tomasello et al. (2005) also postulate a uniquely human motivational precondition in the form of a primary human-specific "motivation to share psychological states with others" (p. 1), which leads to "more deeply psychological levels of identification" (p. 26).[1] It is at this level of *identification* with the mental states of conspecifics that infants can *simulate* the other's intentional actions, attributing the simulated intention automatically to the other (Tomasello, 1999, pp. 73–76).

Tomasello (1999) argues that apes lack the capacity for identification, therefore, they don't simulate and attribute intentions to others either. In his view, this is reflected also in the fact that apes seem not to learn from observing others through imitation, but only through trial-and-error 'emulation' (Tomasello, 1996): they try to reproduce the observed outcome in their own way without attending to or directly re-enacting the particular means action observed. Eventually, through this slow process of (re)discovery, apes manage to acquire the same skill that they observed to produce the desired outcome (or some variant of it).

If one is simply 'blindly copying' an action without understanding the intention behind it, one cannot speak about 'true' imitative learning either, only about "mimicry". Therefore, Tomasello (1996; Tomasello et al., 1993) provided criteria for 'true' imitative learning to help differentiate it from 'pseudo-imitative' re-enactments of others' behaviors produced by 'emulation' or 'mimicry', social learning processes that are also available to many non-human animals.

1. *"The novelty-of-response criterion"*: To avoid confusion with response facilitation, imitative learning should involve "the learning of a new response" (Byrne and Tomasello, 1995) that is not part of the organism's motor repertoire.
2. *"The cognitive transparency criterion"*: Apart from providing a safeguard against confusing imitative learning with 'blind mimicry', this requirement also functions as a *'selection filter'* determining "which aspects of the behavior are relevant for reproduction" (Tomasello, 1996, p. 323). Imitative learning entails "an understanding of both the behavior's goal and its strategy for achieving that goal" (p. 324). To imitatively learn a novel behavioral strategy, the infant must understand "…how the behavior is designed to bring about the goal. This then determines precisely what of the other's behavior it seeks to reproduce" (p. 324). In other words, according to Tomasello we can only speak of 'true' imitative learning, when the underlying causal intentional structure of the other's imitated action is 'cognitively fully transparent' to the learner.

Let us now revisit Meltzoff's (1988) 'magic-box' experiment with Tomasello's criteria in mind. First, the fact that most infants imitated the novel 'head-action', "an unusual and awkward behavior...even though it would have been easier and more natural for them simply to push the panel with their hand" (Tomasello, 1999, p. 82), rules out an emulation account and satisfies Tomasello's "novelty-of-response criterion". Want and Harris (2002), having similarly ruled out emulation, argued, however, that "the children seem to have mimicked or 'blindly' imitated the demonstration, copying exactly the actions...demonstrated" (p. 8).

But 'blind' mimicry implies that the organism copies the behavior "without any regard for its goal-directed nature" (Tomasello, 1999, p. 82). To test this, Carpenter, Nagell, and Tomasello (1998) replicated the Meltzoff (1988) task so that the 'head-action' and its outcome were spatially separated (the light-source was above the box). They found that "the majority of infants both reproduced the unusual action and looked to the interesting result in anticipation — demonstrating that they were not just mimicking" (Tomasello, 1999, p. 82).

Note, however, that this is a rather "weak" test of Tomasello's (1996) full "cognitive transparency criterion" according to which 'true' imitative learning should entail "an understanding of both the behavior's goal *and its strategy for achieving that goal*" (p. 324, emphasis added). Even more strongly, 'true' imitative learning takes place only if the infant understands "*...how the behavior is designed to bring about the goal*. This then *determines precisely* what of the other's behavior it seeks to reproduce" (p. 324, emphasis added). However, it seems entirely doubtful that the 14-month-olds could have reconstructed — through simulation — the underlying intention and rational design behind the model's choice to perform the 'head-action' rather than the apparently more sensible, efficient, and readily available 'hand-action'. Strictly speaking, "the cognitive transparency criterion" should have predicted that infants will *not* imitate the bizarre 'head-action', as it must have remained cognitively opaque to them in terms of the actor's underlying reasons for performing the — apparently non-optimal — means action.

Teleological emulation *versus* rational imitation: The selective interpretive nature of imitative learning in human infants

Meltzoff's (1988) finding that 14-month-olds readily imitate the unusual 'head-action', seemed also unexpected from the point of view of our own theory of the one-year-old's "teleological stance" or "naïve theory of rational action" (Csibra & Gergely, 1998; Gergely & Csibra, 2003). In a series of violation-of-expectation looking time studies (Gergely, Nádasdy, Csibra, & Bíró, 1995; Csibra, Bíró, Koós,

& Gergely, 2003), we have shown that by 12 months infants exhibit a sophisticated ability to attribute goals to observed actions and to evaluate the relative efficiency of the means act in relation to the goal and the physical constraints of the actor's situation. If they know the actor's goal and see a change in situational constraints, young infants can infer what the most efficient new means would be to the goal in the new situation and expect that the actor 'ought to' perform that particular action to achieve the goal[2] (Gergely & Csibra, 2003). On that ground, then, one would have expected that in the Meltzoff (1988) task infants, as rational agents, should have performed the most efficient goal-directed action available to them (using their hand to contact the light-box), instead of imitating the awkward and less efficient 'head-action'.

To clarify this situation, Gergely, Bekkering, and Király (2002) performed a modified version of the Meltzoff (1988) task. They hypothesized that "if infants noticed that the demonstrator declined to use her hands despite the fact that they were free, they may have inferred that the head action must offer some advantage in turning on the light. They therefore used the same action themselves in the same situation" (p. 755). To test this idea, Gergely et al. ran two groups of 14-month-olds varying the situational constraints of the model. In the 'Hands-occupied' condition the model's hands were visibly occupied: she pretended to be chilly and wrapped a blanket around her shoulders holding it with both hands while performing the 'head-action'. In the 'Hands-free' condition, however, after wrapping the blanket around her shoulders, the model placed her hands visibly free onto the table before demonstrating the 'head-action'.

As Figure 1 shows, when the model's hands were occupied, 14-month-olds were much less likely to imitate the 'head-action' (21%). Instead, they illuminated the box by *touching it with their hand* performing the most sensible, simpler, easy-to-perform, and equally effective emulative response available to them, but not to the model (teleological emulation). In contrast, when the model's hands were free, but she still used her head to illuminate the box, 69% of 14-month-olds imitated her 'head-action' ($p < .02$) (replicating Meltzoff, 1988).

A further unexpected finding was that in *both* conditions *all* infants performed the emulative 'hand-action'. Moreover, all subjects in the 'Hands-free' condition who imitated the 'head-action', did so only *after* they had first performed the 'hand-action' that — in all cases — succeeded in illuminating the box. In other words, even after they have experienced that the effect can be brought about by the simpler 'hand-action' as well, most infants in the 'Hands-free' condition remained motivated to imitate the model's demonstrated — though apparently less efficient — 'head-action'.

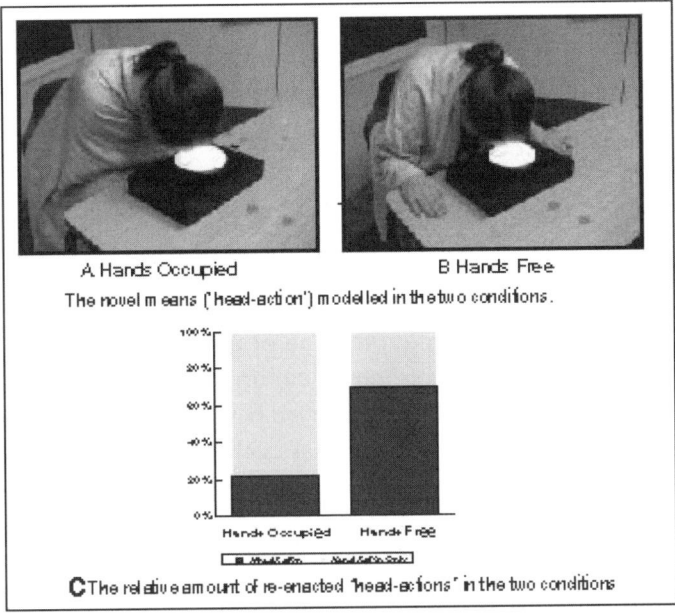

Figure 1.

Let us draw some preliminary conclusions for the two theories of imitative learning described above. First, our findings suggest that imitative learning of novel means is not triggered by identification (as on that basis one could not have predicted a significant difference in imitation between the two context-conditions). Second, our results indicate that imitative learning is not due to automatic behavioral 'copying' of the modeled action. Rather, it is guided and constrained by a top-down *selective interpretive process* involving the *evaluation of the relative efficiency of the means action* as a function of the actor's situational constraints ('Hands-free' *vs.* 'Hands-occupied').

Note, first, that Meltzoff's (1996) theory of the human infant as an "imitative generalist" driven by an innate drive to identify with and act like other humans, contains no mechanism that could account for the selectivity of imitation as a function of the actor's situational constraints. As it stands, Meltzoff's theory predicts automatic copying of *any* observed human action and so it has an *overly broad predictive scope* contradicted by the selective nature of imitative learning demonstrated.

In contrast, Tomasello's theory does include a 'selective filter' in the form of his full 'cognitive transparency criterion'. His model, however, has an *overly narrow predictive scope* as it generates wrong predictions concerning *what* will be imitated. Tomasello's theory predicts that infants will imitate only those behaviors whose underlying intentions and rational design they can fully understand through simulation. Therefore, as it stands, his theory cannot account for the imitative learning of truly *novel* behavioural means that are unpredictable on the grounds of physical-causal efficiency considerations and that, therefore, remain cognitively 'opaque' to the infant.

Cultural learning and human pedagogy

We shall now turn to our own interpretation of the nature of imitative learning and its role in the transmission of human cultural knowledge. We propose that the basic capacity to imitatively 'copy' observed behaviors of conspecifics (present in numerous non-human species as well) has evolved to serve a uniquely human function as a mechanism recruited, directed, and constrained by *pedagogy,* a specialized human-specific cognitive system dedicated to cultural learning. In our view, pedagogy was selected as a primary species-specific cognitive adaptation of mutual design to ensure fast and efficient transfer of relevant cultural knowledge through ostensive communicative 'teaching' manifestations of relevant information by knowledgeable humans for the sake of ignorant learners (Csibra & Gergely, 2005; Gergely & Csibra, 2005a).

What may have been the evolutionary origins of human pedagogy? Elsewhere (Csibra & Gergely, 2005; Gergely & Csibra, 2005a) we speculate that during hominid evolution the original 'simple' goal-driven teleological reasoning capacity of our ancestors about objects as transient tools in the visible presence of goals (answering the question: 'What object could I use to achieve this goal?') was superseded by a more stable functionalist conceptualization in terms of affordance properties (giving rise to "inverse teleological reasoning" answering the question: 'What purpose could I use this object for?'). This eventually led to the practice of tool manufacturing in the absence of directly visible goals as well as to the appearance of mediated tool use (i.e., using tools to make other tools: "recursive teleology"). Such advanced practices posed a learnability problem for the naive juvenile observer for whom they remained cognitively 'opaque' as — lacking perceptual information about the goal — they could not identify which aspects of the observed actions were relevant (and should, therefore, be acquired) and which were incidental. Unguided forms of existing social observational learning mechanisms (including statistical, trial-and-error, and emulation learning) were ill-suited, error-prone and too slow to solve this learnability problem and could not ensure sufficiently high-fidelity successful transgenerational transmission of such cognitively 'opaque' cultural forms and skills. In statistically-based learning mechanisms the local adaptivity of the acquired behavior is ensured by reinforcement, while its evolutionary relevance is ensured by the pattern of environmental invariance it exhibits that is gradually extracted from observed repetitions of contingencies. This makes associative learning a necessarily slow and gradual process restricted to the domain of perceivable repetitive contingencies coupled with reinforcement.

Therefore, the increasing cognitive 'opacity' of complex artifacts and their manufacturing procedures may have provided selective pressure for the evolution of a qualitatively new type of social learning mechanism in the form of pedagogy. In cultural learning one obvious way to overcome the limitations of statistically-based learning mechanisms is to acquire the relevant knowledge directly from another conspecific who already possesses it. As new behaviors, especially cultural activities, are often not transparent as to either their knowledge-base or their function, an active communicative role of the more knowledgeable conspecific may greatly assist the efficient and fast transmission of such culturally relevant information. We propose (Csibra & Gergely, 2005; Gergely & Csibra, 2005a) that Mother Nature's 'trick' to make fast and efficient learning of complex — and, for the learner, cognitively 'opaque' — cultural knowledge possible was to have humans evolve specialized cognitive resources that form a dedicated interpersonal system of mutual design in which one is predisposed to 'teach' and to 'learn' new and relevant cultural information to (and from) conspecifics. We hypothesize that humans possessing cultural knowledge are naturally inclined not only to *use*, but also to *ostensively manifest*[3] their knowledge to (and for the benefit of) naive conspecifics, while the latter are naturally motivated to acquire such knowledge by actively seeking out, attending to, and being specially receptive to the ostensive communicative manifestations of others.

In the design specifications of pedagogical knowledge transfer it is the very fact that a knowledgeable conspecific (a 'teacher') *ostensively communicates* her cultural knowledge by *manifesting* it for the novice (the 'learner') is what ensures the (cultural) relevance of the knowledge transmitted. Since the learner is predisposed to interpret the teacher's ostensive-communicative cues that accompany his knowledge manifestation (such as eye-contact, eye-brow flashing, turn-taking contingency, see Csibra & Gergely, 2005, for a review) as evidence that the manifestation will convey *new* and *relevant* cultural information for him, this allows for fast learning of the communicated content without any further need to test its relevance independently. Furthermore, the built-in presumption of relevance of pedagogically communicated knowledge manifestations also opens the door for the acquisition of knowledge contents that are not only *arbitrary, conventional,* and causally/functionally *non-transparent,* but that sometimes don't seem to (or actually do not) have any obvious adaptive value at all (these being uniquely characteristic species-specific features of many human cultural forms).

We further propose (Csibra and Gergely, 2005) that the human-specific pedagogical inclination to transmit relevant and new cultural information to conspecifics is complemented by a *special kind of receptivity* to benefit from such teaching. Human infants are equipped with specialized cognitive resources that enable them to learn from infant-directed teaching: they 1. show early sensitivity to *communicative and ostensive cues* indicating teaching contexts (such as eye-contact, contingent reactivity, motherese, and hearing one's own name), 2. tend to interpret certain directional actions (e.g., gaze-shift or pointing) occurring in these communicative contexts as *referential cues* to identify the *referents* about which new information will be provided, 3. expect the "teacher" to ostensively manifest *relevant* and *new* information about the referent, and 4. are ready to *fast-map* such information to the referent (see Csibra & Gergely, 2005, for reviewing supporting evidence). Finally, we hypothesize that the infant's 'pedagogical stance' contains the implicit assumption that the information revealed about the referents in such ostensive-communicative teaching contexts consists of *publicly shared* and *universal cultural knowledge* that is *generalizable* and *shareable* with other members of the cultural community.[4]

Imitative learning in the service of human pedagogy: The role of ostensive-communicative cues

It is noteworthy that studies investigating early imitative learning typically present the target behaviors in a rich ostensive communicative-referential context. For example, when a model demonstrates a novel means act (as in Meltzoff, 1988), she typically first establishes *eye-contact* with the infant often also *addressing him by his name* (ostensive cues), then *shifts her eye-gaze or point* to the referent object (referential cues). This is followed by some *communicative-referential speech act* (e.g., "Look, I'll show you something!") before the target action is demonstrated. In fact, this is highly natural and representative of the manner in which human adults manifest to a child new and relevant cultural knowledge for her to acquire.

We hypothesize that in human infants imitative learning is triggered by such pedagogical cues accompanying others' manifestations of cultural information. Furthermore, we argue that the interpretive selectivity guiding what aspect of the modelled behavior will be imitatively learned is directed and constrained by the implicit assumptions of the infant's 'pedagogical stance' that the other's ostensive cues activate. When taking the 'pedagogical stance', infants interpret the other's ostensive communicative gestures as indicating that he is about to manifest 'for' them some significant aspect of cultural knowledge that will be *new* and *relevant* and that, therefore, should be fast-learned.[5]

Let us illustrate how pedagogy works by interpreting the selective imitation finding of the Gergely et al. (2002) study in terms of the inferences invoked by the pedagogical cuing context. First, we assume that 14-month-olds interpret the ostensive-communicative cues of the model as indicating that the other is about to *manifest culturally relevant and new information* for him. Second, the pedagogical context induces in the infant a special attentional and interpretive attitude to apply his knowledge-base and available interpretative capacities (his explanatory schemes or conceptual 'modes of construals') (see Keil, 1995, 2003; Kelemen, 1999a, b; Gergely and Csibra, 2003) to infer what aspect of the manifested behavior conveys *new* and *relevant* information. Third, the pedagogical context triggers a special receptive learning mode to *fast learn* what the infant has inferred to be new and relevant information in the manifested action.

Take the 'Hands occupied' condition. Clearly, the novel outcome including the manifested affordance property of the object (illuminability-upon-contact) is *new* information previously unknown to the infant, so it is going to be retained in memory and reproduced through action. But what about the particular behavioral means ('head-action') performed? Taking the teleological stance towards actions (Gergely and Csibra, 2003) infants can infer that given the physical constraints of the actor (hands occupied), touching the box by her forehead does, in fact, qualify as a sensible, justifiable, and efficient means to the goal. So, since the physical-causal efficiency of the 'head-action' is cognitively 'transparent' (i.e., justifiable, expectable or even predictable) for the infant who sees that the actor's hands are occupied, the fact that she used her head (and not her hands) to touch the box does *not* qualify as part of the *new* information that is being conveyed. Therefore, it is predicted that the infant will *not* imitate the 'head-action' in the 'Hands-occupied' context-condition, but will reproduce the novel information (will illuminate the box) by the most efficient means available to him given his *own* situational constraints: i.e., he will use his (free) hands to illuminate the box.

In the 'Hands-free' condition the situation is different, however. Of course, the goal-state involving the newly experienced affordance of the box is *new* information here, too, so it will be retained and reproduced. In contrast, when setting up a teleological interpretation as to what particular action would constitute under these situational constraints the most rational/efficient means to the goal, given the fact that the actor's hands were free, the infant must have identified the available 'hand-action' as the most efficient (and, therefore, expectable) means that the model 'ought to' perform. Unexpectedly, however, the demonstrator chose not to use her free hands, but performed the unusual 'head-action' instead. We hypothesize that this *perceived mismatch* between the predictable and the actually performed means drew the infants' attention to the *model's contrastive choice* to perform the unexpected 'head-action' as carrying special communicative significance. This contrastive choice then "marked" the 'head-action' as also forming part of the *new* and *relevant* information that the ostensive-communicative manifestation conveyed. As a result, both the new goal *and the new means* were retained and imitated!

Notice the contrast between this analysis and Tomasello's 'cognitive transparency criterion' that predicted that infants would imitatively learn a new action only if its underlying intentions are cognitively fully 'transparent' and interpretable for the infant. On the contrary, our proposed pedagogical interpretation of the ostensive-communicative cues accompanying the action manifestation suggests that imitative learning of a new behavior will occur *precisely* when the choice or particular manner of the action is *unpredictable — i.e., cognitively 'opaque' — to the infant* and, as such, it qualifies as part of the 'new and relevant' information manifested by the ostensive 'teaching' act. (Note that in this model no cognitive 'insight' into *what* makes the manifested skill culturally relevant — apart from it being ostensively manifested — is presumed to be necessary for imitative learning to take place.)

But would then *any behavior that is unpredictable* lead to imitation if presented in a pedagogical context? Well, as it turns out the answer is 'no' and Tomasello is probably right in his intuition that some level of 'cognitive interpretability' is necessary for imitative learning. We have recently run a 'no-effect' control ('Hands-free' condition) in which the same ostensive cues introduced an identical 'head-bending action' without, however, the demonstrator's head actually contacting the box (it stopped 10 cm above it). So the behavior resulted in no observable external effect. In stark contrast to the 69% imitation of the 'head-action' in our replication of Meltzoff (1988), only 7% of the 14-month-olds imitated the very same head-bending action in this 'no-effect' condition. This suggests that (a) the ostensive-communicative cues are in themselves not sufficient to trigger imitation, and (b) the fact that the changed context of the same behavior probably rendered it functionally uninterpretable for these young infants, resulted in the disappearance of its imitation.

So maybe Tomasello's full 'cognitive transparency criterion' should be relaxed into some more general 'schematic cognitive interpretability requirement'. On this account, the behavior should receive an at least partially completed, even if "conceptually shallow or schematic" interpretation (Keil, 2003) in terms of one of the core interpretive "modes of construal" (Keil, 1995; Kelemen, 1999a, b; Gergely & Csibra, 2003) that infants have at their disposal (such as their teleo-functional means-end scheme, causal-physical scheme of contact and force dynamics, or their understanding of distal referential relations as exemplified by eye-gaze, pointing or naming behaviors). In fact, it is in relation to such a schematic and only partially completed cognitive functional interpretation (e.g., that the head-touch behavior functions as a means to a goal) that the particular choice of the behavior manifested as the means remains cognitively 'opaque' to the infant. If such an apparently unjustifiable behavioral choice is, nevertheless, ostensively manifested in a pedagogical context, infants will interpret this as conveying significant and relevant cultural knowledge that is new for them and so should be retained and imitatively reproduced (even though it may remain cognitively 'opaque' to them).

This 'pedagogically guided social learning strategy' may be seen as a developmental example of what Keil (2003) refers to as "the benefits of being [conceptually] shallow" (p. 372). He points out that "people…rapidly decide which domain of causal patterns is relevant and then use their own schematic knowledge of relations and patterns to constrain explanations on the fly….Adults and children alike amplify their understandings by relying on the division of cognitive labour that is intrinsic to all cultures….One advantage of lean causal representations — Keil emphasizes — may be rapid development" (pp. 371–2).

Recently, we also ran a further control study that was identical to the original 'Hands-free' condition, except for the fact that — following the ostensive-communicative cues — the demonstrator manifested *both* the (unusual) 'head-action' and the (predictable) 'hand-action'. Again, we found that imitation of the 'head-action' has practically disappeared as a function of this contextual change: only one of 14 fourteen-month-olds imitated the less efficient means act demonstrated (the 'head-action'), while all subjects performed the predictable 'hand-action'. It seems, therefore, that the ostensive manifestation of both the head- and hand-actions 'sanctioned' both actions as culturally equally acceptable and relevant alternative means to the goal. Since in this way the pedagogically transmitted information did not compete with considerations of physical efficiency, the infants' choice of behavior was fully determined by the latter, and no imitative learning of the less effective 'head-action' took place.

The potency of the ostensive-communicative demonstration context in socially inducing fast learning of the relevant function of new artifacts has also been elegantly demonstrated by Deb Kelemen and her colleagues' recent studies on the social determinants of the early understanding of artifact functions (DiYanni & Kelemen, 2005; Casler & Kelemen, 2005). For example, Casler and Kelemen (2005) have shown that 2.5-year-old children rapidly form a teleo-functional representation of a novel instrumental tool after only one single ostensive demonstration. In their studies, children were presented with two tools that were physically equally affordant for a new task (turning on a light box). The children were first allowed to explore the relevant physical affordance properties of the two tools (they put both into slots), but then they saw only one being chosen and demonstrated to perform the new function. At 2.5 years of age, children repeatedly returned to the demonstrated tool as "for" the task, both immediately and after a multi-day delay, despite the ready availability of the alternative. Children were also found to dissociate, preferring to use the alternative when asked to perform a different function (crushing up crackers). Casler and Kelemen (2005) argue that after only one single demonstration indicating the new artifact's functional use in a pedagogical context, "children will construe the tool as for that particular purpose and…avoid using it for another feasible purpose". Furthermore, the two-year-olds appeared to view the demonstrated function as an intrinsic property of the object that should be readily recognizable by others as well. This is shown by the fact that they also expected *another person,* who was absent during the demonstration and was unfamiliar with the two new tools, to choose to use for the new function the same tool that the children had seen contrastively chosen by the demonstrator earlier. This provides support for our hypotheses that (a) pedagogical cues trigger fast learning, and (b) the infant's 'pedagogical stance' contains a "universality assumption" that the cultural contents conveyed through ostensive-communicative manifestations constitute publicly shared and generalizable knowledge.

But is it really the case that the kind of inferences and interpretations underlying the selective nature of imitative learning are triggered only if the observed target action is manifested in a pedagogical context? To find out we have recently run a new version of the Gergely et al. (2002) study (Király, Csibra, & Gergely, 2004). Half of the subjects were presented with the 'head-action' in either the 'Hands-free' or the 'Hands-occupied' context-conditions demonstrated with rich ostensive-communicative cues as before. The rest of the 14-month-olds participated in an "incidental observation" situation in which they observed the very same 'head-action' in either the 'Hands-free' or the 'Hands-occupied' context-condition, but without being exposed to any ostensive-communicative cues by the model. Our findings indicate that the pedagogical demonstration context does make a qualitative difference. In the pedagogical demonstration situation we have replicated (now the third time) the same pattern of selective imitation of the 'head-action' as in Gergely et al. (2002). Furthermore, the 'head-action' was imitated in the 'Hands-free' condition significantly more when preceded by ostensive-communicative cues than when only incidentally observed in a non-communicative context. In fact, while we did find some imitation of the 'head-action' in both of the two 'incidental observation' conditions as well, the selective degree of imitation present in the pedagogical cuing condition has disappeared: there was no differential imitation evoked in the "Hands-free" *versus* "Hands-occupied" context-conditions when no ostensive-communicative cues were present.

Conclusions

We reviewed recent evidence revealing (a) the selective interpretive nature of imitative learning in human infants and (b) the role of ostensive-communicative cues in constraining and guiding the infant's selective interpretation of what is the new and relevant cultural information conveyed by the other's manifestation that should be fast learned. We argued that these findings pose problems for current theories of human imitative learning whose predictive scope is either too broad or too narrow to account for the type of selectivity that characterizes imitative learning in infants. We proposed a new theory of human cultural learning in which imitation is seen as a basic mechanism that has been recruited, guided and constrained by the human-specific adaptation for 'pedagogy', a complex cognitive system of mutual design that is dedicated to the fast and efficient transmission of cultural knowledge in humans. We argued that the selective interpretive nature of early imitative learning can be explained as a result of the implicit assumptions built into the infant's 'pedagogical stance' that constrain and guide imitative learning, and that is activated by the ostensive-communicative cues of knowledgeable others who manifest new and relevant cultural information for the infant to learn.

Acknowledgment

This research was supported in part by a Fellowship of the J. S. Guggenheim Memorial Foundation to the first author, and by grants from the Hungarian National Science Foundation (OTKA #T034567) and The Leverhulme Trust.

Notes

1. For a critical analysis of this position, see Gergely & Csibra (2005b).

2. For example, after repeatedly seeing an actor approach its goal by jumping over an obstacle, infants show surprise (look longer) when — following the removal of the obstacle — the actor performs the previous jumping action again to get to the goal (this time, however, jumping over nothing). In contrast, when the actor *changes* his behavior in a justifiable manner approaching the goal through the most direct straight-line path that has become available (rational goal-approach), the infants look significantly less (showing no sign of surprise) at this novel (but sensible) action (Gergely et al., 1995; Gergely & Csibra, 2003).

3. The ostensive *manifestation* of a motor skill involves a saliently transformed manner of motor execution when compared to its primary functional *use*. Think of the difference between hammering a nail in *vs.* demonstrating to a novice *how* to hammer a nail in. Manifestations involve slowed-down, schematic, exaggerated, or sometimes only partially executed transformations of

the primary motor program that foregrounds and thus helps to identify the relevant and new information for the novice to acquire.

4. See Csibra and Gergely (2005) for arguments showing that many early emerging social cognitive capacities — such as social referencing (Egyed, Király, & Gergely, 2004), protodeclarative pointing, or word learning — can be usefully reinterpreted as examples of cultural learning through pedagogy.

5. Note that these assumptions are directly analogous, if not identical, to the Gricean pragmatic assumptions of ostensive communication as spelled out in Sperber and Wilson's (1986) relevance theory. In our view, however, pedagogy is a primary adaptation for cultural learning and not a specialized module dedicated to the recovery of speaker's intent in linguistic communication that has evolved later as a sub-module of human theory of mind (Sperber and Wilson, 2002).

References

Byrne, R. W., & Tomasello, M. (1995). Do rats ape? *Animal Behaviour, 50,* 1417–1420.

Carpenter, M., Nagell, K., & Tomasello, M. (1998). Social cognition, joint attention, and communicative competences from 9 to 15 months of age. *Monographs of the Society of Research in Child Development, 63(4).*

Casler, K., & Kelemen, D. (2005). Young children's rapid learning about artifacts. *Developmental Science, 8,* 472–480.

Csibra G., & Gergely, G. (1998). The teleological origins of mentalistic action explanations: A developmental hypothesis. *Developmental Science, 1:2,* 255–259.

Csibra, G., & Gergely, G. (2005). Social learning and social cognition: The case of pedagogy. In M. H. Johnson & Y. Munakata (Eds.), *Progress of Change in Brain and Cognitive Development. Attention and Performance XXI.* Oxford: Oxford University Press.

Csibra, G., Bíró, S., Koós, O., & Gergely, G. (2003). One-year-old infants use teleological representations of actions productively. *Cognitive Science, vol. 27*(1), 111–133.

DiYanni, C., & Kelemen, D. (2005). Using a bad tool with good intention: How preschoolers weigh physical and intentional cues when learning about artifacts. *Manuscript under revision.*

Egyed, K., Király, & Gergely, G. (2004). Object-centered versus agent-centered Interpretations of referential attitude expressions in 14-month-olds. Poster presented at the *14th Biennial International Conference on Infant Studies,* May 2004, Chicago, IL, USA.

Gergely, G., & Csibra, G. (2003). Teleological reasoning about actions: The naïve theory of rational action. *Trends in Cognitive Sciences, 7,* 287–292.

Gergely, G., & Csibra, G. (2005). A few reasons why we don't share Tomasello et al.'s intuitions about sharing. A commentary on Tomasello et al.'s "Understanding and sharing intentions: The origins of cultural cognition." *Behavioral and Brain Sciences, 28,* 701–702.

Gergely, G., & Csibra, G. (2006). Sylvia's recipe: Human culture, imitation, and pedagogy. In S. Levenson & N. Enfield (Eds.), *Roots of Human Sociality: Culture, Cognition, and Human Interaction* (pp. 229–255). Oxford: Berg Publishers.

Gergely, G., Bekkering, H., & Király, I. (2002). Rational imitation in preverbal infants. *Nature, Vol. 415,* p. 755.

Gergely, G., Nádasdy, Z., Csibra, G., & Bíró, S. (1995). Taking the intentional stance at 12 months of age. *Cognition, Vol. 56*, No. 2., 165–193.

Goodall, J. (1986). *The chimpanzees of Gombe*. Cambridge, Mass.: Harvard University Press.

Heyes, C. M. (1993). Imitation, culture and cognition. *Animal Behaviour, 46*, 999–1010.

Heyes, C. M., & Galef, B. G. (1996). *Social learning in animals: The roots of culture*. NY: Academic Press.

Keil, F. (1995). The growth of understandings of natural kinds. In D. Sperber, D. Premack, & A. Premack (Eds.), *Causal cognition* (pp.234–267). Clarendon Press.

Keil, F. (2003). Folkscience: coarse interpretations of a complex reality. *Trends in Cognitive Sciences, 7*, 368–373.

Kelemen, D. (1999a). Function, goals and intention: children's teleological reasoning about objects. *Trends in Cognitive Sciences, 12*, 461 — 468.

Kelemen, D. (1999b). The scope of teleological thinking in preschool children. *Cognition, 70*, 241–272.

Király, I., Csibra, G., & Gergely, G. (2004). The role of communicative-referential cues in observational learning during the second year. Poster presented at the 14th Biennial International Conference on Infant Studies, May 2004, Chicago, IL, USA.

Meltzoff, A. N. (1988). Infant imitation after a one week delay: Long term memory for novel acts and multiple stimuli. *Developmental Psychology, 24*, 470–476.

Meltzoff, A. N. (1996). The human infant as imitative generalist: A 20-year progress report on infant imitation with implications for comparative psychology. In C. M. Heyes & B. G. Galef (Eds), *Social learning in animals: The roots of culture* (pp. 347–370). NY: Academic Press.

Meltzoff, A. N., & Moore, M. K. (1977). Imitation of facial and manual gestures by human neonates. *Science, 198*, 75–8.

Meltzoff, A. N., & Moore, M. K. (1989). Imitation in newborn infants: Exploring the range of gestures imitated and the underlying mechanisms. *Developmental Psychology, 25*, 954–62.

Meltzoff, A. N., & Moore, M. K. (1997). Explaining facial imitation: theoretical model. *Early Development and Parenting, 6*, 179–92.

Sperber, D., & Wilson, D. (1986). *Relevance: Communication and Cognition*. Oxford: Blackwell.

Sperber, D., & Wilson, D. (2002). Pragmatics, modularity and mind-reading. *Mind & Language, 17(1)*, 3–23.

Thorpe, W. H. (1963). *Learning and instincts in animals*. London: Methuen.

Tomasello, M. (1996). Do apes ape? In C. M. Heyes & B. G. Galef (Eds), *Social learning in animals: The roots of culture*. NY: Academic Press.

Tomasello, M. (1999). *The cultural origins of human cognition*. Boston: Harvard University Press.

Tomasello, M., & Call, J. (1997). *Primate cognition*. Oxford: Oxford University Press.

Tomasello, M., Kruger, A. C., & Ratner, H. H. (1993). Cultural learning. *Behavioral and Brain Sciences, 16*, 495–552.

Tomasello, M., Carpenter, M., Call, J., Behne, T., & Moll, H. (2005). Understanding and sharing intentions: The origins of cultural cognition. *Behavioral and Brain Sciences, 28*, 675–735.

Want, S. C., & Harris, P. L. (2002). How do children ape? Applying concepts from the study of non-human primates to the developmental study of 'imitation' in children. *Developmental Science, 5(1)*, 1–13.

Whiten, A., Goodall, J., McGrew, W. C., Nishida, T., Reynolds, V., Sugiyama, Y., Tutin, C. E. G., Wrangham, R. W., & Boesch, C. (1999). Cultures in chimpanzees. *Nature, 399*, 682–685.

File Change Semantics for Preschoolers
Alternative naming and belief understanding

Josef Perner and Johannes L. Brandl
University of Salzburg

We develop a new theory of the cognitive changes around 4 years of age by trying to explain why understanding of false belief and of alternative naming emerge at this age (Doherty & Perner, 1998). We make use of the notion of discourse referents (DR: Karttunen, 1976) as it is used in File Change Semantics (Heim, 2002), one of the early forms of the more widely known Discourse Representation Theory (Kamp & Reyle, 1993). The assumed cognitive change exists in how children can link DRs in their mind to external referents. The younger children check whether the conditions for a DR match the conditions of an external entity (an implicit/procedural understanding of reference). The older children, in addition, have an explicit understanding of reference in virtue of making explicit identity assertions. This involves the metarepresentational ability of representing that different DRs represent the same external referent, which — we argue — is required for alternative naming and for the false belief task.

Developmental data to be explained

We develop our theory with a concrete goal in mind, namely to explain why an alternative naming and the false belief task are mastered at the same age. In the standard false belief task (Wimmer & Perner, 1983) a story character Max puts a piece of chocolate into the kitchen cupboard. In his absence the chocolate is unexpectedly transferred to the drawer of the kitchen table. When he comes back he wants to get his chocolate. Children are asked where he will look for the chocolate. Almost all young 3-year olds predict that he will go to the kitchen table, while most 5-year olds will correctly predict that he will go to look in the cupboard (see Wellman, et al., 2001, for a meta-analysis of a large number of existing studies).

The alternative naming game started out as a synonyms task (Doherty & Perner, 1998): "this is a bunny," "this is a rabbit" (quasi-synonyms). It soon transpired that children's problems were the same whether one used those (quasi)-synonyms or super- or subordinate category terms (e.g., "animal"-"dog", or "dog"-"poodle": Perner, Stummer, Sprung, & Doherty, 2002). In this game it is first established that children are familiar with both terms used, e.g., "rabbit" and "animal," and that they know that the particular item is a rabbit and that it is an animal. This is also explicitly pointed out to them. Then they are instructed to play the following game:

> If the puppet (child's partner in the game) is asked what this is and he says "it is an animal" then you have to say what it is in different words. You have to say "it is a dog". But if the puppet says "it is a dog," then you have to say "it is an animal".

This is called the "production version" of the game, because children have to produce the alternative name. In another version the roles of puppet and child are reversed and the child has to judge whether the puppet had used the correct alternative expression. Children master both versions of the alternative naming game and the false belief task at about the same age. The young 3 year olds who fail the false belief task tend to repeat what the partner had just said (or judge the partner's repetition of their own expression as admissible), while those who pass false belief also switch to the correct alternative name and judge the partner's performance correctly. Why should there be a developmental relationship between the alternative naming games and the false belief task?

We provide an answer to this question in terms of Heim's (2002) *file change semantics,* which introduces the notion of discourse referents in a very concrete way in terms of a filing system where each discourse referent is instantiated by a particular file card.

File change semantics

We start our excursion into file change semantics with one, albeit foreshortened, example from Heim (2002, p. 226):

(1)   (a) A woman was bitten by a dog. (b) It jumped over a fence.

This little story is encoded on file cards, where every card represents one of the entities mentioned. The changes to the file are governed by a simple rule, which captures the familiarity rule of definite descriptions and works, with exceptions, for various kinds of referential expressions (demonstratives, indexicals, descriptions) that occur in non-negated simple sentences (see Karttunen, 1976):

FILE CHANGE RULE: For every indefinite, start a new card. For every definite, update an old card.

Upon hearing sentence (a) containing two indefinites, which suggests the need for two discourse referents, two new cards (1 and 2) are created and the information pertaining to each discourse referent is encoded on the respective card (see below). Sentence (b) contains one definite and one indefinite. Accordingly the information pertaining to the definite is used to update the existing card 2 while the information pertaining to the indefinite is encoded on a new card 3:

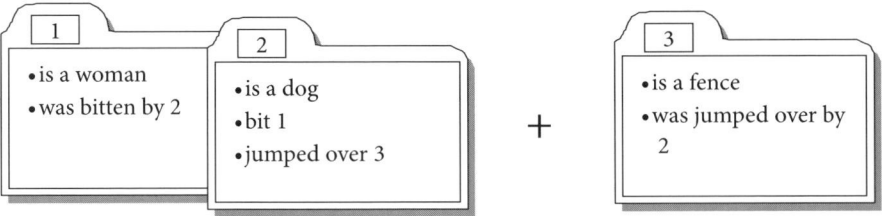

File card management and alternative naming

The two critical statements in the alternative naming game are the pair of sentences:

(2)   (a) "This is a dog."
      (b) "This is an animal."

Before being able to apply Heim's rule to these sentences we need to clear up the preliminary question whether a demonstrative, like "this," supported by a pointing gesture, fixes a referent or not. If it does, we would have to extend Heim's rule and make up a card for the referent picked out by "this" alone, and upon hearing "a dog" Heim's simple rule would have us introduce a second card. However, there are good arguments that demonstratives do not fix referents on their own. Imagine the dog has just rolled around in a mud puddle. I point to it and say "this." What is my referent? Most likely the dog, but it really depends on how I continue. If I say "…is a mess," then my referent is the dirt on the dog (or both) but not just the dog. Hence, in the naming game the demonstrative by itself does not warrant starting a new card. A card is started only upon hearing "a dog". That is, for our purposes the sentence "this (+pointing) is a dog" could be glossed as: "A dog is there (location pointed at)", and the indefinite "a dog" triggers the introduction of a file card. Similarly, the sentence "this (+pointing) is an animal" can be glossed as: "An animal is there." Upon hearing the indefinite in the second sentence a second card is opened up saying that it is an animal and that it is in location L, resulting in:

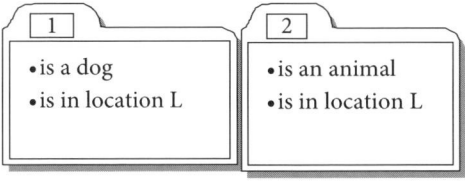

Now imagine a child, equipped with such a discourse filing system, has to play the alternative naming game. The child relates the two cards correctly to the same external referent (the dog is the external referent; thus she has procedural knowledge of the fact that "the dog" and "the animal" refer to the same entity). Yet, the child does not realize this fact within the declarative information of the discourse, because the file cards do not show this fact. So when the partner (in the production version of the game) calls it "an animal" the child, realizing that she has to say something pertinent concerning the same referent, looks up card 2 and tries to find suitable information. Unfortunately, the card only says that it is an animal. So most children erroneously repeat what the partner had called it, or if they are particularly concerned about not repeating what the partner had said they may give some other information encoded about the animal or refuse to answer. And this is what happens for most children younger than 4 years before they pass the false belief task.

Before moving on to the older children and what they need to acquire in order to play the game more successfully, let us look at some control conditions for the alternative naming game. For instance, in the *colour-colour game* children are shown a picture of a football, which is part blue and part green, and they are instructed to say in response to the question "Which colour does this have?" the other colour than the one named by the partner. From the instructions, e.g., "this football is blue and green," they will have started a file card like that:

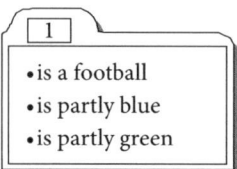

When their partner answers the question with, "it is green," children look up the football file and search for alternative colour info, which they find and can say, "blue". Similarly, a single file card provides all needed information for the *name-colour game*. If one player says what colour the football is (which in this case is only green) then the other player has to say that it is a football, or the other way round. So, if the confederate decides to call the colour, "it is green," the child knows to search for a sortal specifying what this referent is and finds: "is a football". And indeed, even the young three year olds perform quite well on these control conditions (Perner, et al., 2002).

What seems to be needed for playing the alternative naming game correctly is some information on the file cards, that they are simply a means for establishing a reference to a real external referent. Kamp & Reyle (1993, p. 257) speak of "asserted identity" in this case. In their system (where x and y are discourse referents) it "is expressed by the condition **x is y**, which asserts that the individuals repre-sented by x and y coincide." As this quote makes clear, an asserted identity is a metarepresentational assertion (in the sense of Pylyshyn, 1978). Hence our claim that children cannot employ asserted identities before they master the false belief task goes well with the claim in Perner (1991) that mastery of the false belief task depends on metarepresentational understanding.

Kamp and Reyle distinguish asserted identity from what they call merely "stip-ulated identity," which they notate as "x = y". When an identity is stipulated this just means that x and y are different notations for the same discourse referent. In this way greater notational flexibility is achieved than in file change semantics, where each discourse referent is, by definition, represented by a different file card. We leave aside such stipulated identities here, but we will introduce asserted identity claims into file change semantics. The only difference to Kamp's system here is that a (non-stipulative) identity assertion, for instance **1 is 2,** has to be encoded on the cards 1 and 2, respectively. Because this kind of condition is of central importance for our developmental claim we put "® is same as…" in doubly framed boxes on the relevant file cards (where ® stands for "reference information"):

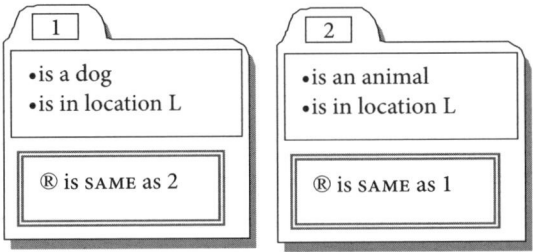

The older children, who — by hypothesis — possess the capability of asserting identities, can now make better sense of the game instructions. When trying to find information on what else the mentioned item is, they are not limited to in-formation on the same card (discourse referent) but can consult other cards with the same external referent. So when the partner called the item "an animal" then the child, picking up card 2, gets the information that card 1 has the same external referent and can, therefore, also use information on that card as pertaining to the same referent, i.e. telling her that *it* is also a dog.

File change semantics and the false belief task

We now try to show with file change semantics that the false belief task, too, re-quires the use of non-stipulative identity assertions, like the alternative naming game. We argue that this commonality accounts for the observed developmental correlation between these tasks. Identity assertions are required under the assumption that beliefs create perspectives (points of view) that may be captured in terms of discourse representation structures with their own set of discourse referents (file cards). Hence we will introduce a set of cards that encodes Max's false beliefs in our example. The information encoded on these cards does not match the conditions in the external world, which makes it impossible to find a coherent set of external anchors for these discourse referents by using the normal anchoring procedure. For this reason the discourse referents describing Max's view of the world can be coherently anchored only by linking them — via identity assertions — with corresponding discourse referents describing the child's own view of the world.

This is what we want to arrive at, but we develop our argument from the bottom up. We start by showing how children can successfully reason about a person's (Max's) actions in pursuit of his goals without using file cards that specify the point of view of this person. This works as long as there is no conflict of goals, and as long as the beliefs do not deviate from external circumstances. Then we build in the necessary complications that arise from conflicting desires and false beliefs.

To start our argument, we apply file change semantics at first to a *true belief story*. We take a story that differs from the false belief story rehearsed above only in so far as Max observes the chocolate being moved from the cupboard to the drawer. Hence he knows (and has a true belief) that the chocolate is in the drawer. In order to keep our file simple we restrict it to those file cards that are relevant for answering the test questions ("Where will Max go to get his chocolate?") and we start at a late point in the story, where most of the file already exists. Thus we avoid the interesting but complicating effect of distinguishing referents for different times. We enter the scene when the child has begun thinking about the answer to the question. In particular, she has realised that Max wanting to get his chocolate implies that he needs to be close to where the chocolate is, in other words, within reaching distance of the chocolate. The following file encodes the relevant objective story details, that there is Max (1), a chocolate (2), a cupboard (3), and a drawer (4) of the kitchen table.

OBJECTIVE STORY EVENTS:

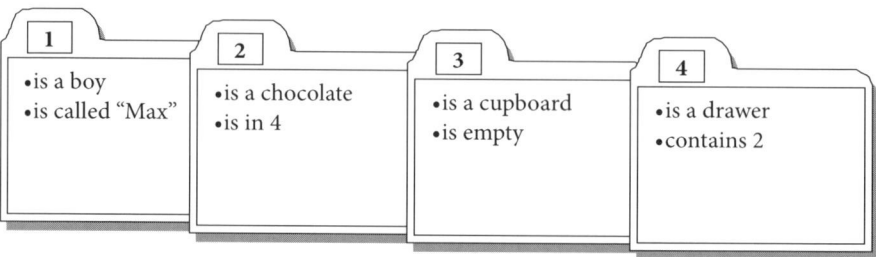

1	2	3	4
•is a boy •is called "Max"	•is a chocolate •is in 4	•is a cupboard •is empty	•is a drawer •contains 2

Now let us return to the task of answering the question about where Max will go in search of his chocolate. In order to make the requested behavioural prediction one needs more than a representation of story facts. One also needs to know at least what Max's goal is. Without goal, no behaviour. The easiest way to bring goal information into the filing system is by taking the goals to be something "objective", i.e., as something that *needs* or *ought* to be done.

Teleological (objective goal) reasoning

There is some evidence that young children reason about what people (or animate entities in general) will do, not in terms of people's subjective desires, but in terms of some objective goal, i.e., something that (in a very loose sense) should happen. This form of understanding goal directed action is akin to what Csibra and Gergely (1998) called *teleological reasoning*. They see its onset as early as 9 months of age. This way of understanding people's reasons for acting may persist up to 3 or 4 years (Yuill et al., 1996; for a defence of this position against seeming counterevidence see Perner, Zauner, & Sprung, 2005). This kind of approach may underlie early "desire" reasoning (Wellman, 1990). It captures an intuition expressed by non-introspectionist simulation theorists (Gordon, 1995), who see the origin of beliefs and desires in objective distinctions between facts and non-facts, and between what is needed and not needed, respectively. For instance, when engaged in cooperative activities people know what others will do at a particular juncture because at that point in time a particular action is *needed* and one assumes that the person responsible for that action will carry it out. This provides a basis for predicting when each person will do what, without any thought about what each of them *wants*.

Back to our true belief story: When told that Max *wants* to get his chocolate, "objectivist" children take this to mean that *Max being next to his chocolate* is something that *should happen*. They can combine this knowledge of what *should be* with how they know the world works with rules like the following:

> GETTING-CLOSE RULE:
> IF C is in L, AND P moves (from where P is) to location L,
> THEN P will be close to C.

This knowledge needs to be combined with a practical reasoning rule:

> GOAL→ACTION RULE:
> IF G is *to be* (i.e., is a goal) AND person P can bring about G by doing action A
> THEN P will do A.

However, before they can apply these rules to our story the rules need to make contact with the story entities by substituting the variables in the rules with the discourse referents. For this we need to add the goal information onto our file cards (preceded by the "♦" symbols).

OBJECTIVE GOALS + STORY EVENTS:

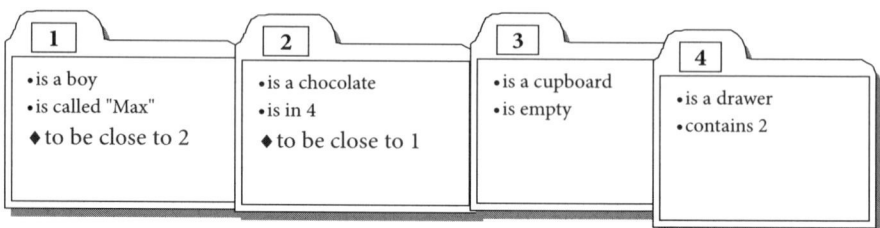

With this addition to the file, the Goal-Action rule can be applied by setting G = *1 will be close to 2*. Then the child needs to search his general knowledge about the world for rules whose consequents match the condition in this instantiation of G (i.e. __ close to __), check whether the non-action antecedents of this rule can be made to match reality by a suitable variable instantiation. If they do, except for an action to be carried out, then children can predict that this action in the antecedent will be what someone will do. In our case the child will hit upon the Getting-Close rule. It matches the goal specification by setting P = *1* and C = *2*. The antecedent of this rule suggests that if *2 is in L* and if *1 moves to L* then *1 will be close to 2*. A look up on card 2 tells us that 2 is in 4, hence variable L = 4, and the needed action is specified as, *1 move to 4*. Success — almost.

In order to give an answer in terms of the actual story characters and locations, children need to determine the external referents of 1 and 4. This is easy because only MAX satisfies the specification of card 1 as being a boy and being called "Max", and only the DRAWER satisfies the specifications on card 4 of being a drawer and containing 2, which uniquely specifies the CHOCOLATE as its external referent. So, finally children will be able to point out that Max will move to the kitchen drawer. This answer is perfectly correct in the true belief story, where Max witnessed the transfer of the chocolate to the kitchen drawer. We see that reasoning with objective goals provides a powerful — albeit far from perfect — tool for understanding people's actions.

Evidently the success of objective-goal reasoning for predicting people's actions is possible only when people's motivating forces can be understood as an objectively valid goal for the given context and when their view of the world does not diverge from the predictor's own (objective) description of the world. Action predictions based on such an objective framework break down when characters with different views of the world are involved and pursue incompatible goals. For instance, if beside Max there were also Mary, who — unlike Max himself — wants him to be at a safe distance from the chocolate, then encoding these opposing desires with objective goals would result in a contradiction, e.g., on card 1:

Card 1:
♦ 1 to be close to 2
♦ 1 to be distant from 2

Which action children will predict in this case depends on which goal information happens to be used. If it is the first one, the prediction will be correct that Max will go to where the chocolate is, if it is the second piece of information the prediction will be the opposite. What is evidently needed is a way to link what should happen specifically to Max and thereby to what he will do.

Generally speaking we need to move from a purely objective view of what needs to be done and what is the case to person-specific, subjective perspectives of what has to be done and what is the case. How children acquire an understanding of perspectives (points of views) is a question too big to be addressed here in any detail. Let us mention only that in principle there seem to be two routes an explanation of this achievement might take, by introducing subjective perspectives within the conventions of our filing system. One option is to encode beliefs and desires explicitly on the already existing file cards, e.g. on two of the cards in the true belief story:

Card 1:	Card 2:
•is a boy	•is a chocolate
•*wants* to be close to 2	•is *wanted* by 1 to be close to 1
•*thinks* (knows) 2 is in 4	•is *thought* by 1 to be in 4

If one takes this route, the practical reasoning rule has to be adjusted to making action predictions for a particular person on the basis of what that person wants and thinks. It has yet to be shown, however, whether this strategy suffices for explaining more complex phenomena, like the step from an earlier implicit understanding of false belief to a later explicit understanding. We can think of arguments both for and against this strategy, but eventually it will be largely an empirical issue of whether this option or the one we favour can better account for the data, some of which we will mention below.

Our preferred option, which we will pursue from here onwards, assumes that a subset of file cards describes the subjective perspective of each relevant story character (for whom there are indications that his/her subjective view needs to be considered).

Practical reasoning with point of view

True belief story. In order to bring in Max's point of view in the true belief story we introduce file card 5* that contains a separate subset of file cards (cards 51 ... 54) to express Max's subjective preferences and view of the world.[1]

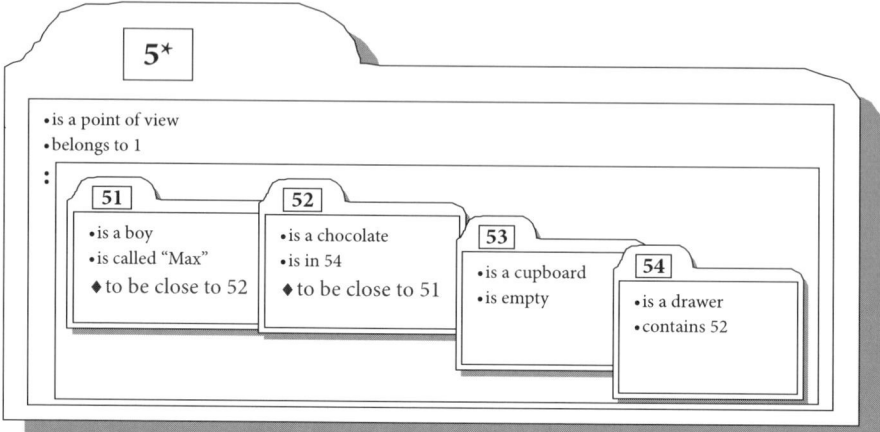

With this addition children can account for differences in desire. The objective goal has become a desire. It is not yet a desire in the ordinary sense, though, which presumably includes a higher-order subjectivity within the person's point of view, i.e., a self-ascription that the person him/herself considers as a subjective prefer- ence. By representing goals as goals within a person's perspective we have gone only one step closer to seeing goals as something subjective. However, with the person's perspective taken into account the goal still remains an objective good. In what follows we will use the term "desire" in a broad sense, covering both "per- spectival" goals as well as fully subjective, self-ascribed desires.

With this change the Goal-Action Rule has to be amended to take the actor's point of view (PoV) into account:

> GOAL→ACTION RULE for POINTS OF VIEW:
> IF within person P's PoV, G is *to be* AND P can bring about G by doing action A,
> THEN P will do A.

The content of cards 51–54 is the same as that of cards 1–4. Hence we can immedi- ately see that this rule in conjunction with cards 51–54 will bring the same results in predicting Max's action as the original Goal-Action reasoning with file cards 1–4: a correct prediction in the true-belief story and an incorrect one in the false belief story. The only difference is, that children can now account for differences between Max's goals and Mary's competing goals in a more complicated story. If Mary wants Max to keep away from the chocolate no contradiction arises because this goal can be encoded on a different subset of file cards specifying Mary's perspective. Furthermore, when asked what Mary will do, children will not answer that she will help Max to get close to the chocolate, since within her point of view Max being close to the chocolate is not a goal.

False belief story. The next question of interest is whether a subset of file cards specifying Max's point of view enables children to appreciate a false belief as well as the subjectivity of desire. Endowed with the facility to represent Max's perspective and the subjective goal-action rule, the ability to cope with false belief problems seems immanent. Provided the child understands how beliefs are formed, then all she needs to do is to use cards 51–54 to encode Max's falsely believed information. We thus get file card 5** for the false belief story.

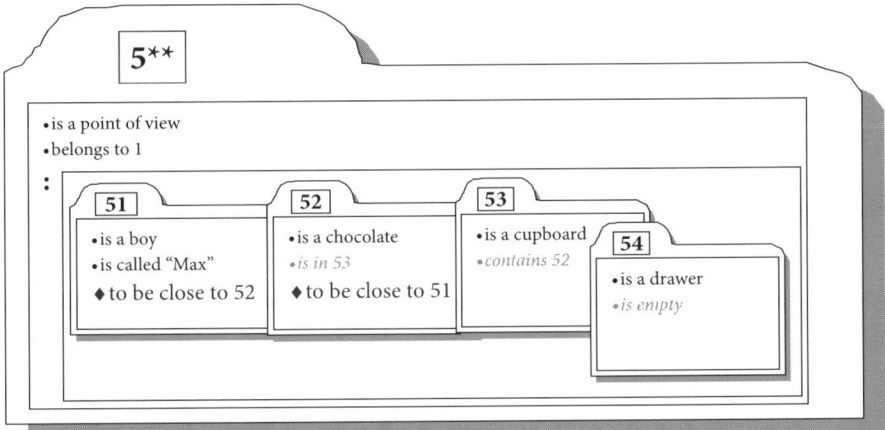

Applying the Goal→Action Rule for Points of View in conjunction with the Getting-Close Rule to 5** the seemingly correct answer will emerge that *51*(Max) *will move to 53* (the cupboard). However, children need to determine the respective external referents of discourse referents 52–54. Here the situation has crucially changed from 5* to 5**. The set of discourse referents composing 5* contained, like the original file cards 2–4, only correct factual information. Hence the external anchoring procedure could find a coherent set of external entities satisfying the conditions on the cards: the CHOCOLATE, the CUPBOARD, and the DRAWER, respectively. This is no longer possible now.

For instance, a 'point-at-able' location that corresponds to discourse referent 53 needs to be determined. This involves trying to find for the discourse referent an entity in the story that satisfies the conditions specified on the file card in conjunction with the conditions specified on cross referenced cards. For card 51 this works nicely: there is only one entity that is a boy called Max, and so MAX becomes the external referent for card 51 as much as for card 1. But now, if we try to do the same for card 53 we get a problem: 53 should be something that is a cupboard and contains something (52), which is a chocolate. Unfortunately the only thing, which satisfies the condition of being a cupboard fails to satisfy the condition of containing a chocolate. That means there is no coherent anchoring for cards 52, 53 and 54 to external referents.

Children dabbling in practical (belief-desire) reasoning with points of view, will be confused at this point and are likely to fall back on their earlier, usually successful strategy of using file cards 1–4 instead of 51–54. Unfortunately, this leads again to the wrong answer in the false belief task. There is, however, also another possibility.

Precocious "implicit" understanding of false belief. Ironically, children, who are not yet experienced in reasoning with points of view may be led to a correct answer by sheer luck. Consider the point, where children have arrived at the conclusion that *51*(Max) *will move to 53* (the cupboard). When looking for an external anchor for 53, they may simply check the first, most prevalent condition, "is a cupboard" and uncritically take the CUPBOARD as the external referent of card 53, which fortuitously leads to the correct answer. The use of such half-baked belief-desire reasoning could explain the precocious appearance of — what has been called — "implicit" understanding of false belief (Clements & Perner, 1994). It has been found that children of about 2 years and 11 months to 3 years and 2 months, who practically all give the typical wrong answer to the false belief test question, namely that the protagonist will go for the desired object to where the object presently is, show some signs of understanding. When the protagonist is invisible and will reappear through one or the other of two doors in search of the desired object, then these children look "in expectation" to the door in front of the empty location, where the protagonist mistakenly thinks his object still is (Clements & Perner, 1994, 2001; Ruffman, Garnham, Import, & Connolly, 2001). This precocious understanding has been termed "implicit", because like blindsight patients' knowledge of objects in their blind field, it only shows in eye movements or spontaneous action (Perner & Clements, 2000), but cannot be used for discourse about the story (the traditional way of assessing understanding).

Furthermore, Clements & Perner (2001) asked children to put a mat at the door where the protagonist will reappear in search of the desired object. Among the young 3-year olds there were many who answered the standard question wrongly but who put the mat correctly to where the mistaken protagonist will actually reappear provided they moved the mat quickly without much deliberation. Those children who hesitated in apparent deliberation did not show this effect. They put the mat where they also said the protagonist would reappear.

It is tempting to speculate that these early signs of understanding false belief are based on an uncritical use of reasoning with points of view. Children's attempt to decipher the external referent for the belief discourse referent 53 makes them think of the possibility that MAX will go to the CUPBOARD, and so they look there in anticipation, or even unreflectively move the mat there. But for giving an answer in the ongoing discourse or if they deliberate too long about where to move the mat, they can't find a consistent answer and fall back to the old, reliable teleological reasoning and give the wrong answer with conviction (Ruffman et al., 2001).

What is needed to enable children to make the correct prediction with conviction and to fully understand why they make this prediction, is the ability to make (non-stipulative) identity assertions, as we shall see next.

Mature belief-desire reasoning (with asserted identity)

Finally we come to our explanation of how the false belief task is actually solved by mature belief-desire reasoning with asserted identity. In order to be able to coherently anchor cards 52–54, explicit information about their external referents has to be provided by non-stipulative identity information that links these cards to the original card set 1–4, as shown on card 5.

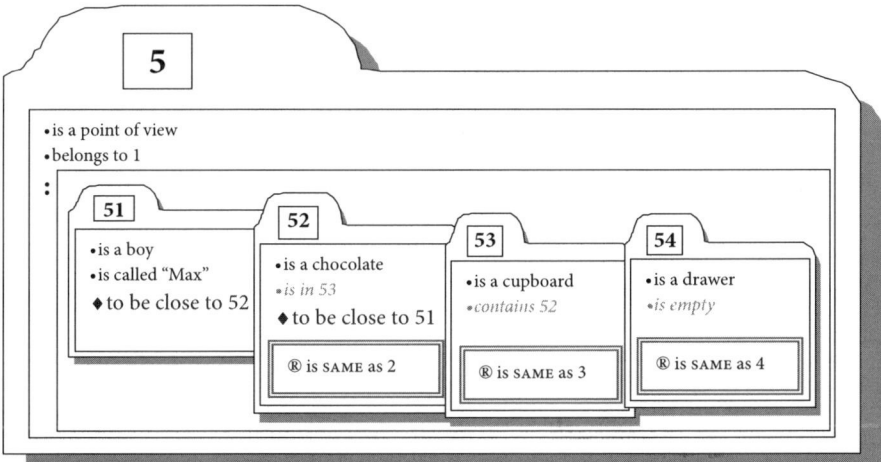

So for card 53 the anchoring information in the doubly outlined boxes marked "®" says that it has the same external referent as card 3 (the empty cupboard). This allows children, who can have and use such information, to uniquely determine the external referent as: THE EMPTY CUPBOARD, and they can, finally, give the correct answer to the test question: Max will go to the *cupboard* in search of his chocolate.

Correct verbal answers to the test question typically emerge around the age of four years, when children also become proficient at the alternative naming game.

Summary of our developmental hypothesis

Our developmental claim is that children below the age of about 4 years cannot make or understand or even represent (non-stipulative) identity assertions that involve the ability to link discourse reference in a meta-representational way. This capacity is required for correct performance on the alternative naming game as well as for passing the false belief test. Identity assertions are needed for somewhat different reasons in the two tasks, however. In the alternative naming game the rules of language lead to different discourse referents for the same external entity. Although the child can anchor the two discourse referents to the same external referent, an assertion of identity is required for understanding that two different discourse referents for the same external referent are used (that they are actually about the same thing). Once this is mastered, children can make sense of the instructions to answer the same question about the same item (what is this?) differently from what the other player had said.

In the false belief task identity assertions are required for finding external referents for the discourse referents in the first place. This is a particularly virulent problem in the case of false beliefs because false beliefs result in conditions that are incompatible with the external world. Hence the child cannot use his own anchoring procedures, which rely on these conditions for finding external referents for each discourse referent such that the conditions stipulated for each discourse referent are met by the corresponding external referent. Because of the falsity of the belief these conditions cannot be made to match. Hence the discourse referents figuring in false belief descriptions can only be externally anchored with the help of information about asserted identities.

Implications for Making Minds

Starting from an empirical puzzle — why alternative naming is developmentally related to understanding false belief — we arrived at a possible solution highlighting the crucial role of discourse referents and the use of anchoring information.

By linking the growing understanding of the mind (in particular the understanding of false beliefs) to discourse referents we also encourage researchers to reconsider their view of how language development influences children's theory of mind. There is increasing evidence that general language competence has a positive influence on theory of mind development (Astington & Jenkins, 1999; Ruffman, Slade, Rowlandson, Rumsey, & Garnham, 2003), rather than any particular syntactic developments as deVilliers and deVilliers (2000) have claimed. Most dramatically deaf children raised by hearing parents suffer from a language delay of several years that is also reflected in their late understanding of false beliefs (Peterson & Siegal, 1995; Gale, deVilliers, deVilliers, & Pyers, 1996). These findings fit our theory in so far as it suggests that progress in understanding beliefs relates to a discourse competence, which is a fairly general linguistic ability. It rests on the ability to update ones file-cards according to a file change rule that distinguishes between definite and indefinite referential expressions (see above). Presumably, this rule is closely connected to the practice of listening to stories and other intensive language uses.

Combining these insights with the intuition that the specific characteristic of the human mind depends essentially on linguistic communication, we would advise anyone in the business of *making* artificial systems with human-like *minds* to build in discourse referents. Moreover, if the mind to be built is supposed to appreciate the subjectivity of different views it will have to be able to handle asserted identities that genuinely enlarge its knowledge base instead of merely applying the knowledge the system already has. And it might further be speculated that introducing this novel feature into the architecture of a system presupposes a form of self-reflexive awareness on the part of the system that goes hand in hand with the emergence of consciousness. In this way our solution to a fairly small empirical puzzle could be seen as an important step in explaining why only systems enjoying conscious mental states are capable of developing a theory of mind, without which no true understanding of other minds is possible.

Acknowledgment

The authors express their gratitude to Mike Martin and Alan Garnham for suggesting that a solution to the theoretical problems encountered with an earlier account (Perner, Brandl, & Garnham, 2003) might be found in discourse representation theory and file card semantics.

Note

1. Card 5* introduces the novel element ":" to mark that the discourse referent 5* is characterized by the complex structure within the box containing the subset of file cards. We take this notation from Kamp (1990) for specifying a complex proposition p to have the structure of a formally anchored discourse representation structure (DRS), "p: DRS."

References

Astington, J.W., & Jenkins, J.M. (1999). A longitudinal study of the relation between language and theory-of-mind development. *Developmental Psychology, 35*, 1311–1320.

Clements, W.A., & Perner, J. (1994). Implicit understanding of belief. *Cognitive Development, 9*, 377–397.

Clements, W.A., & Perner, J. (2001). When actions really do speak louder than words — but only implicitly: Young children's understanding of false belief in action. *British Journal of Developmental Psychology, 19*, 413–432.

Csibra, G., & Gergely, G. (1998). The teleological origins of mentalistic action explanations: A developmental hypothesis. *Developmental Science, 1*, 255–259.

de Villiers, J., & de Villiers, P. (2000). Linguistic determination and the understanding of false beliefs. In P. Mitchell & K. J. Riggs (Eds.), *Children's reasoning and the mind* (pp. 191–228). Hove, East Sussex: Psychology Press.

Doherty, M., & Perner, J. (1998). Metalinguistic awareness and theory of mind: Just two words for the same thing? *Cognitive Development, 13*, 279–305.

Gale, E., de Villiers, P., de Villiers, J., & Pyers, J. (1996). Language and theory of mind in oral deaf children. In A. Stringfellow, D. Cahana-Amitay, E. Hughes, & A. Zukowski (Eds.), *Proceedings of the 20th annual Boston University Conference on Language Development. Volume 1* (pp. 213–224). Somerville, MA: Cascadilla Press.

Gordon, R.M. (1995). Simulation without introspection or inference from me to you. In M. Davies & T. Stone (Eds.), *Mental Simulation: Evaluations and applications* (pp. 53–67). Oxford: Blackwell.

Heim, I. (2002). File change semantics and the familiarity theory of definiteness. In P. Portner & B. H. Partee (Eds.), *Formal semantics: The essential readings* (pp. 223–248). Oxford: Blackwell Publishing.

Kamp, H. (1990). Prolegomena to a structural account of belief and other attitudes. In C. A. Anderson (Ed.), *Propositional attitudes: The role of content in logic, language and mind* (pp. 27–90). Stanford, CA: Center for Study of Language and Information, Lecture Notes Series.

Kamp, H., & Reyle, U. (1993). *From discourse to logic. Introduction to modeltheoretic semantics of natural language, formal logic and discourse representation theory.* Dordrecht, Boston, London: Kluwer Academic Publishers.

Karttunen, L. (1976). Discourse referents. In J. McCawley (Ed.), *Notes from the linguistic underground (Syntax and Semantics, vol. 7)* (pp. 363–385). New York: Academic Press.

Perner, J. (1991). *Understanding the representational mind.* Cambridge, MA: MIT Press. A Bradford book.

Perner, J., & Clements, W.A. (2000). From an implicit to an explicit theory of mind. In Y. Rossetti & A. Revonsuo (Eds.), *Beyond dissociations: interaction between dissociated implicit and explicit processing* (pp. 273–293). Amsterdam: John Benjamins.

Perner, J., Stummer, S., Sprung, M., & Doherty, M. (2002). Theory of mind finds its Piagetian perspective: Why alternative naming comes with understanding belief. *Cognitive Development, 17*, 1451–1472.

Perner, J., Brandl, J., & Garnham, A. (2003). What is a perspective problem? Developmental issues in understanding belief and dual identity. *Facta Philosophica, 5*(2), 355–378.

Perner, J., Zauner, P., & Sprung, M. (2005). What does 'that' have to do with point of view? The case of conflicting desires and 'want' in German. In J. W. Astington & J. Baird (Eds.), *Why language matters for theory of mind* (pp. 220–244). New York: Oxford University Press.

Peterson, C.C., & Siegal, M. (1995). Deafness, conversation and theory of mind. *Journal of Child Psychology and Psychiatry, 36*, 459–474.

Pylyshyn, Z.W. (1978). When is attribution of beliefs justified? *The Behavioral and Brain Sciences, 1*, 516–526.

Ruffman, T., Garnham, W., Import, A., & Connolly, D. (2001). Does Eye Gaze Indicate Implicit Knowledge of False Belief? Charting Transitions in Knowledge. *Journal of Experimental Child Psychology, 80*, 201–224.

Ruffman, T., Slade, L., Rowlandson, K., Rumsey, C., & Garnham, A. (2003). How language relates to belief, desire, and emotion understanding. *Cognitive Development, 113*, 1–20.

Wellman, H.M. (1990). *The child's theory of mind.* Cambridge, MA: MIT Press. A Bradford Book.

Wellman, H.M., Cross, D., & Watson, J. (2001). Meta-analysis of theory of mind development: the truth about false belief. *Child Development, 72*, 655–684.

Wimmer, H., & Perner, J. (1983). Beliefs about beliefs: Representation and constraining function of wrong beliefs in young children's understanding of deception. *Cognition, 13*, 103–128.

Yuill, N., Perner, J., Pearson, A., Peerbhoy, D., & van den Ende, J. (1996). Children's changing understanding of wicked desires: From objective to subjective and moral. *British Journal of Developmental Psychology, 14*, 457–475.

In the series *Benjamins Current Topics (BCT)* the following titles have been published thus far or are scheduled for publication: